CW00953603

# FIRST-CLASS PASSENGERS ON A SINKING SHIP

# FIRST-CLASS PASSENGERS ON A SINKING SHIP

## ELITE POLITICS AND THE DECLINE OF GREAT POWERS

RICHARD LACHMANN

**VERSO**
London • New York

First published by Verso 2020
© Richard Lachmann 2020

1 3 5 7 9 10 8 6 4 2

**Verso**
UK: 6 Meard Street, London W1F 0EG
US: 20 Jay Street, Suite 1010, Brooklyn, NY 11201
versobooks.com

Verso is the imprint of New Left Books

ISBN-13: 978-1-78873-407-3
ISBN-13: 978-1-78873-409-7 (UK EBK)
ISBN-13: 978-1-78873-410-3 (US EBK)

**British Library Cataloguing in Publication Data**
A catalogue record for this book is available from the British Library

**Library of Congress Cataloging-in-Publication Data**
A catalog record for this book is available from the Library of Congress

Typeset in Minion by Hewer Text (UK) Ltd, Edinburgh
Printed and bound by CPI Group (UK) Ltd, Croydon CR0 4YY

For my children,

Madeleine and Derrick

# Contents

# Preface

I began thinking of writing a book about US decline at the end of the George W. Bush administration and finished it in the early months of Donald Trump's presidency. My concern, then and now, has not been with the men elected president, and not much with the voters who elect them. It is not that elections do not matter; they do, although, as I will try to explain, only in limited and occasional ways. Much of American domestic policy, and almost all of US foreign policy, is determined by elites who are only somewhat constrained by voter preferences and decisions. What seemed remarkable and worthy of sociological inquiry was not Bush's own personal stupidity or vicious-ness but the lack, until late in his presidency, of a credible challenge to his policies from any significant power base. As for Trump, we will see if the level of opposition shown in the first years of his presidency is sustained, if it weakens or intensifies. In any case, most of his substan-tive policies were proposed by earlier Republican politicians at the behest of the elites who fund them, which is why most Republican members of Congress voted to repeal Obamacare and to enact tax cuts that funneled two-thirds of the benefits to the top 1 percent, regard-less of their constituents' disapproval and dismay.

Barack Obama and Hillary Clinton, who seemed destined to succeed him, certainly offered programs to mitigate and reverse aspects of American decline, both at home and as the dominant geopolitical power. I wrote the bulk of the substantive chapters during the Obama presidency and saw little sign that his policies, to the extent that he actually could legislate and implement them, would do anything more than cushion the effects of decline on ordinary Americans. The accomplishments of the Obama years are no small thing for those who gained access to health care and other social benefits or were protected from financial fraud or danger to their health and safety at work and in the environment. However, what Obama offered were gifts from on high, and he did not create political coalitions that could push for further advances or challenge elite power.

Nothing Obama did, or Hillary Clinton might have done, posed a significant challenge to elites' capacities to serve their own interests at the expense of their nation's hegemony and of their fellow citizens' well-being. Indeed, a narrow elite has been able to prevent policy shifts that would endanger their ability to enrich themselves in the pursuit of fossil fuels that are altering the earth's environment in ways that will cause mass extinctions and render the planet unable to support the current human population of 7 billion. Non-elites, perhaps not in America but certainly in much of the world, will be not just impoverished but killed by global climate change.

As I will argue, it is time to move beyond the fruitless hope that there is a plausible path to reverse or even slow American decline. Instead, the choices that remain are, as they were for inhabitants of the declining Dutch and British hegemons, about who will suffer the effects of decline. In the past, the costs of decline were spread widely, exempting only a narrow, privileged elite. National decline, therefore, becomes decline in most people's standard of living and sense of well-being. As such, it provokes varying responses, including anger, resignation, solidarity, collective action, mutual animosity, militarism, racism, religiosity, and, yes, plans for reform.

Those reactions do not act directly to produce significant social change. Most often, the actors are inchoate, and their rage and pain are diverted into support for politicians and policies that further elite interests. When anti-elite forces focus their energies on electoral politics, their influence is uneven and of limited efficacy. The small achievements of popular forces in post-hegemonic Britain and the Netherlands illustrate the highly limited parameters of reform and redistribution unless and until those reactions create or revivify political organizations that can challenge elites. However, even when discontent is channeled into mass organizations, those organizations act on a domestic political field on which other forces are arrayed and which is affected by actors located in places abroad that are within or escaping the nation's hegemonic sphere. All this needs to be taken into account as we trace the varying paths, through organizational structures and contingent events, that lead from the emotions provoked by decline to stasis or transformative actions.

Our analysis, therefore, needs to focus on the question of whether the loss of hegemony can in itself disrupt fossilized domestic or global politics in ways that would undermine elite power. That will allow us to identify the narrow range of plausible political strategies and to be honest about what can actually be accomplished in this moment by engaging with American citizens.

This, then, is a book that aims to be precise in its analysis of how we arrived at the present situation, and how America's trajectory compares with those of past hegemons. To the extent that I have accomplished that task, this book, by drawing on both historical comparison and contemporary evidence, reaches a pessimistic but realistic conclusion.

I had conflicting emotions as I worked on this project. As a sociologist, I feel enormously privileged to have a front-row seat in observing a major historical transformation, and I hope this book, which is directed primarily, but certainly not exclusively, at social scientists and historians, succeeds in addressing the decline of the United States in rigorous analytical terms. At the same time, as someone who has spent my entire life in a First World democracy (however limited) and who would like my children to have that same option, I regard this country's present trajectory with horror.

I believe any contribution I can make as a social scientist and a citizen has to be grounded in my capacity for precise analysis and a willingness not to let my hopes and desires for a better future lead me to empty exhortations or to draw implausible conclusions about what political action or an improbable deus ex machina might produce. Our energies are limited and they should not be squandered. A realistic assessment of elites' vulnerability can help us to focus our intellectual and organizational efforts where they can be most effective. For that reason, analysis must precede exhortation. I have tried, in this book, to bring my energy and abilities to the former task. I hope my contribution helps to map the terrain for those with the ability to inspire others to action.

I have benefited from friends' and colleagues' advice and their careful readings of portions of this book. I gratefully acknowledge the help of Jeffrey Alexander, Joel Andreas, Matt Baltz, Robert Brenner, Jonah Brundage, Bruce Carruthers, Steve Casey, Vivek Chibber, Tom Crosbie, Georgi Derluguian, G. William Domhoff, Barry Eidlin, Emily Erikson, Robert Fishman, Julian Go, Jeff Goodwin, Phil Gorski, John Hall, Greg Hooks, Andrew Horvitz, Ho-fung Hung, Ron Jacobs, Meyer Kestnbaum, James Mahoney, Aaron Major, Michael Mann, Eugene Matiash, David McCourt, Mark Mizruchi, Ann Orloff, Stephen Pampinella, Beth Popp-Berman, Isaac Reed, Dylan Riley, Fiona Rose-Greenland, Ian Roxborough, Michael Schwartz, Beverly Silver, Ori Swed, Cihan Tugal, Nicholas Wilson, and Kevin Young. All of these readers and advisors improved the clarity of my argument and alerted me to books, articles, and data sources of which I was not aware and which helped fortify this book. Of course, these helpers are not miracle workers, and there are no doubt errors of fact and interpretation from which they could not save me and for which I alone am responsible.

I appreciate the research assistance and suggestions I received from my graduate assistants at the University at Albany who participated in an ongoing project on depictions of war casualties: Abby Stivers, Lacy Mitchell, Ian Sheinheit, Jing Li, and Mishel Filisha. Some of the results of that project and of our thinking are presented in chapter 7.

I benefited from the questions and comments of audiences at McGill University; Emory University; University of California, Berkeley; Binghamton University; Johns Hopkins University; New York University; Stony Brook University; Northwestern University; the Graduate Center of the City University of New York; University Institute of Lisbon; University of Porto; Fudan University (Shanghai, China); Renmin University (Beijing, China); and Zhejiang University (Hangzhou, China).

Brief portions of chapter 1 are drawn from the first chapter of *States and Power*; portions of chapters 3 and 4 from the fifth chapter of *Capitalists in Spite of Themselves*; and portions of chapter 5 from the second chapter of *States and Power* and from the fourth chapter of *Capitalists in Spite of Themselves*. Part of chapter 2 was previously published as "Greed and Contingency: State Fiscal Crises and Imperial Failure in Early Modern Europe" in *American Journal of Sociology* 115, no. 1 (July 2009): 39–73. An earlier version of chapter 1 was published as "Hegemons, Empires, and Their Elites" in *Sociologia, Problemas e Práticas* (Portugal) 75 (2014): 9–38; a version of chapter 6 as "From Consensus to Paralysis in the United States, 1960–2012" in *Political Power and Social Theory* 26 (2014): 195–233; and a version of chapter 7 as "The American Military: Without Rival and Without Victory" in *Catalyst* 1, no. 3 (2017): 117–48.

An extensive bibliography for the book is accessible online at the following address: https://v.versobooks.com/lachmann_bibliography.pdf.

# Introduction: The Problem of Decline

A specter is haunting the United States—the specter of decline. Discussion of decline leapt in 2016 from academic treatises to the forefront of public debate as the winning presidential candidate made his slogan "Make America Great Again," which implied America was no longer great, as it once had been. Trump built his platform on the notion that drastic action was needed to recover from a decline brought on by America's own government. The 2008 crisis and the government's response made obvious the extent of economic and political inequality in the United States, and the absolute decline in wealth and well-being for a growing fraction of Americans.

Evidence of decline is manifest to those of us living in America in the first decades of the twenty-first century. Spending on infrastructure has stagnated as bridges collapse, water and sewer pipes and dams burst, air and road traffic become ever more snarled, and passenger trains on a shrinking network struggle to reach early-twentieth-century speeds. From the arrival at the airport to the high-speed train or subway trip into town, a visit to most countries in Europe and East Asia can seem to an American like a journey to a Tomorrowland, never to be realized in the United States outside of Disney World.

Student achievement at the primary, secondary, and university levels has fallen from the top ranks. US students, who attend ever more decrepit schools, are performing less well than their peers in countries with much lower levels of income or educational spending. The United States, which pioneered mass higher education with the GI Bill of 1944 and held the lead in the percentage of its population with university degrees for the following five decades, has now fallen to fourteenth among developed nations.[1]

The United States does spend lavishly in two sectors, health care and the military, but its relative standing in both realms has been falling for decades. The United States is now thirty-fourth among nations in life expectancy.[2] Beckfield and Morris report,

> People living in the United States today can expect to live shorter and sicker lives, compared to people living in any other rich democracy. This "health gap" between the US and its peer countries is growing over time, as Canadian, British, Australian, French, German, and Swedish death rates among people aged 45–54 continue falling, and the US fails to keep pace with such changes . . . the US level of [health] inequality is far higher than we observe in most European countries, and the prevalence of poor health is on par with the former Soviet-bloc states of Central and Eastern Europe.[3]

This is the case despite the fact that medical spending in the US was 17.1 percent of GDP in 2013, almost 50 percent above the next highest country, France, at 11.6 percent. Per capita and adjusted for differences in the cost of living, the United States spent $9,086 in 2013, 44 percent above the runner-up, Switzerland, at $6,325 (Commonwealth Fund 2015).[4]

--------

1  Jacob S. Hacker and Paul Pierson (*American Amnesia: How the War on Government Led Us to Forget What Made America Prosper* [New York: Simon & Schuster, 2016], 33) note that the entire increase in African American high school graduation rates since the 1980s is an artifact of the federal government's decision not to include prisoners in its statistics on educational attainment. The huge increase in prisoners since the '70s, many of whom are high school dropouts, raises the graduation rate for the declining share of the population not in prison.

2  Lawrence R. Jacobs and Theda Skocpol, *Health Care Reform and American Politics: What Everyone Needs to Know* (New York: Oxford University Press, 2010), 21.

3  Jason Beckfield and Katherine Morris, "Health," in *Pathways: State of the Union: The Poverty and Inequality Report, 2016*, 58–64, retrieved May 17, 2016; see also Steven Woolf and Laudan Aron, *US Health in International Perspective: Shorter Lives, Poorer Health* (Washington, DC: National Academies Press, 2013).

4  Commonwealth Fund, *US Healthcare from a Global Perspective* (2015), retrieved May 17, 2016.

Why does the United States get such a poor return on its health care spending, or, to ask the question another way, why is it so expensive to provide worse care than people get in other wealthy and not-so-wealthy countries? It is not because Americans use so much health care; Americans, in fact, go to the doctor less and spend fewer days in the hospital than people in other OECD countries. Instead, Americans pay much more for doctors, drugs, medical devices, and hospital stays than anywhere else on Earth because Congress has repeatedly rejected cost controls and forbids the federal government from negotiating prices.[1] America also devotes more than twice as large a share of its medical spending to administrative costs as any other OECD nation.[2] This is so because multiple for-profit insurance companies, each with their own set of procedures and reimbursement schedules, need to hire armies of administrators to process their distinctive forms, while hospitals and doctors' offices hire medical "coders" who seek to classify the care provided to patients in ways that maximize reimbursements, leading insurance companies to hire yet more administrators to check and challenge the bills submitted by hospitals and physicians. Of course, none of that contributes in any way to patients' health and longevity.

The US military has become ever less able to win wars, even as its advantage in spending and in the amount and sophistication of its armaments has widened over its actual and potential rivals to a level unprecedented in world history. America's only unambiguous military victories since World War II came in the first Gulf War of 1991, a war with the strictly limited objective of expelling Iraq from Kuwait, and in various "police actions" against pathetically small and weak opponents in the Dominican Republic in 1965, Grenada in 1983, and Panama in 1989. The US war in Korea had an ambiguous result, while Vietnam was a clear defeat. In both those wars, the United States faced significant enemies backed by the rival superpower, and in Korea fought hundreds of thousands of Chinese troops as well. None of

---

1  Hacker and Pierson, *American Amnesia*, 273–81.
2  Michael Mueller, Luc Hagenaars, and David Morgan, "Administrative Spending in OECD Health Care Systems: Where Is the Fat and Can It Be Trimmed?" in *Tackling Wasteful Spending on Health* (Paris: OECD Publishing, 2017), table 6.2, retrieved April 23, 2017.

those conditions hold for the wars in Iraq and Afghanistan, which, even though they did not end in outright defeat, failed to achieve most of the objectives for which they were fought. Any single defeat can be attributed to particular and ad hoc circumstances, but America is unique among the world's dominant powers of the past five hundred years in its repeated failure to achieve military objectives over decades. Those failures are even more extraordinary because they occurred in the absence of a rising military rival and as America's ability and willingness to produce and pay for the weapons needed for military supremacy remained undiminished.

Outside of the lavishly, if ineffectively, funded military and medical realms, the outlook is bleak. At the very moment when further investment is needed for infrastructure,[1] scientific and industrial research and development,[2] education, and environmental repair, the capacity of the federal and of state and local governments to muster those funds is weakening. Following the Bush tax cuts, federal receipts fell in 2004 to 16.3 percent of GDP, the lowest level since 1951.[3] To hold spending steady as tax revenues decline, public debt has increased vastly since 2000, mirroring American families' use of credit to sustain their spending in the face of stagnant incomes. Federal debt as a percentage of GDP more than doubled from 31.7 percent in 1981 to 67.7 percent in 2008, and then after the Great Recession, federal debt further increased to 101.8 percent of GDP in 2015.[4] Private debt, held by individuals and firms, increased as a percentage of GDP at an even faster rate in those three decades, and right before the financial crisis totaled four times the federal debt.[5] "Between 2000 and 2007—the total [of household debt] doubled to $14 trillion and the household

---

1   American Society of Civil Engineers, *Making the Grade: 2017 Infrastructure Report Card* (2017), retrieved March 14, 2017.

2   National Academies, *Rising above the Gathering Storm: Energizing and Employing America for a Brighter Economic Future* (Washington: National Academies Press, 2007).

3   Office of Management and Budget, *Historical Tables-Budget of the US Government, FY 2017* (2016), table 1.2, retrieved February 26, 2017.

4   Ibid., table 7.1.

5   Federal Reserve, *Statistical Release Z.1, Flow of Funds Accounts of the United States* (2010), table D.3.

debt-to-income ratio skyrocketed from 1.4 to 2.1."[1] However, the fastest increase in debt was on the part of financial firms, which rose from 19.7 percent of GDP in 1979 to 117.9 percent in 2007.[2]

Many commentators have described America's decline, and many have proposed solutions.[3] America's loss of military and economic supremacy, and its citizens' continued fall from the first rank in education, health, and well-being, have been accompanied by numerous suggestions of policies that could reverse the process. Yet increasingly those proposals are put forward with a resigned belief that they will not be heeded because the United States is no longer capable of mustering the political will to actually appropriate the revenues needed and has lost the organizational capacity to bring large-scale projects to completion. In essence, American progressives and realists express political options as a series of regrets:

*Yes, we know the economic leader of the twenty-first century will develop a green energy sector, and that to do so will require massive*

--------

1    Atlif Mian and Amir Sufi, *House of Debt: How They (and You) Caused the Great Recession, and How We Can Prevent It from Happening Again* (Chicago: University of Chicago Press, 2014), 4. After dipping during the financial crisis, household debt surpassed its 2008 peak in early 2017. Mortgage debt made up two-thirds of the total, but the fastest increases in recent years have been in student debt and auto loans (Federal Reserve Bank of New York, *Household Debt Surpasses Its Peak Reached During the Recession in 2008* [2017], retrieved May 18, 2017).

2    David Kotz, *The Rise and Fall of Neoliberal Capitalism* (Cambridge, MA: Harvard University Press, 2015) 129.

3    Porter and Mykleby (2011), for a well-publicized recent example, mix dire descriptions of the current US trajectory with grandiloquent if vague proposals for domestic investment and a rethinking of a military-dominated foreign policy. Building America's Future (*Building America's Future: Falling Apart and Falling Behind* [2011]), a bipartisan group headlined by Edward Rendell, former Democratic governor of Pennsylvania; Arnold Schwarzenegger, former Republican governor of California; and Michael Bloomberg, the billionaire former mayor of New York who has belonged to both parties and been an independent at various points in his career, advocate for higher infrastructure spending directed at mass transit and high-speed rail in large metropolitan areas. While totally rational, and necessary for America's economic competitiveness, such a plan would require raising gas or other taxes and/ or shifting spending from rural areas that are overrepresented in the Senate to urban areas. The authors have nothing to say about how political support for such measures could be mobilized, nor have they sought to enlist business interests that suffer from road, port, and airport congestion.

*governmental investment, efficiency mandates, and taxes on fossil fuels, but America lacks China's resources and the EU's willingness to tax and regulate, so such a sector cannot really grow here.*

*Of course, we understand that a government-directed and -financed universal health care system is the best (perhaps the only) way to lower health care costs and improve outcomes, but the insurance, pharmaceutical, and hospital industries will never allow that here, so America will have to continue to pay more for worse outcomes.*[1]

*Every country with better educational results has a single national system and recognizes teachers' professional worth with high levels of autonomy and pay,*[2] *but America has a tradition of local control, and in any case we can't afford to pay enough to get capable professionals, so we had better settle for closely supervising teachers by testing their pupils on basic academic skills, even though students who pass those tests are not prepared for university education or international competition.*

When commentators do not fall into despair about the consequences of a supposedly unique American approach to politics and governance, they indulge in magical thinking, hoping for a savior or for the spontaneous eruption of a social movement. Barack Obama certainly embodied such hopes in 2008 as his supporters projected onto him personal qualities that would allow him to single-handedly overcome partisan divisions and enact needed reforms. Obama returned the favor, telling those who attended his rallies, "We are the people we have been waiting for."

Ralph Nader's book *Only the Super-Rich Can Save Us!*, a utopian novel that imagines billionaires undermining corporate power and

---

1   Elisabeth Rosenthal, in *An American Sickness: How Healthcare Became Big Business and How You Can Take It Back* (New York: Penguin, 2017), offers a comprehensive overview of the mechanisms that make American health care more expensive than anywhere else in the world, although she has little to say about how health care firms maintain their privileges and block reforms.

2   Steven L. Paine and Andreas Schleicher, in *What the US Can Learn from the World's Most Successful Education Reform Efforts* (McGraw-Hill Research Foundation, 2011), offer a summary of the research supporting this claim.

revitalizing citizen action, shows the extent to which progressive plans are based on hopes for elite generosity rather than realistic plans for political mobilization.[1] It is especially revealing, and depressing, that this book was written by the American who has been more successful than any other at building citizen organizations over the past half century. In any case, the contributions from liberal billionaires such as Tom Steyer, a hedge fund manager who spent tens of millions of dollars in the 2014 and 2016 elections on ads criticizing Republican climate change skeptics to little effect, were overwhelmed by spending from the Koch brothers and their allies for federal and state-level candidates committed to gutting environmental protections, weakening unions, and making it difficult for African Americans and other Democratic constituencies to vote in future elections.[2]

"Tea Party" adherents believed that by electing a collection of retired corporate executives, self-satisfied heirs, career politicians, and assorted oddballs they would achieve a dramatic reduction in government spending that would revive the economy while returning government to what they imagine the Founding Fathers intended when writing the Constitution.

Periodically, a new third party is seen as the engine of change. Before he placed his hopes on the superrich, Ralph Nader thought that his third-party presidential candidacy would disrupt the two-party duopoly on power and, in some never-specified way, open a space for progressive politics.[3] Thomas Friedman, the most prominent US newspaper columnist of the early twenty-first century, advocated for

--------

1   *Only the Super-Rich Can Save Us!*, New York: Seven Stories, 2009. As we will see in chapter 6, Nader's newly adoring view of the superrich reflects the shift in recent decades of progressive efforts away from mass organizing and toward soliciting funds from the rich and their foundations to establish think tanks and Washington offices devoted to lobbying Congress and federal agencies—Skocpol (in "Government Activism") offers the best analysis of this shift.

2   Jane Mayer, *Dark Money: The Hidden History of the Billionaires Behind the Rise of the Radical Right* (New York: Doubleday, 2016); Theda Skocpol and Alexander Hertel-Fernandez, "The Koch Network and Republican Party Extremism," *Perspectives on Politics* 14, no. 3 (2016); Hacker and Pierson, *American Amnesia*.

3   G. William Domhoff, in *Changing the Powers that Be: How the Left Can Stop Losing and Win* (Lanham, MD: Rowman & Littlefield, 2003), offers the most persuasive critique of third-party strategies.

a third party on the stage of the next presidential debate to look Americans in the eye and say: "These two parties are lying to you. They can't tell you the truth because they are each trapped in decades of special interests. I am not going to tell you what you want to hear. I am going to tell you what you need to hear if we want to be the world's leaders, not the new Romans."[1]

Friedman does not explain how such a party would be organized, or how it would finance itself while flouting the "special interests" that fund the two existing parties. Nor does he discuss how and why a third party would be able to overcome the obstacles that Obama, who also pledged to tell the truth, challenge special interests, and overcome gridlock, was unable to surmount. Tea Party activists, though they in fact operate within the Republican Party, believe that a new, purer party could renew the nation in (unspecified) ways that even a purged and revitalized Republican Party cannot achieve.

Another popular trope finds the potential for political transformation in new technologies. Claims that the internet (or Twitter or cell phones) might foster effective political movements that can replace defunct or shrunken unions and mass organizations have yet to be realized.[2] Nor is Donald Trump's use of Twitter a sign that it can serve

---

1  Thomas Friedman, "Third Party Rising," *New York Times*, October 3, 2010.

2  Kay Lehman Schlozman, Sidney Verba, and Henry E. Brady, *The Unheavenly Chorus: Political Voice and the Promise of American Democracy* (Princeton: Princeton University Press, 2012), chapter 16; and Matthew Hindman, *The Myth of Digital Democracy* (Princeton: Princeton University Press, 2008).

Jennifer Earl and Katrina Kimport (*Digitally Enabled Social Change: Activism in the Internet Age* [Cambridge: MIT Press, 2011]), in perhaps the most comprehensive and precise study of online mobilization, conducted a massive survey of sites that make possible online protests such as petitions, letter-writing campaigns, email campaigns, and boycotts. They find that the web has drastically lowered the costs, in time, effort and money, of participating in social movements. The web fosters what they call "five-minute activists" (184), people who quickly sign a petition, send an email, or pledge to join a boycott. They show that as activism has migrated to the web, the role of social movement organizations has declined. The book is a catalogue of online activities mixed with paeans to "theory 2.0" models (e.g., 13). The authors track and report the number of signatures various sites gathered but have almost nothing to say about the effects of those petitions. They identify new digital repertoires of contention and show that they tend to facilitate "short, sporadic, episodic, and enduring campaigns" that often have no political content and instead pursue a

as an organizing tool. Twitter worked for Trump because "one group is as intoxicated by Twitter as Mr. Trump is: journalists." Thus, old-style broadcast media amplified each of his tweets, ensuring that "the social

wide variety of tactics to seek redress (table 8.1). The authors' examples of such isolated online efforts focus on expressing resentments and complaints, often from the participant's experiences as a consumer rather than as a citizen. The book concludes by asking, "What does a new repertoire offer to internet studies?" (188), not what the online repertoire offers to politics.

Leah A. Lievrouw (*Alternative and Activist New Media* [Cambridge: Polity, 2011]) asserts that "the rise of new, transnational social movements and radical politics [are] facilitated by global digital networks" (151). She says that the internet has been used to mobilize activists to disrupt meetings of international organizations such as the World Bank, IMF, and World Trade Organization, G8 and G20 summits, and the World Economic Forum, to produce and distribute radical content, and to engage in "hacktivism," efforts to disrupt mainstream websites. Lievrouw's focus is on the techniques of internet mobilization, and she has nothing to say about whether activists' disruption of meetings has had any effect on whether the global agencies have been less able to enact their preferred policies.

Caroline W. Lee (*Do-It-Yourself Democracy: The Rise of the Public Engagement Industry* [Oxford: Oxford University Press, 2015]), in contrast, finds that the growing realm of "deliberative democracy" has become a consumer product, provided by an industry of professionals, that offers an "activism [that] is small in scope and aligned with sponsors' goals" (226). She concludes that since opportunities for deliberation usually are not accompanied by the significant resources that would be needed to actually address problems, "the results are ultimately disappointing" (226). Instead of making it possible to increase taxes on corporate profits or the rich, "participants are encouraged by the notion that social profits are tantalizingly within their grasp with a little elbow grease and a neighbor's helping hand" (226).

Hacker and Pierson (*American Amnesia*) say "electronic organizing ... could become a powerful weapon for diffuse interests" (351) but recognize that "online participation can be thin and sporadic" and "the flexibility to move from one issue to another" can lead participants to quickly move on to a new issue, while "organizations ... face a constant tension between responding to the concerns of their most active supporters and building the broader coalitions needed to achieve lasting political success" (352).

Zeynep Tufekci (*Twitter and Tear Gas: The Power and Fragility of Networked Protest* [New Haven: Yale University Press, 2017]) argues that internet mobilization is limited by online movements' lack of decision-making mechanisms to develop effective responses to police repression or to formulate new positions as the political terrain shifts. She says social movements are effective to the extent that they can frame debates and can signal potential disruptive and electoral power. The internet is good for framing, but much less so for creating real disruption, since flash mobs dissipate quickly. Also, she argues that internet mobilizations have little electoral effect since politicians rightly discount calls and petitions generated online. Tufekci notes that governments can use the internet themselves to overwhelm citizens with information, both real and fake. And, of course, governments can use the internet to affect other countries' politics, as Russia did in the 2016 election and continues to do.

media platforms that were once heralded as democratic tools could also be used to undermine democratic norms."[1]

So far, the internet is most effective as a fundraising tool, as was the previous technological innovation, direct mail, which was pioneered in George McGovern's 1972 presidential campaign. Yet, the funds raised online or through the mail continue to be overwhelmed by money collected the nineteenth-century way, from corporations and wealthy individuals that buy the votes of candidates and officials of both parties.

Even when political hurdles are cleared and a new program is instituted, the state's weakened organizational capacity hampers implementation. Compare Medicare, which went into operation, covering 19 million citizens, only eleven months after Lyndon Johnson signed it into law in 1965, with President Obama's 2010 health care legislation. The recent law was written with a four-year delay before its government-supervised health care plans would take effect. That long delay was partly an effort to game the accounting rules of the Congressional Budget Office but also reflected the president's and Congress's shared belief that the government could not implement such a plan any faster. That belief turned out to be more than justified when the Obama administration postponed the implementation of some elements of the law from 2014 to 2015 and the online system to register applicants for government-subsidized insurance failed to operate properly for several months.

Or, compare the 2009 stimulus with government jobs programs during the New Deal or with the 2009 stimulus spending in China. In the absence of agencies capable of preparing engineering or architectural plans and managing corps of newly hired workers, the "shovel-ready" projects undertaken in the US in 2009–10 were small-scale and incremental, focused mainly on repaving roads and repairing existing infrastructure, paying for existing state and local workers who otherwise would have been laid off, and passing out tax cuts to be spent on consumer goods in the private sector. The sum effect of the stimulus spending was to merely slow the rapid decay of American

---

1   Amanda Hess, "Trump, Twitter and the Art of His Deal," *New York Times*, January 15, 2017.

roads, bridges, dams, and schools, with virtually no progress toward building the new transportation, utility, and other networks needed for international competitiveness or even to sustain existing levels of economic production. The contrast with the monumental dams and other projects constructed in the New Deal, and with the high-speed rail lines, subways, airports, and city centers accelerated by the Chinese stimulus, reveal a decline in the capacity of the US government to plan and execute large-scale projects that parallels the loss of ability to administer benefits.

## DECLINE PAST AND PRESENT

The United States is not the first dominant power to undergo decline, nor is this the first book to place American decline in comparative and historical perspective. I have written this book, and hope you will read it, because it makes a new argument about how nations decline. Decline is not inevitable; it is not determined by grand historical cycles and does not conform to a universal clock. Some great powers— Habsburg Spain, France under Louis XIV and then under Napoleon, and the Dutch Republic—lost their geopolitical or economic dominance within decades. In contrast, Britain maintained its dominance over more than a century that spanned the transition to industrial capitalism. America's ongoing decline comes after less than seventy years of dominance.

The struggle among the great European powers for geopolitical and economic dominance over the past five hundred years coexisted with the development of the capitalist world economy. This fundamental reality sets these centuries of strife apart from the conflicts of the precapitalist era. For that reason, I confine my analysis in this book to the polities that have vied for dominance since 1492. Until 1945, the competition was among European states, albeit ones with empires of colonies beyond Europe. When one declined, another European power rose to supplant it.

The United States since 1945 is different in two ways. First, it lacks the formal empire of previous great powers. Second, in its decline it will not be replaced by another Western power. No European country, nor the EU as an entity, seeks or is capable of asserting global hege-mony. The United States today is in decline mostly vis-à-vis non-West-ern countries, above all China, that were objects of, rather than partic-ipants in, the great power rivalries centered on Europe and pursued in part through colonization. Whether the United States is succeeded by China, or American hegemony is followed by a multipolar or anarchic world, the five-century era of global power centered on and organized by Westerners is coming to an end.

While this book is about the decline of great powers, it is an error to analyze those polities as unitary entities. Rather, they—like all polities—are amalgamations of institutions, each of which is controlled by an elite capable of guarding its own interests. That means we cannot predict a polity's military, economic, or geopolitical success from its absolute or relative resources because competing elites, in pursuit of their own interests, divert those resources in ways that undermine their polity's ability to carry out policies needed to achieve or maintain dominance. Put another way, "state" policies emerge out of elite conflict more often than they are expressions of a unitary ruler's (whether conceived as a capitalist class or a state manager) design that it is able to impose upon its subjects.

Elite conflict over, and appropriation of, resources explains why the richest and most powerful polities often failed to attain or sustain dominance. Dominant powers do not decline because they lack the resources to fulfill their geopolitical and economic ambitions. Rather, decline is the result of internal political dynamics that are specific to each great power and that can be understood and explained only if we trace the ways in which elites seek and attain the capacity to protect their own particular interests.

Elite conflict destabilizes each polity's internal politics. Conditions that allow a polity to achieve dominance can be undermined or forti-fied by the ways in which domestic conflicts restructure elite and class relations. As domestic social structures change, great powers enhance or weaken their capacities to respond to opportunities and threats from rival powers.

Specifically, when polities conquer other lands, creating formal or informal empires, or when a polity achieves hegemony, relations among existing elites are transformed and new elites are created in the lands the imperial or hegemonic power comes to dominate. As elites moved to protect their particular institutional interests on the new terrains created by imperialism or hegemony, they appropriated resources and stymied rival elites' institutions in ways that weakened their home polity and undermined the welfare of the home population. These elite actions thus blocked further expansion or even the maintenance of their home polity's dominance. This process did not happen in the same way in each empire or hegemon. The specific trajectories of expansion and decline were determined by the overall structure of elites and the ways in which elite and class conflict transformed those structures and thereby altered the openings for future conflicts.

My working hypothesis is that contingent chains of elite conflict and structural change determined the viability of modern empires, their relative geopolitical and economic standing, whether they became hegemons, and how long and in what form their hegemony endured. Yet we need to remember that each polity existed in a world in which they competed with varying degrees of hostility against rival powers.

The long time span and growing geographic scale over which great powers competed requires us to be aware of how the requisites of dominance changed. The sorts of resources and organizational capacities that great powers must mobilize to achieve and sustain global dominance have changed over the five hundred years from when the Habsburgs created the first modern empire, to the centuries when the Netherlands and then Britain wielded military power and capitalist hegemony (and France and Germany failed to do the same), to the heyday of American power now reaching its end. Similarly, the techniques elites used to withdraw resources from central control have varied over time and from polity to polity, in part because the organizations elites control and the methods for maintaining elite organizational power have changed over time and differ across polities.

It is the variability in how international geopolitical and economic power has been built, and the variability in how elites have fortified themselves against the interests of non-elites and rival elites, that render universal theories of decline inadequate to the tasks of explanation and prediction. However, the struggle over resources and powers is continual. Therefore, if we want to compare great powers and understand the forces that led to their rise and decline, we need to analyze how elite conflicts affected domestic social relations that, in turn, shaped each polity's ability to project power in the world, thereby recasting global economics and geopolitics.

The global economy and international relations thus are artifacts of long historical sequences of elite and class conflicts within multiple polities. Of course, some polities matter more than others, and hegemons matter the most of all. The global architectures hegemons create, or the stalemates or disorder generated by multiple powers in conflict, form the terrains on which states oppose one another and on which elites struggle for advantage within and beyond their home polities.

Invocations of past greatness, or of a unique national spirit and destiny, did not save Britain, the Netherlands, Spain, or France from defeat and decline, and they will not further American interests today. In those past moments of political decision, some commentators saw what was needed to stave off, or at least slow, decline. The problem never was, and today in America it is not, lack of knowledge or understanding of how to counter the loss of world power. In each instance, decline is a result of elites' capacity to guard their particular and immediate interests regardless of the broader and long-term consequences for their country. If we want to understand the decline of great powers past and present, we need to explain how some elites manage to escape the restraints and control of national governments, popular forces, and rival elites. That is my task in this book.

## THE ANALYTIC TASK AHEAD

My overriding goal in this book is to explain why the United States will not be able to sustain its global dominance, and to contrast its relatively brief period of hegemony with Britain's far longer era of leadership and the Netherlands' similarly short hegemony. Spain and France will also figure in the comparisons as polities that were not able to parlay their military dominance (for Spain in the sixteenth century, and for France in the seventeenth century and then again under Napoleon) into economic or geopolitical hegemony.

The first step in our analysis is to understand what hegemony is, who exercised it, and for how long, since that is the subject of our study. The myriad typologies and definitions of empires, great powers, and hegemons pose the danger of drawing our attention to too many polities over too many historical eras. In chapter 1, I will first seek to explain how hegemony under capitalism differs from the forms of dominance exerted by earlier empires, and also by the empires that have existed concurrently with each successive hegemon. This is especially important since we need to disentangle the long era of British hegemony from the even longer existence of the British Empire, the short era of Dutch hegemony from the centuries of Dutch Empire, and both from the never-hegemonic empires of Spain and France. Chapter 1 will also address the problem of how to identify elites within a hegemon and how to analyze relations among elites whose power is grounded in institutions that exist solely in the home territory with those whose structural locations are external to the home polity and those whose positions span domestic and international sites. This is necessary because our goal in the following chapters is (1) to trace changes in relations among elites in each hegemon or failed hegemon, (2) to identify the conflicts that transform those relations, and (3) to determine how the institutions that are artifacts of those conflicts facilitate or hinder each polity's capacity to maintain global hegemony. I hope the conceptual apparatus developed in chapter 1 can clarify the historical accounts and comparisons presented in the rest of the book.

This book asks questions that numerous previous authors have also sought to answer. Obviously, I would not have written this book (or it would have been a very different sort of book) if I thought past work was adequate. Chapter 2 reviews the main strands of theories on decline and presents their contributions and shortcomings.

Chapters 3 through 5 look at the internal dynamics of the two European hegemons and their challengers. Chapter 3 explains why Spain and France, despite their military dominance on the Continent, were unable to translate military power into hegemony. The answer is found in the internal dynamics of elite conflict in the two polities, and in how elite relations at home affected the acquisition of colonies and rendered Spain and France unable to funnel colonial revenues into the central treasury or to leverage military power in Europe and beyond into economic growth or control over international markets.

The Netherlands was much more successful at using its resources to capture colonies and to construct the first instance of hegemonic control over the European economy. Chapter 4 explains how that was accomplished and also how the elite structure that was created in the Netherlands' rapid rise from Habsburg colony to independence was then reinforced as the Dutch took colonies and gained hegemony. The durability of Dutch elite relations, in turn, had the unintended effect of locking the Netherlands into state policies and economic practices that prevented the Dutch from winning subsequent wars and preserving its economic hegemony. Thus, this chapter offers an explanation for the Dutch rise to and fall from hegemony that is grounded in the formation and robustness of elite relations within metropolitan Netherlands and in its empire.

Chapters 3 and 4 both raise the issue of reform. Some political figures and intellectuals understood what was needed to allow Spain, the Netherlands, or France to enhance its global military and economic position and to stave off decline. I explore why ideas for reform never moved beyond the realm of policy debate and were not implemented.

Chapter 5 examines what has been, up to now, the longest-lasting hegemon of the capitalist era: Great Britain. Again, I undertake a close analysis of elite relations and trace how they changed in the centuries from the sixteenth-century Henrician Reformation, through the 1640–51 English Revolution and Civil War, and during the creation of the British Empire in the eighteenth century and its drastic expansion in the nineteenth. I identify the moments when Britain undertook reforms that allowed it to preserve its hegemony in the transition to industrial capitalism, and explain how the elite structure of Britain itself and of its empire had the flexibility to respond to geopolitical and economic challenges.

My goal in this chapter is to explain how Britain, which by any objective measure was weaker than the United States in its era of hegemony, exercised control over the global economy and preserved a Pax

Britannica for far longer than its American successor. The chapter concludes by explaining how British elite relations became ossified at the height of Britain's world hegemony, causing the Empire and its capacities to atrophy in the last decades of the nineteenth century, and opening a period of rivalry among the declining hegemon and its challengers that culminated in two world wars and a global depression.

Chapters 6 through 8 focus on the United States. Chapter 6 begins in the early 1960s, when the United States was at the peak of its global power and elites were linked in ways that led or compelled them to harmonize their interests. I identify the forces that undermined elite coordination and allowed the emergence of autarkic elites who are able to paralyze any policy reforms that could endanger their privileges or their command over specific state powers and resources. I examine how elites became increasingly able to manipulate or paralyze governmental regulation and policymaking, and how such self-dealing and paralysis combined with the decline of unions and of locally based mass organizations to allow for the rise of right-wing politics that culminated in Trump's election.

Chapter 7 focuses on the US military. I am not the first to note that America's overwhelming (and after 1989 unprecedented) edge over all other powers has yielded only limited capacity to impose US interests around the world. The explanation of that conundrum requires us first to specify the weaknesses within the US military. Second, we need to identify the elites who set military and foreign policy, and explain how their interests and demands determine the ways in which US military and diplomatic resources are employed abroad. The gentlemen's agreement that C. Wright Mills found between economic and military elites in the 1950s has been disrupted by the transformation of economic elites in the subsequent half century. At the same time, increasing popular aversion to American war casualties has imposed real restraints on what the US government can attempt abroad. As we trace the changing interests and interactions among elites and against popular forces, we will be able to understand the real, though increasingly limited, power the United States exerts abroad, and to discuss how those limits shape elites' perceptions of, and capacities to push for, their foreign interests.

Elites, of course, are able to further their interests through economic as well as diplomatic-military means. Chapter 8 examines the bases of US economic hegemony since 1945 and how elites have been able to harness that power to further their collective and particular interests. Tensions—between the general interests of the nation, the particular interests of capitalists or of a power elite, and the specific interests and capacities of individual elites that are located both within the United States and abroad—have been resolved in various ways in the past half century. Chapter 8 traces that change and explores the implications of the fragmentation of elite interests on US economic competitiveness in manufacture and finance.

America's inability, up to this date, to enact policies that could halt and reverse, or even slow, decline points to the silliness and fantasy in most proposals for reform offered in the United States in recent years (such as those by Ralph Nader and Thomas Friedman, which we outlined at the outset of this chapter). What is needed instead is a sober and honest assessment of how inevitable decline will affect Americans' standard of living and the capacity of the US state. How does the loss of hegemony transform elite and class relations within formerly dominant polities, and what sorts of political choices are opened by those structural changes? That is the topic of the final chapter of this book. I begin that task by examining how the standard of living and the relative distribution of income and wealth changed in the Netherlands and Britain after their eras of dominance ended.

I also compare the social welfare initiatives taken by those two states and examine the geopolitical policies adopted by those states in their decades of decline. That comparison will prepare the ground for the book's concluding pages, in which I will offer my predictions on the degree to which inequality will deepen or be mitigated, social welfare programs will be gutted or strengthened, and the United States will rely on military interventions in an attempt to sustain hegemony. I will also speak to the future possibilities of a vital electoral democracy in America and the prospects for social movements to affect electoral and non-electoral politics.

Readers can approach this book in a number of ways. Those who are interested only in tracing and explaining American decline can read the introduction and then skip straight to chapter 6 and read to the end of the book. Those who want to see how America compares with previous hegemons should read chapters 3 through 5 as well. Finally, those who want to explore the theoretical bases of my analysis and see how my argument compares with the many others who have addressed the problem of decline will want to read chapters 1 and 2. For those readers, it is best to read the entire book in order.

All polities, including hegemons, are limited ultimately by their internal structures as well as by international competitors. If we want to understand why polities achieve and lose, or never attain, hegemony, we need to look systematically at their internal conflicts and at the state institutions and social structures that are created by the interplay over time of domestic conflicts and international rivalries. Sociology came into existence as a discipline in order to explain the fundamental and long-term changes Marx, Weber, and Durkheim each believed were occurring in their lifetimes.

No polity, and no elite, can pursue a policy, goal, or ambition at will. The outcomes of each initiative are determined by structures of social relations. Such structural analysis is the core concern and methodology of sociology as a discipline. It is what I as a sociologist seek to bring to the study of decline, and what sets this book apart from the many existing theories of decline (and it is on these structural grounds that I debate with the sociologists and others who address this question). Each hegemon's history and future prospects must be studied by examining the social forces that discipline and channel each actor's and each nation's hopes and desires.

# I. Hegemony Past

# 1

# Hegemons, Empires, and Their Elites

There have been numerous empires and great powers in world history but, at most, a few hegemons. What is a hegemon and how is it different from an empire or from a single power or group of dominant or great powers? How do hegemons differ from empires in the ways they rule the territories they control, in the ways they affect the rest of the world, and in how they decline?

An empire, in Julian Go's definition, is "a sociopolitical formation wherein a central political authority ... exercises unequal influence and power over the political (and in effect sociopolitical) processes of a subordinate society, peoples, or space."[1] This chapter does not offer a critical review of the myriad definitions of empire.[2] Those definitions all agree that empires differ from non-imperial polities in that they exert power over territories and peoples beyond their core polity, and that the essential dynamic of an empire is produced by the interaction between the core's efforts to sustain or expand and deepen its rule over peripheries and the peripheries' efforts to weaken or end the core's rule over them.[3]

---

1   Julian Go, *Patterns of Empire: The British and American Empires, 1688 to the Present* (New York: Cambridge University Press, 2011), 7.

2   For a review of the literature on empires, see George Steinmetz, "The Sociology of Empires, Colonies, and Postcolonialism," *Annual Review of Sociology* 40 (2014).

3   Jane Burbank and Frederick Cooper (*Empires in World History: Power and the Politics of Difference* [Princeton: Princeton University Press, 2010]) also see empires as "polities that maintain distinction and hierarchy as they incorporate new people." They contrast empires with nation-states on this basis: "The empire-state declares the non-equivalence of multiple populations ... the nation-state tends to homogenize those inside its borders and exclude those who do not belong, while the empire reaches outward and draws, usually coercively, peoples whose difference is made explicit under its rule" (8). Valerie A. Kivelson and Ronald Grigor Suny

I want to step back from definitional debates to make a basic point that will guide the analysis in this book. Empires exert a different sort of control than do hegemons, even though each hegemon had an empire and used it as one of the cornerstones of its hegemony. Those differences determine the sorts of pressures empires and hegemons endure internally and from those they subjugate, as well as the opportunities they derive from their power, and most importantly give rise to different internal political dynamics. Imperial elites are different from hegemonic elites.

Empires use their power to extract resources from their colonies and dependencies and, in so doing, change the social structures of the lands they control. At the same time, imperial metropoles themselves are changed by their domination of territories and peoples beyond their cores. Specifically, in the course of ruling other lands, empires and hegemons change the elite and class structures of both their metropoles and the lands they conquer or dominate. Social structural changes create opportunities for new elite and class conflicts that, in turn, produce further structural changes. My working hypothesis is that contingent chains of elite conflict and structural change determined the viability of modern empires, their relative geopolitical and economic standing, whether they became hegemons, and how long and in what form their hegemony endured.

## EMPIRES IN THE ERA OF CAPITALISM

Looking at the centuries from 1492 to the present, which overlap the era of capitalism and are the subject of this book, there have been six empires that have conquered or dominated enough lands beyond their immediate region to vie for global economic or geopolitical

---

(*Russia's Empires* [New York: Oxford University Press, 2017]) draw a similar contrast between empires and nation-states. "The more a state institutionalizes difference and maintains a hierarchy among its people between the ruling group or institution and the rest of the people, the more it approaches the ideal type of empire. The more a state attempts to homogenize its population, reduce difference and hierarchy, and bring the rulers in line with the people, the more it approaches the ideal type of a nation-state" (77).

dominance: Spain, France, Portugal, the Netherlands, Britain, and the United States.

The Austro-Hungarian, Ottoman, and Russian empires confined their conquests to adjacent lands, albeit, in the cases of the Ottomans and Russians, lands that spanned two continents and, for Russia, comprised the single largest polity in the modern world. None of these three empires were able, or even sought, to parlay their collection of dependencies into military power beyond Eurasia or into any form of economic dominance. The Soviet successor to the Russian Empire did, after 1945, attain a measure of global influence, but beyond Eastern Europe it was not an empire by any definition and never seriously vied with the United States for global dominance. Portugal was never a contender for geopolitical power in Europe; indeed, it was ruled by Spain from 1580 to 1640. Both before and after those decades, Portugal depended on Spain for (often ineffectual) military help in fending off Dutch efforts to seize its American and Asian colonies. Portugal's trade with its colonies was dominated by the Spanish and later by the Dutch and then the British.[1] Germany, Italy, and Belgium had some non-European colonies (and Japan had Asian colonies), but far too few to contend for global power. Germany and Japan's twentieth-century failed attempts at dominance were confined to their home continents.

As this brief accounting of modern empires makes clear, each empire did not exist in a vacuum. Each of those polities' struggles for dominance was fought on a global stage against multiple rivals at the same time as capitalists within each polity sought to attain or preserve control over sectors of production, commerce, and finance against established or emerging rivals. Conflicts among great powers and resistance from the dominated shaped geopolitics, while economic competition and exploitation cast and recast the world capitalist system. Thus, each power's dominance was constantly challenged by (1) rival geopolitical powers, (2) the extent to which its capitalists faced competition from capitalists in other polities, (3) metropolitan

---

1 John Lynch, *Spain 1516–1598: From Nation State to World Empire* (Oxford: Blackwell, 1991), 429–85; *The Hispanic World in Crisis and Change, 1598–1700* (Oxford: Blackwell, 1992), 149–57.

elites' self-serving efforts, and (4) resistance from elites in subordinate territories and from non-elites in both the metropole and colonies.

I will have very little to say, in this chapter and throughout the book, about how subjected peoples are affected by hegemonic or imperial domination. I do not seek to minimize the suffering that those who have been exploited by hegemons and empires endure. The contribution of this book does not lie in adding to the rich literature on the victims of domination. Instead, I seek to analyze how dominant powers and their elites are transformed by their efforts to expand and maintain the realms in which they exercise power. Empires and hegemons, unfortunately, did not decline because they were brutal, and exposing that brutality does not help much in understanding their declines, although, as I will show, massive cruel violence was an essential element in the rise and continuation of imperial and hegemonic power.

Elites make empires, and empires create new elites and change the structure of relations among old and new elites. If we want to understand how empires change over time, and how hegemons emerge, develop, and decline, we need to study the causal relations between elite conflict, elite structure, and class relations. Before we can begin that task, we need to define elites and differentiate them from classes, and elite conflict from class conflict.

## WHAT IS AN ELITE?

An elite is a group of rulers who inhabit a distinct organizational apparatus with the capacity to appropriate resources from non-elites. According to this definition, elites are similar to ruling classes in that both live by exploiting producing classes. However, elites differ from ruling classes in two significant ways: First, although in Marx's theoretical framework the fundamental interest of the ruling class is to reproduce its exploitative relation vis-à-vis the producing class, in my elite model this interest is complemented by an equally vital interest in guarding its existing power from, and extending its power at the expense of, rival elites. Second, each elite's capacity to pursue its interests derives from the structure of relations among various coexisting elites as much as from interclass relations of production.

Elite conflict is the primary threat to elite capacities; yet the interests each elite seeks to defend are grounded in their relations with the producing classes. Elite *capacities* change primarily when the overall structure of elite *relations* changes.[1] The outright defeat and elimination of a rival elite is rare, and when it happens it produces a decisive change in overall social structure. More commonly, elite conflict ends in stalemate or produces incremental changes in elite powers and relations that only gradually transform the overall social structure of a society.

Oftentimes, elites resolved their conflicts and fended off challenges from non-elites by combining themselves and their organizational capacities into a single institution. That was the main process that animated state formation. States were not, for the most part, created when kings used force to eliminate enemies on the battlefield or sent bureaucrats or soldiers from a capital to tax and control the hinterland. Force played a much greater role in the formation of empires than of states, yet elite combination and joint rule over complex imperial institutions was as much a part of the dynamic of empires as conquest and elimination. When multiple elites entered into a single institution, they often retained specific powers and exercised control over elements of that institution. Thus, it is a mistake to see states or empires as unified and operating under the direction of a single ruler or elite, or setting policy according to a single logic.

Elites assert and exercise through their institutions a combination of economic, political, military, and ideological powers as they seek to guard their interests against both rival elites and the non-elites from whom they extract resources. While the mix of those powers varies among elite institutions, almost never does an elite survive by relying exclusively or even primarily on a single form of power. It is an error, especially in the precapitalist world, to contrast political and economic institutions.[2] Even in the modern era, elites inhabit institutions that

1   For further discussion of this model see Richard Lachmann, *Capitalists in Spite of Themselves: Elite Conflict and Economic Transitions in Early Modern Europe* (New York: Oxford University Press, 2000), chapter 1.

2   Indeed, that is an error Marx never made. Michael Mann (*The Sources of Social Power*, volumes 1–4 [Cambridge: Cambridge University Press, 1986–2013]) builds his historical analysis upon the ways in which the four forms of power that he identified are combined by various sorts of elite and popular actors and the institutions they inhabit.

simultaneously are state-like and imbricated in production in civil society. Elites in each society were able to mobilize particular combinations of powers in their institutions. Their conflicts with each other and with non-elites were fought on terrains that were in part and simultaneously economic, political, ideological, and military. However, elites combined and exercised those powers in quite different ways in pre-state polities, ancient empires, modern empires, and nation-states. Those differences produce the different dynamics of each of those social formations. That is why we will learn little about the dynamics of empires and hegemons in the capitalist world of the past five hundred years from studying ancient empires.

In sum, elites are defined by the organizations they inhabit, organizations that mobilize a combination of powers. Ultimately, the capacities of those organizations are determined by their position in the overall structure of a polity in which multiple elites jostle to appropriate resources from non-elites. For that reason, elites and their organizations occupy very different positions in empires, nation-states, or hegemons. If the polity they inhabit gains or loses an empire, or attains or surrenders hegemony, elites come to assume different opportunities and capacities as the number of elites changes along with relations among those elites. The fundamental dynamics of ancient imperialism, modern imperialism, and capitalist hegemony generate particular sorts of elite relations and conflicts. We need to identify the basic dynamics of each type, and, in that way, we will be able to highlight what is unique about the hegemons of the past five hundred years. That will lay the theoretical basis for the analysis, in the rest of this book, of the specific dynamics of each hegemon and allow us to determine why each lost hegemony and how that loss affected and was affected by elite and class relations in the former hegemon.

## ELITES IN ANCIENT AND MODERN EMPIRES

Ancient empires had very different elite structures than modern empires. Precapitalist empires were characterized by two domestic elites at home (aristocrats/landowners and citizen-soldiers/generals/emperors), and an additional provincial elite in each of the conquered lands that was kept in line largely by military force. Modern empires were shaped and managed by multiple elites. Two of those elites—capitalists and state officials—were fundamentally different from the elites of precapitalist empires, even as those modern elites, like their ancient predecessors, were sustained in their imperial endeavors by their home country's military power. In modern empires, where older elites—most often landed aristocrats and military officers—played key roles along with capitalists and civilian state officials, those older elites differed fundamentally from the armed men and landowners of precapitalist empires because (1) they wielded much greater infrastructural power than their ancient counterparts, and (2) they had to share imperial power with modern capitalists and state officials.

*Capitalists*, unlike merchants in ancient empires, did not have to wait until imperial armies had conquered new lands to control trade routes and extract revenues from foreign lands. Capitalists enjoyed a high degree of autonomy for two reasons. First, unlike merchants in precapitalist empires, who often engaged in commerce as a secondary activity to their primary military, officeholding, or landholding positions, capitalists were genuinely separate elites at home because they had independent organizational capacities to appropriate resources from non-elites. Second, capitalists were able to engage in commerce with their counterparts from other polities, which gave them further leverage at home.

*State officials* in modern empires differed from their ancient counterparts in that they could deploy strong nonmilitary organizational capacities that gave them "infrastructural power"[1] to penetrate conquered societies. This gave modern imperial administrators means in addition to the threat of force that they could use to manipulate local elites, and, in some cases, to interact with and extract resources directly from the mass of subjects in the lands they conquered.

Capitalists and state officials had varying effects on metropoles and colonies, and on the place of their empire in the world economic and geopolitical system. Those variations, across time and space, had little to do with the resources and capacities those elites initially commanded as they began their imperial conquests and instead were

---

1   Mann, *Sources of Social Power*, volume 1, 11.

determined mainly by three factors: the number of elites, their location, and the overall structure of their relations.

*Number*: Imperialism created new elites at home and in the colonies. Some of the colonial elites were people from the metropole who came to the colonies as permanent settlers or temporarily as administrators, soldiers, merchants, landlords, slaveholders, and/or capitalists. Indigenous elites often were incorporated into the empires that conquered their homelands, either retaining their existing organizational bases (which would be altered significantly by their new place in an empire) and/or being recruited into new colonial organizations created by the conquering empire.

The mere addition of new elites to the existing number of elites disrupted existing elite relations in modern empires. This prevented the stalemates between two metropolitan elites that characterized ancient empires, and that were rarely affected by distant provincial elites. Modern empires thus had more complex dynamics than ancient empires, if only because they had more elites, which created more complex elite structures that had more points for conflict and therefore for change.

In addition, capitalism itself was more dynamic than any previous economic system, and the global reach of both capitalism and modern geopolitics ensured further opportunities for conflict and structural change. The extent to which capitalists cooperated, came into conflict with each other and with other elites, or sought to achieve autarkic positions varied among empires and over the course of each hegemonic cycle. I address the implications of that process at the end of this chapter.

*Location*: Some colonial elites became permanent settlers in colonies while others left the metropole only temporarily or moved among colonies, and others were involved in colonial rule and exploitation without ever leaving home. Of course, indigenous elites remained located in their colonies of origin. As we will see below, settlers enjoyed more autonomy than officials and capitalists who were only temporarily based in colonies. Empires with settler colonies had very different dynamics than those empires without such colonies, although the very different trajectories of the Spanish and British empires remind us that this factor exerted its causal force in interaction with the number and structure of relations among elites.

*Structure*: Multiple elites in different and often shifting locations made possible varying and changing alliances among elites. Those alliances, in turn, shaped the elite conflicts that then eliminated elites, created new elites, changed the strategic meanings of each elite's location, and altered the structure of elite relations, which in turn opened new possibilities of alliance and conflict.

## TYPES OF MODERN EMPIRES

Modern empires varied in the extent to which colonial elites were autonomous from metropolitan officials. Similarly, while colonial elites in ancient empires had little effect on the metropole's economy or politics, some modern colonial elites have had a strong influence over the metropole.

Table 1.1 situates ancient and modern empires along these two dimensions.

**Table 1.1: Structural Relations Between Imperial Metropoles and Colonial Elites**

|  |  | Colonial Elites' Level of Autonomy from Metropolitan Officials | |
|---|---|---|---|
|  |  | **High** | **Low** |
|  |  | Spanish American colonies | Dutch colonies |
|  | **High** | British settler colonies | British India & other non-settler colonies |
| **Colonial Elites' Influence on Metropole's Economy and/or Politics** |  | French colonies | US formal and informal colonies |
|  | **Low** | German colonies | Napoleonic empire |
|  |  | Ancient empires | Nazi empire |

The empires in each quadrant had significantly different dynamics. We will begin with the lower left quadrant, the empires whose colonial elites enjoyed the most autonomy from the metropole and also had the least influence on metropolitan economy and politics. This will allow us to understand the essential differences between ancient and modern colonial elites, and also to see how Germany, an empire that never sought geopolitical or economic dominance, differed from the ones that pursued such ambitions. Next, we will focus on the upper left quadrant to see how colonial elites can affect elite relations in the metropole even when they retain a high degree of autonomy.

We will then look at two cases of almost pure colonial exploitation, the Napoleonic and Nazi European empires in the lower right quadrant. While geopolitical forces (i.e., defeat in war) quickly felled both empires, had they endured, both Napoleon's and Hitler's empires would have transformed the structure of elite relations in the metropole. Early signs of those changes provide a basis to speculate on the sort of imperial polity that would have developed, and to compare that structure and the dynamics of that quadrant to those in the upper right quadrant.

The three polities in the upper right quadrant are the three capitalist hegemons of the last three centuries: the polities that are the core comparison of this book. I will reserve detailed analysis of those three cases, and of the Spanish and French empires, for the rest of this book. My goal, in the concluding sections of this chapter, is to contrast hegemons to the other cases and to offer a series of hypotheses about how hegemonic social structure and the resulting dynamic of elite conflict differ from the other three types. This will also allow us to adjudicate among various definitions scholars have previously proposed for hegemony and in that way clarify how my approach differs from theirs.

## AUTONOMOUS COLONIAL ELITES

Elites in the conquered territories of ancient empires enjoyed autonomy mainly because those empires lacked the infrastructural capacity to control those elites' behavior or to appropriate much of the surplus local elites extracted from non-elites.[1] Empires prevented rebellions in conquered territories by using exemplary terrorism, such as the Athenians' massacre of men and enslavement of women on Lesbos and Melos or the Romans' crucifixion of thousands of defeated slaves at the end of the Third Servile War in 73–71 BC, which led to an abrupt end of such uprisings. However, empires lacked enough soldiers or material resources to occupy or repeatedly invade its colonies, hence the decision to use extreme violence in suppressing rebellions.

The everyday administrators of conquered territories were either local elites, who were co-opted into service to the empire in return for a large share of the surplus expropriated from non-elites, or administrators from the metropole to whom the imperial court also had to concede a large share of the revenues appropriated from locals. If metropolitan administrators were allowed to serve in a single colonial locale for long periods, they tended to ally (and often intermarry) with local elites. The danger to rulers was greater if they appointed generals, who controlled armed men who could be marched to the capital to overthrow the ruler, as local administrators. On the other hand, civilian administrators who could not back their decrees with armed force were less of a threat both to the ruler and to the locals from whom they were expected to extract resources and obedience. If imperial officials were rotated among colonies frequently, they lacked local knowledge and became heavily dependent on local elites in controlling and taxing non-elites. In any case, colonial elites achieved a high degree of autonomy from the metropole.[2]

----

1    The discussion of ancient empires in this section draws mainly on studies of the Roman Empire from Keith Hopkins, "The Political Economy of the Roman Empire," in *The Dynamics of Ancient Empires: State Power from Assyria to Byzantium*, eds. Ian Morris and Walter Scheidel (New York: Oxford University Press, 2009), 178–204; Perry Anderson, *Passages from Antiquity to Feudalism* (London: New Left Books, 1974); G. E. M. Ste. Croix, *The Class Struggle in the Ancient Greek World: From the Archaic Age to the Arab Conquests* (Ithaca: Cornell University Press, 1981); Colin Wells, *The Roman Empire* (Stanford: Stanford University Press, 1984); Kevin Greene, *The Archaeology of the Roman Empire* (London: Batsford, 1986); and more generally on Mann, *Sources of Social Power*, volume 1, chapter 9; and Lachmann, *Capitalists in Spite of Themselves*, 7–15.

2    China at first glance appears different from Western empires in the longevity of its bureaucracy, which spanned multiple dynasties. However, Chinese bureaucrats also oscillated between eras of rapid rotation among posts in which they ceded much

Rulers' attempts to deepen control over colonies and over colonial elites were stymied by several factors beyond their lack of resources and infrastructural capacity. First, rulers exercised only limited power over rival metropolitan elites. Ancient rulers enjoyed what Mann describes as "despotic powers [that were] virtually unlimited,"[1] i.e., emperors could expropriate or kill any individual they targeted. However, emperors sparked rebellions if they did not maintain the support or at least the quiescence of most of the members of metropolitan elites, and they could do so only by sharing the fruits of their conquests and rule. Each ruler also needed to enrich loyalists at the court to prevent palace coups or assassination, and to give colonial elites enough of the local surplus to ensure they did not rebel. These imperatives of imperial survival mired ancient empires in perpetual fiscal crisis. Even in times of relative financial stability, those empires lacked the resources as well as the technological means to build an infrastructure that would have allowed rulers to create their own organizations capable of collecting revenue or ruling conquered territories without depending on armed forces or local elites.

Second, ancient empires, indeed all polities until the advances in transportation and communication of the nineteenth century, faced severe logistical limits in waging military campaigns more than a few days' march from home. Their capacities for transporting provisions were highly limited, especially at sites not directly accessible by ships from sea. Animals, like humans, ate more in a week than they could carry. As a result, armies had to feed themselves and their animals by pillaging farms and urban storehouses as they fought. This restricted war and conquest to settled agricultural areas with surpluses capable of producing enough food to support both the farmers and the marauding troops. As a result, armies either focused their efforts on

---

power to local landlords and being allowed careers in single localities where they forged links to local elites. Dingxin Zhao, in *The Confucian-Legalist State: A New Theory of Chinese History* (Oxford: Oxford University Press, 2015), argues that the separation of bureaucrats' political and ideological power from landlords' economic power was the key to the bureaucracy's longevity. That separation also ensured a high degree of autonomy for local landlord elites while minimizing their influence on the central state.

1   Mann, *Sources of Social Power*, volume 1, 113.

rape, murder, and pillage, in the hope their exemplary violence would terrify locals into paying tribute after the soldiers left, or the soldiers remained in the conquered lands with only episodic communication from and limited control by rulers in the metropole. This meant that resident colonial administrators had a high degree of autonomy from the metropole, while over time soldiers and civilian administrators established familial and economic ties with locals.

Colonies' geographic, communicative, and organizational distance from the metropole also meant that premodern colonial elites had little influence over the metropole's economy and politics. Colonial elites' links with metropolitan elites declined over time as invaders combined with local elites, as discussed above. The backward colonial economies were not significant markets for metropolitan producers. Colonies sent raw goods and slaves to the metropole. As those flows waxed and waned, the metropolitan economy experienced booms and busts, but class relations and the level of production in the metropole remained unchanged by the actions of elites in the colonies.[1]

The combination of high autonomy for colonial elites and low influence on the metropole did not entirely end with the creation of modern empires that were linked together through capitalist trade and production and through modern infrastructural advances that allowed for rapid communication. The German Empire consisted of colonies in Africa and the western Pacific, and concessions in China. The colonies were established in the 1880s and '90s, and all were lost during or at the end of World War I. Geopolitically, they were insignificant. Britain and the other great powers regarded Germany as a threat in Europe but not elsewhere, and so were willing to compromise with

---

1    The extent of control the Ottomans were able to exert in their empire was not much greater than what the Romans had achieved 1,500 years earlier. Like the Romans, "the Ottomans understood well the limits of their rule, in terms of both the geographical reach of their control and their limited manpower, and fashioned an empire that was based on organizational diversity . . . accepting of multiple systems of rule, multiple negotiated frontiers, laws and courts, forms of revenue management, and religious diversity" (Karen Barkey, *Empire of Difference: The Ottomans in Comparative Perspective* [Cambridge: Cambridge University Press, 2008], 70). This resulted in an empire with a high degree of autonomy for provincial elites, but also an imperial court that was largely invulnerable to influence from outside.

the Germans' desire for an empire by conceding them lands in Africa, the Pacific, and China.[1]

The German Empire's marginality to its economy and to world geopolitics meant that conflicts among colonial elites could play out without the confounding effects of heavy interventions from central authorities or from capitalists based in the metropole. The German state had the resources and infrastructural capacity to monitor what their agents were doing in the colonies and to intervene to force a change in policy. Yet the central state did not utilize that capacity, and metropolitan elites did not exert enough pressure to make the state do so. This allows us, with the help of Steinmetz,[2] to understand a key mechanism through which colonial officials, though not settler or local/comprador elites who are discussed in the following sections, gained autonomy from the metropole.

What does Steinmetz find? First, colonial officials did not arrive in conquered lands as individuals. Rather, they came as representatives of elites transplanted from home and maintained their distinct identities in the colonies. The three principal metropolitan German elites, "the nobility, the propertied bourgeoisie, and the Bildungsbürgertum (i.e., the educated middle class),"[3] arrived in the colonies with distinct forms of capital that they deployed to gain control over the German colonial government. The main terrain of struggle was over "native policy." Each elite made claims to "ethnographic expertise" based on the sort of cultural capital they brought to the colonies from Germany.

Steinmetz shows how "drawn-out contests between different fractions of a splintered dominant class may prevent a field from being settled while enhancing its autonomy, as field-specific modes of action

1   Bernard Porter, *The Lion's Share: A Short History of British Imperialism 1850–1983*, second edition (London: Longman, 1984), 101–11; Patrick K. O'Brien, "The Security of the Realm and the Growth of the Economy, 1688–1914," in *Understanding Decline: Perceptions and Realities of British Economic Performance*, eds. Peter Clarke and Clive Trebilcock (Cambridge: Cambridge University Press, 1997), 49–72.

2   George Steinmetz, "The Colonial State as a Social Field," *American Sociological Review* 73 (2008); *The Devil's Handwriting: Precoloniality and the German Colonial State in Qingdao, Samoa, and Southwest Africa* (Chicago: University of Chicago Press, 2007).

3   Steinmetz, *Devil's Handwriting*, 597.

become more systematic and clearly defined,"[1] and provide a basis for colonial elites to "enhance their autonomy from the metropolitan state over time."[2] In other words, while the three German elites fought with one another over how to deal with natives, they fought on the basis of expert knowledge, which they claimed was refined through firsthand experience in ruling over the particular natives of the colonies they inhabited.

As each elite asserted expert knowledge, it gained control of particular colonies: the military-nobility in Southwest Africa, the *Bildungsbürgertum* in Samoa, and eventually in Qingdao, China, as well. Merchants achieved dominance nowhere. Claims of expertise shielded colonial elites from their putative superiors in Berlin, from the metropolitan elites that lobbied officials back in Germany, and from elites in other colonies who, because they ruled different sorts of natives, had different expertise that could not be automatically transferred to another colony.

Once an elite gained control of a colony, it was able to prevent metropolitan Germans from interfering in colonial policies directly or from exerting indirect influence by allying with one colonial elite against the others in return for policy decisions or a share of the colonial spoils. This was evidenced in the growing capacity of colonial officials to take actions that were inimical to the admittedly marginal interests of metropolitan capitalists, or even to the central German government's minor geopolitical interests in its colonies. It is also demonstrated by the very different native policies officials pursued in Southwest Africa, Samoa, and Qingdao, differences that cannot be derived from economic or geopolitical considerations. At the same time, colonial officials' particular expertise and their organizational bases gave them no leverage against elites in the metropole. Unlike the colonies or quasi-colonies of Britain, France, Spain, the Netherlands, Portugal, and later the United States, German colonies did not affect elite relations back home. German colonial elites, in other words, deepened their autonomy by isolating themselves from metropolitan interests.

---

1    Steinmetz, "The Colonial State as a Social Field," 600.
2    Ibid., 591–2.

Colonial officials in other empires' colonies were not able to construct and act on their claims of expertise unimpeded, as we will see below. The metropolitan governments in London and Paris (and Brussels, Rome, and Washington) created central agencies to manage (with varying degrees of success) the officials they posted in their colonies, even when those men in the field claimed expertise in managing natives. Decades later, the Nazis overruled diplomats, military officers, and businessmen to set "native policy" for the conquered lands of Europe and enforced tight control over German officials in those lands. Uniquely, German colonies' economic and geopolitical insignificance magnified the power of colonial officials' cultural claims but also guaranteed their isolation from metropolitan politics. The effect of that absence on the dynamics of the entire empire can best be understood in comparison to the empires in the upper half of table 1.1, whose colonies did affect the metropole's political economy.

## COLONIAL ELITES IN THE METROPOLE

Valuable and geopolitically crucial colonies captured the interest, and provoked the intervention, of elites back home. Yet in the Spanish, French, and British empires, listed in the upper left quadrant of table 1.1, colonial elites retained a high degree of autonomy even as they profoundly affected social relations back in the metropole. How was that accomplished?

Some of the colonies seized by the French, Spanish, and British were immensely valuable, and the riches that could be taken from them were quickly apparent to elites in the metropole. Metropolitan elites vied with one another to control colonies by planting their representatives in offices and on landed estates in the conquered lands. The multiple elites in metropolitan Spain and France did not each create a distinct colonial elite in their image, differentiated by forms of cultural capital (as in the German colonies) or by distinct organizational apparatuses. Rather, Spanish and French kings, great nobles, clerics, and state officials each granted a welter of concessions to men journeying to the colonies in return for up-front payments or promised shares of future revenues. While the monarchs were, at least in theory, the ultimate arbiters of conflicting colonial claims, kings often ceded that power or specific colonial concessions to metropolitan elites in return for revenues or domestic political support, further undermining metropolitan leverage over colonial elites.

High levels of conflict among metropolitan elites were a necessary but not sufficient condition for colonial elites to achieve autonomy from the metropole. As James Mahoney[1] demonstrates through his comparison of Spanish American colonies, the colonies' pre-conquest social structure shaped colonial elites' organizational capacities and thereby determined whether they could sustain their autonomy against efforts by monarchs and other metropolitan elites to reassert (or often to assert for the first time) control over colonial officials and resources.

Mahoney finds that Spanish American colonial elites were more unified in territories where they were able to plant themselves in rich, complex, and densely settled precolonial societies. Colonial elites magnified their control over indigenous peoples where they could appropriate already-existing complex systems of rule and where the conquered peoples were populous enough to supply sufficient labor to work plantations and mines. In those colonies, Spanish conquistadors were able to establish what Mahoney labels "higher levels" of "mercantilist colonialism." Mahoney's detailed histories of each colony show that, where a high level of mercantile colonialism was established, there was a tight linkage that in practice amounted to a fusion of officials, clerics, landlords, and merchants. In territories (such as what later became the southern cone countries of Chile, Argentina, and Uruguay) where indigenous peoples were few and scattered and did not have a complex polity, Spanish conquistadors were unable to extract enough resources to sustain themselves in significant numbers. In those territories, the colonial elites had little leverage over the crown and other metropolitan elites, and in the eighteenth century the Spanish crown was able to insert new elites that competed with and subordinated the earlier settlers.

Mahoney identifies a different mechanism for Spanish American elite autonomy than does Steinmetz for German colonial elites.

---

1 James Mahoney, *Colonialism and Postcolonial Development: Spanish America in Comparative Perspective* (Cambridge: Cambridge University Press, 2010).

However, those mechanisms reflect the particular elite structures in the two metropoles and the two empires' organizational capacities. German colonial elites did not have to leverage the political infrastructures of the lands they conquered because they arrived with far more sophisticated (bureaucratized) organizations than did the Spanish conquistadors, possessed far better technologies to communicate with one another and back to the metropole, and wielded far more deadly military technology in the nineteenth century than the Spanish did in their centuries of American rule (in the oft-quoted words of the mediocre British poet Hilaire Belloc, "Whatever happens, we have got / The Maxim gun, and they have not").

Beyond the different capacities German and Spanish elites brought to their colonies, they arrived holding different positions in the overall elite structure of the two empires. German colonists came from already distinct metropolitan elites, defined more by their sort of cultural capital than by a matrix of structural relations between colonial offices and metropolitan institutions.

In contrast, Spanish colonists held offices and controlled *encomiendas* and other concessions that overlapped and brought them into conflicts with one another. As long as Spanish colonial elites had to appeal to the Habsburg monarchs, or to other elites to whom the crown had ceded colonial authority, to clarify and guarantee their jurisdictions, they remained limited in their assertions of autonomy.[1] However, where there were rich and complex indigenous social organizations that Spanish conquistadors could appropriate, colonial elites were able to rapidly structure themselves in ways that reduced their organizational and ideological dependence on their metropolitan patrons. In terms of winning autonomy, the conquistadors' social appropriations of pre-conquest indigenous structures served the same purpose as the more gradual German colonial elites' construction of expertise and British settler colonists' creation of national identities and institutions (above all representative assemblies). Similarly, French colonial elites unified themselves and guaranteed their autonomy by building slave institutions on islands where they had

---

1  John H. Elliott, *Empires of the Atlantic World: Britain and Spain in America, 1492–1830* (New Haven: Yale University Press, 2006), 353–68 and passim.

exterminated the indigenous population. However, when and where slaves rebelled (most notably in Haiti), the colonial elites again became dependent on the metropole and had to surrender autonomy to save themselves.

The structures of rule created in the first moment of colonization mattered for subsequent economic development[1] as well as for the room imperial rulers back in the metropolitan capital enjoyed to restructure colonial rule. The complexity of metropolitan elite relations in Spain and France in the sixteenth through eighteenth centuries meant that colonial elites often had multiple patrons whom they could play off against one another for further autonomy. As the wealth produced in the colonies increased, metropolitan elites themselves gained an advantage in their struggles with one another to the extent that they could win the (at least temporary) loyalty and financial support of colonial elites. This, of course, gave colonial elites greater leverage in their negotiations with monarchs and other metropolitan elites for autonomy and to keep a larger share of the revenues they generated. The colonies with less dense indigenous societies and weak colonial elites contributed little to and had little influence on the metropole.

Colonial elites' deals with metropolitan elites were often significant, and at times proved decisive, in the outcomes of French and Spanish metropolitan elite conflicts. That is how colonial elites affected the structure of elite relations for the empires in this quadrant. The sort of transformation was very different from that which occurred in hegemons (discussed below). The Spanish and ancien régime French empires did not create new metropolitan elites; instead, they affected the balance of power among existing elites.

How did colonial elites' interference in metropolitan elite conflicts matter for Spain and France's ability to compete geopolitically and in the world economy? I will present a detailed answer to that question in chapter 3. However, what we must note here is that the stability and

---

1   Mahoney's goal in his book is to explain post-independence economic and social development. He is less concerned with the effects of colonial rule on the metropole. However, I have taken advantage of his prodigious historical research and the structure of his argument to draw conclusions about the metropole.

autonomy of elites in Spanish and French colonies, while initially made possible by elite instability in the metropoles, then helped to sustain and deepen elite conflicts in France and Spain. In that sense, the French and Spanish metropoles were uniquely disordered among the empires and hegemons discussed in this book and represented in table 1.1.

Colonial elite unity and metropolitan elite disorder weakened Spain and France's geopolitical positions. While all the great powers attempted to seize one another's colonies from the initial colonization of the Americas through World War II, Spain and France were uniquely vulnerable because their especially autonomous colonial elites at times were able to ally, or threaten to ally, with rival powers against their nominal rulers, seeking better terms from a new master or greater concessions from their current monarch. Britain had a similar vulnerability, but only with their settler colonies, most notably the Americans, whose victory was sealed with French support. Germany's colonies were not vulnerable in the same way, since Britain, which acquiesced in and at times facilitated Germany's colonial acquisitions, did not see value in antagonizing the German state by interfering in its colonies. This reduced German colonial elites' leverage over the state, and therefore the extent to which those elites or the fate of their colonies entered into German metropolitan politics.

Similarly, British settler colonists did not win their autonomy due to a general lack of capacity on the part of metropolitan officials. Britain's non-settler colonies, above all India, are in the opposite quadrant in table 1.1 from British America even though all were part of a single empire. While Britain's overall imperial capacity to monitor and project force was common to the settler and non-settler colonies,[1] those two groups of possessions differed fundamentally in the numbers

---

1   The British Empire's capacities did differ over time, as Julian Go reminds us. However, imperial capacities also varied across the empire at the same time. The American colonies gained independence in the same years as the British East India Company was subordinated to the state, and Canada, Australia, and New Zealand had their greatest leverage at the height of British hegemony. To solve that seeming conundrum we need to analyze the dynamics of hegemons, as we will do on a theoretical level at the end of this chapter, and in terms of Britain's particular history, as we will do in chapter 5.

and self-organization of Britons in each colony. In India and the other non-settler colonies, Britons were few and remained highly dependent on metropolitan power and capital of all varieties. (I will discuss the implications of that dependency in the section on hegemons below.)

American and other British settler colonial elites, unlike German colonial administrators or Britons in India, did not plan to return home and therefore assumed identities based on their American social positions and the sorts of capital they could accumulate in the colonies.[1] The growing numbers of British settlers in America built their own organizational capacities that progressively lowered their governmental, military, and economic dependence on Britain and, as the 1776 revolution demonstrated, gave them the ability to subvert and challenge officials shipped over from the metropole. In the nineteenth century, settlers in Canada, Australia, and New Zealand achieved a high degree of autonomy and got major concessions from Britain without having to mount their own wars of independence.

British settler colonists strengthened their autonomy by weakening two sources of leverage that European metropolitan governments exerted in other colonies. First, as British settlers created their own governments and were able to limit the number of officials appointed by the crown rather than chosen by the settlers themselves, Britain lost the ability to play settlers against each other in the competition for lucrative offices, as the Spanish and French were able to do at first in their colonies.[2] As the Spanish and French crowns sold colonial offices, they too lost that leverage, and colonial elites won increasing autonomy.

--------

1   T. H. Breen's *The Marketplace of Revolution: How Consumer Politics Shaped American Independence* (New York: Oxford University Press, 2004) shows how colonial Americans' growing wealth created a culture of consumerism that allowed boycotts of British goods in the 1770s to create an American identity, transcending both local differences and their status as British subjects, that became a foundation of popular resistance. The sort of cultural capital Breen describes is very different from the expertise Steinmetz analyzes; however, both American consumerism and German colonial native policy contrasted local knowledge and practices to the uninformed dictates or unjust demands of metropolitan officials.

2   Elliott, *Empires of the Atlantic World*, 237–45.

Second, settlers also reduced their dependence on the British state and its armed forces by exterminating rather than subjugating the natives. Indeed, the British recognized this point of pressure by at times encouraging Native American attacks on defiant American colonists, and native policy became a key issue for American revolutionaries. As long as settlers did not become dependent on native labor (a problem the southern American colonies solved with slaves), Britain remained limited in the leverage it could gain from native attacks. New Zealanders lost little autonomy when they had to call on British troops to defeat Maori rebellions, while British settlers in southern Africa were limited in their assertions of autonomy by economies organized on the basis of cheap native labor.

Finally, American colonies, like the Spanish and some French colonies, were of such importance as a market for British manufacturers that those businessmen in the metropole intervened with their parliamentary representatives to repeal the Stamp Act.[1] The path from colonial customer to metropolitan influence was more direct in Britain than in France or Spain because, first, British manufacturers had greater leverage in a parliamentary system than Spanish or French merchants had with their absolutist monarchs. Second, Britain encroached on French and Spanish colonial markets, diminishing the importance of colonial markets for continental manufacturers and merchants, which in turn diminished those metropolitan elites' leverage over the central government.

Let us summarize our findings in this and the previous section with a Boolean analysis.

We can see that colonial elites were able to attain autonomy through various mechanisms. Any one mechanism was enough to attain autonomy: German colonial elites' cultural capital of expertise in native management, the slave institutions created by French colonists in the Caribbean and British settlers in the southern colonies, the national identities created by British settler colonists, or the complex indigenous institutions that Spanish conquistadors appropriated to build their own unified social networks and system of rule. Colonial elites were unable to exercise autonomy only in those Spanish colonies

---

1   Ibid., 316.

where natives were scattered and complex social institutions did not exist, and, as we will see below, in the Napoleonic and Nazi European empires and in hegemons' non-settler colonies.

Table 1.2:  **Boolean Truth Table of Colonial Elite Autonomy**

| Colonies | Four Mechanisms | | | | Outcome: Colonial Autonomy |
| --- | --- | --- | --- | --- | --- |
| | I | C | N | S | |
| German | 0 | 1 | 0 | 0 | 1 |
| French | 0 | 0 | 0 | 1 | 1 |
| British Settler | 0 | 0 | 1 | 0 | 1 |
| British Settler (American South) | 0 | 0 | 1 | 1 | 1 |
| Spanish Strong Mercantile | 1 | 0 | 0 | 0 | 1 |
| Spanish Weak Mercantile | 0 | 0 | 0 | 0 | 0 |

I = complex indigenous structures appropriated by colonizers
C = colonial elites create cultural capital
N = settlers create national identity
S = settlers create slave institutions

Colonial autonomy did not translate automatically into influence in the metropole. The pathways through which colonial elites exerted influence on the metropole and the issues on which that influence made a difference varied across empires and eras. Thus, we need to analyze the full elite structure of each empire if we want to explain why colonial elites had influence on some issues and with some metropolitan elites while being marginal at other times and places. I undertake that task in chapters 3 through 5.

## PURE IMPERIAL EXPLOITATION[1]

Napoleon and Hitler's European empires, like Spain's American empire, conquered existing societies with dense populations and complex indigenous social institutions. Like the conquistadors, Napoleon and Hitler's armies, especially the latter, relied on local collaborators to raise revenues, to corral strategic materials and manufactured goods, and, in the case of the Nazis, to round up Jews for extermination. Napoleon differed from Hitler in his ambition to transform the societies he conquered, and obviously in the goals he had for his conquered dominions. Yet the dense and complex local societies did not provide an opening for the Napoleonic or Nazi elites sent to administer and loot conquered lands to win autonomy. Those two empires stand as polar opposites to the Spanish Empire, or to France's non-European colonies, even during the Napoleonic era.

The key difference between the Napoleonic and Nazi empires and all others lies in their extreme dominance by a single military or military-party elite in the metropole. That single elite was able to exercise tight control over the men they sent to rule and exploit the conquered lands. As a result, neither capitalists nor civilian state officials in those two empires were able to gain independent access to conquered lands. This weakened the leverage of capitalists and state officials both at home and in the conquered lands. Nor could the "colonial" elites of the Napoleonic and Nazi empires exploit divisions among metropolitan elites in the way that Spanish American elites did. Napoleon had built on the achievements of the revolutionary governments that preceded his in suppressing the aristocracy and subordinating capitalists, while the Nazi Party achieved tight control over the pre-Nazi civil service, intimidated the military, and confined capitalists and landowners to an ever more

---

1   The discussion of the Nazi empire in this section relies upon Mark Mazower, *Hitler's Empire: How the Nazis Ruled Europe* (New York: Penguin, 2008); Gotz Aly, *Hitler's Beneficiaries: Plunder, Racial War, and the Nazi Welfare State* (New York: Metropolitan, 2005); Peter Fritzsche, *Life and Death in the Third Reich* (Cambridge: Harvard University Press, 2008), chapter 3; and Nicholas Stargardt, *The German War: A Nation under Arms, 1939–1945, Citizens and Soldiers* (New York: Basic, 2015). The discussion of Napoleonic France relies on the materials presented below in chapter 3.

marginal role. Mann[1] notes that, after World War II, landowners were eliminated as a significant class in Germany, and attributes that to Nazi policies that fatally weakened the Junkers' political and economic bases of power. Mann hypothesizes that, had the Nazis remained in power, the existing capitalist class would have met the same fate, under a postwar state-controlled economy.

The military elite of the Napoleonic Empire and the Nazi Party were on paths to becoming single ruling elites, forcing capitalists, landowners, and civilian state officials (and in Germany the military command as well) into subordinate positions that would have left them somewhat privileged but not elites in the sense of having independent organizational capacities to extract resources, and the power and autonomy that went with such capacities. The high administrative capacities of both the Napoleonic and Nazi regimes ensured that the officials and soldiers sent to rule conquered European lands remained under close surveillance and tight supervision, unlike the ancient Roman or Ottoman colonial elites. French revolutionary ideology and Nazi racial doctrines also made occupying elites loath to establish ties with local conquered elites that could have provided a basis for resistance against metropolitan edicts. Napoleon and Hitler's defeats cut off that process. The sudden elimination of Napoleon's army and the Nazi Party created structural room for the reemergence of capitalists and new state elites in both countries. A new corps of state officials and a new capitalist elite in post-Napoleonic France became the central actors in sustaining and expanding France's non-European empire in the nineteenth and twentieth centuries.

Would a single elite, organized within the Napoleonic state or the Nazi Party, have been able to sustain a monopoly on power in the metropole and the conquered lands if Napoleon and Hitler had won their wars? The answer for France seems almost certainly to be no. Napoleon was far less able than Hitler to suppress resistance in conquered lands, and the need to accommodate local actors would have provided a basis for the French military elite in each conquered territory to develop interests and organizational capacities separate

---

1   Michael Mann, *Fascists* (Cambridge: Cambridge University Press, 2004); see also Dylan Riley, "Enigmas of Fascism," *New Left Review* 30 (2004).

from the metropolitan ruling elite. The Nazis' success in rapidly conquering much of Europe, and unprecedented capacity and willingness to use massive terror, ensured little resistance in its empire, blocking a potential basis for division between party officials in Germany and abroad.[1] The Nazi empire, had it survived, would have become the only empire with a single elite, eliminating elite conflict as a basis for structural change in the foreseeable future. In that way, the Nazi empire was unique in world history, and on its way to creating an actual "end of history" in its domains.

We need, however, to remember that empires never exist in a vacuum. Unlike the ancient empires, which were bordered by deserts and sparsely inhabited woodlands, the Nazi empire was part of the modern world. The war making that created it also inevitably brought it into contact with the forces that destroyed it. Nor could the Nazi regime make peace with its enemies, since continual conquest was necessary to bring in enough loot to sustain the German economy and to sustain the regime's ideological hegemony at home.[2] As a pure empire without elite conflict, the Nazi regime was a short-lived anomaly, indicative of how the elite structure of metropoles remained the ultimate limitation on colonial elites' autonomy and on the ways in which they could affect metropolitan politics and economics.

--------------

1   Riley contrasts "a regime of collaboration with the ruling class" in France with "the war against the Soviet Union [that] was from the beginning a war against the entire Soviet political class" (Dylan Riley, "The Third Reich as Rogue Regime: Adam Tooze's *Wages of Destruction*," *Historical Materialism* 22 [2014], 343). However, the majority of the loot taken in war came from the East and, as Riley emphasizes, conquest in the East was central to Nazi ideology and the basis of a link with the old German elites. The weight of German desire and power always faced east, making it unlikely, though not impossible, that an emergent elite of German occupiers in France and the other Western lands could have become a counterweight to a combined domestic and Eastern ruling party elite in a postwar Nazi Europe.

2   Adam Tooze, *The Wages of Destruction: The Making and Breaking of the Nazi Economy* (Harmondsworth: Penguin, 2007). Riley challenges Tooze's view of Germany as economically backward and therefore forced to play a weak economic hand to inevitable defeat once Hitler decided on a war of conquest. In contrast, Riley sees Germany's war of Eastern conquest as the result of Germany being locked out of imperial expansion by Britain's ability to hold its empire and by the Bolshevik Revolution, "which at a stroke removed a vast zone of potential economic expansion from what was arguably the most dynamic capitalist power of the day: Germany" (Riley, "Third Reich as Rogue Regime," 348).

## HOW HEGEMONS ARE DIFFERENT

We are now ready to address the question with which this chapter opened: how hegemons are different from empires and dominant or great powers. My goal in this book is to explain why particular polities have gained or lost (or never managed to achieve) geopolitical and economic advantage over all other societies in the world. I am not trying to explain why one polity merely held first place, became wealthy, or became a military "great power." Rather, I want to understand how one polity achieved and held leverage that allowed it to shape the operations of the world capitalist system and geopolitical order to its singular advantage.

Hegemony is not just a quantitative or qualitative edge over rivals. Rather, hegemony is institutionalized—in networks of finance, trade, and production, and in geopolitical alliances and the capacity to project military power throughout the world—to reinforce and further expand the hegemon's advantage over rivals. *Thus, a polity can be said to be hegemonic only as long as it is able to enforce a system of geopolitical and economic relations that advantages it over all other polities.*

My definition is similar to Immanuel Wallerstein's, who describes the difference between empire and hegemon as follows:

> A hegemonic power is quite different from a world-empire. The political superstructure of a world-economy is not a bureaucratic empire but an interstate system composed of allegedly sovereign states. And a hegemonic state is not simply a strong state, not even simply the strongest single state within the interstate system, but a state that is significantly stronger than other strong (strong, not weak) states . . . that one state is able to impose its set of rules on the interstate system, and thereby create a world political order as it thinks wise. In this situation, the hegemonic state has certain extra advantages for enterprises located within it or protected by it, advantages not accorded by the "market" but obtained through political pressures.[1]

1   Immanuel Wallerstein, *The Modern World-System*, volume 2 (Berkeley: University of California Press, [1980] 2011), xxii. Elsewhere, in "The Three Instances of Hegemony in the History of the Capitalist World Economy" (in *The Essential Wallerstein* [New York: New Press, (1983) 2000], 255), Wallerstein defines "hegemony in the interstate system [as] that situation in which the ongoing rivalry between the so-called 'great

Giovanni Arrighi argues that there have been four hegemons since the advent of the capitalist world-system: Genoa, the Netherlands, Britain, and the United States. Arrighi and Silver define hegemony similarly to Wallerstein as

> something more than domination pure and simple: it is the *additional* power that accrues to a dominant group by virtue of its capacity to lead society in a direction that not only serves the dominant group's interests, but is also perceived by subordinate groups as serving a more general interest.[1]

Michael Mann uses the "two-power standard" for hegemony, i.e., possessing more than the next two powers.[2] He contends that only the United States has been hegemonic. Britain's

> power within Europe had always been limited and dependent on alliance with other great powers. It had the largest imperial segment across the world and the biggest navy, but these were only quantitative differences. True, the pound sterling, tied to gold, was still the linchpin of world finances, but the British were no longer powerful enough to run the system by themselves.[3]

Mann uses the term "hegemonic" "in the Gramscian sense of routinized leadership by a dominant power over others, which is regarded by the

powers' is so unbalanced that one power can largely impose its rules and its wishes (at the very least by effective veto power) in the economic, political, military, diplomatic, and even cultural arenas."

1   Giovanni Arrighi and Beverly J. Silver, *Chaos and Governance in the Modern World System* (Minneapolis: University of Minnesota Press, 1999), 26.

2   Mann, *Sources of Social Power*, volume 2, 264. George Modelsk and William R. Thompson, in *Leading Sectors and Global Politics: The Coevolution of Global Politics and Economics* (Columbia: University of South Carolina Press, 1996), define dominance as controlling more than 50 percent of any sector of commerce. They find that Britain and the Netherlands never achieved that standard in more than a few sectors. The Dutch dominated Baltic shipping (1500–1680) and in Asia (1590s to 1690s). Britain dominated American sugar production (1650s to 1750s), textiles (1660s to 1730s), tea exports (1719–25), the slave trade (1690s to 1700s), raw cotton consumption (1790–1880), pig iron production (1800–80), and railroad construction (1830–40).

3   Mann, *Sources of Social Power*, volume 3, 211–12.

latter as being 'legitimate' or at least 'normal.' "[1] Mann's definition is close to Arrighi and Silver's, although they come to different conclusions about who has exercised hegemony and for how long. We will examine and evaluate the bases for those claims in the substantive chapters on the Netherlands, Britain, and the United States.

Mann, like Wallerstein and Arrighi, is precise in his terminology. He sees hegemony as the extreme case in an array of types ranging from direct empires that are creations of mainly military power, to indirect empires, to informal empires built on military power (gunboat empires), to informal empires through proxies, to economic imperialism and finally to hegemony, which combines economic, political, and ideological, but not military, power. Mann rightly acknowledges that "actual empires . . . typically combine several of these forms of domination."[2] For Mann, the ideological sphere is necessary to achieve Gramscian hegemony. That is the basis of his unwillingness to view the Netherlands and Britain as hegemonic, despite their dominance and world-shaping power in geopolitics and the economy.[3]

My definition of hegemony differs from Mann's in that I see coercion playing as much of a role as consent in sustaining hegemony. While Mann sees the "rules of the game" that favor the hegemon as a product of "diffuse, not authoritative power,"[4] my analysis of elite relations allows for hegemony to emerge from coercion. In other words, my notion of hegemony, like those of Wallerstein and Arrighi, encompasses all the elements of "informal empire" in Mann's typology, including military coercion.

Since Mann allows that, in reality, empires can include all these ideal types, our differences are only secondarily ones of definition. Rather, we differ in our explanations for the loss of hegemony,

---

1  Mann, *Sources of Social Power*, volume 4, 87.
2  Ibid., 87.
3  Wallerstein's volume 4 of *The Modern World-System*, in addressing the development of a geoculture of centrist liberalism, offers an implicit criticism of Mann's volume 4 published two years later. Wallerstein finds that liberalism was initially centered in Britain, thereby offering evidence for Gramscian hegemony in the British era of world dominance.
4  Mann, *Sources of Social Power*, volume 4, 87.

dominance, or empire. Mann is mainly concerned with identifying the strength and coherence of an empire's ability to marshal economic, political, military, and ideological power. My analysis focuses on conflicts among elites in the metropole and in the formal and informal territories of an empire, or of the entire globe beyond the hegemon's metropole, as the source of structural changes that can undermine a hegemon's capacity to mobilize resources or can produce what Mann calls "incoherence" among the four types of power. Wallerstein and Arrighi look to the dynamics of the world-system to explain hegemons' decline.

Chapter 2 reviews the answers a range of authors in addition to Wallerstein, Arrighi, and Mann give to the question of why hegemons lose hegemony, and I will present what I see as the shortcomings of their analyses. The typology of empires in table 1.1 identifies the conditions in which hegemony can develop and points to the dynamics that can then undermine hegemony. Only where colonial elites had a low level of autonomy could a polity attain the coherence to set a global strategy and mobilize resources necessary to vie for hegemony. The high degree of elite conflict and institutional incoherence in early modern Spain and France and within their empires doomed the efforts of the Habsburgs and Louis XIV to parlay their commanding military and geopolitical positions in Europe into hegemony. Napoleon and Hitler were able to impose coherence and discipline in their metropoles and empires, but the fact that their empires in their short lives were pure creations of a unitary metropolitan elite led inevitably to a military rather than an economic strategy for creating dominance that brought on the combined responses of the other great powers, ensuring France and Germany's defeats. The similar military foci of the Habsburgs and Louis XIV can also be analyzed as emanations of the limits imposed by high levels of elite autonomy and conflict in the Spanish and French metropoles and early modern empires.

Paul Kennedy,[1] among many other scholars, has argued that hegemony in Europe was impossible, that each effort to attain it led the

---

1   Paul Kennedy, *The Rise and Fall of the Great Powers: Economic Change and Military Conflict from 1500 to 2000* (New York: Random House, 1987).

other powers to unite to defeat the putative continental hegemon. However, we need to take the analysis a step back and ask why Spain, France, and (in the twentieth century) Germany took that route while the Netherlands and Britain took their quests for power beyond Europe and constructed global hegemonies, as did the United States in the twentieth century. Strategies of European conquest were not dictated by geography or by unusually martial national cultures. Rather, continental militarism was the only path open to metropolitan elites who were divided among themselves (or under Napoleon and Hitler melded into one) and unable to subordinate colonial elites or create a sufficient non-European empire before engaging rival powers geopolitically or economically.

The quest for hegemony is made possible in the first instance by conditions internal to each polity, just as internal conditions fore-closed the possibility of hegemony in other polities. I hypothesize that colonial elites in the three hegemons, during what Go labels the phases of "hegemonic assent" and "hegemonic maturity," had low levels of conflict because they were bound together in institutions that within the metropole regulated elite relations in ways that reduced conflicts and stabilized the distribution of resources and power. Those institutions structured the ways in which metropolitan elites achieved concessions and exercised power in colonies, both formal and infor-mal. Polities with such elite unity were better able to mobilize resources for seizing colonies and then holding them against rival elites. Colonial elites from such polities were more closely integrated with, and subor-dinated to, metropolitan elites, which facilitated the extraction of resources by the metropole and also allowed the metropole to leverage their colonial and neocolonial holdings to create hegemony in produc-tion, trade, and finance.

The stability of relations among elites is what distinguishes the three polities that became hegemons from all other modern polities that amassed empires but did not achieve hegemony. While Napoleonic France and Nazi Germany also had stable elite relations, because one elite achieved total control within the metropole, the identity of that single elite—a military or party elite—combined with the previous absence of a significant empire to dictate a military strategy of conquest that precluded the construction of global hegemony. The ancient

Roman and Ottoman empires also had elite stability but lacked the infrastructural capacity to penetrate their colonial holdings in a way that could transform them and impose economic as well as geopolitical hegemony.

We can summarize this discussion with another Boolean truth table.

**Table 1.3: Boolean Truth Table of Elite Structure and Hegemony**

| Empires | Characteristics of Elite Structure | | | | Achieved Hegemony |
|---|---|---|---|---|---|
| | C | A | U | I | |
| Spanish | 1 | 1 | 0 | 0/1 | 0 |
| French | 1 | 1 | 0 | 0 | 0 |
| Dutch | 0 | 0 | 0 | 0 | 1 |
| British | 0 | 0 | 0 | 0 | 1 |
| US | 0 | 0 | 0 | 0 | 1 |
| Napoleonic | 0 | 0 | 1 | 0 | 0 |
| Nazi | 0 | 0 | 1 | 0 | 0 |
| Ancient empires | 0 | 1 | 0 | 1 | 0 |

C = high level of elite conflict in metropole
A = high level of colonial elite autonomy from metropole
U = unitary elite dominant in metropole
I = lack infrastructural capacity to control colonial elites

Four factors can prevent a polity, even one with an extensive empire, from achieving global hegemony: (1) a high level of elite conflict in the metropole, (2) a high level of colonial elite autonomy from the metropole, (3) a unitary elite that achieves dominance over all other elites, in essence eliminating them as elites, in the metropole, and (4) the lack of infrastructural capacity to control elites in conquered or dominated lands. In ancient empires, the lack of infrastructural capacity allowed colonial elites to achieve a high level of autonomy, foreclosing the possibility of hegemony. For early modern Spain and

France, high levels of elite conflict in the metropole allowed a high level of colonial elite autonomy, again blocking the creation of hegemony. Napoleon and Hitler ruled polities that were blocked from hegemony by the single factor of a unitary elite. Only the Netherlands, Britain, and the United States did not face a single structural factor that could have prevented the hegemony that all three achieved.

Why did the three hegemons each lose hegemony? If the overall structure of my argument is correct, hegemony itself must have created one or more of the four factors that blocked hegemony for the other empires. I hypothesize that hegemony affected the first factor, that it disrupted stable elite relations and heightened elite conflict in the metropole. The question then becomes: Through what process did hegemony affect metropolitan elite relations?

Hegemony brought great wealth, but it also restructured the political economy of the metropole and of the capitalist world as a whole. Indeed, each hegemon created a new system of capitalist production, exchange, and finance.[1] Profit margins widened during periods of hegemonic expansion, increasing the total pool of wealth and income. This meant that elite and even class conflict were not zero-sum games during those periods. This temporarily reduced elite conflict, creating conditions for further hegemonic expansion—a virtuous cycle.

Elites were not just passive beneficiaries of growing profits during periods of hegemonic expansion. Rather, and this is one way in which capitalism differs from previous social forms, capitalists within the hegemon were best able to capture markets throughout the world and to widen their profit margins through cooperation and coordination of the particular forms of production that each controlled. Such gains from cooperation contrast with the situations of elites in precapitalist empires, whose power was largely political and therefore could not be shared or melded as becomes possible under capitalism.

Virtuous cycles end as dominant capitalists come under competitive pressures from new entrants in rival polities. Capitalists in the hegemon then increasingly employ political means to maintain or expand their rate of profit. This turn to the political shattered the bases

---

1   Giovanni Arrighi, Kenneth Barr, and Shuji Hiseada, "The Transformation of Business Enterprise," in *Chaos and Governance in the Modern World System*, 77–150.

for elite cooperation and resulted either in inconclusive and heightened elite conflict or in elites' successful creation of autarkic organizations that allowed privileged elites to solidify their authority over
sectors of the state and economy that they walled off from rival elites.

While no elite in a hegemon achieved the unitary power of the
ruling elite in Napoleonic France or Nazi Germany, elites in the
Netherlands and recently in the United States succeeded, as we will
see in subsequent chapters, in appropriating sectors of the economy
and the state for their exclusive benefit. Elites' success in preserving
their particular privileges precluded the reinvestments and strategic
shifts necessary to maintain hegemony. Britain maintained its hegemony longer than the Netherlands or the United States because the
balance of elite forces was more durable than in the other two
hegemons.

The rest of this book is devoted to weighing the theoretical assertions in this chapter against the historical evidence from Spain, France,
and the three hegemons. We will need to trace the specific chains of
contingent action that led the three polities to achieve and lose hegemony, and the other two powers to fall short. In so doing, we will also
be able to explain the particular relations of power that were left after
the end of hegemony and so elucidate the choices that were open to
elites and non-elites in the Netherlands and Britain as they underwent
decline, and the actual choices the United States now faces.

# 2

# Money and Military Success, 1500–1815

Global dominance, as we will discuss in detail in later chapters, confers huge benefits upon the citizens and government as well as the elites of each hegemon. Yet various theories of decline see dominance as ultimately more costly than beneficial to the hegemon. In other words, these theories contend that the global forces or internal factors that create the conditions for a polity to dominate the world economically and/or geopolitically set in motion dynamics that ensure the hegemon's inevitable subsequent decline. Different theories identify different causes of decline. Some authors acknowledge hegemons as special, with particular dynamics of their own, while others explain dominant powers' decline in terms of broader theories of great powers, ruling elites, or ecosystems.

What are the claims made by existing theories of decline, and where have they gone wrong? We can group past work on the decline of great powers into four categories: (1) theories that the profits from hegemony or empire finance generous social benefits and/or liberal values that shade into cultural decadence, which then render once-dynamic elites or peoples self-satisfied and soft and sap their will to go abroad and fight to maintain their dominance, (2) environmental/demographic theories, (3) world-system theory that locates the decline of the dominant core polity in the crisis at the end of each stage of the world economy, and (4) assertions that empires cost more to maintain than they return and hence lead to economic decline in the metropole.

The common problem with all four explanations is that they do not examine the internal politics of each hegemon/empire/great power with sufficient seriousness and rigor. As we examine each set of theories in this chapter, we will see that all these authors pay inadequate attention to the dynamics of conflict and the struggle for resources and power among the multiple elites and non-elite groups *within* each polity. That failure is caused either by a theory's assumption that the rulers or citizens of dominant powers are helpless in the face of inexorable demographic, environmental, fiscal, or cultural forces, or because those theories misidentify the crucial actors in each polity.

## DECADENCE AND DECLINE

Empires and hegemons impose human as well as financial costs on their home populations. One strain of argument contends that the wealth realized through dominance renders the ruling elites and/or the population at large soft and decadent, unwilling to endure the hard service and casualties, or to commit the atrocities, necessary to rule conquered peoples and to fend off rivals.

This line of argument has roots in the elite theory first developed by Vilfredo Pareto and Gaetano Mosca. Pareto proposes a life cycle theory for "the rise and fall of elites." Arguing by analogy with living organisms, Pareto contends that each elite decays over time, becoming "softer, milder, more humane and less apt to defend its own power." At the same time, "as [the ruling elite's] power wanes, its fraudulent practices increase" [i.e., it appropriates more of its society's income], leaving it more vulnerable to popular rebellion, led by a more vigorous middle class that then becomes the new elite.[1] Since all elites decline inevitably and in pretty much the same way in Pareto's telling, he is unable to account for differences in the longevity of elites, nor for why some elites are able to assemble larger dominions than others before they become soft and weak.

Mosca contrasts elites whose power is built upon military force and those who derive their power from economic wealth. In this, he anticipates C. Wright Mills's distinction among economic, military, and political elites in the United States. Mosca and Mills both note

---

1   Vilfredo Pareto, *The Rise and Fall of the Elites* (Totowa, NJ: Bedminster Press, [1901] 1968), 59, 69.

that these elites sometimes cooperate and sometimes fight one another. Mosca finds cooperation between the (military) aristocracy and economic elite in England during the seventeenth and eighteenth centuries. In France, the aristocracy's unwillingness to accommodate the bourgeoisie led, in Mosca's view, to the 1789 revolution.[1] Ancient Rome offers a third possibility: There the aristocracy adopted policies that served to weaken the middle class. The aristocracy thus was able to prevent a challenge to its political dominance but also inadvertently starved the economy, leading ultimately to the fall of the Roman Empire.[2] Similarly, Mills, while most famous for his analysis of how cooperation among American elites rendered them practically invulnerable to challenge from below, also describes, though he offers no mechanism to explain, the emergence of new elites in what he identifies as five epochs of American history.[3] Mills does go beyond Mosca in his contentions that bureaucratic methods of recruitment and promotion ensure that capable new men are recruited into the elite, and (somewhat in contradiction) that the common backgrounds of the men who head government agencies and big corporations and their career movements among organizations minimize conflicts among elites.

Mosca and Mills's limitations are mirror images of each other. Mosca is unable to explain why some elites, like the British, are better able to maintain their vigor and to accommodate challengers than were French or Roman elites. Mills accounts for the continuing strength of the American power elite, but he did not extend his insightful focus to the institutional sources of elites' power and the organizational mechanisms that allow them to coordinate their interests to explain how differences among elites can emerge or why non-elites vary in their capacity to challenge elites' national or global hegemony. I undertake that essential task in this book.

Daron Acemoglu and James A. Robinson argue economic decline is caused by political events that create institutions (a term they never

---

1   Gaetano Mosca, *The Ruling Class* (New York: McGraw Hill, [1896] 1939), 381–93.

2   Ibid., 366–70.

3   C. Wright Mills, *The Power Elite* (New York: Oxford University Press, 1956), 269–76.

define) that undermine entrepreneurship, which they believe is the source of economic growth. They contrast "extractive and inclusive economic institutions."[1] The former allow rulers to control much of a society's surplus, but at the cost of stifling individual initiative and thereby retarding economic growth. Inclusive institutions encourage entrepreneurship and foster economic growth. Acemoglu and Robinson argue that rulers are willing to accept slow or no economic growth in return for maintaining political control because, were they to allow

> economic institutions that create incentives for economic progress [those institutions might] simultaneously redistribute income and power in such a way that a predatory dictator and others with political power may [lose control of their polities and thereby] become worse off.[2]

Thus, initially small differences in political and economic institutions, caused by key events such as the English Civil War and the Glorious Revolution, lead to large differences in economic growth and prosperity as interactions between economic and political institutions create virtuous or vicious cycles. In Acemoglu and Robinson's view, European exploitation of much of the rest of world mattered less because of the resources extracted from colonies and more because colonialism and slavery (and other forms of exploitation) created permanent political and economic institutions in post-independence societies that blocked innovation and entrepreneurship.

Acemoglu and Robinson focus on explaining why countries become and then remain rich and poor; thus, they examine the divergence of British and Spanish colonies in the Americas. Their book does not attempt to address why countries that have become rich through virtuous cycles decline, but their overall argument suggests that political events can undermine institutions that promote entrepreneurship and thereby lead to economic decline. As I will show in

---

1   Daron Acemoglu and James A. Robinson, *Why Nations Fail: The Origins of Power, Prosperity, and Poverty* (New York: Crown, 2012), 73–6.
2   Ibid., 84.

later chapters, entrepreneurship (in the sense that Acemoglu and Robinson mean) did not decline in the Netherlands and Britain, nor is it declining in the United States now, although (as Arrighi shows) it focuses more on finance than production. Rather, we need to look for the sources of decline in other sorts of institutions or by looking with more depth and precision at what Acemoglu and Robinson so vaguely label economic and political institutions.

Some recent work on America has turned away from Mills's institutional analysis and returned to Pareto and Mosca's focus on elites' or citizens' moral strength. The most prominent such commentator is Niall Ferguson, who has abandoned serious historical research in an effort to become tutor to American imperialists, drawing on supposed lessons from the British Empire, much as Greek scholars hoped to instruct Roman conquerors. Ferguson's key argument is that "a peculiarity of American imperialism—perhaps its principal shortcoming—is its excessively short time horizon."[1] Americans' quick departures from foreign trouble spots matter mainly, in Ferguson's view, because potential local collaborators are unwilling to work with the United States if it will soon depart, leaving them at the mercy of anti-American forces. The British, he claims, were easily able to recruit local allies since they announced and gave the impression of planning to stay forever. Similarly, Ferguson says the United States succeeded in Germany, Japan, and Korea, where they have maintained forces for decades.

Why did Americans not stay long enough in Iraq and Afghanistan, or in Vietnam, to accomplish their goals? Ferguson gives two reasons. The first reflects on the general public, the second on the elite:

Besides the obvious constraint imposed on American administrations by the electoral system, which requires that overseas interventions show positive results within two or at most four years, an important explanation for this chronic short-windedness is the difficulty the American empire finds in recruiting the right sort of people to run it. America's higher educational institutions excel at

---

1   Niall Ferguson, *Colossus: The Rise and Fall of the American Empire* (New York: Penguin, 2004), 13.

producing very capable young men and women. Indeed, there is little question that the best American universities are now the best in the world. But few, if any, of the graduates of Harvard, Stanford, Yale or Princeton aspire to spend their lives trying to turn a sun-scorched sandpit like Iraq into the prosperous capitalist democracy of Paul Wolfowitz's imaginings. America's brightest and best aspire not to govern Mesopotamia but to manage MTV; not to rule the Hejaz but to run a hedge fund. Unlike their British counterparts of a century ago, who left elite British universities with an overtly imperial ethos, the letters most ambitious young Americans would like to see after their names are CEO, not CBE (Commander of the Order of the British Empire).[1]

Note first that Ferguson does not even attempt to offer a comparison to the attention span or tolerance for casualties of the nineteenth-century British public. If he had, he would have had to acknowledge that Britain, as we will see in chapter 5, did not endure high casualties in those places where its troops fought for extended periods, in part because it too had regular elections. In the rare instances where British casualties were high in the century from the final defeat of Napoleon to the outbreak of World War I, wars were short.

Ferguson's criticism of US university graduates for not being willing to sacrifice income and comfort to serve the empire is similarly ahistorical and ignores the very different rewards available to twenty-first-century Americans and nineteenth-century Britons (or mid-twentieth-century Americans) embarking upon careers. Derek Bok provides the needed perspective and context by comparing American graduates of the late twentieth century with those who, like Bok, entered the workforce in the decades after World War II, when, in fact, many graduates of elite universities did pursue careers in the diplomatic corps or the CIA that sent them abroad for extended terms.

---

1   Ibid., 204. Ferguson's hopes that Americans would be willing to spend, or lose, their lives in imperial service abroad were mocked, decades before he expressed them, in the Vietnam War–era bumper sticker "Join the Army! Travel to exotic distant lands. Meet exciting, unusual people. And kill them!"

All over the country . . . speakers . . . would be exhorting graduating classes to devote their lives to improving society by helping the poor, defending the environment, fighting for racial justice, and pursuing other worthy ends [to which Ferguson would add, serving in Iraq, Afghanistan, or other outposts of the American empire]. The more I thought about this yearly ritual, the more hollow, even hypocritical these speeches seemed. In fact, notwithstanding the commencement rhetoric, society was making it extremely difficult for graduating students to follow the advice of the speakers. Moreover, the problem was steadily growing worse, much worse.

When I graduated from Harvard Law School in 1954, I could have taken a job with a Wall Street firm for $4,200 a year . . . I could have gone to the Justice Department [or the State Department or CIA] for almost as large a salary as private law firms were offering. Or else, by giving up only a few hundred dollars in starting pay, I could have become a teacher and devoted myself to helping young people [which Bok did as a professor at Harvard Law School, rising to president of Harvard University in 1971].

By 1987, the outlook for graduating law students was radically different from the one that I had encountered. They could teach school for approximately $16,000 per year. They could work for the Justice Department for $25,000. Or they could join a Wall Street firm at a starting salary of $65,000 to $70,000.[1]

Since Bok wrote those words, the chasm between public service and private employment has widened even further, and graduates of colleges like Harvard now can earn even more if they bypass law or other professional schools and go straight to Wall Street. By contrast, nineteenth-century graduates of Oxford and Cambridge who were not in line to inherit landed or industrial fortunes found that they could realize higher incomes by going abroad than they could at home. Whether or not nineteenth-century Oxbridge graduates had an "imperial ethos" is debatable (and the ambiguous evidence will be reviewed in chapter 5). Even more debatable is whether

1  Derek Bok, *The Cost of Talent: How Executives and Professionals Are Paid and How It Affects America* (New York: Free Press, 1993), v.

nineteenth-century Britons stationed in the empire were more committed to "spreading commerce, Christianity and civilization"[1] than Americans stationed abroad during the Cold War were to furthering "capitalism" and "democracy." Determining levels of ideological commitment is a slippery and ultimately frustrating task. It is more useful to take a sociological approach and do the hard work of examining the institutional factors that determined who was recruited to diplomatic or military positions abroad and what resources were available to them and to their opponents. That is the task I undertake for Spain, France, the Netherlands, and Britain in chapters 3 through 5, and for the United States in chapter 7.

The problem with Ferguson is not that he compares present-day Americans to nineteenth-century Britons, but that he makes an essentialist argument, attributing the differences to unchanging national cultures or characters. It is his inflated sense of Britain's capacity to generate imperialists, and his exaggerated belief in what supposedly selfless and well-trained imperialists can accomplish, that leads him to assert, as he did in *Empire*,[2] the book he wrote as a companion to a television series, that the British Empire, and British world hegemony, were felled by the deus ex machina of two world wars rather than by internal weakness, colonial resistance, or world capitalist dynamics. In Ferguson's analysis, it is the American rather than British empire that is "accidental," won at low cost by a nation that was unwilling to pay the costs or to perform the dirty deeds necessary to preserve what fell into its lap. Ferguson believes the British were willing to make sacrifices greater than those of other great powers and so could be undone only by overwhelming outside force rather than internal decline. The Americans, in contrast, are so soft that they are declining even as their military edge remains overwhelming.[3]

--------

1   Ferguson, *Colossus*, 208.
2   Niall Ferguson, *Empire: The Rise and Demise of the British World Order and the Lessons for Global Power* (New York: Basic, 2002).
3   Ferguson's call for Americans to make greater financial and human sacrifices for empire is echoed by Donald and Frederick W. Kagan, *While America Sleeps: Self-Delusion, Military Weakness, and the Threat to Peace Today* (New York: St. Martin's, 2000); Max Boot, *War Made New: Weapons, Warriors, and the Making of the Modern World* (New York: Gotham, 2006); and Victor Davis Hanson, *The Father of Us All: War and History, Ancient and Modern* (New York: Bloomsbury, 2010), although these authors place more emphasis on the willingness to die than on military budgets.

Michael Mann[1] offers reasons why America's military, political, economic, and ideological assets are less suited to pacifying conquered territories than were Britain's. Mann's focus on America's incoherence among its sources of power provides a structural explanation for the United States' difficulty in recruiting reliable locals to do most of the fighting and administering of conquered lands that is more grounded historically than Ferguson's focus on Americans' supposed quickness to leave. (Ferguson forgets that America's South Vietnamese allies were every bit as corrupt and cowardly as the twenty-first-century Afghan or Iraqi governments, even though it appeared that the United States was prepared to stay in Vietnam indefinitely.)

Yet even Mann falls into temptation and steps away from his careful structural analysis to evoke similar national cultural differences to those in Ferguson's narrative when he discusses Americans' supposed unwillingness to engage in the "ferocious exemplary repression" that Mann sees as an essential ingredient for maintaining direct or indirect imperial control over conquered peoples. Mann contends that "the lack of an imperial American culture makes for further weaknesses. American kids are not brought up to be as racist, as stoic in combat, as self-denying in crisis, or as obedient to authority as British kids once were."[2] Mann could have accurately added "or as American kids once were." Certainly, early-twentieth-century Americans were brought up to be racist and had no trouble perpetrating ferocious exemplary repression in their conquest of the Philippines,[3] or in their earlier

---

Stephen Brooks and William Wohlforth, in *America Abroad: The United States' Global Role in the 21st Century* (New York: Oxford University Press, 2016), argue that the United States retains an overwhelming military edge over rising China and will do so for decades, mainly because of America's long investment in advanced military technologies that China has no prospect of equaling. Thus, for Brooks and Wohlforth, the only way in which the United States can lose global dominance is to surrender it by pulling back from "globe-shaping deep engagement" (191) with the world due to a mistaken belief that US military investment saps the overall economy, or from an exaggerated assessment of the consequences of American overreach in Iraq.

1   Michael Mann, *Incoherent Empire* (London: Verso, 2003).

2   Ibid., 25, 27.

3   Julian Go, *American Empires and the Politics of Meaning: Elite Political Culture in the Philippines and Puerto Rico during US Colonialism* (Durham: Duke University Press, 2008).

enslavement of Africans and extermination of Native Americans (as Mann notes in volume 2 of *The Sources of Social Power*), or in later interventions in Latin America, or in attacks on civilians as well as soldiers in World War II, Korea, and Vietnam. If American soldiers have been gentler since Vietnam, it is the result of a historical process that needs explanation, not the product of inherent differences in national culture.

Conversely, Michael Mandelbaum argues that the United States failed in its efforts under presidents Clinton, Bush, and Obama to transform Haiti, Somali, the successor states to the former Yugoslavia, Afghanistan, and Iraq because "in all human endeavors culture matters" and those lands "were dominated by social and political loyalties too narrow" to sustain the sorts of political democracies Mandelbaum believes the United States was trying to create.[1] Mandelbaum remains convinced that the United States has the capacity to dominate the world militarily, but that it was an error of hubris, born from America's triumph over the Soviet Union, to believe that its military power would allow it to remake societies that lack the "Western" cultural and institutional characteristics of the defeated Axis powers that became US allies after 1945.

Mandelbaum's focus on the alien cultures of the lands and peoples the United States failed to subdue absolves him of any need to explore if and how the US military and other capacities have changed relatively or absolutely over the past half century. Nor does he need to examine American motives and interests since he sees US foreign policy as guided by noble if unrealistic goals rather than elite or class interests. Indeed, the only American interests he identifies are security from attack and global peace.

Niall Ferguson joins many others in making one further argument about how what he views as American self-indulgence threatens its continued world dominance. In addition to America's attention deficit, which leads it to leave countries before they are pacified, and its manpower deficit (the lack of a draft, which results in too few troops being available to occupy foreign countries), the United States, in

---

1   Michael Mandelbaum, *Mission Failure: America and the World in the Post-Cold War Era* (New York: Oxford University Press, 2016).

Ferguson's view, suffers from an economic deficit that he attributes entirely to rising future social benefits, above all Social Security and Medicare. He contends (inaccurately) that taxes would almost have to double to pay those obligations, and praises Margaret Thatcher for reducing the indexing of British old age pensions to inflation. Ferguson claims that, by cutting the real value of future old age benefits, Thatcher reduced Britain's unfunded liabilities to 5 percent of GDP through 2050 vs. 105 percent for France and 110 percent for Germany.[1] (David Cameron seemed not to have gotten Ferguson's good news, since he committed to further cutting Britain's supposedly now-almost-fully-funded benefits.)

Ferguson and Paul Kennedy suggest that similar benefit cuts in the United States are necessary to prevent growing deficits that would otherwise compel future cuts in military spending.[2] Thus, Ferguson is suggesting that liberal democracy produces social benefit overstretch, and that, rather than nonexistent imperial overstretch, will undermine American imperialism. Kennedy, somewhat challenging the thesis of his 1987 book (discussed later in this chapter), argued that growing deficits, due mainly to rising entitlement spending, would in themselves accelerate American economic decline and also make it impossible for the United States to pay for the imperial obligations expanded by the Bush Doctrine.

In fact, as we will discuss in detail in chapter 6, US social programs are modest compared to almost all of Europe, and the main cause of the federal deficit is tax cuts, which have gone mostly to the wealthy and corporations. Overall federal spending in 2008 as a percentage of GDP was no higher than in 1968, while military spending as a percentage of GDP declined by more than half in those decades. The United States, in reality, could easily afford both vastly expanded military spending and existing social benefits with only modest tax increases.

Despite the inaccuracy of his calculations, Ferguson's focus on social benefits adds to his narrative of American inattention and

1    Ferguson, *Colossus*, 273.
2    Niall Ferguson, "Niall Ferguson on Why Barack Obama Needs to Go," *Newsweek*, August 19, 2012; Paul Kennedy, "American Power Is on the Wane," *Wall Street Journal*, January 14, 2009, A13.

decadence. He echoes the political claims of most Republicans and a not inconsiderable number of Democrats who see the federal budget deficit as an "existential threat" to US prosperity. The proposal to solve it by cutting social programs rather than raising taxes or cutting defense spending is not original to Ferguson. Indeed, he is unusual in giving priority to increased military spending rather than tax cuts, along with deficit reduction, from the proceeds of cuts in social programs.

The focus on social spending and budget deficits moves attention away from the supposed shortcomings of an American elite that would rather go to Wall Street than Iraq and toward the mass of Americans who have won supposedly unsustainable benefits by playing the electoral system. The view that America's too-vibrant democracy has produced overly generous benefits is argued most prominently by Peter Peterson, who was successively CEO of Bell & Howell (a major military contractor), commerce secretary in the Nixon administration, CEO of Lehman Brothers, and cofounder of the Blackstone Group (a private equity firm that focuses on leveraged buyouts). Peterson also was chairman of the Council on Foreign Relations and of an eponymous foundation he created to publicize the "deficit crisis." Peterson, who embodied the meritocratic recruitment, organization jumping, and self-dealing Mills attributed to the power elite, was remarkable less for his decades-long dogged focus on federal deficits, and for the wealth that allows him to hire "intellectuals" and publicists, than for the respectful attention his selective presentations of budget data have won from politicians and journalists. One very rich man's fixation became the obsession of majorities in Congress and the dominant frame for viewing the budget and economy among journalists and economists.[1]

The evidence for a unique American aversion to foreign and military service is weak. Nor has there been a recent increase in governmental spending in the United States. The temporary jump in spending in the early years of the Obama administration in response to the

---

1   Hacker and Pierson (*American Amnesia*, chapter 6) go into detail about Peterson's career and his bankrolling of anti-deficit and other right-wing organizations.

financial collapse of 2008 has receded, and the long-term decline of government spending as a percentage of GDP has resumed. Ferguson, coming out of the academic world, and Peterson, as the epitome of the businessman-politician, are merely the latest incarnations of an intellectual tradition that grounds national decline in the essential weakness or developing self-indulgence of the nation's people. However resonant politically, and however much attention these views receive in the media, they are not supported by evidence. These arguments appear to work only by abstracting current American conditions from both past US history and from the sorts of careful comparisons of other countries' historical trajectories that I attempt to offer in this book.

## DEMOGRAPHY AND ECOLOGY

Just as past social movements gave rise to ambitious totalizing theories, most notably Marxism, which arose in the midst of bourgeois and working-class mobilization, so too has the environmental movement, which has been gathering force since the 1970s, given rise to authors who see environmental exploitation and degradation as the master explanatory variable of societies' rise and fall. Most environmentalists rightly see the entire globe as a single ecosystem and so focus their attention on the consequences to all of humanity of overpopulation, pollution, resource overexploitation, global warming, and species extinction. Others, engaged in local struggles, write about the disproportionate impact of pollution on communities targeted by "environmental racism." Neither sort of analysis can help us understand differences among the sort of large polities that vied for global dominance.

Jared Diamond stands out for his effort to find environmental causes for the decline of individual societies and to explain how some societies were able to avoid or reverse environmental degradation.[1] He is concerned with cases of "collapse," catastrophic declines in

---

1    Jared Diamond, *Collapse: How Societies Choose to Fail or Succeed* (New York: Penguin, 2005).

population that either kill off every member of society, force the survivors to migrate to another ecological zone where life can be sustained, or leave a diminished population living at a much lower level of material comfort and social sophistication. The fundamental cause of each collapse, in Diamond's analysis, is population growth that leads to overexploitation and irreversible damage of the natural environment. Collapse happens only when environmental damage is exacerbated by the fragility of the local ecosystem, which prevents recovery, and/or cyclical climate change (such as the Little Ice Age of 1400–1800), attacks from hostile neighbors, and failure by the collapsing society to realize what was happening and mend its ways. Thus, in Diamond's view, humans can repair as well as cause environmental damage.

The entities about which Diamond writes are, for the most part, isolated societies that were unable to draw resources from abroad once they had degraded and exhausted their environments. His one case of an advanced, large-scale society that collapsed, the Maya in the ninth century, also did not depend on "trade with external societies."[1] His model, therefore, is hard to adapt to empires or economic hegemons, which prosper by extracting resources from, and exporting the consequences of their environmental exploitation to, distant lands.

Diamond is as interested in identifying, and drawing lessons from, societies that avoided environmental catastrophe as he is in finding commonalities among those that collapsed. Diamond argues that knowledge about the environment, whether it comes from common citizens who see the effects of rising population on their local environments or national leaders who have the perspective to see how local farming, logging, mining, and industry combine to undermine national ecosystems, has the potential to inform effective policies that can prevent or remediate environmental harm before it causes societal collapse. Diamond's attention to knowledge is hortatory; he wants to encourage societies, leaders, firms, and ordinary people to become environmental stewards.

---

1   Ibid., 160. Diamond briefly (13–14) discusses the fall of the Roman Empire but merely raises it as a subject for study without offering any evidence or conclusions on the role of environmental degradation in its fall.

Unfortunately, Diamond is less effective in explaining why some act to prevent environmental harm and others do not. His one case of environmental repair in a large-scale historical society is Tokugawa Japan, which reforested much of the country and halted population growth in the eighteenth century. Diamond argues that Japanese rulers husbanded the nation's forests because "they expected their own Tokugawa family to remain in control of Japan . . . Peace, political stability, and well-justified confidence in their own future encouraged Tokugawa shoguns to invest and to plan for the long-term future of their domain." Similarly, Diamond looks to Japanese peasants' secure land tenure as a reason they limited births. On the other hand, Joaquín Balaguer, the dictator who was later elected president of the Dominican Republic, pursued pro-environmental policies even though he was in a precarious position and "constantly maintained a delicate balancing act between the military, the masses, and competing scheming groups of elites." Security in office or property did not shape Balaguer's policy; rather, Diamond concludes that Balaguer "really did care about the environment" and presumably was able to rise above his personal interests.[1]

Diamond's book is typical of much environmental analysis: precise on how humans' short-term interests lead to environmental exploitation and on how environmental degradation threatens human survival, while vague on when and how states, interest groups, or social movements generate policies that limit pollution, population, or resource extraction. In discussing China and Australia, Diamond sees hopeful signs of new attitudes toward the environment on the part of the Communist Party and the Australian public respectively, but offers no way of explaining why those attitudes have changed to the limited degree they have. Nor does he identify factors that might further or impede the implementation of pro-environmental policies. He lauds "admirable leaders" who had the foresight to see the need to limit population and pollution and "courageous people . . . who decided which of their core values were worth fighting for, and which no longer made sense." Diamond acknowledges that individuals and corporations often have an economic interest in cutting costs and

----

1   Ibid., 305, 346, 348.

extracting resources in ways that degrade the environment, and rightly argues that "government regulation [is] necessary for the enforcement of moral principles" such as the protection of the environment for the collective good.[1] But Diamond offers no explanation for why such regulations are imposed in some places and times, beyond his praise of courageous and farsighted leaders and publics.

Diamond's model, and environmentalist analyses more broadly, need more *sociology*. We can only understand, as his subtitle puts it, "how societies choose to fail or succeed," why some modern societies act on broadly available knowledge of how humans degrade and can restore ecosystems, and why most do not, if we can move past hortatory appeals to become better citizens of Planet Earth. Instead, we must identify the conditions under which rulers, states, or environmental parties and movements have been able to overcome interests and practices that lead to environmental degradation. The knowledge of good environmental stewardship is available and widely known; so (as we noted above) is understanding among hegemonic powers today and in past centuries of how to produce economic growth, reform militaries, and enhance governmental fiscal and organizational capacities. What requires analysis is why actors are unable to implement policies that reflect their knowledge of environmental, economic, or geopolitical realities.

Ian Morris presents an even darker view of humans' future than does Diamond. Morris constructs a "social development index" that is a combination of greater energy use, urbanization, information technology (literacy rates multiplied by speed of communication), and war making (measured by "size of forces, the speed of their movement, their logistical capacities, the range and destructiveness of their striking power, and the armor and fortifications at their disposal").[2] Morris shows that his index of energy alone yields almost the same graph as his four-factor index. Thus, his elaborate model is not far from the definition of modernization, offered in the 1970s, as the moment when the use of inanimate energy exceeds that of animate

--------

1  Ibid., 440, 485.
2  Ian Morris, *Why the West Rules for Now: The Patterns of History, and What They Reveal about the Future* (New York: Farrar, Straus & Giroux, 2010), 633, 620.

energy.[1] The development of these four factors allowed humans to break through various "ceilings" from the end of the Ice Age through the Industrial Revolution. The societies or polities (Morris is vague on the definitions or boundaries of leading regions of the world) that broke through ceilings to become dominant did so because they were geographically favored with the particular factors that mattered for that transition. Advantage shifted from the hilly lands west of Mesopotamia to the river valleys of China and finally to the coal-rich British Isles on the Atlantic. The varying advantages and disadvantages of particular places overwhelmed the genius or stupidity of the rulers and scientists and technicians of each society. Morris says history is made by "maps," not "chaps."[2]

Morris argues that geographic advantage does not necessarily allow societies or humanity to smash through a ceiling.

> Societies rarely—perhaps never—simply get stuck at a ceiling and stagnate, their social development unchanging for centuries. Rather, if they do not figure out how to smash the ceiling, their problems spiral out of control. Some or all of what I call the five horsemen of the apocalypse . . . famine, disease, migration, and state collapse— [which are worse if they coincide with the fifth horseman] climate change—will drive development down, sometimes for centuries, even into a dark age.[3]

Morris offers no basis to explain or predict why humans get smart in some moments of crisis but not others. He does have an explanation for where humans can exercise their smartness (this is his geographic determinism) but it is on a huge scale (West and East, not Netherlands or Britain). He also has no explanation for when innovations emerge. Throughout most of the book, he argues that turning points could have happened a century or more earlier or later; decades do not matter for his explanations.

--------

1   Marion J. Levy, Jr., *Modernization: Latecomers and Survivors* (New York: Basic, 1972).
2   Morris, *Why the West Rules for Now*, 29.
3   Ibid., 560.

Morris identifies dangers that could halt and then reverse human social development in the twenty-first century: Migration could create a new wave of disease, population growth could reach the limit of energy resources, and, most dangerously, resource shortages and global warming could lead to an environmental collapse and/or nuclear war among powers competing for resources. Morris ends his book by asserting that these problems can be solved by smart humans who will figure out how to limit nuclear weapons and advance green technologies. Morris subscribes to the idea of the "Singularity," the notion that computers will become so powerful they will equal human brains or incorporate human brains, erasing the line between people and machines, and presumably giving humans the intellectual fire-power to come up with the needed solutions.

Unfortunately, the problems Morris says now threaten human society are not problems that can be solved with smart technological inventions, except perhaps if some method of environmental engineering is developed to neutralize carbon dioxide in the atmosphere or if innovations lower the cost of green energy drastically. However, even that would not address overpopulation or competition for resources. All these problems require political solutions, and nowhere in the book does Morris offer explanations for how new state institutions came into existence except to say that wars led to increases in political scale, or that the limited reaches of the biggest polities left some areas (like Britain) with the autonomy to innovate. Neither of those mechanisms is of help in identifying pathways that can lead to global political solutions today.

As we will see in later chapters, dominant powers did not decline because of general environmental or economic collapse; indeed, none of Diamond's cases are of hegemonic powers. Rather, population growth has a direct effect on social relations, undermining states before or instead of its eventual effects on the environment's carrying capacity.

Jack Goldstone[1] is more helpful to our task of explaining the decline of great powers. His goal is to explain "state breakdowns" in

---

1  Jack Goldstone, *Revolution and Rebellion in the Early Modern World* (Berkeley: University of California Press, 1991).

early modern Europe, both those that led to full-fledged revolutions (England in the 1640s and France in 1789) and those in which weakened states survived: the French Frondes of the 1640s and the concurrent rebellions in the Spanish Habsburg Empire. While Spain's heyday came before the 1640s and Britain's after, and France was a contender, though never a hegemon, in both the 1640s and 1789, Goldstone's analysis is useful in pointing to ways in which rapid population increase can weaken state capacity and undermine great powers' ability to compete economically and geopolitically on a global scale.

Goldstone's central argument is that rapid population increase, as occurred through much of Europe in the sixteenth century and then again from 1750 to 1850, caused inflation (especially of food prices), social mobility, and a decline in state revenues that in combination destabilized the governing regime. Inflation in the pre- or proto-capitalist societies of the early modern world reduced government revenues (as opposed to twentieth-century inflation, which raises revenues from progressive income taxes). States were largely unsuccessful at addressing the loss of revenues, and so their capacity, both domestically and abroad, fell, even as their stratagems to raise new revenues alienated elites who lost privileges, rising groups that were locked out of government, and masses that were hit with higher taxes. Inequality rose during these periods, as some elites gained from inflation while much of the middle class and most urban workers and peasants lost ground. Non-elites reacted to declining incomes and to the geographic mobility forced on them by agrarian crises by mobilizing against both government and elites and by openness to "ideologies of rectification and transformation." Goldstone finds that "factional conflict within the elites, over access to office, patronage, and state policy, rather than conflict across classes, led to state paralysis and state breakdown."[1]

---

1   Ibid., 460, 461. Peter Turchin, *War and Peace and War: The Life Cycles of Imperial Nations* (New York: Pi Press, 2006); *Ages of Discord: A Structural-Demographic Analysis of American History* (Chaplin, CT: Beresta Books, 2016); and Turchin and Sergey A. Nefedov, *Secular Cycles* (Princeton: Princeton University Press, 2009) make a similar argument. Unlike Goldstone, who seeks to identify particular historical moments when overpopulation leads to state breakdown, Turchin sees demographic expansion leading to state breakdown, economic crisis, war, and then population decline as a regularly recurring cycle. Turchin writes about the increasing number of elites, but by that he means increases in the number

Goldstone is careful to note that his is a theory of the causes of state breakdown: "The model allows that the precise responses to these pressures varied with the capacity of the state to react, elites to organize, and of popular groups to mobilize."[1] Goldstone's model leaves open the question of whether the rewards of hegemony increase states' capacities to respond to demographic pressures more than geopolitical constraints restrict them. The model also undertheorizes divisions among elites and therefore has difficulty accounting for elites' varying organizational capacities, and for the very different structural effects of state breakdowns.[2] For these reasons, Goldstone's model is of limited use in explaining how hegemons, or indeed any polity, change after they go through a period of rapid population increase.[3] However, Goldstone's model is highly valuable in alerting us

---

of individuals who are elite, which he defines as having high incomes, not specific elites defined by distinct organizational bases, as I do. *Ages of Discord*, which focuses on the United States, suffers from his inability to identify a clear mechanism for elite overproduction. He argues that, as elites gain a rising share of national income, a society can support more elite individuals because "A favorable economic conjuncture for the employers enables large numbers of intelligent, hard-working, or simply lucky workers to accumulate wealth and then attempt to translate it into social status. As result, upward mobility into the ranks of the elites will greatly surpass downward mobility" (15). But, if wealth becomes more concentrated when population rises, as Turchin argues, how do more people achieve "elite" incomes? Turchin never answers that, nor does he identify structural positions those elites create or take over.

1   Goldstone, *Revolution and Rebellion*, 462.

2   This is the crux of my disagreement with Goldstone in *Capitalists in Spite of Themselves*, where I offer accounts of the English and French revolutions that are at odds, in many respects, with Goldstone's analysis.

3   Paul Kennedy, in *Preparing for the Twenty-First Century* (New York: Random House, 1993), identifies rapid population growth, mainly in the Third World, as the greatest source of instability in coming decades. Yet Kennedy offers only vague prescriptions for dealing with the consequences of population growth and has even less to say on what factors might account for differences in countries' capacities to address those consequences. Goldstone, in "The New Population Bomb: The Four Megatrends That Will Change the World" (*Foreign Affairs* 89, no. 1 [2010]), finds that almost all population growth from now until global population stabilizes around 2050 will be in poor, predominantly Muslim countries.

Goldstone argues that rapid population growth combined with urbanization will destabilize already weak governments and create openings for terror networks. Unlike Kennedy, Goldstone offers policy recommendations: primarily proposals to encourage immigration from poor to rich countries and efforts to draw middle-income countries, such as Turkey, into leadership roles in international

to the pressure that demography can exert on states. Therefore, we must examine each hegemon to see if demographic pressures hit it at any point in the eras when it contested for, held, or lost dominance. General ecological crisis will be an issue for future hegemons or aspirants to world power. For past and present hegemons, human population exerts its influence directly, along the pathways Goldstone identified for the early modern world.

## WORLD-SYSTEMS THEORY: CRISES AND THE DECLINE OF HEGEMONS

Marx and Lenin, and many of those who followed in their analytical footsteps, have little to say about the decline of hegemons since they see formal and informal colonies as an unalloyed gain for countries with such territories. Colonial loot, along with appropriated peasant lands, is, in Marx's view, the main source of the "primitive accumulation" of capital.[1] For Lenin, the continuing transfer of wealth from colonies both fuels imperial powers' further capitalist development and quiets class conflict in rich countries by subsidizing workers' standard of living. Lenin argues that imperial powers first gained relative advantage by seizing "ownerless territory," but by the end of the nineteenth century "the world is completely divided up," and powers then could gain formal or informal control over additional territories only

---

organizations. That, in turn, he believes, would fortify efforts to strengthen weak governments in poor countries with rapidly rising populations: Goldstone identifies NATO's involvement in Afghanistan as having the potential to demonstrate the West's ability to help Muslim countries or, if the intervention fails, to further antagonize millions of Muslims in Afghanistan and beyond.

1   Karl Marx, *Capital*, volume 1 (New York: International Publishers, [1867] 1967). The essence of Marx's view of colonialism's contribution to capital accumulation is summarized in the wonderful passage from chapter 31 of the first volume of *Capital*, which Immanuel Wallerstein used as the epigraph to the first volume of his *Modern World-System*: "The discovery of gold and silver in America, the extirpation, enslavement and entombment in mines of the aboriginal population, the beginning of the conquest and looting of the East Indies, the turning of Africa into a warren for the commercial hunting of black-skins, signalised the rosy dawn of the era of capitalist production. These idyllic proceedings are the chief momenta of primitive accumulation. On their heels treads the commercial war of the European nations, with the globe for a theatre."

by taking them from one another through war or other means unspecified by Lenin. Each power's success in that competition "is a calculation of the strength of those participating, their general economic, financial, military strength."[1]

Lenin does not weigh the relative contribution of economic, financial, or military strength to the outcome of great power conflicts. (Such calculations are the province of Paul Kennedy, discussed in the next section, who believes empires are not profitable in the long term.) Lenin's repeated discussion of finance capital would suggest that the country or countries that dominated finance also gained control of territories, but he sees military conflict as important. While Lenin documents Britain's growing edge over other powers in the nineteenth century, he never suggests that one power is hegemonic in that or any previous century, nor that a single power would predominate in the future (perhaps because he thought capitalism would not last much longer). As a result, Lenin leaves unresolved the question of why some great powers were unable to adapt to the shift from industrial to financial capitalism and to the new geopolitics of a world in which almost all non-European territories were owned or dominated by a capitalist power, while others, like Germany, Japan, and the United States, benefited from that transition.

This is where world-systems theory makes its contribution. Immanuel Wallerstein and Giovanni Arrighi are able to explain not just the relationship between core and peripheral polities, but why there is a hierarchy within the core. Wallerstein and Arrighi also identify a dynamic in the world-system that they contend accounts for the cyclical decline of each hegemonic core country and its replacement by a successor.[2]

1  V. I. Lenin, *Imperialism: The Highest Stage of Capitalism* (London: Pluto, [1917] 1996), 234, 267.

2  While Wallerstein, in *Modern World-System*, first developed both the theoretical framework of world-systems theory and offered a sustained application to the history of world capitalism from its origins in the sixteenth century to the eve of World War I British hegemony, it is Giovanni Arrighi, in *The Long Twentieth Century: Money, Power, and the Origins of Our Times* (London: Verso, 1994) and *Adam Smith in Beijing: Lineages of the Twenty-First Century* (London: Verso, 2007), who specifically addresses the problem of hegemony and offers the most sophisticated explanation for the decline of each hegemon and its replacement by a successor. For that reason, my discussion here will focus mainly on Arrighi's arguments.

Each hegemon in the world-system—which Arrighi identifies as successively the Genoese city-state, the Dutch Republic, Britain, and the United States—has operated on a greater geographic scale at home and controlled a greater expanse of the globe than its predecessor. Geographic expansion, as Arrighi citing David Harvey explains, is a "spatial fix" for the crises caused by "the accumulation of capital over and above what can be reinvested in the purchase and sale of commodities without drastically reducing profit margins."[1] Geographic expansion, of the hegemon's home polity (note that each hegemon has a significantly larger home territory than its predecessor) and also in imperialist control over trade routes, colonies, and dependent nations, opens new spaces for profitable investment. However, the expanding scope of capitalist investment and production spurs "uneven development" as backward territories take advantage of lower labor costs and newer facilities to undercut and out-compete the hegemon. "At this point, capitalist agencies tend to invade one another's spheres of operation; the division of labor that previously defined the terms of their mutual cooperation breaks down; and competition becomes increasingly vicious."[2] Capitalists respond by keeping their resources liquid, loaning their capital to governments, firms, and individuals in financial crisis. For a few decades, financialization seems to create a new boom, as it did during Britain's Belle Époque of 1896 to 1914 and for the United States from the 1980s to 2008. But the relief is temporary and the prosperity highly concentrated as "the underlying over-accumulation crisis" intensifies and "exacerbates economic competition, social conflicts, and interstate rivalries to levels that it was beyond the incumbent centers' power to control."[3]

While the crises are inevitable, the responses by capitalists, states, and popular forces are highly variable across space and between each historical epoch. The interactions among classes and states determine the levels of violence and chaos that accompany each crisis and transition, and mold the new hegemonic order that emerges. Hegemonic powers are tempted to use the massive financial resources they attract

1   Arrighi, *Adam Smith in Beijing*, 216–17.
2   Ibid., 232.
3   Ibid., 232.

for military buildups and wars that can stymie rising rivals' ambitions. Thus, Britain vastly expanded its navy, conquered the bulk of Africa, and carved out the largest concession in China in an effort to block France, Germany, and Japan from leveraging their rising industrial might to challenge its geopolitical and economic hegemony. Of course, Germany and Japan responded militarily in an attempt to break out of the secondary positions to which they were confined by British control over finance and empire. Britain won the two world wars, yet lost the peace to the United States, which followed the model of military intervention the British themselves had pioneered in the Napoleonic Wars: Wait until the other combatants have exhausted themselves, then intervene late in the war, and finish as the only nation left with most of its military and financial resources intact, and thus in a position to dictate the terms of peace.

Arrighi shows that militarism and imperialism are not merely governmental reflexes but actions tailored to address specific opportunities and crises created by the world capitalist system. His focus on financialization allows him to explain why certain states temporarily gain extraordinary resources to finance military buildups and wars that cannot be derived from regular economic measures or Tillyesque conceptions of state capacities. At the same time, the outcomes of wars between hegemons and their challengers cannot be explained simply from the workings and cycles of the world-system. In recognizing that, Arrighi provides a basis to go beyond cyclic theories of capitalism and the world-system. Most crucially, Arrighi brings popular forces into the history of capitalism and imperialism as actors capable of challenging pro-capitalist policies at home and of blocking imperialist grabs for territory abroad.

The United States, even more than Britain in its heyday, saw a high level of worker mobilization during its rise to hegemony. Arrighi shows how unionization and less organized forms of worker power maintained high wages that cut into profits. Arrighi also notes that popular mobilization limits US intervention abroad, but he does not provide the detailed analysis needed to specify why Americans' anti-war mobilization has varied over time and among wars, nor how US foreign policy has been affected by shifting levels of domestic opposition to intervention and to American casualties, which we will examine in chapter 7. Arrighi therefore remains vague on how such limits curtail present-day US hegemony.

Arrighi is far clearer on how foreign competition in the core and resistance in the periphery undermined US capacity to sustain a world order under its control. Even though it does not face a military rival with any possibility of supplanting it, the United States today is, in other crucial respects, weaker than Britain was a century ago, having become a debtor nation while Britain was still able to rely on revenues and soldiers from its pliant empire, above all from India, in the world wars. Arrighi specifies the ways in which the United States, like hegemons before it, seeks to leverage military, economic, and geopolitical advantage, and therefore how weakness in one realm undermines strategies in the other spheres. Thus, the US wars in Vietnam and Iraq, designed to blunt geopolitical challenges from Third World liberation movements and uppity oil states, instead emboldened their undefeated targets and created budget and trade deficits that weakened the US economy. While foreign creditors so far have not been able to use American demand for capital to mold US foreign policy, China joined other foreign states and private investors to demand the US government take steps to protect the value of their investments in the 2008 financial crisis.[1]

Arrighi, aided by the sophistication of his world-systems analysis, shows the strengths but also the persistent limitations of that model. He is able to specify what is needed in each era to achieve hegemony in the world-system. However, Arrighi, like Wallerstein and Lenin before him, is less successful in explaining why particular countries achieve hegemony in the first place while others fail. From his world-systemic perspective, Arrighi often ignores the internal conflicts within each core country that set the policies that determine its (changing) position in the world-system. Instead, the countries themselves are often presented as unified actors. We read about the interests and actions of "the Netherlands," "Britain," and "the United States."

We need to look deeper and more systematically within the countries that are the main units of analysis in world-systems theory and

---

1  Daniel W. Drezner, "Bad Debts: Assessing China's Financial Influence in Great Power Politics," *International Security* 34, no. 2 (2009).

identify the actors whose conflicts produced the policies in each country that resulted in the achievement or loss of hegemony. In fact, hegemons, like empires, contain multiple, competing elites. The actors in world history are elites and classes, not polities. Elite and class conflict repeatedly change the structure of each polity and thereby change each polity's capacity to vie for or sustain hegemony. While the world-systems approach can recognize and address elite and class conflict, I take issue with Wallerstein and Arrighi's efforts to synchronize structural change within polities to the cycles of the world-system. As a result, Arrighi is unable to explain why Britain's hegemony lasted so much longer than that of the Netherlands or the United States, nor how Britain was able in essence to succeed itself as hegemon over two successive eras that spanned the transition to industrial capitalism.

George Modelski recognizes that Britain reached two peaks of hegemony:[1] one in the eighteenth century, grounded in its settler colonies and undone by the American Revolution and declining profits in the East India Company, and a nineteenth-century hegemony built mainly on industry and supported by its South Asian colonies. In between the twin peaks, Modelski sees a period of decline. Thus, Modelski acknowledges that a hegemon can succeed itself by reforming and reconfiguring its empire. However, Modelski, like the world-systems theorists, fails to explain why the British government was able to reform while rivals did not. Modelski pays little attention to the actors and events that built or undermined hegemony. Indeed, Modelski neglects even to mention the nationalization of the East India Company. In chapter 5 we will see how dynamics internal to Britain and its empire produced two eras of hegemony, and why that hegemony was lost once temporarily and then permanently.

As I hope to demonstrate in later chapters, the politics of each empire or hegemon were idiosyncratic. We will spend the rest of this book tracing contingent chains of conflict and structural change to determine their effects on each hegemon and putative hegemon's capacity to set and enforce global rules of the game. Once we have done that sort of historical

---

1   George Modelski, *Long Cycles in World Politics* (Seattle: University of Washington Press, 1987).

analysis, we then can return to world-systems theory to help us understand the consequences of those decisions in determining the shifting positions of those polities in the world economy and geopolitics.

## THE COSTS (AND BENEFITS) OF EMPIRE AND HEGEMONY

Paul Kennedy views formal and informal empires as money-losing burdens that sap great powers' economic vitality.[1] Kennedy's position is the opposite of Lenin's in his assessment of the contribution of formal and informal imperialism to a great power's economic prosperity. While acknowledging that great powers do extract riches from colonies, Kennedy argues that the costs of guarding colonies, dependencies, and trade routes from rival great powers outweigh the benefits of empire. The greatest powers—which he lists as Habsburg Spain, the Netherlands, France, Britain, the United States, and the Soviet Union—came to have strategic interests in so many places in the world that they felt forced to commit military and financial resources to locales and conflicts that could not be justified on economic grounds.

All of this matters because, as the cost of foreign commitments increases, great powers come to suffer from what Kennedy calls "imperial overstretch." As resources are diverted from productive investment to the military costs of empire, the dominant power's economy declines until it is no longer able to afford the military needed to sustain its global position. That, in Kennedy's view, was the cause of each previous great power's decline—and, he predicted, so it would be for the United States.[2]

--------

1   Kennedy, *Rise and Fall of the Great Powers.*
2   Robert Gilpin, in *War and Change in World Politics* (Cambridge: Cambridge University Press, 1981), makes a similar argument, albeit with more theoretical abstraction and less historical evidence than Kennedy. Gilpin also subscribes to the view that in dominant powers, "social values, attitudes, and behaviors change in ways that undercut the efficiency of the economy and the dedication of individuals and groups to the commonweal" (165). In addition, the people of a dominant power believe in the "goodness and benefits of the status quo" and so "neither concedes to the just demands of rising challenges nor makes the necessary sacrifices to defend its threatened world" (166). This latter argument anticipates Niall Ferguson, although Ferguson never concedes that challengers to Britain or the United States make just demands.

Kennedy gives little weight to the internal fiscal organization or political dynamics within great powers, and has little to say about differences in governmental form and state–civil society relations among great powers because they do not figure into his analysis. "There are no stunning contrasts [among the great powers] in evidence here; success and failure [at raising revenues] are to be measured by very narrow differences."[1]

Kennedy makes a second argument, directed specifically at the strongest great power of each era, about why imperialism is costly rather than beneficial. He contends that the leading power of any era will come under increasing challenge from second-level powers that will temporarily set aside their own differences and unite to ensure they do not have to suffer under the putative hegemon's rule. Kennedy's focus on geopolitics makes the vital contribution of highlighting the ways in which wars affect the leading power or hegemon differently from lesser powers.[2]

Kennedy's historiography leaves little room for contingency. The costs of maintaining empires or hegemony increase inexorably, the resulting economic decline (or at least slowing growth and loss of economic leadership) is inevitable, and the rise of a new power or set of competing powers marks each era since 1500.

Kennedy's model differs not only from Marxist views of imperialism's profitability but from the fiscal-military model, the dominant sociological model of state formation and competition.[3] Charles Tilly, the foremost exponent of this model, argues that rulers gained revenue and access to armed men (and later to conscripts) as they

1    Kennedy, *Rise and Fall of the Great Powers*, 72.
2    Daniel H. Nexon and Thomas Wright, in "What's at Stake in the American Empire Debate" (*The American Political Science Review* 101, no. 2 [2007]), argue that empires are undermined as their formal and informal colonies gain capacities to coordinate resistance to the metropole. However, their focus on center-periphery relations slights the role colonial elites play. Nexon and Wright assume that the imperial rulers have a unified interest in holding colonies within their geopolitical orbit and in extracting revenues. However, as I hypothesize in the previous chapter and will demonstrate substantively in the rest of this book, colonial and metropolitan elites have distinct interests that can reduce imperial capacity even in the absence of, and certainly prior to, colonial rebellions.
3    Kennedy, while blithely dismissing the need to examine states' internal institutions and dynamics, never cites, let alone addresses, Tilly or any other scholar of state fiscal policy.

added territories to their polities within Europe and as they accumulated colonies elsewhere in the world. Rulers' ability to defeat and absorb rival European polities or to win colonies in the rest of the world depended partly on their political skills in building alliances and winning support from rich and powerful subjects but, more decisively, was determined by the relative concentrations of capital and coercion that rulers found in their territories and that varied across Europe. At first, the advantage lay with capital-rich polities, like Italian city-states. Mercenaries, paid for by rich cities with tax revenues and loans, could be mobilized more quickly, and were better armed, than bands of feudal retainers. In the sixteenth century,

> The increasing scale of war and the knitting together of the European state system . . . gave the warmaking advantage to those states that could field great standing armies; states having access to a combination of large rural populations, capitalists, and relatively commercialized economies won out.[1]

As a result, dominance passed to states that combined capital and coercion that they used to consolidate large territorial states within Europe and also conquer global empires.

The fiscal-military model sees state formation and territorial conquest as path dependent.[2] States, once launched on their

---

1   Charles Tilly, *Coercion, Capital, and European States* (Oxford: Blackwell, 1990), 58.

2   Other scholars follow a similar path-dependent logic while giving emphasis to different factors than Tilly. Thomas Ertman, in *The Birth of the Leviathan: Building States and Regimes in Medieval and Early Modern Europe* (Cambridge: Cambridge University Press, 1997), distinguishes states along two dimensions: their absolutist or constitutional political regimes, and their patrimonial or bureaucratic state structures. He argues that states became embedded in their typological cell when they were drawn into geopolitical competition; thus, the timing of their entry into European wars in crucial. Ertman's argument in this regard parallels Wallerstein's contention that states' characters and their class relations become fixed at the moment when they are incorporated into the world-system. Similarly, Bruce Porter, in *War and the Rise of the State: The Military Foundations of Modern Politics* (New York: Free Press, 1994), and Brian Downing, in *The Military Revolution and Political Change* (Princeton: Princeton University Press, 1992), argue that wars forced rulers to reach accommodations with subjects that then set the future social and political arrangements of each state.

particular trajectories, were not diverted by later contingent events. Tilly contends that the particular paths of state formation that European rulers adopted at home shaped their strategies of colonial conquest and governance. "European colonizers exported a very similar system to conquered territories outside Europe."[1] As a result, the European states with the greatest supplies of capital and coercion created the largest and most lucrative empires. Just as early modern European rulers needed to conquer and thereby appropriate neighbors' coercion and capital-containing territories in order to attain the scale needed to protect themselves against similarly aggrandizing rivals, Europeans in later centuries had to follow the same imperative on a world scale. Those who conquered colonies in Asia, the Americas, and Africa gained new sources of capital and coercion that could be employed in wars for additional colonies and back in Europe.

The fiscal-military model offers a coherent account for the expansion of European states and their global empires. However, in explaining defeat, Tilly's analysis becomes somewhat tautological. He posits that "states that lost wars commonly contracted" and conversely that there is a positive two-way relationship between winning wars and state revenues.[2] States able to recruit the most men into their armed forces and/or able to raise the most revenues won wars, and as those states won wars they increased the territories they ruled and thereby gained access to more coercion and capital. This virtuous cycle continued unless a polity was defeated and lost territory to a larger rival and/or revenues were lost due to internal rebellions or tax strikes. Strikes and rebellions, in turn, were sparked by sudden increases in tax burdens. Tilly does not explain why popular resistance broke the virtuous cycle of revenue increase and military victory in some polities but not others.[3]

--------------

1   Tilly, *Coercion, Capital, and European States*, 49.
2   Ibid., 28 and passim.
3   Rational choice theorists offer an explanation for the varying importance of rebellions on states' fiscal strength. They contend that rulers weigh the benefits of increasing taxes, which could finance potentially profitable wars, with the risk that subjects would rebel. Taxpayers can choose whether to submit to higher taxes, use bribery or subterfuge to reduce their personal tax burdens, or engage in collective action to roll back tax increases.
   Rulers' and subjects' decisions on whether to cooperate or fight were based on their (often inadequate) information about "the anticipated reactions of other actors"

## TESTING KENNEDY'S AND TILLY'S CLAIMS

We can test both of Kennedy's claims—(1) that great powers did not differ in their ability to raise revenues, and (2) that dominant powers lost wars when military costs reduced their rate of economic growth and/or their rivals united to attack its hegemonic position—as well as the fiscal-military model's claim that states with greater revenues will seize European territories and/or colonies from opponents with lesser revenues.

I confine the analysis in the rest of this chapter to Spain, the Netherlands, France, and Great Britain: the four powers that attempted

---

(Edgar Kiser and April Linton, "The Hinges of History: State-Making and Revolt in Early Modern France," *American Sociological Review* 67 [2002], 889). Past experience guided decisions. If a ruler was successful in raising taxes in the past, he was likely to try again when he wanted or needed to fight the next war. Subjects evaded taxes if the ruler's agents lacked the information to calculate the tax burden or enough personnel to collect what was due. As kings built bureaucracies capable of gathering such information, subjects then had to either pay what was demanded or rebel. Bureaucratization spurred rebellion.

Failure resulted in learning. Kiser and Linton describe repeated or catastrophic failures as "hinges of history" that forced actors to change strategies and led states down different paths of state formation. Rational choice theorists argue that agreements on the levels of taxes often extended, at least implicitly, to the decision of whether or not to go to war and also to how the spoils of war were to be divided. Both king and elite could, potentially, benefit from pooling their resources to fight wars that would take territories or trade routes from rival polities. The elite hesitated to contribute its resources because it feared that the king would monopolize the spoils of war. When the king and elite agreed on rules that gave the elite a say in the decision to start a war and in the distribution of the spoils of war, then the elite was more willing to approve taxes and also to loosen restrictions that preserved elite control over the economy. Elite economic controls retarded economic growth, and so when such controls were loosened the economy grew, making it easier for the polity to afford wars.

See Richard Lachmann, "Greed and Contingency: State Fiscal Crises and Imperial Failure in Early Modern Europe," *American Journal of Sociology* 115, no. 1 (2009) for a fuller discussion and critique of the fiscal-military and rational choice model and for a fuller test of those theories than I offer in this chapter. In essence, I argue that the rational choice model is inadequate because it oversimplifies the ruler-elite dynamic. Laurent Rosenthal, in "The Political Economy of Absolutism Reconsidered" (in *Analytic Narratives*, ed. Robert Bates et al., [Princeton: Princeton University Press, 1998], 64–108), presents aristocrats, non-noble landowners, and merchants as part of a single elite. He argues that differences among those actors can be ignored because all elites are equally open to crown "bribes and threats" and equally able to engage in "free riding." Kiser, too, does not distinguish among groups of tax-paying subjects. I will demonstrate the problems with those assumptions as I analyze actual elite dynamics in the following chapters.

both to achieve dominance within Europe and to build global empires. I ignore Austro-Hungary, Russia, and Portugal. As I noted in chapter 1, while the former two created large European or European-Asian empires, neither sought colonies distant from the contiguous territories under their control. Portugal, while it had a global empire, was never a contender for geopolitical power in Europe. I examine the trends in those four polities' revenues from 1515 to 1815, the centuries when they were in contention for dominance in Europe and for colonies around the world. The following century was the era of British hegemony, when great power rivalries were modulated. I examine Kennedy's claims about the United States in chapter 7. I finish this chapter with a look at the relationship between revenue and territorial conquest for the same four countries, again from 1515 to 1815.

## STATE REVENUES: AMOUNTS AND TRAJECTORIES

Did states' revenues expand progressively except when undermined by territorial losses or domestic rebellion, as Tilly contends? Is Kennedy correct that there were no significant differences in states' fiscal capacities? Tables 2.1 and 2.2 provide the data needed to answer these questions. Table 2.1 presents governmental revenues of the four main European military powers from the sixteenth century through the end of the Napoleonic Wars. The figures for France, the Netherlands, and Spain are converted into British pounds based on the silver content of each currency; the figures are then adjusted for inflation. Table 2.2 converts those data into per capita figures.

Table 2.1 shows that Kennedy is wrong; there were dramatic differences among the four states' fiscal capacities. One polity had a clear and massive advantage over its rivals in each period from the Spanish arrival in the Americas to the end of the Napoleonic Wars. At the start of the sixteenth century, France retained its long-standing advantage of being the largest and most effective European state, collecting more than three times as much as Spain and fourteen times as much as England. Even in per capita terms, as table 2.2 indicates, France had a clear advantage over Spain and especially over England.

Table 2.1:  Governmental Revenues of Britain, France, the Netherlands,
and Spain 1515–1815 (in thousands of British pounds,
adjusted to 1500–49 purchasing power)

| Years | Britain | France | Netherlands | Spain |
|---|---|---|---|---|
| 1515 | 126 | 1,800 | | 558 |
| 1560s | 149 | 631 | | 1,099 |
| 1580s | 173 | 1,500 | 156 | 1,862 |
| 1600s | 214 | 992 | 361 | 1,794 |
| 1630s | 218 | 3,429 | 819 | 1,679 |
| 1650s | | 4,194 | | 2,131 |
| 1670s | 517 | 4,500 | 1,887 | 1,411 |
| 1720s | 1,846 | 5,139 | 1,417 | 1,574 |
| 1750s | 1,951 | 5,574 | 1,693 | |
| 1780s | 4,670 | 8,554 | | |
| 1790s | 10,714 | | 1,290 | |
| 1805 | 11,042 | | 1,983 | |
| 1810 | 14,400 | | | |
| 1815 | 19,947 | 14,890 | | |

Sources: Lachmann, *Capitalists in Spite of Themselves*, table 5.4 for government
revenues in British pounds, 1515–1790s; British data, 1805–15, from Michael
Mann, "State and Society, 1130–1815: An Analysis of English State Finances."
*Political Power and Social Theory*, volume 1 (Greenwich, Conn.: JAI Press, 1980),
193. French 1815 data is for 1814 and from Michel Bruguière, "Finistère," in Jean
Tulard, ed., *Dictionnaire Napoléon* (Paris: Fayard, 1987). Dutch 1805 data is for
1801 and from Marjolein T'Hart, "The United Provinces, 1579–1806," in Richard
Bonney, ed., *The Rise of the Fiscal State in Europe, c. 1200–1815* (Oxford: Oxford
University Press, 1999), 312. Inflation index from Robert C. Allen, "The Great
Divergence in European Wages and Prices from the Middle Ages to the First
World War." *Explorations in Economic History* 38 (2001), 426.

Table 2.2:  Per Capita Governmental Revenues of Britain, France,
the Netherlands, and Spain 1515–1815 (in British
pounds, adjusted to 1500–49 purchasing power)

| Years | Britain | France | Netherlands | Spain |
|---|---|---|---|---|
| 1515 | 0.05 | 0.11 | | 0.08 |
| 1600s | 0.05 | 0.05 | 0.24 | 0.22 |
| 1720s | 0.34 | 0.27 | 0.75 | 0.21 |
| 1805 | 1.20 | | 0.94 | |
| 1815 | 2.17 | 0.55 | | |

Sources: Table 2.1 for government revenues; Lachmann, *Capitalists in Spite of
Themselves*, table 5.3 for population. Per capita figures are derived by dividing 1515
revenues by 1500 population levels, 1600s revenues by 1600 population, 1720s
revenues by 1700 population, and 1805 and 1815 revenues by 1800 population.

Spain's conquests in the Americas decisively shifted the fiscal balance for the entire second half of the sixteenth century. Spain collected almost twice as much revenue as France did (except in the 1580s, when France briefly came close to parity as it extracted revenues to fight its Wars of Religion). Throughout, England remained a distant third, with revenues a tenth of those of Spain and less than a quarter of France's. Spain then stagnated: Its revenues in the 1580s constituted a peak that went unequaled until it was slightly exceeded in the 1650s, before Spanish revenues crashed in the following decades.

The Netherlands vaulted ahead of Britain in the 1600s and surpassed Spain to take second place to France by the 1670s. However, the Dutch state then stagnated fiscally in the eighteenth century. French revenues more than doubled from the 1580s to the 1630s and then almost doubled again from the 1650s to the 1780s, giving France a lead that it sustained until the last decade of the eighteenth century. Britain made the most dramatic gains in the period from 1720 to 1815; its revenues increased almost 900 percent from the 1750s to 1815, when it finally had greater revenues than any other European state, a lead that it, in turn, held through the nineteenth century.

If we look at table 2.2 as a measure of state capacity, we see a somewhat different story. France's sixteenth-century advantage was lost to both Spain and the new Dutch state in the seventeenth century. Spain's gains were due largely to revenues from its American colonies, which quickly stagnated. Indeed, per capita revenues for Spain and the Netherlands in the 1600s were similar to those of France and Britain a century later. The Netherlands' gains in state capacity were largely internal and accelerated throughout the seventeenth century. Dutch per capita revenues reached unprecedented levels by the early eighteenth century, almost four times those of France and Spain, and more than twice those of Britain. It was only in the first years of the nineteenth century that Britain took first place in per capita revenues, an amount that then almost doubled by the end of the Napoleonic Wars. France's per capita also doubled during the war, albeit from a much lower level, and remained about half those of the Netherlands.

Britain's history, as reflected in both tables, supports Tilly's model, but the other three countries experienced prolonged periods of stagnation when existing revenues and populations that could be tapped to form armies failed to produce new increases in revenue. Finally, Spanish revenues fell by almost a third from the 1640s to the 1720s, as that empire's sources of capital and coercion proved ever less effective at extracting new revenues or even sustaining existing levies on the people and commerce within its territories. Thus, the four powers differ significantly in their fiscal capacities, and the fiscal-military model is unable to account for those differences.

## REVENUES AND MILITARY SUCCESS

We can test Tilly's claim that polities with more revenue take territories from rivals with less fiscal capacity. We can also see whether Kennedy is correct that lesser powers ally and succeed in defeating the dominant power of each era. If we want to test those claims, we cannot look simply to victory or defeat in individual wars, because those terms are ill suited for describing what happened at the end of most early modern European wars, which were inconclusive and ended with treaties that more often than not returned all or most conquered territories to their prewar rulers. Unconditional victory in war was a twentieth-century development.[1] Thus, extending Andreas Wimmer and Brian Min's data set on victory and defeat in wars in the nineteenth and twentieth centuries back an additional three hundred years would not help us adjudicate between Tilly's and Kennedy's claims.[2]

Instead, we need to look at each polity's success in winning territory through war. I have compiled a data set of each change in territorial control in Europe and of colonies on other continents (presented in tables 2A and 2B respectively in the appendix).[3] Table 2.3 offers a summary of those changes, highlighting the periods when each of the four powers experienced significant territorial gains and losses in Europe and beyond in the three centuries from 1500 to 1815. Table 2.3

--------

1   Eric Hobsbawm, *The Age of Extremes: A History of the World, 1914–1991* (New York: Pantheon, 1994), 44–9.

2   Andreas Wimmer and Brian Min, "From Empire to Nation-State: Explaining Wars in the Modern World, 1816–2001," *American Sociological Review* 71, no. 6 (2006).

3   The tables exclude those instances where a great power seized territory from a rival during a war but then returned the territory in a peace treaty at the end of that war. All territorial changes (de facto and de jure) that lasted beyond the end of a war are contained in those tables.

also identifies periods of territorial stasis and specifies anomalies in the relationship between states' fiscal resources and territorial gains predicted by the fiscal-military model.

**Table 2.3:  Eras of Military Dominance, Territorial Gains and Losses, and Anomalies, 1500–1815**

SPAIN:

1500–1580s: conquered lands in Europe; seized colonies in Americas from natives and from Portugal

1590–1648: no land gains [**anomaly**: richest, then second richest, power]; loss of Netherlands [**anomaly**: Spain's budget five times that of Netherlands]

1659–78: losses in Europe to France

1633–1814: losses of colonies to other powers [**anomaly**: most losses to comparably rich Netherlands and Britain, not richer France]

1810–25: most American colonies independent

FRANCE:

1516–59: expelled British from France, gains in Italy

1659–78, 1735, 1768: added territories along its borders [**anomaly**: richest, but no gains during most of this period]

1605–77, 1763–95: seized colonies [**anomaly**: richest, but no gains during most of this period]

1758–97: lost most America colonies to Britain [**anomaly**: France richer]

1797–1810: conquered much of Europe, but all lost by 1815 [**anomaly**: gains came after Britain became richest]

NETHERLANDS:

1609: de facto independence from Spain [**anomaly**: Spain's budget five times greater]

1605–87: seized colonies [**anomaly**: third richest, then second to France]

1664–77: lost most American colonies to Britain [**anomaly**: Netherlands' budget three times greater]

1714: added Guelders to homeland

1783–1814: lost many colonies to Britain

BRITAIN:

1559: lost holdings in France

1714: gained Gibraltar

1610–72: seized colonies [**anomaly**: poorest of four powers]

1739–1763: seized colonies [**anomaly**: poorer than France, even with Spain]

1783: lost American colonies

1783–1815: seized colonies from France, Spain, and Netherlands, but also lost colonies to same three powers [**anomalies**: took most colonies from France while French had larger budget and were militarily dominant in Europe; lost colonies mainly to poorer Netherlands and after Britain achieved military dominance in Europe]

The fiscal-military model is not supported by the data. Five out of the eleven European changes of territory in table 2A among the four great powers went to the state with the bigger budget at that time, four to the poorer state, and two were between states with almost equal budgets. Outside of Europe, twenty-four of the colonial switches among the four great powers in table 2B went to the richer polity and nineteen to the poorer.

More significant than the mixed picture of territorial changes among the four powers is the inability of the fiscal-military model to account for the long periods when the leading fiscal and military powers made no territorial gains at all, despite their advantages over rivals with lesser resources. The richest power of each era did not add territories during most of its years of fiscal supremacy, and the powers that accumulated territories as often as not had smaller budgets than rivals who failed to add to their holdings or lost lands to poorer powers.

Kennedy's model is of only limited help in explaining the anomalies generated by the fiscal-military model. Some, but not most, Spanish and French military reverses occurred because lesser powers united to thwart those dominant powers' ambitions. Kennedy's contention that imperial costs led to economic decline is unsupported by the evidence in any of the four cases.

*Spain*: Spain made almost all of its conquests in the sixteenth century, when it was vastly outspent by France. In the 1580s, when it had the largest budget, Spain gained temporary control over Portugal and Portuguese colonies. Most challenging to the fiscal-military model, Spain lost military dominance within Europe, exemplified by its loss of control over its richest territory, the Netherlands, and its colonial acquisitions came to an abrupt halt in the 1590s, the moment at which its revenues increased from 120 percent to 200 percent of that of its leading rival, France. Spain lost territories in Europe during the seventeenth and eighteenth centuries to the richer France but surrendered colonies elsewhere in the world mainly to Britain and the Netherlands, which had budgets similar to that of Spain until Britain's fiscal resources expanded dramatically in the latter half of the eighteenth century. Spain's capacity to seize and hold colonies, contrary to the fiscal-military model, did not correlate with its fiscal resources.

Spain became a target of the combined forces of lesser powers in the fifteenth century and during the Thirty Years' War of 1618–48, and Kennedy is able to demonstrate that several Spanish defeats in Europe occurred because "Spain was fighting on three fronts simultaneously, and with her enemies consciously aiding each other, diplomatically and commercially if not militarily,"[1] thus accounting for Spain's inability to gain territory after 1590. Most critically, the Dutch were able to win independence and to take American and Asian colonies from the far wealthier Spain with English and French aid, while Spain was simultaneously fighting France, Sweden, and various German polities.

Kennedy offers little evidence that "imperial overstretch" affected the Spanish economy and sapped the Habsburgs' future capacities to pay for war. The fiscal weaknesses Kennedy identifies—the great autonomy of each Habsburg territory except for Castille, which provided the bulk of royal revenues, the tax exemptions enjoyed by aristocrats and corporate bodies, and the monopolies that retarded economic growth and commerce—all were artifacts of the Habsburg Empire's formation. If these weaknesses were deepened by Spain's efforts after to preserve and expand the empire, Kennedy does not explain how. Above all, Kennedy has nothing to say about the dramatic decline in Habsburg revenues from their American colonies in the first half of the seventeenth century, precisely the period when it suffered its most significant military and territorial losses in Europe.

*France*: France was, by far, the richest European state from the 1630s until the 1790s. France made modest gains to its national territory at several points during those centuries, while it made unprecedented conquests under Napoleon *after* Britain had achieved a decisive fiscal advantage. France, despite having a population and receipts that equaled those of its three main rivals combined, was unable to achieve any geopolitical gains in the period from the 1680s to the 1750s. During that era, France gained neither territory within Europe (except for taking Lorraine from the Habsburgs in 1735), nor expanded its colonies, nor did it gain control over any new trade routes. France lost many of its colonies in the second half of the eighteenth century,

---

1   Kennedy, *Rise and Fall of the Great Powers*, 49.

while it retained a decisive fiscal advantage over Britain. Ancien régime France's huge fiscal edge yielded some territory in Europe (although the revolutionary fervor of Republican troops and Napoleon's leadership produced far more). France was singularly unable to translate revenues into colonies.

Kennedy contends that France's two efforts to achieve continental hegemony (1660–1714 and 1793–1814) were blocked by broad coalitions of the other great powers and lesser states, desperate to avoid living under French hegemony. He argues that France's ability to fight against those broad coalitions deteriorated as the costs of prolonged wars sapped the French economy.

While Kennedy sees similarities in the failures of France's two efforts to achieve hegemony, there were crucial differences between the two eras. Napoleon was confronted by a unified and totally mobilized coalition of all the other European states, while the coalition against Louis XIV was less solid, with Britain and various other powers allied at times during that half century with France.[1] France's economic and demographic advantage over the other powers was greater in the earlier period than under Napoleon.[2] Kennedy's model would predict greater French successes under Louis XIV than under Napoleon, yet the opposite happened. Ancien régime France added territories along its borders but managed to hold no other European territories and added few colonies from the 1630s to the 1780s. Napoleon, for a time, held much of Europe, even as he lost most of the remaining French colonies to Britain.

Kennedy offers no analysis of how military spending, as opposed to France's perennial "fiscal immaturity,"[3] weakened French economic growth. He steps outside his model in an effort to explain the anomaly of ancien régime France's meager territorial gains. He argues that France failed to follow a consistent continental or maritime strategy. "Torn between fighting in Flanders, Germany, and northern Italy on the one hand and in the Channel, West Indies, Lower Canada, and the

---

1    Ibid., 100–6, 121–39.

2    Massimo Livi Bacci, *The Population of Europe* (Oxford: Blackwell, 1999), 8.

3    Kennedy, *Rise and Fall of the Great Powers*, 83. This claim of French fiscal immaturity contradicts his general claim that there were "very narrow differences" in the great powers' fiscal capacities.

Indian Ocean on the other, French strategy led repeatedly to a 'falling between stools.'"[1] Kennedy describes but does not explain why France dithered under Louis XIV, achieved clarity of purpose under the weaker Louis XVI when it focused its military resources to aid the American Revolution, and then achieved its greatest gains under Napoleon.

*Netherlands*: The Netherlands achieved de facto independence from Spain when its budget was a fifth that of its ruler. The Dutch took most of their colonies from the natives of those territories rather than from previous European conquerors. The few colonies they seized from rival powers were taken at moments when the Dutch had lower state revenues than those rivals, and the Dutch lost most of its colonies to the British at a time when the Dutch state enjoyed triple the revenues received by the British. During the first two Anglo-Dutch Wars the Netherlands had the added advantage of having France as an ally. The Dutch took Guelders province from the Spanish Netherlands and made it a permanent part of their nation in 1714 when Spanish and Dutch revenues were almost equal, during a time when the vastly richer French were unable to make any additions to their homeland. The Dutch did much with relatively little and lost the most colonies at the apex of their fiscal development.

Kennedy argues that Dutch efforts to sustain great power status were doomed by that small country's inability to afford both the land forces needed to defend itself against France and naval forces to protect its coast, colonies, and European and international trade routes from British and Spanish attacks. The Netherlands' inherent strategic weaknesses forced it into an alliance with Britain. That alliance weakened the Dutch commercially due to frequent British-enforced trade embargoes against France and British demands that the Netherlands supply troops for land wars against France, burdens that then further retarded Dutch economic growth.[2]

In fact, the main Dutch geopolitical reversals happened before it allied with Britain and while it maintained a fiscal advantage over all its rivals except France. The Dutch were able, until Napoleon's

---

1   Ibid., 89.
2   Ibid., 86–8.

invasion, to fend off both the French (the wealthiest of the four powers) and the Spanish on land, where Kennedy locates their greatest geopolitical weakness, while losing colonies and trade routes to the poorer British in sea battles. The Netherlands' economic decline occurred in the eighteenth century, decades after the Dutch had significantly reduced their military commitments.[1]

*Britain*: Britain took colonies from rivals when it had the smallest budget of the four main powers and lost colonies in the late eighteenth century as its revenues began a dramatic rise, mainly to the Dutch and Spanish, whose revenues were stagnant then. Britain gained much with little and less when they had more.

Kennedy explains Britain's ability to capture colonies from its richer European rivals in terms of that island nation's geographic remove from continental wars, which allowed the British to concentrate their resources on building a navy that could be diverted from Europe to colonize lands and to capture existing colonies from rivals preoccupied with European wars. Kennedy ignores the fact that the navy was created to defend Britain from invasion and could be sent to capture colonies only because Britain had an army that could neutralize its enemies on the Continent. That is why Britain was able to seize colonies from other powers even when it was at peace with those rivals in Europe; indeed, Britain took colonies from France just after its American defeat.

## HOW KENNEDY GOES WRONG

How can we account for Kennedy's explanatory failures? How can we construct an explanation that is able to account for the actual fiscal and geopolitical trajectories of Spain, France, the Netherlands, and Great Britain? Kennedy's model fails to explain so many of the great powers' territorial gains and losses because he ignores the dramatically varying capacities of each power to actually assert centralized control over the tax collectors, soldiers, and other officials under its

1   Jonathan Israel, *The Dutch Republic: Its Rise, Greatness, and Fall, 1477–1806* (Oxford: Clarendon, 1995).

nominal control. Nor does Kennedy address or attempt to explain the varying abilities of colonial trading companies, merchants and banks, or colonial administrators and settlers to launch diplomatic or military missions and create incidents that committed their metropoles to foreign wars that made neither economic nor geopolitical sense.

As we will see in later chapters, when we examine Spain, France, the Netherlands, and Britain (and then the United States), the problem was not the availability of resources: Colonies yielded enough revenues to pay for the general costs of fighting wars against other European nations and controlling empires. Rather, European powers lost wars and colonies because they were unable to gain central control over the troops and weapons their budgets bought, or to ensure that colonial profits and domestic taxes actually arrived in the central treasury. If we want to explain both military defeat and economic decline, we must look at hegemons' and failed hegemons' internal dynamics. Empires, formal and informal, matter as much for their effects on the structure of elites that determine state policies and capacities within each hegemon as for their contributions to economic growth and their role in animating wars among great powers.

# 3

# Spain and France: Military Dominance Without Hegemony

In the last chapter, I asked whether military success was explained by a polity's fiscal advantage over rivals. My answer, in a word, was no. This chapter seeks to explain the reasons for the anomalies between revenues and territorial conquest by getting at the dynamics of elite conflict and structural change. Specifically, I ask why Spain and France were unable to meld the fruits of their military conquests into a coherent empire that could funnel resources to the metropole and thereby fuel economic growth and further military success. In order to answer this question, we need to ask and answer a further question: Who controlled the conquered lands and the revenues extracted from them?

Habsburg Spain and France under both Louis XIV and Napoleon demonstrate the limits of empires and of geopolitical power. Those polities sought to achieve military dominance within Europe and to use their continental power to amass a greater collection of colonies than their European rivals. Spain held sustained military dominance in Europe for longer than any other polity since Rome, and it conquered an empire that remained significantly larger than its rivals until the loss of most of its American colonies during the 1811–36 wave of independence revolutions, when it was eclipsed by Britain's imperial expansion beginning with the defeat of Napoleon. France was unable, during either era of European military dominance, to build a significant empire beyond the Continent, and its military conquests within Europe were, except for modest expansions of its border, only temporary.

## THE LIMITS OF MILITARY POWER

As we saw in the previous chapter, Spain built the largest and most lucrative empire of its European rivals in the sixteenth century when it seized most of Latin America, much of what today is the western half of the United States, some Caribbean islands, and the Philippines. From 1580 to 1640, during the union with Portugal, the Habsburgs also held a string of coastal trading ports in Africa, India, and Southeast Asia. In addition, the Spanish monarch as Habsburg emperor ruled the Low Countries (present-day Netherlands, Luxembourg, and Belgium) and much of what became Germany and Italy.

These conquests allowed the Spanish crown to increase its revenues by 233 percent from 1515 to the 1580s, at which point it exceeded, for the first time, the income of the French monarch. However, the 1580s were the fiscal high point for the Habsburgs. Thereafter, Habsburg revenue, controlling for inflation, stagnated. By the 1720s, Spanish revenue was only 31 percent of France's, 85 percent of Britain's, and only 4 percent above that of the Netherlands, its former colony.[1]

Spain's military success came to an end in the seventeenth century. Money did not buy military victories for the Habsburgs, as we saw in the previous chapter. Spain lost its most lucrative and strategically important European territories in the early and mid-seventeenth century to the combined forces of Dutch rebellion and French interventionism. The Dutch also took some of Spain's richest Caribbean holdings in that period. Spain ceded the southern Netherlands (Belgium), Naples, Milan, and Sardinia to Austria in 1714, Sicily to the Holy Roman Empire in 1720, and Tuscany and Parma to Austria in 1735. While most of those lands fell to the Austrian Habsburgs, we must remember that the Austrian and Spanish branches of the family had divided their holdings into separate polities two centuries earlier and, during the seventeenth and eighteenth centuries, competed and at times fought with each other for territory and influence within Europe. Spain's American colonies almost all were lost in a wave of independence movements from 1808 to 1833.

France sought hegemony within Europe twice: under Louis XIV and then Napoleon. Louis achieved little success, taking only some

---

1   These data are from table 2.1 on page 89.

lands bordering France, much of which remains part of the Republic to this day. Napoleon created the greatest European empire since Rome and until Hitler, seizing lands that constitute present-day Belgium, the Netherlands, Portugal and Spain, and much of Italy and Germany. The accomplishments of these two rulers were quite different beyond Europe: Louis XIV expanded French holdings in North America, the Caribbean, and India, mainly by defeating indigenous peoples rather than taking already existing European colonies. Napoleon did little to challenge Europeans beyond the Continent (anticipating Hitler's strategy), taking only minor possessions in the Americas and Africa.

In essence, success in Europe did little for colonization, and colonial empires contributed little to Spain and France's battles to rule Europe. The contrast with Britain, to be discussed in chapter 5, and the United States, examined in later chapters, could not be sharper, while the Netherlands occupies an intermediate position. This chapter first examines the dynamics of the Spanish Empire. The subsequent sections perform the same task for France under Louis XIV and then for the Napoleonic era. This chapter concludes by identifying the commonalities in the Spanish and French dynamics and uses them to assess the efficacy of the typology of empires I developed in chapter 1.

## SPAIN

### The Empire the Habsburgs Built

The Habsburg Empire is often presented as the product of marital deals and demographic luck: Ferdinand married Isabella, uniting Castile and Aragon; their daughter Joanna was married to Philip I, son of Maximilian and Mary, whose marriage had united the thrones of Austria and Burgundy and the Holy Roman Emperorship. The luck was the well-timed death of Joanna's elder brother, ensuring she and her son Charles would inherit the Spanish throne along with that of Austria. Further demographic luck came when Portuguese king Sebastian died in 1578 without a direct heir, allowing Philip II to claim the Portuguese throne when Sebastian's uncle Cardinal Henry died in 1580.[1] Later, the entire male line of the kingdom of Hungary and

---

1   Lynch, *Spain 1516–1598*, 429–85.

Bohemia died off, letting that crown fall to the next generation of Habsburgs. While the Spanish and Austrian crowns were separated, (and the increasingly divergent interests of the Austrian Habsburg/ Holy Roman Empire rulers became peripheral to the future of the Spanish Habsburgs and their empire), the Spanish line kept Burgundy and was aided in taking what became the Netherlands due to the leverage of the Holy Roman Emperor.

Accounts of dynastic shenanigans obscure the essential deals that convinced elites in the European territories united under Spain to go along with Habsburg sovereignty. In each place, the Habsburgs selected the largest aristocrats as their main elite ally. The crown then provided the military muscle (or respected the dominant elite's existing military forces) that enabled that elite to subordinate rival elites and exploit peasants and towns. These deals reflected the Habsburgs' accurate appraisal of their limited military and organizational capacity relative to nobles.

Castilian aristocrats had provided the armed forces needed to reconquer Muslim Spain and were rewarded with the lion's share of the lands seized in the centuries-long struggle.[1] "Since the late Middle Ages, successive Castilian kings and queens had coaxed the nobility away from rebellion by giving it effective control over the internal economy and local politics of Castile."[2] Crown efforts to limit aristocratic authority with corps of bourgeois officials sparked the fourteenth-century Castilian Civil War. The king was killed and replaced by his half brother, who returned high state and clerical offices to the aristocratic families that claimed those posts. The new king also revoked towns' autonomous rights in the aftermath of that Civil War. Aristocrats thus regained control over those towns that had sided with the monarchy in the Civil War. Subsequent crown efforts to check aristocrats' power by supporting peasant demands during the spate of uprisings from 1460 to 1472 were countered as aristocrats crushed all the uprisings.[3]

---

1    Ibid., 1–26.

2    Carla Rahn Phillips, *Ciudad Real, 1500–1750: Growth, Crisis, and Readjustment in the Spanish Economy* (Cambridge: Harvard University Press, 1979), 77.

3    Stanley G. Payne, *A History of Spain and Portugal* (Madison: University of Wisconsin Press, 1973), 141–69.

King Ferdinand and Queen Isabella and their Habsburg successors learned from those failed efforts. They did not provoke further noble or peasant uprisings in Castile. As they moved to incorporate other kingdoms within an imperial monarchy, these monarchs did so by preserving all the privileges of the incumbent nobilities. The kingdom of Aragon, which itself was a combination of Aragon, Catalonia, and Valencia, and later Portugal, was brought into the Iberian empire not by conquest but instead through accords between the Castilian monarch and the aristocracies of each of those kingdoms. Aragonese and Portuguese nobles recognized the Castilian monarch's right to wear plural crowns in return for royal recognition of the aristocracies' broadest claims of ancient rights to tax exemptions, local judicial authority, and power for their representative bodies to veto royal initiatives.[1]

The Spanish crown did realize fiscal as well as dynastic benefits from its alliance with provincial nobilities. The Habsburgs succeeded in challenging the power of the clergy, thereby claiming a growing share of clerical tithes and appropriating much of the church's property. Crown appropriations of clerical powers and properties began during the Castilian Civil War and continued in the following centuries. The crown was able to weaken the church for two reasons. First, clerics lost land and tithe rights when they backed losing parties in the fourteenth-century civil war. Second, the pope granted the crown the power to appoint all Spanish bishops and the right to receive a growing share of clerical revenues in recognition first of Ferdinand and Isabella's reconquest of Spain, then of their successors' vigor in combating Protestants, Jews, and Muslims through warfare and through the Inquisition, and finally of the crown's efforts to convert heathens in the Americas.[2]

---

1   M. L. Bush, *Renaissance, Reformation, and the Outer World* (London: Blandford, 1967), 48–58; Henry Kamen, *Spain 1469–1714: A Society of Conflict* (London: Longman, 1991), 17–32; Lynch, *Spain 1516–1598*, 67–8 and passim; Lynch, *The Hispanic World in Crisis and Change*, 17–52; Daniel H. Nexon, *The Struggle for Power in Early Modern Europe: Religious Conflict, Dynastic Empires, and International Change* (Princeton: Princeton University Press, 2009), 147–9, 228–30; Payne, *History of Spain and Portugal*; Pierre Vilar, *La Catalogne dans l'Espagne moderne: Recherches sur les fondements économiques des structures nationales* (Paris: SEVPEN, 1962), volume 1.

2   Bush, *Renaissance, Reformation, and the Outer World*, 44–8, 58–61; Lynch,

The Spanish Church became, after the Castilian peasantry, the largest source of crown revenues in the seventeenth century. Averaging revenues from 1621 through 1640, Castilian taxes (which fell almost exclusively on peasants and laborers) yielded 38 percent of crown revenues, followed by 15.6 percent from the Spanish Church, and only 10.7 percent from American bullion.[1] The crown's clerical revenues came, however, at a political cost. Much like the English crown following the Henrician Reformation, discussed in chapter 5, Spanish monarchs found that in allying with aristocrats to weaken the clergy, they lost a potential counterweight to the great nobles or to local landlords. Before they were weakened by the crown-aristocrat alliance, clerics and urban merchants were the only groups with either the administrative capacity or the local knowledge and political authority to reap the full benefits of clerical lands and tithes for the crown. Instead, the crown had to turn to aristocrats to manage and tax clerical properties. Much clerical land was leased to nobles on favorable terms, with corrupt payments passing between nobles and clerics who often were related to one another.[2]

Aristocrats in Iberia cemented their control over localities by creating familial alliances that were built upon clear hierarchies of aristocratic titles. These chains of lineages, capped by regional magnates or provincial estates, gained increasingly clear control over land, peasants, towns, and clerical offices as they won concessions from the crown and defeated peasants.[3] By the seventeenth century, each Spanish province was ruled by an aristocratic autarky.

The way in which Habsburg territories had been amalgamated allowed aristocrats to maintain hereditary control over officer positions in the military and over their armed retainers. The crown's limited financial resources meant that the Habsburgs could not create a parallel professional army with the potential to dominate and eventually incorporate or replace the disparate noble armed forces. Habsburg rulers, like their counterparts elsewhere in Europe, did have

---

Spain 1516–1598, 1–26, 342–85; Payne, *History of Spain and Portugal*, 205–6.

1   Kamen, *Spain 1469–1714*, 218.

2   Lynch, *Hispanic World in Crisis and Change*, 348–82; Phillips, *Ciudad Real*, 110.

3   Lynch, *Spain 1516–1598*; Vilar, *La Catalogne dans l'Espagne moderne*.

varying amounts of money to hire mercenaries, but such hired guns would switch sides or disappear the moment the crown lacked the cash to pay and provision them. As a result, the bulk of Habsburg and, indeed, of all European armies were amalgams of armed men controlled by aristocrats. Often, aristocrats came to battle but then held back their men if they disagreed with their nominal ruler's plans. Thus, victory in battle (and even more in a war that was a series of battles often separated by months or years-long gaps and that extended over years and even decades) often had less to do with the commander's strategic plan or tactical skill than with a ruler's financial resources and the degree to which he possessed the political ability and/or leverage to convince the aristocrats he supposedly ruled to bring their armed men to the battlefield and then to fight with dedication and courage in harness to the ruler's strategy and command.[1]

### WHO CONQUERED THE AMERICAS?

The system of rule, and of empire-building, that the Habsburgs used in Spain and then elsewhere in Europe was applied to the opportunities for conquest that became apparent with the first reports of Columbus's explorations of the new continent. Spain's lack of a centralized army and navy and the crown's chronic fiscal crisis were circumvented by the decision to allow private actors, mainly aristocrats but also urban merchants, to pay for expeditions to America.

We need to acknowledge that the initial conquerors and settlers of Spanish, and of most other European colonies, in the Americas, Asia, and Africa were private entrepreneurs. Schoolbook stories about Queen Isabella pawning her jewels to pay for Columbus's journey in 1492 mask the true source of funds for American exploration and conquest.

---

1   See Richard Lachmann, "Mercenary, Citizen, Victim: The Rise and Fall of Conscription in the West," in *Nationalism and War*, ed. John A. Hall and Siniša Malešević (Cambridge: Cambridge University Press, 2013), 44–70, for a fuller discussion of the limits of centralized control in early modern European armies.

Resources for conquest and settlement came, for the most part, from private individuals ... The crown and its officials had met some of the small cost of Columbus's first voyage, but merchants and nobles flocked to lend support to his much larger second expedition of 1493, and they provided the funds for all later ventures. Partnerships of merchants, nobles and soldiers competed for royal licenses to explore and to organize new settlements, guaranteeing shares of their gains to the crown. Capital to provide the ships and their stores, and the colonists' armament, was raised in Spain itself for the early expeditions, but by 1506 a few of the colonists had accumulated sufficient fortunes from the gold of Española to mount the conquests of Cuba, Jamaica and Puerto Rico ... The series of expeditions after 1516 which culminated in Cortes's conquest of Mexico were backed by Cuban resources; and the wealth of Mexico paid for the northward and southward extension of exploration and gave some backing to the conquest of Peru. The net investment of Spanish resources in the New World itself, therefore, was significant only in the first fifteen years after Columbus's arrival.[1]

Spanish and then Spanish American entrepreneurs' access to private capital determined their capacity to finance voyages and to hire soldiers who, like the ancient Romans, made use of exemplary terrorism to subdue the peoples whose lands they conquered. To be sure, European rulers granted the entrepreneurs charters that were supposed to limit the conquistadors' autonomy in the new colonies; however, for the first centuries of European conquest and rule, the monarchs back home contributed little or no money and very few troops to control and develop the colonies they nominally ruled. In essence, monarchs granted men with ships, money, and guns monopoly rights to conquer, loot, and exploit territories and the people who lived there (and also to import new laborers from Africa to replace the native Americans the conquerors had killed in genocidal campaigns and with the spread of European diseases). In return, European monarchs demanded that colonizers pay taxes and that colonies trade

1   Ralph Davis, *The Rise of the Atlantic Economies* (London: Weidenfield and Nicholson, 1973), 39–40.

only with their "home" European country. Such demands were hard to enforce, and European monarchs were at best only partly successful. In this and the following two chapters, we will trace and explain the differences in the extent to which first monarchs and then states were able to exert control over "their" colonists. That will then allow us to understand the dynamics and ultimate fates of the Spanish, French, Dutch, and British empires.

## How the Colonists Achieved Autonomy and Retarded Spain's Economy

The Habsburgs rewarded New World explorers and conquerors, and adjudicated among their competing claims, by awarding *encomiendas*. An *encomienda* was a grant over the indigenous people in a territory. The holder of the *encomienda* got the right to the forced labor of the indigenous people within the territory of the grant as well as to any gold and silver already held by the natives or which the natives could be compelled to mine for their overlord. (The *encomienda* holder was also supposed to see to the natives' conversion to Christianity.)

Charles V and his ministers realized within two decades of the conquests of Mexico and Peru that Ferdinand and Isabella, and then Charles himself, had given away the store in granting *encomiendas* to the colonists. Holders of the grants quickly drafted the natives under their control to find treasure. The rigors of mining combined with the introduction of European diseases to wipe out the native populations on the Caribbean islands conquered by the Spanish and then to kill off more than 80 percent of the indigenous population of Mexico.[1] Charles V, perhaps prodded by his clerical retainers, seems to have become disturbed at the deaths of so many heathens before they could be converted to Christianity. But he exhibited far more distress over his meager 26 percent share of American treasure shipped back to Spain. Charles V sought to solve both problems in the 1540s by narrowing the privileges granted to colonists. *Encomiendas* were made to expire upon their holder's death. Charles V transferred control over indigenous labor from the holders of *encomiendas* to state officials. However, the crown's need for revenue

---

1   Ibid., 54.

led it to sell extensions on *encomiendas,* turning them, like venal offices, into permanent rights.[1]

Restrictions on colonists' *encomiendas,* if they could have been sustained, should have allowed the crown to become the main beneficiary of treasure mined from the vast new deposits discovered at Potosi, Peru, in 1545 and at Zacatecas, in northern Mexico, in 1546. However, Charles V's representatives in Mexico and Peru remained totally dependent upon the settler oligarchies for the resources necessary to work the new mines because the Spanish crown remained mired in a permanent fiscal crisis. Just as Ferdinand and Isabella had to rely upon private capital to explore and conquer America (and then reward the financiers and conquistadors with *encomiendas*), so too bankrupt Charles V had to call upon American capital to open and operate the new Mexican and Peruvian mines. Charles V's successors were also dependent upon capital from the colonial oligarchy to mine the deposits discovered in Mexico in the 1670s.

Capital trumped control over corvée labor in the mines of Mexico and Peru. The great mines of the 1540s and 1670s, as well as the lesser mines discovered in between, all were controlled by the American financiers who paid for the mining equipment (and for the German technicians who immigrated to Mexico and Peru to set up and operate the pumping and crushing machines). Silver was extracted from low-grade ores using the mercury amalgamation process. The two largest known deposits of mercury were in Spain; American mine owners quickly gained control over Spanish mercury production. State officials became glorified press gangs and crew bosses for the mine owners, supplying masses of indigenous laborers who were trained and provisioned at the mines.[2]

Ferdinand and Isabella's decisions to grant *encomiendas* and thereby create an American oligarchy would not have been

--------

1   Olivier Caporossi, "Adelantados and Encomenderos in Spanish America," in *Constructing Early Modern Empires: Proprietary Ventures in the Atlantic World, 1500–1750,* eds. L. H. Roper and Bertrand van Ruymbeke (Leiden, Netherlands: Brill, 2007), 55–77.

2   Lynch, *The Hispanic World in Crisis and Change,* 229–347; John J. TePaske and Herbert S. Klein, "The Seventeenth-Century Crisis in New Spain: Myth or Reality?," *Past and Present* 90 (1981); Davis, *Rise of the Atlantic Economies,* 50–53.

irredeemable if their royal successors had had the resources to finance new mines on their own, or even to create and reward an independent corps of officials in America. The crown never was able to generate a surplus large enough to pay the huge start-up costs of new mines and certainly could not weather the frequent losses that mine owners incurred when the amount of silver or gold that could be extracted with existing technology fell off. Thus, the bankrupt Spanish crown had to surrender the lion's share of American treasure to the only elite willing and able to finance the great mining enterprises in Mexico and Peru.

The crown received between 25 percent and 30 percent of the gold and silver mined and stolen in America from the start of significant treasure imports in 1503 until 1580. The crown's share fell with the vast increase in mining output after 1580, dropping to the 15 percent range, and then catastrophically (for the crown) to 10 percent or less after 1615. For the five years from 1656 to 1660, the crown received 600,000 pesos of treasure out of 51.6 million produced, little more than 1 percent. Expressed in different terms, the crown's share of American gold and silver amounted to 4 percent of royal income in 1510, rose to 7.5 percent in 1577, and then to a peak of 16 percent of receipts in 1591. The crown's take then declined to an average of 6 percent of income for 1621–40 and fell to an insignificant 1 percent for 1656–60.[1] American elites took advantage of the Habsburgs' weakness and preoccupation during the Thirty Years' War against the Netherlands, France, and Britain (and at the end of the war with the revolt of Portugal) to withhold an ever-greater share of declining bullion production, sealing Spain's doom in its fight to retain its European empire.

Could Spanish monarchs have undermined the American oligarchs by offering competing mining concessions or land grants to rival elites in Europe? Charles V and his successors laid the basis for such a strategy by granting the merchants of Seville a monopoly on

1   Dennis O. Flynn, "Fiscal Crisis and the Decline of Spain (Castile)," *Journal of Economic History* 42, no. 1 (1982): 142; Lynch, *Hispanic World in Crisis and Change*, 270, 283.

trade with the Americas.[1] As long as the crown maintained control over the military and merchant fleets sailing to America, it could have used its naval hegemony to concentrate all the advantages of transatlantic trade on a merchant elite in Seville. Then most of the profits from American mines and plantations would have accrued to Seville, leaving the American oligarchs in a perpetual state of underdevelopment and dependence on Spain for finished goods and mining and farming equipment. American oligarchs never would have generated the surplus to develop and operate the new mines. Instead, the Seville merchants would have been the nexus of Spanish American wealth, much as London merchants were the primary beneficiaries of British American colonial settlements. A powerful commercial elite in Seville could have been a counterweight to the entrenched rural nobility of Spain, allowing the crown to play competing elites against one another as French kings were able to do so well.

The Seville merchant elite never became a major political or economic force within Spain. The crown lost the dual opportunities to subordinate American settlers to a metropolitan commercial elite and to create a counterweight to the rural aristocracy. Seville's trade monopoly did not foster much industry within Spain because land and labor remained locked in feudal relations of production under aristocratic control as a result of earlier Habsburg deals with large aristocrats. Seville became nothing more than an entrepôt, sending American gold and silver on to the real centers of European production (mainly France and the Netherlands, and later England) and receiving manufactured goods (and even French agricultural products) for shipment back to Spanish America.[2]

American treasure, in the absence of opportunities for productive investment, stimulated inflation within Spain that further reduced the possibilities for constructing domestic manufactures that could compete with the cheaper products of established industries in the relatively low-inflation economies of France, the Low Countries, or

---

1   Elliott, *Empires of the Atlantic World*, 108–14; Davis, *Rise of the Atlantic Economies*, 62–3.

2   Davis, *Rise of the Atlantic Economies*, 143–56; Henry Kamen, "The Decline of Spain: A Historical Myth," *Past and Present* 81 (1978); Wallerstein, *Modern World-System*, volume 1, 187–99.

Britain.[1] The Spanish crown, under constant fiscal duress and without the immediate possibility of profiting from new domestic industries, milked transatlantic trade as a cash cow.

American settlers built direct commercial relations with trading partners beyond Spain as a way to avoid high Spanish taxes and to compensate for the dearth of Spanish entrepreneurs with the capital and know-how to develop American ventures. American settlers met their needs for agricultural and manufactured goods by building domestic industries. The 1630s were the turning point. Silver shipments to Spain through official channels dropped off abruptly, along with trade. Dutch and British piracy disrupted official convoys, while merchants from those nations became ever more aggressive at undercutting the official markets of Seville. By 1686, only 5.5 percent of Spanish American trade was with Spain (and an additional 17 percent with Genoa), compared to 39 percent with France and the remaining 37.5 percent with Britain, the Low Countries, and Hamburg.[2]

Britain cemented its position as the dominant investor in and market for Latin America when France's defeat in the Seven Years' War removed it as a significant military or economic presence in the Americas. Immediately after the war, Britain, in an effort to funnel Spanish American and French Caribbean commodities through Britain, passed the Free Port Act of 1765, which allowed Spanish and French colonial elites to dock their ships at British colonial ports without threat of seizure and without having to pay duties. Spanish efforts to force colonial administrators to compel their colonies to trade exclusively with Spain failed first because Spain lacked the bureaucracy and political leverage to enforce dictates in the Americas. Second, Spain's support for France in aiding the revolutionaries in the Thirteen Colonies led to British naval actions that fatally disrupted direct trade between the Americas and Spain and bankrupted some colonial elites, opening the way for final dominance by British merchants and financiers in Spanish America.[3]

---

1   Anthony Pagden, *Lords of All the World: Ideologies of Empire in Spain, Britain and France c.1500–c.1800* (New Haven: Yale University Press, 1995).

2   John Lynch, *Bourbon Spain 1700–1808* (Oxford: Blackwell, 1989), 20.

3   Wallerstein, *Modern World-System*, volume 3, 193, 212–20.

Spanish American commercial separation from the mother country was matched by Mexican and Peruvian political autonomy from Madrid. The share of Mexican state revenue shipped to Madrid or to the new colony in the Philippines fell from 55 percent in 1611–20 to 21 percent by 1691–1700.[1] In Peru, state revenues declined 47 percent from 1650 to 1700, and remittances to Spain fell 79 percent.[2] Spanish colonialism became a significantly lighter burden on Mexico and Peru in the course of the seventeenth century.

Seville's own merchants were rapidly displaced as managers and beneficiaries of the entrepôt's American trade by Genoese who outclassed their Spanish competitors in their access to capital and their commercial connections to markets throughout Europe. The Habsburgs welcomed the Genoese since they had a far greater capacity to buy state debt than did the hapless Spanish merchants of Seville.[3] The political and financial benefits of servicing crown debts then accrued to the Genoese, further retarding the Seville merchants' development as a national elite.

Seville merchants were blocked at every turn by the rigidity of Spanish elite and class relations. They were unable to mobilize the factors of production and the political power necessary to take advantage of the opportunities to spur manufacture opened by American treasure and American markets. The Seville merchants gained neither financial nor political leverage over the imperial government or any measure of control over American oligarchs and the colonial governments. The weakness of the Seville merchant elite, which could have acquired the wealth and power of the aristocracy and clergy through real hegemony over Spanish American markets, extinguished the Habsburgs' last opportunity to foster political realignment within Spain.

James Mahoney,[4] as we discussed in the previous chapter, identifies another factor beyond the structure of elite relations within Spain that stymied Habsburg efforts to better control its American colonists:

------------

1    TePaske and Klein, "The Seventeenth-Century Crisis in New Spain," 133.
2    Lynch, *Bourbon Spain 1700–1808*, 13.
3    Giovanni Muto, "The Spanish System: Centre and Periphery," in *Economic Systems and State Finance*, ed. Richard Bonney (Oxford: Clarendon, 1995), 231–59.
4    Mahoney, *Colonialism and Postcolonial Development*.

the already existing complex systems of rule in the pre-conquest indigenous societies that provided the personnel and social institutions that the conquistadors could appropriate for their own colonial governments. Mahoney accurately notes that, in the southern cone of Latin America, where indigenous societies were less dense and complex, colonial elites were unable to create regimes that could resist the efforts of eighteenth-century reformist Bourbon kings to impose tighter control in those colonies. Thus, in the southern cone, the Bourbons succeeded in empowering their appointed intendants to extract greater revenues, to invite in Spanish investors and merchants, and to actually run the colonial governments. In the older colonies, the intendants proved to be far less effective because the local elites had such control over the economies and over the colonial governments that they could not be bypassed or weakened with a divide-and-rule strategy. Spain's core colonies remained largely removed from the Spanish metropolitan economy through the eighteenth century because during their time under Habsburg rule, elites were established that could not be eliminated by Bourbon liberal reforms. Liberalism mattered ultimately mainly for the former peripheries, by creating an opening for a new commercial elite in Argentina. For the rest of the Spanish colonial world, liberalism arrived too late.

We now have an answer, for the Spanish Empire, to the question I posed at the start of this chapter: Why was Spain unable to meld the fruits of its military conquests into a coherent empire that could funnel resources to the metropole and thereby fuel economic growth and further military success? The structure of relations between crown and elites, established in the formation of the Habsburg's European empire, was reproduced in the Americas. This was not a matter of institutional isomorphism. As we saw above, the Habsburgs thought they were creating a different system in their New World colonies by rewarding new men, who were not extensions of the great provincial aristocracies of Spain, with *encomiendas*. Rather, chronic fiscal crisis and the Habsburgs' lack of governmental infrastructure made it impossible to police the conquistadors' exploitation of *encomiendas* or to block them from establishing direct trade links with rival European powers.

We are left with one more set of questions to answer: Why did the Spanish empire survive in such a weakened form? Why did highly autonomous colonial elites hold off in their efforts to attain independence until decades after their North American counterparts succeeded in breaking away from Britain?

### The Benefits of Being a Spanish Colonial Elite in a World Economy, and Why Finally Independence Was Achieved

Even as domestic aristocratic oligarchies undermined the Spanish crown's opportunities to turn its American colonies into an engine of economic growth for the metropole, the Spanish crown sought to exploit the limited openings that remained to profit from its empire. Spain's perpetual fiscal crisis ensured that the metropolitan government had little capacity to create a bureaucracy or military force that could directly rule and tax the American colonies. Instead, the Spanish crown adopted strategies similar to (if less effective than) those of French monarchs, discussed later. The crown sold venal offices in the Americas. Those offices provided one-time cash infusions for the crown when first sold but were unable to generate continuing revenues, except when holders had to pay fees to renew their rights to offices or to pass the positions on to their heirs, since the crown lacked the resources to create a bureaucracy to supervise American officeholders and to audit the taxes those officials were supposed to collect.

Venality reduced the number of American offices over which the crown retained the right of appointment, which had the effect of limiting opportunities to reward elites in Spain with American sinecures. It also further weakened Spain's capacity to administer its colonies.[1] As a result, the flow of influential and rich Spaniards—most often the younger sons of aristocrats or merchants—to the Americas declined, and white and mestizo elites in the Americas tightened their control over the governments and economies of the colonies and became ever more separate from Spanish elites.

Spanish American elites' unity, however, was disrupted by the crown's efforts, within the limited channels still possible in the

---

1   Josep M. Delgado Ribas, "Eclipse and Collapse of the Spanish Empire, 1650–1898," in *Endless Empire: Spain's Retreat, Europe's Eclipse, America's Decline*, eds. Alfred W. McCoy, Josep M. Fradera, and Stephen Jacobson (Madison: University of Wisconsin Press, 2012), 43–54.

seventeenth and eighteenth centuries, to profit from its colonies. The crown's fatal combination of a perpetual need for money, which led it to sell multiple offices and concessions in the Americas, and an inability to enforce decrees in its colonies spurred the formation of new elites who challenged the oligarchies of *encomienda* holders. Sales of offices and grants of lands and privileges to clerical orders and to military companies, all of which were motivated by the crown's desire to generate revenues in the Americas, had the effect of creating divisions among American elites. Venal offices had overlapping powers and revenue rights, which conflicted with the powers of offices granted to the original conquistadors. This created conflicts among "regular versus secular clergy, order against order, creole against native-born Spaniard, [and] a state-controlled church all too often impervious to state control."[1]

The multiplication of elite positions, identities, and interests inadvertently created reasons for colonial elites to retain their ties to the empire and held back struggles for independence. As the crown sold more and more venal offices, granted new privileges to both regular clergy and those from orders, and sought to encourage creoles to serve in military companies by creating *fueros*, corporations that accorded special legal and income rights to its military officers and to a lesser extent to enlisted men,[2] a welter of overlapping and competing privileges and rights created conflicts among formerly cohesive colonial elites. Venal offices were most attractive to American-born elites, who were mainly creoles and saw the prestige and privileges of those offices as a basis to challenge the autarkies formed by descendants of the original conquistadors.

The crown, however, was not able to benefit much from the growing discord among colonial elites because, by the end of the seventeenth century, the colonial elites, through their connections with Spanish landowners and merchants, had as much influence over the royal government as the crown had over colonial affairs. The colonies' high degree of autonomy from Spain, and their easy access to markets in Europe, ensured growing wealth for the Spanish American elites

---

1   Elliott, *Empires of the Atlantic World*, 201.
2   Ibid.

who controlled mines, lands, and trade networks within the Americas, making them valued allies for poorer elites within Spain.

Spanish American elites sought advantage in their conflicts with rival elites by appealing to the authority of the crown and by building connections with elites in Spain with whom they were connected and who had influence in the royal government.[1] This dynamic was similar to that between provincial venal officials and the crown in France,[2] as we will see later. As a result, Spanish American elites, especially more recent notables who achieved wealth and position through venal office or other crown appointments, rather than as land or mine owners or merchants, had an interest in remaining subjects of the Spanish crown and thus favored continued colonial status.

Spanish rule remained light during the eighteenth century, despite the appointment of intendants, and the laws and decrees formulated by the king and his agents in the Americas could be undercut or circumvented. Spanish Americans used the leverage they gained from their great wealth over elites within Spain to repeatedly block crown initiatives that might have increased taxes on *encomiendas* or on trade within the Americas and with Europe, or that would have limited the autonomy of American officials to make policies and to disregard the proclamations of *peninsulares* (men who had been born in Spain and came to the Americas with royal appointments and lacked an independent economic base in the colonies or ties to American-born elites). Thus, dynamics internal to settler society created a basis for Spanish American elites' long-term (nominal) loyalty to the crown.

Ironically, even though the provincial autarkies encouraged by the Habsburg's empire-building strategy undermined Spain's ability to compete militarily or economically with the other great powers after the sixteenth century, the dominant elites in each colony were still able to use their alliance with Spain's rulers, court officials, and metropolitan elites to strengthen their control over rival elites and non-elites within colonies. That is why most of the empire remained intact long

---

1   Jeremy C. A. Smith, "Europe's Atlantic Empires: Early Modern State Formation Reconsidered," *Political Power and Social Theory* 17 (2005): 101–50.

2   William Beik, *Absolutism and Society in Seventeenth-Century France: State Power and Provincial Aristocracy in Languedoc* (Cambridge: Cambridge University Press, 1985).

after Spain lost the capacity to vie for European or global dominance. Spain's army (or as much of it as the crown could afford, fiscally and geopolitically, to ship to the Americas) was still able to suppress uprisings in Peru in the 1780s and in Venezuela in 1812–13.

The American independence movements were sparked by Spain's late-eighteenth-century efforts to increase control over American elites.[1] However, the success of those movements was the result of a set of conjunctures. Napoleon's invasion of Spain, and his replacement of the Bourbon king with his brother Joseph in 1808, left Spain unable to reinforce troops in America and disrupted trade between the colonies and Spain. It also fatally undermined the Spanish crown's legitimacy and thereby heightened conflict among colonial elites who could no longer count on the crown to adjudicate among their relative powers.[2]

Britain filled the vacuum, at the expense of both Spain and France, becoming, and remaining for the rest of the nineteenth century, the dominant economic force in Latin America. The colonial elites' privileges and offices, which, as we saw above, had all been defined in relation to king, were thrown into doubt, removing the prime reason colonial elites had for remaining loyal to Spain. The Cádiz Cortes, which sought to create a new government to challenge the French occupation and included few American representatives, wrote a constitution in 1812 that would have had the effect of reducing Latin American autonomy. This spurred demands for independence that the shrunken and disorganized Spanish army in America (which in any case the new government in Spain lacked the funds to reinforce) was unable to prevent. By 1821, all of Spanish America, except for Cuba and Puerto Rico, was independent.[3]

The independence of its American colonies permanently demoted Spain from the ranks of great powers. However, that demotion was mainly one of perception. Spain had surrendered military

---

1   James Mahoney and Matthias vom Hau, "Colonial States and Economic Development in Spanish America," in *States and Development: Historical Antecedents of Stagnation and Advance*, eds. Matthew Lange and Dietrich Rueschemeyer (New York: Palgrave Macmillan, 2005), 92–116; Lynch, *Bourbon Spain*, 329–74.

2   Wallerstein, *Modern World-System*, volume 3, chapter 4.

3   Elliott, *Empires of the Atlantic World*, 369–402.

preeminence a century earlier. Spain's empire never made it a leading economic power, nor did it provide the resources that could have helped Spain in its military competition within Europe. Most fatefully, Spain's empire retarded rather than developed its economy. In the era of global capitalism that coincided with Spain's imperial formation, Spain was never a contender for control of global markets; it was a bystander and then a loser as trade became centered on and controlled by other European polities.

## FRANCE

### Louis XIV and the Limits of Vertical Absolutism

Elsewhere,[1] I described seventeenth-century France as a vertical absolutism. I used that term to describe the results of Louis XIV's strategy of creating or allying with venal and provincial elites in order to undermine the ability of great nobles and the church to extract revenues from peasants and towns and, in the case of nobles, to field armies that could challenge the crown. Vertical absolutism was successful in that it prevented the consolidation of aristocratic oligarchies like those that formed in Spanish provinces. Instead, multiple French elites jostled for the rights to collect taxes and rents from the peasantry. By the time of the Fronde, the simultaneous peasant and aristocratic rebellions of the 1640s that all ended in failure, and which came after a century and a half of crown manipulation of provincial elites and the relocation of aristocratic power within venal offices, each elite's authority came to rest upon royal grants of "privileges which were subject to differing interpretations and which were defined in reference to the king."[2]

The crown, as it weakened nobles and clerics who could mount challenges at the national level, empowered officials and lesser landlords to appropriate revenues and to exercise state-like powers at the local level. Thus, even though France was the richest state from the 1630s, when it surpassed Spain, until it was overtaken by Britain in the 1790s,[3] Louis XIV and his successors, like their Bourbon

---

1  Lachmann, *Capitalists in Spite of Themselves*.
2  Beik, *Absolutism and Society*, 219.
3  Table 2.1 on page 89.

counterparts in Spain, were limited by constant fiscal crises caused by the crown's growing obligation to pay or divert revenues to venal officials and by the mounting debt incurred in repeated wars. As we noted in chapter 2, nominal tax receipts do not take into account the ability of various elites to appropriate "state" revenues for themselves. The proliferation of venal offices served to encumber much of French state revenue before it reached the central treasury. Therefore, a growing share of royal revenues was not available to pay for wars, the development of a central bureaucracy, or other royal initiatives.

Venality and the crown's encouragement of overlapping elite powers and privileges affected both economic development within France and the ways in which the French overseas empire was formed and linked to the metropolitan economy. This is not the place to offer a detailed explanation for France's relatively late (compared with Britain) capitalist development.[1] Suffice it to say, in most of France, perpetual elite conflict and the overlapping jurisdictions engendered by vertical absolutism ensured that most farmland never became private property with a single owner in full control of the land and its output, as happened in seventeenth-century England. Crown stratagems that divided elites and ensured tax collectors' access to peasant production also perpetuated legal rights that became insurmountable barriers for those seeking to enclose their property. French farmers remained limited in their control over land throughout the entire ancien régime. No single elite enjoyed a monopoly of control over land that would have justified capital investments in improvements that could have produced significant increases in yields.

Ancien régime landlords were driven by the exigencies of their situation to create tenancy and sharecropping systems that compounded the other bitter fruits of vertical absolutism, leaving most of rural France economically backward and unable to function as a source of demand for urban merchants and manufacturers or for colonial plantations and industries. Lack of domestic demand, and competition from wealthier and more vibrant competitors in Britain and the Netherlands, kept France's commercial and financial elites

---

1   For my full analysis, see Lachmann, *Capitalists in Spite of Themselves*, chapter 6.

small and relatively capital poor. In any case, the best returns on wealth in France went to purchasers of government debt and venal offices, so the holders of capital in France had little incentive to invest in real industries. Only smaller, politically excluded merchants and land-owners invested in industry and agriculture because they were excluded from the more lucrative opportunities within the absolutist state.

## The Empire French Absolutism Made

Private entrepreneurs launched France's empire, like those of the other European powers. France was held back in the initial push to colonize the Americas, Asia, and Africa by its relatively small naval and commercial fleets. As a result, Spain and Portugal got what at first were the most lucrative American colonies with easily exploited gold and silver mines, and the Portuguese, Dutch, and British seized the best Asian trade routes and then the key colonies in Indonesia and India. France's *Compagnie des Indes orientales*, charged with coloniz-ing India, was not protected by France's limited navy and could not afford to purchase its own ships. When the Dutch refused to supply the French Asian settlements, the company failed.[1]

Why did France, despite its lead over its European rivals in the size of its state revenues, fail to build a larger and more cohesive or more lucrative empire? The answer to this question is found in the nature of the French absolutist state, described above, in the limited size and wealth of the French entrepreneurial elite and their rational orienta-tion toward the more lucrative opportunities in state finance and offices, and in the happenstance of the timing of the Wars of Religion in France.

French colonies were concentrated in the Caribbean and in North America. The northern colonies were perpetual economic losers, partly because the French state, in thrall to a mercantilist theory that regarded a growing domestic population as essential to France's

1   Pierre H. Boulle, "French Mercantilism, Commercial Companies and Colonial Profitability," in *Companies and Trade: Essays on Overseas Trading Companies during the Ancien Régime*, eds. Leonard Blussé and Femme Gaastra (Leiden, Netherlands: Leiden University Press, 1981), 97–117.

economic and military primacy, discouraged emigration.[1] The British government took the same view; however, settlement in French North America was further reduced by "Richelieu's decision to exclude foreigners (together with his refusal of Protestant settlement)."[2] That proved to be the crucial restriction and fundamentally handicapped French North American settlement in its competition with the British. Even if there had been more settlers, there was insufficient demand in France's underdeveloped domestic market for the crops that could be grown or foraged in North America,[3] and little was produced because so little French capital was enticed to invest in those colonies. The small population of France's northern American colonies, and the extreme poverty of the slaves who made up the bulk of the inhabitants in the Caribbean colonies, together ensured that the empire would create little demand for French manufactured goods. In contrast, the larger and more prosperous British North American colonies provided a crucial customer base for British domestic manufacture.[4]

The Caribbean was far more promising, since it was well suited for sugar plantations, for which there was a highly lucrative market in France and elsewhere in Europe. However, profits were smaller than they could have been, or were for Britain's Caribbean colonies, because the French colonies were perpetually undercapitalized since there were better investments for the politically connected at home. The French colonial ventures were poorly run since, again, skilled administrators could make better and more lucrative careers at home, and there was little royal financial support or military protection against

---

1   Jeremy C. A. Smith, "Europe's Atlantic Empires" and "A Deliberate Imperialism: France in the Americas in the Eighteenth Century," in *Revolution, Society and the Politics of Memory: The Proceedings of the Tenth George Rudé Seminar on French History and Civilization*, eds. Michael Adcock, Emily Chester, and Jeremy Whiteman (Carlton, Victoria: University of Melbourne, 1996).

2   Leslie Choquette, "Proprietorships in French North America," in *Constructing Early Modern Empires: Proprietary Ventures in the Atlantic World, 1500–1750*, eds. L. H. Roper and Bertrand Van Ruymbeke (Leiden, Netherlands: Brill, 2007), 130.

3   Smith, "A Deliberate Imperialism."

4   Eric Hobsbawm, "The Crisis of the Seventeenth Century," in *Crisis in Europe, 1560–1660* (London: Routledge and Kegan Paul, [1954] 1965); Wallerstein, *Modern World-System*, volume 2, 103–4.

attacks from the Spanish.[1] In other words, the superprofits from offices and loans available within the absolutist state in France starved the colonies of investment and skilled personnel.

The profits that were generated from the relatively undercapital-ized and poorly managed French Caribbean plantations did little to stimulate the metropolitan French economy and contributed almost nothing to royal finances. This lack of synergy between the colonial and metropolitan was the result of two factors: first, the temporal misfortune that the Wars of Religion occurred at the same time as the development of the Caribbean sugar economy, and second, the funda-mental nature of the French royal government, which regarded colo-nies as they approached decisions at home: as a search for opportuni-ties to reward allies and to generate immediate revenues.

French Caribbean colonization became established at the same time as the Wars of Religion. The main French Atlantic ports were under the control of Protestant forces, and French kings and/or the Catholic League kept those towns under siege, which prevented the Protestant merchants there, or Catholic merchants elsewhere, from controlling trade with the Caribbean. This provided an opening for the Dutch, who became both the principal purchasers of sugar from the French colonies and the main suppliers of slaves to those islands.

A century later, Jean-Baptiste Colbert was able to temporarily divert the sugar trade to French ports when he established the *Compagnie des Indes occidentales*, gave it a monopoly on sugar in the French Caribbean, and demanded that all sugar produced on the *Compagnie's* plantations be shipped to French ports. Colbert backed that demand with French naval power, which was used both to intim-idate colonial planters and to offer protection against British piracy. However, the costs of deploying naval ships in the Caribbean over-whelmed the income from sugar, and the *Compagnie* never made a profit and closed in less than a decade.[2] France's Caribbean colonies were crippled economically again when Britain's blockade during the

1   Philip Boucher, "French Proprietary Colonies in the Greater Caribbean," in *Constructing Early Modern Empires*.
2   Robin Blackburn, *The Making of New World Slavery: From the Baroque to the Modern, 1492–1800* (London: Verso, 1997), 279–86.

Seven Years' War disrupted the growing commerce between France's Atlantic ports and its African and American holdings.[1]

The *Compagnie des Indes occidentales*' trade monopoly came too late to dent Dutch control over the sugar trade within Europe. The Dutch had already established a sales network that the merchants in France were unable to duplicate, and so they had to resell the sugar, and thus surrender much of the ultimate profits, to their Dutch rivals. The Dutch, Portuguese, and British profited further from the French sugar colonies because they controlled the trade routes and coastal forts in Africa, which meant that they ran the slave trade that supplied the only source of labor for sugar plantations.[2] The king, Colbert, and key members of provincial *parlements* financed the *Compagnie du Cap-Vert et du Sénégal*, the firm that received the French monopoly on trade with Africa. However, they never invested enough to build a network of forts to compete with the Dutch; indeed, they sought to rely on Dutch and Portuguese forts for access to slaves and on the Dutch for ships to transport the slaves to America.[3]

The French crown had to take such a heavy-handed, and ultimately too costly, approach to creating and enforcing a monopoly on the Atlantic sugar trade because it had already lost control of the Caribbean colonies themselves. Nicolas Fouquet, the self-enriching *surintendant des finances* who was ultimately imprisoned by Louis XIV for corruption (and for amassing a fortune that rivaled the king's), granted Caribbean colonial charters to his allies, who were given land grants and governorships of colonies at the same time. These privileged colonists used their official positions to ensure that tax rates were kept low, allowing them to retain almost all the profits from their plantations. The *Compagnie des Indes occidentales*' monopoly did not disturb land rights or control over offices within the colonies. Throughout the late seventeenth and eighteenth centuries, planters were able to keep the rate of the *octroi* (the export tax) extremely low, ensuring that the crown continued to realize almost no revenues from

---

1  Wallerstein, *Modern World-System*, volume 3, 72–3.

2  Sidney Mintz, *Sweetness and Power: The Place of Sugar in Modern History* (New York: Viking, 1985).

3  Kenneth J. Banks, "Financiers, Factors, and French Proprietary Companies in West Africa, 1664–1713," in *Constructing Early Modern Empires*, 79–116.

the colonies. Offices remained in the hands of the colonists.[1] Plantation owners had leverage over colonial policy because they were from the same families as the great financiers and venal officials in France.[2] In that sense, French, like Spanish, colonists had more power within the metropole than metropolitan officials and capitalists had over the colonies.

Because the sugar colonies yielded almost no revenues for the crown and did little for the overall French economy, it was easy and sensible for the crown to subordinate its colonial policies to larger geopolitical concerns. Thus, Louis XIV deepened planters' autonomy in an effort to enlist their support for his quixotic effort to capture Spain's American colonies during the War of the Spanish Succession.[3] The failure of that scheme, and the crown's lack of leverage within the colonies, reinforced Louis XIV's focus on expanding France's boundaries within Europe. France's main strategy beyond Europe was to undermine Britain's control over its colonies rather than to capture new lands for France. Thus, France supported Indian princes in their efforts to repel the British East India Company, efforts that were decisively defeated at the Battle of Plassey in 1757. Thereafter, Britain was the sole European power able to exercise de facto and then de jure control over an increasingly unified Indian polity,[4] even as France and Portugal periodically lost and regained minor concessions on the subcontinent. France's sole success was in aiding the American Revolution,[5] which, as we will see in chapter 5, struck a major blow against Britain's "first empire." However, France's strategic success "turned out to be chimerical" because France lacked the international trade networks and industrial base that made Britain the most attractive and indeed the only realistic commercial partner for the now independent United States.[6] French military forces were largely

---

1   Blackburn, *Making of New World Slavery*, 292–8.
2   Smith, "Europe's Atlantic Empires;" D. K. Fieldhouse, *The Colonial Empires: A Comparative Survey from the Eighteenth Century* (New York: Delacorte, 1965).
3   Blackburn, *Making of New World Slavery*, 292–8.
4   Immanuel Wallerstein, "Does India Exist?" in *The Essential Wallerstein* (New York: New Press, [1991] 2000), 310–14.
5   Wallerstein, *Modern World-System*, volume 3, 217–18.
6   Ibid., volume 3, 83, and chapter 2, passim.

withdrawn from its colonies, and the opportunities for further colonial expansion outside Europe were blocked until the nineteenth century.

By the time France got its colonies in Africa and Southeast Asia in the nineteenth century, it was too late to matter for the already settled geopolitical and economic competition with Britain, and the colonies were useless for fending off the rising economic challenges from the United States and Germany. France's nineteenth- and twentieth-century empires did not make significant financial or manpower contributions to France's wars with Germany, although they did enrich certain French capitalists who, along with strata of colonial officials and settlers, were adamant about retaining the empire even in the face of armed independence movements after 1945.

Napoleon was the exceptional French ruler who was able to extract significant revenues and recruit soldiers from his conquered lands. We need to explain how he alone managed to accomplish that, and why he too built a European empire at the expense of his American holdings.

*Napoleon's Exceptional Empire*
Napoleon's strategy of imperial expansion was based on his accurate perception of: (1) France's weak position militarily and economically beyond Europe, (2) Britain's dependence on continental European markets, which could be undermined by the imposition of a continental blockade, and (3) France's ability to self-finance its wars by looting the territories it conquered (a policy that anticipated the Nazi's ad hoc war finances and that mirrored Britain's relationship with its empire).

France after 1789 had three advantages over Britain. First, it was able to field an unprecedentedly large army because it instituted mass conscription. This allowed France to outlast enemies and to tolerate high casualties, since it could replenish its armies repeatedly, while other European nations relied on much harder to replace aristocrats and their retainers, or much more expensive mercenaries. Second, the Revolution and the flight and exile of many nobles eliminated the hereditary officer corps, allowing for the rapid promotion of soldiers and lower-level officers by merit.[1] Napoleon was the outstanding example of that, and his military genius gave France its third advantage.

The Revolution transformed French elite structure. The aristocracy and venal officials were swept away. While much of the capitalist landowner class and urban bourgeoisie survived the Revolution and indeed prospered in the Napoleonic era, a new unified elite dominated the state and military. This allowed Napoleon to ensure that his military realized most of the fruits of conquest. By 1809, when the largest landowners in France, many of whom were former nobles, had incomes of 11–50,000, and the very richest 100–150,000 francs per year, Napoleon's generals received salaries of 100–200,000 francs per year and the top marshals realized 1 million per year.[2] Conquered lands were looted and taxed. Under the pre-Napoleonic revolutionary governments, tax revenues from occupied European territories accounted for at least a quarter of total revenues between 1792 and 1799,[3] an amount that did not include food and other provisions looted from the occupied territories.

Taxes in conquered lands became even more important under Napoleon. The revolutionary government's default on debt in 1797 closed the possibility of taking out loans until after Napoleon's final defeat, although Napoleon was able to revive tax farms. Napoleon also limited paper money, cutting off another indirect way to finance deficits. Instead, Napoleon relied on indemnities and extraordinary taxes he imposed on conquered lands. These revenues "covered one-third of France's budgeted expenditure, in addition to the maintenance of the army abroad."[4] In addition, France used foreigners from conquered

---

1   Lachmann, "Mercenary, Citizen, Victim;" Alan Forrest, "*La patrie en danger*: The French Revolution and the First *Levée en masse*," in *The People in Arms: Military Myth and National Mobilization since the French Revolution*, eds. Daniel Moran and Arthur Waldron (Cambridge: Cambridge University Press, 2003).

2   Louis Bergeron, *France under Napoleon* (Princeton: Princeton University Press, [1972] 1981) 122–38.

3   Richard Bonney, "The Eighteenth Century II: The Struggle for Great Power Status and the End of the Old Fiscal Regime," in *Economic Systems and State Finance*, ed. Richard Bonney (Oxford: Clarendon Press, 1995), 352.

4   Ibid., 357; see also Kennedy, *Rise and Fall of the Great Powers*, 132–5.

lands in its armies,[1] further extending its manpower advantage over its enemies. However, the heavy tax burden combined with damage and disruption from war undermined the economies of the occupied lands. This weakened the efficacy of the continental blockade by reducing the ability of other countries to serve as trading partners with France. The war and French occupation also decisively weakened the Netherlands, which made Britain the undisputed economic hegemon. Britain's economic expansion as a manufacturer and emergence as the trading and financial hegemon so strengthened British tax receipts that it was able to finance the huge costs of the war, including the subsidies to its allies that ultimately created the coalition able to defeat Napoleon.[2]

Napoleon's policy of bleeding conquered lands to support his military and to enrich his key subordinates in the army and occupation administrations meant that local elites in those countries (who were excluded from sharing in, and indeed whose wealth was a main source of, indemnities and extraordinary taxes) had no interest in supporting the new governments Napoleon imposed in the conquered lands. This was a contrast with the Dutch and British approach, discussed in the following two chapters, of creating ways for selected elites to benefit from the colonial regime. Napoleon's fiscal strategy ensured that his officers and administrators would remain loyal to the metropolitan government and to Napoleon personally. Although Napoleon's empire lasted for too brief a period to predict what would have happened over the long term in the face of never realized contingencies, French occupying forces and administrators did not develop ties to local elites. This had the advantage of preventing conflicts between, indeed preventing even the development of separate, metropolitan and (European) colonial elites. The disadvantage was that none of the local elites in the occupied countries developed an interest in collaborating with French administrators. Napoleon's invasions sparked rebellions in many of the occupied countries, rebellions that the British supported financially and that sapped the strength of Napoleon's armies beyond the damage inflicted in Russia and before the coup de grâce

---

1   Kennedy, *Rise and Fall of the Great Powers*, 132–5.
2   Bonney, "The Eighteenth Century," 377–86.

administered by Britain at Waterloo. The Spanish resistance was key in undermining Napoleon by diverting and killing so many of his soldiers, emboldening Britain to finally intervene directly with its own land forces, and fatally weakening the continental blockade.[1]

The French revolutionary governments and then Napoleon understood that their advantages were best deployed in continental Europe. Efforts to take colonies were doomed to failure by France's weak navy and by the logistical difficulties of provisioning armies on other continents. These limitations first became apparent and consequential in Napoleon's defeat in Egypt in 1801.[2] France confined its efforts at weakening the British Empire to aiding rebellions, thus following the pattern set with ancien régime France's aid to the American War of Independence. However, the French Republic and Napoleon were never able to duplicate the earlier American success and instead followed the pattern of failure set in its intervention in India. France's effort to aid the 1798 Irish rebellion ended with its defeat at Bantry Bay in 1797.[3]

France's low capacity to project power and to administer beyond Europe also doomed efforts to defeat the Haitian Revolution. The sugar planters of Saint-Domingue (the future Haiti) were harmed by the French royal government's trade deals with Britain (the Eden Treaty of 1786) and with the new US government (the Franco-American Convention of 1787). The French government, in essence, traded away the interests of the sugar plantation owners for those of domestic silk and wine producers. While both agreements did not survive the outbreak of the revolution, they spurred the plantation owners to seek representation in the 1787 Estates General and then in the successor National Assembly. However, metropolitan investors in Saint-Domingue had been disempowered if not decapitated in the

------

1    David Bell, *The First Total War: Napoleon's Europe and the Birth of Warfare as We Know It* (Boston: Houghton Mifflin, 2007); Thomas M. Huber, "Napoleon in Spain and Naples: Fortified Compound Warfare," in *Compound Warfare: That Fatal Knot*, ed. Thomas M. Huber (Fort Leavenworth, KS: US Army Command and General Staff College Press, 2002), 91–112; Kennedy, *Rise and Fall of the Great Powers*, 129, 134.

2    Kennedy, *Rise and Fall of the Great Powers*, 125–6.

3    Wallerstein, *Modern World-System*, volume 3, 82–3, 244–6.

Revolution, and so the planters had no leverage in the decisions of the revolutionary government. This led the white settlers to push for greater autonomy and for the mulattoes to appeal to the National Assembly for equal rights. The split between whites and mulattoes, and the diminution of French authority, created an opening for the first and "the most successful slave rebellion in the history of the capitalist world-economy."[1] France's inability to project power across the Atlantic, combined with an ill-fated British intervention that led to a British-French competition for slave support in Saint-Domingue, ensured the failure of efforts to restore white dominance.[2]

In light of France's ultimate inability to penetrate and control the settler society in its richest colony, Saint-Domingue, Napoleon's decision to sell Louisiana (which became all of seven and parts of eight more states) to the United States in 1803 for $15 million that could be used for European wars was rational. Napoleon's imperial plans reflected France's highly limited commercial and geopolitical position in the Americas, Asia, and Africa. Of course, in the end, and for contingent as well as structural reasons, Napoleon's strategy of European domination proved impossible to sustain, as would Hitler's similar plan in the next century. However, well before Napoleon gambled and lost in Europe, different global strategies of building hegemony had been foreclosed by the nature of the French state and by France's early concessions to the aristocratic and financial elites that financed the first colonies in the Caribbean and Africa.

Napoleonic France was fundamentally different from Spain and from ancien régime France in that the Revolution had swept away many of the old elites, which allowed a new state elite to consolidate itself and become a unitary elite that could shape and profit from conquest without having to share resources and decisions with autonomous colonial elites. As we noted in chapter 1, this is what made the Napoleonic and Nazi empires different from all other empires, ancient and modern, formal and informal.

---

1   Ibid., 241.
2   Ibid., 240–6.

## Failed Hegemonies: Strong Colonies in Weak Empires

We now are in a position to answer the question posed at the start of this chapter: Why were Spain and France unable to meld the fruits of their military conquests into a coherent empire that could funnel resources to the metropole and thereby fuel economic growth and further military success? Those two polities, which each were for a time (twice, in the case of France) the dominant military power in Europe, either failed to harness that power to build a significant empire outside of Europe (France) or created an empire that quickly declined as a contributor of taxes or trade with the metropole (Spain).

Spanish and French colonization reflected the state's relationship to metropolitan elites. In both cases, state formation had been accomplished by ceding authority to elites in return for pacifying provinces (often by ending armed challenges that had been mounted by aristocracies) or for supplying funds that the royal government was unable to extract itself. In some ways, the process was very different in Spain and France. The Habsburgs recognized dominant elites in each province, while the French kings constructed a vertical absolutism that left multiple elites vying for power and resources in conflicts that the crown simultaneously adjudicated and spurred in return for a share of the resources those elites extracted. However, the Spanish and French states both surrendered, or, to be more accurate, never achieved, the capacity to mobilize money and armed men and to promulgate and administer laws and regulations independent of the various elites that each held pieces of those "state" powers.

The limits that Spanish and French rulers faced at home were reproduced in their colonial projects. Thus, Spain almost immediately gave near monopolies on land and power in each colony to the entrepreneurs who supplied the men and money for conquest. The French created multiple and overlapping charters and privileges in each of their colonies. Neither monarchy was able to force settler elites to obey high officials sent from the capital. This failure was partly due to the weak capacities each ruler developed in the process of domestic state formation, and partly was the legacy of the concessions made to convince entrepreneurs to invest in, and settlers to voyage to, distant colonies.

The patterns of elite conflict and state formation in Spain and France also precluded the development of single or even of competing elites capable of dominating trade with the colonies and thereby using the profits from colonial production to fan demand for and to support investment in domestic industries. Instead, colonial trade was funneled through capitalists in rival polities, preventing any Spanish or French city from becoming a trading entrepôt or global financial center as Amsterdam and London did. Instead, Spain became ever more dependent on foreigners to finance state debt, while French finance became almost entirely the pursuit of the superprofits from state debt and state offices available only to the politically connected.

Finally, domestic and colonial elite structures in both Spain and France interacted in each empire to allow colonial elites to influence metropolitan politics even as those same colonial elites enjoyed high degrees of autonomy from the metropole. Spanish and French colonial elites had far more sway over metropolitan politics and state policy than did their counterparts in the Netherlands and Britain (and much more than the colonial elites in the Napoleonic empire) for three reasons: First, as we saw above, the imperial center had little infrastructural capacity to rule its colonies; however, this was true of many empires and fundamentally mattered for Spain and France only in conjunction with the other elements of metropolitan and colonial elite relations. Second, elite autarky in Spain and unresolved elite conflict in France made it impossible for the crown or any other elite to resolve disputes over imperial policy, and indeed metropolitan elites appealed to colonial elites for aid in metropolitan elite conflicts. The flow of influence was at least as much from colonies to metropole, and the appeals for allies went both ways. Finally, divisions or autarky in the metropole gave colonial elites the autonomy to develop trade relations with rival European powers. In the end, the Spanish Empire existed mainly in name rather than practice and enriched Spain's rivals. France's empire became a shrinking sideshow in the unresolved elite conflicts at home, and once the Revolution recast French elite structure, the winning military elite largely abandoned its overseas empire and turned its resources to European conquest.

Spain and France thus clearly fit in the category of empires that were stunted by the double handicaps of high colonial autonomy from metropolitan officials and high influence of colonial elites over the metropole's economy and politics. Of course, Spanish and French weakness did not exist in a vacuum. Their inabilities to control and profit from their empires created openings for the Netherlands and Britain. How those two polities developed the capacities to exploit global opportunities, and how their hegemonies ultimately were undone, are the topics of the following two chapters.

# 4

# The Netherlands: Elites vs. Hegemony

The Dutch were the first hegemonic power, in the senses that I (and Wallerstein and Arrighi) define hegemony in chapter 1.[1] As such, the Netherlands, like Britain and the United States later, "fears no economic competition from other core states. It, therefore, tends to favor maximal openness of the world-economy. This policy is one which some historians have called informal empire (that is, noncolonial and eventually even anti-colonial imperialism)."[2] Of course, the Netherlands also had a formal empire, and it was the first European polity that figured out how to generate consistent and long-term profit from its global empire. Our goal in this chapter is to analyze the process by which the Dutch achieved hegemony and the methods they used to accumulate an empire and rule it in a way that differed from the un-, or merely episodically, profitable ways of the Spanish and French. We also need to figure out how that empire related to the Netherlands' hegemonic position in the global economy of the seventeenth century. We then must explain why this global empire and Dutch hegemony were unable to sustain themselves, even though the Dutch state had greater financial resources than its rivals and dominated the existent global trading and financial networks. Finally, we need to identify the factors that prevented the Dutch from adopting the reforms that some Dutch politicians

---

1    Michael Mann, who defines hegemony by the "two-power standard" (*Sources of Social Power*, volume 2, 264), i.e., possessing more than the next two powers, argues that only the United States has been hegemonic (although Britain was hegemonic in naval power, and briefly in manufacturing). For Mann, the Netherlands never was hegemonic in any respect. Arrighi argues that Genoa was hegemonic before the Netherlands.

2    Wallerstein, *Modern World-System*, volume 3, 200.

(accurately) identified as solutions to the challenges posed by Britain.

## BUILDING HEGEMONY

How did the Dutch become hegemonic, and what did that have to do with its formal and informal empire? For Wallerstein, the necessary first step was to become the leading agricultural and manufacturing entity in the world, producing "so efficiently that they are by and large competitive even in other core states ... Marked superiority in agro-industrial productive efficiency leads to dominance of the spheres of commercial distribution of world trade, with correlative profits accruing both from being the entrepôt of much of world trade and from controlling the 'invisibles'—transport, communications, and insurance. Commercial primacy leads in turn to control of the financial sectors of banking (exchange, deposit, and credit) and of investment (direct and portfolio)."[1] "It was the point at which the rising power had all three advantages [in production, commerce, and finance] that  corresponded to the moment of true hegemony."[2] Wallerstein thinks that the Netherlands maintained simultaneous dominance in those three spheres only between 1625 and 1675.

Dutch agricultural and then manufacturing supremacy was built on two legs, in Wallerstein's analysis: dominance of Baltic fisheries and agricultural innovation. The Dutch invented a superior fishing boat, which allowed them to catch and sell fish, above all the "rich trade" in herring, more cheaply than anyone else. Their huge fish industry spurred the development of a large salt industry and also led to further improvements in shipbuilding, which later gave the Dutch a crucial advantage in building a transoceanic merchant fleet. Shipbuilding became ever more efficient as it grew in scale (partly with the use of

---

1   Wallerstein, *Modern World-System*, volume 2, 38.
2   Ibid., xxv; Jan de Vries and Ad van der Woude, *The First Modern Economy: Success, Failure, and Perseverance of the Dutch Economy, 1500–1815* (Cambridge: Cambridge University Press, 1997), 412 and passim, see 1672 as the end of Dutch hegemony. Modelski (*Long Cycles in World Politics*, 42) gives 1608–42 as the period of Dutch "oceanic supremacy."

power from windmills first built for drainage projects) and spurred the development of "ancillary industries in Amsterdam—rope yards, biscuit bakeries, ship chandlering, and the construction of nautical instruments and sea charts."[1] Profits from herring and later from other sources allowed the Dutch to pay for wood imports from Germany needed to build more and better ships than its rivals.[2]

The need to drain marshlands "led to the invention of windmills and the flourishing of the science of engineering."[3] Poor soil quality forced the Dutch to shift from grain production, which they made up by importing grain from abroad, to growing industrial crops, to horticulture, most famously of flowers, and to livestock husbandry.[4] "Between 1600 and 1750, [the Dutch and the English] each experienced an agricultural revolution in which output per worker reached and exceeded Belgian levels."[5] The Dutch grew the crops needed for dyes and so were able to assert control of that most lucrative stage of textile manufacture against Britain in the seventeenth century. An index of Dutch agricultural production rose from 100 in 1510 to 243 in 1650, and more slowly to 305 in 1810.[6]

The Dutch created and benefited from a virtuous cycle. Dutch shipbuilding efficiency made it possible to undercut rivals engaged in long-haul shipping in the North Sea, the Mediterranean, the Americas, and Asia. This added business spurred more shipbuilding and encouraged further technical innovation and economics of scale, widening the Dutch advantage. As a result,

> Dutch shipping dominated the world carrying trade in the seventeenth century. It grew tenfold from 1500 to 1700. As of 1670, the

1  Wallerstein, *Modern World-System*, volume 2, 43; see also Bas van Bavel, *Manors and Markets: Economy and Society in the Low Countries, 500–1600* (Oxford: Oxford University Press, 2010), chapter 7.

2  Jonathan Leitner, "An Incorporated Comparison: Fernand Braudel's Account of Dutch Hegemony in a World-Ecological Perspective," *Review* 30 (2007).

3  Wallerstein, *Modern World-System*, volume 2, 40.

4  Leitner, "An Incorporated Comparison"; de Vries and van der Woude, *The First Modern Economy*, chapter 6.

5  Robert C. Allen, *The British Industrial Revolution in Global Perspective* (Cambridge: Cambridge University Press, 2009), 61.

6  De Vries and van der Woude, *The First Modern Economy*, 233.

Dutch owned three times the tonnage of the English, and more than
the tonnage of England, France, Portugal, Spain, and the Germanics
combined. The percentage of *Dutch-built* ships was even greater.
Dutch shipping reached its heyday, in fact, only in the second half of
the seventeenth century, the Dutch having used the occasion of the
English Civil War to establish "undisputed ascendancy in the world's
carrying trade."[1]

The commercial networks that the Dutch created for fish, grain,
industrial crops, and textiles provided the basis for Dutch dominance
of shipping in general and then allowed Amsterdam to become the
controlling entrepôt of the most profitable commodities in the global
market. The Dutch centralized in Amsterdam warehouses the major
supplies of key commodities, allowing merchants to release limited
amounts of each commodity upon markets in ways controlled to
maximize profits.[2] The Dutch were able to do this because they were
the beneficiaries of key geopolitical shifts. Giovanni Arrighi aptly
summarizes the bases of Dutch commercial hegemony in seventeenth-century Europe. Taking advantage of an opening in the
world-system left by the decline of the Spanish empire and with it of
Genoese financial hegemony, the Dutch developed a strategy and built
the organizations that were suited to their location "in the place and at
the time that were both just right to catch 'the wind actually blowing.' "[3]

"When Antwerp fell to the Spanish in 1585, the European spice
market was transferred to Amsterdam."[4] Skilled craftsmen and
merchants with capital also migrated to the Netherlands to escape
instability and persecution. This sped urbanization and increased the
stock of capital in the Netherlands. Spain's virtual abandonment of the
reconquest of the northern (Dutch) Netherlands in favor of war with
France in 1590 allowed the Dutch to decisively capture the Baltic trade
from the English and the Hanseatic League, thereby expanding their
share of the "bulk" Baltic trade in grain, timber, salt, and herring, and

--------

1   Wallerstein, *Modern World-System*, volume 2, 46; see also Angus Maddison,
*The World Economy* (Paris: OECD, 2006), volume 1, 79.
2   De Vries and van der Woude, *The First Modern Economy*, 667–72.
3   Arrighi, *Long Twentieth Century*, 133.
4   Wallerstein, *Modern World-System*, volume 2, 46–7.

to gain access to the "rich" trade in bringing "spices, sugar, dyestuffs, Mediterranean fruit and wine, and Spanish American silver . . . to the North."[1] Spain's withdrawal also allowed the Dutch to blockade the southern ports of the Netherlands, thereby ending Antwerp's role as a major port and center of manufacture to Amsterdam's benefit,[2] and further accelerating the flow of skilled craftsmen and rich merchants to Amsterdam. The Dutch-Spanish truce of 1609 gave Dutch merchants access and then control over trade in the Mediterranean, valuable because it gave Dutch merchants a new customer base, and also key to blocking rival merchants. The Dutch increased the dominance and profitability of the Amsterdam spice market because they gained control over trade and production of the valuable spices grown in Asia through the creation of the Dutch East India Company (*Vereenigde Ooost-Indische Compagnie*; hereafter VOC), a chartered company given a monopoly if it could enforce it against rival non-Dutch firms. VOC did so by limiting production of spices in Asia, buying the surplus, and fixing prices.[3]

The exchange at which the carefully controlled supply of spices, futures in spices and other commodities, and contracts and insurance for shipping were traded was institutionalized as the Amsterdam Bourse. The Bourse, "the first stock exchange in permanent session," made Amsterdam "the central money and capital market of the European world-economy."[4] The Amsterdam Bourse also became the site for trading in VOC stock, the most valuable firm by far in the Netherlands, in shares of other chartered companies, and in government bonds. Because the Netherlands was the only European polity that did not default on state bonds, the Amsterdam Bourse and Dutch state bonds attracted capital from throughout Europe.

........................................................

1   Israel, *Dutch Republic*, 312.
2   Julia Adams, "Trading States, Trading Places: The Role of Patrimonialism in Early Modern Dutch Development," *Comparative Studies in Society and History* 36 (1994): 327–32.
3   J. L. van Zanden, *The Rise and Decline of Holland's Economy: Merchant Capitalism and the Labour Market* (Manchester: Manchester University Press, 1993), 67–87; Chris Nierstrasz, *In the Shadow of the Company: The Dutch East India Company and Its Servants in the Period of Its Decline (1740–1796)* (Leiden: Brill, 2012).
4   Arrighi, *Long Twentieth Century*, 142.

Bourse financiers made money by acting as brokers for investors from throughout Europe, by trading on their own accounts,[1] and by loaning capital drawn from the Netherlands and beyond to borrowers throughout Europe. Dutch bankers determined interest rates for much of Europe, and their evaluation of borrowers' creditworthiness determined the ability of firms and governments to attract investment throughout Europe. Thus, Amsterdam became the first financial hegemon of the capitalist world economy.

Wallerstein and Arrighi offer clear descriptions of the building blocks of Dutch hegemony and show how each aspect of Dutch advantage created or reinforced the other elements of Dutch power. They have less to say about why the Dutch, rather than any of its rivals, achieved those advantages. We hear that the Dutch had a unique agricultural system and was unusual in its capacity to reclaim lands, but Wallerstein says little about the origins of the Dutch land tenure and governance systems. We know that the Dutch state's creditworthiness was vital to its financial hegemony, but not how the Netherlands achieved fiscal stability and, unique among its rivals, avoided default on its debt. Arrighi shows how the Dutch benefited from geopolitical openings but does not explain why it was they and not the British or French who did so. As we will see later in this chapter, Wallerstein and Arrighi's inability to explain why the Dutch were able to exploit the opportunities that were available in the seventeenth century limits their abilities to find the reasons for Dutch decline in the eighteenth century.

ELITE CONSOLIDATION AND THE ORIGINS OF DUTCH ADVANTAGE

The northern Netherlands came under the sovereignty of an independent count after the collapse of the Carolingian empire. The count and lesser aristocrats exercised only weak control over the peasants who

---

1   Pit Dehing and Marjolein 't Hart, "Linking the Fortune: Currency and Banking, 1550–1800," in *A Financial History of the Netherlands*, eds. Marjolein 't Hart, Joost Jonker, and Jan Luiten van Zanden (Cambridge: Cambridge University Press, 1997), 37–63.

tilled their lands. Peasant freedom was the result of the ways in which the northern Netherlands were settled and ruled. Dutch farmland in large part was reclaimed from the sea, as Wallerstein points out. However, what mattered as much as that environmental reality was the class identity of the people who organized and controlled those projects.

Reclamation work was initiated and financed almost exclusively by peasants, who elected their peers to drainage boards (*waterschappen*) to plan the dikes and canals needed to reclaim lands and control flooding. To raise revenues, the counts of Holland sold land to intermediaries, who often resold it to peasants, keeping only tithe rights. Thus, in most of the northern Netherlands, nobles and other landlords exercised no juridical control over peasants or land, receiving only rents and tithes, leaving peasants free to manage their collective affairs with little interference from above.

The absence of feudalism in the northern Netherlands shaped elite as well as class relations. Elites, lacking power over land and peasants, withered in political and economic importance. The clergy was an unusually weak elite in all Dutch provinces: They exercised little legal authority, collected few tithes, did not enjoy benefices, and had to depend upon fees from religious services for their income.[1] Both contributing to and as a consequence of those weaknesses, there were relatively few clerics in residence in the northern Netherlands. Each province of the Dutch Republic sold lands once owned by the Catholic Church and by exiled Catholic nobles in the decades following the Spanish withdrawal from the northern Netherlands after 1590.[2] Those property transfers further consolidated agricultural lands in the hands of urban merchants and rich peasants in Holland and Zeeland, the two wealthiest Dutch provinces.

The nobility was the dominant elite in the less populous and poorer Dutch provinces. "In Friesland and Groningen, the rulers were gentleman farmers. Gelderland was dominated by rural nobles, whereas

---

1   Jan de Vries, *The Dutch Rural Economy in the Golden Age, 1500–1700* (New Haven: Yale University Press, 1974), 41–3.

2   Ibid., 337–41.

hedge squires governed in Overijssel and neighboring Drenthe."[1] Those noble elites were the main beneficiaries of the sale of Catholic lands after 1590 in their provinces. The unitary elites of those provinces exercised only limited, non-feudal control over peasants, deriving income from renting the land they owned and from political offices.

In Holland, by far the richest province of the northern Netherlands, the nobility was a weak elite. Noble families were easily bankrupted by war or other extraordinary expenses since they received relatively little income from their lands. "In Holland, around 200 families comprising the province's nobility, in 1500, possessed approximately 5 per cent of the total cultivable land . . . The church too lagged behind, owning under 10 per cent."[2] Noble and clerical weakness, and the ongoing shift of land and agricultural income to urban merchants and peasants, meant that farmers themselves, as landowners or long-term tenants, had the freedom and interest to improve land and to switch to whichever crops were most lucrative in the domestic urban and international markets to which Dutch farmers increasingly were linked. As urban merchants came to own more and more of the lands once held by nobles, clerics, and peasants, those merchants realized a growing and eventually majority share of the ever-rising agricultural profits that came from the shift to high-margin crops.[3]

The weakness of the nobility and clergy also shaped the sort of state that developed during the northern Netherlands' long struggle for autonomy and then independence from the Habsburgs. The absence of feudal agrarian relations in Holland and the other northern Netherlands provinces, and the resulting paucity of elites (few nobles, a weak clergy, hardly any "state" officials in Holland and Zeeland, and almost nothing but nobles in the other provinces), short-circuited the opportunities for factional conflict. As a result, Dutch urban merchants were able to achieve hegemony within their

---

1  Marjolein 't Hart, *The Making of a Bourgeois State: War, Politics, and Finance during the Dutch Revolt* (Manchester: Manchester University Press, 1993), 25.

2  Israel, *Dutch Republic*, 108.

3  De Vries and van der Woude, *The First Modern Economy*, 202; Pepijn Brandon, "Marxism and the 'Dutch Miracle': The Dutch Republic and the Transition-Debate," *Historical Materialism* 19, no. 3 (2011): 123–5.

towns. Towns gained charters of autonomy, and urban elites institutionalized their power in return for paying set quotas of taxes to the
ruling counts and later to the Habsburgs. Urban oligarchies further
cemented their power by granting guilds strong charters and monop-
olistic privileges.[1] Despite their internal cohesion, Dutch guilds
lacked the elite allies necessary to leverage their disruptive street
potential beyond economic concessions into a political role in urban
or state organs.

Urban oligarchies forged links across towns and developed cohesive interests because they needed to cooperate on a broad scale to
complete the massive dike and canal projects that were needed as
much to preserve existing towns, farmlands, and their water supplies
from flooding or salinization as they were to open new lands and
waterways for settlement and transport. The Dutch gained control
over North Sea trade because urban oligarchies joined together to
finance warships and harness the navies of the various towns and
provinces into a cohesive force that defeated the Hanseatic League,
held off the British, and then confronted the Spanish.

The merchant-regent elite of Holland and the elites of other Dutch
provinces faced their ultimate threat from Spain. Spain made increasing fiscal demands on Holland to support the costs of defending the
entire Netherlands and for war against France. Beginning in the 1550s,
and continuing until 1648, when the United Provinces won Spanish
recognition of their independence in a formal peace treaty, Holland—
with greater or lesser support from the other provinces—resisted
those demands. The struggle against Spain drew popular as well as
elite support because it also addressed Dutch Protestants' desire for
religious freedom against the fanatical efforts of Spain to impose
Catholic conformity upon all Habsburg subjects. The Eighty Years'
War between Spain and the Dutch was marked by periods of intense
and brutal conflict, years of less violent resistance, and times when
Spain offered truces in hopes of regaining the financial and military
means to recapture the northern Netherlands.

The Dutch won their war for independence in part because Spain
became progressively weaker in the sixteenth and seventeenth

---

1   Israel, *Dutch Republic*, 119–21 and passim.

centuries, as we saw in the previous chapter. The Dutch also were aided by Spain's enemies, France and Britain. Yet the Dutch did not merely outlast an exhausted Spain to become an independent backwater, as did Portugal. The Dutch emerged from their war as a major military and colonial power and with Amsterdam as the financial and industrial capital of Europe.

War with Spain consolidated the Amsterdam-Holland merchant oligarchy's capacity to pursue its interests globally. First, as we noted above, the war with Spain undermined Amsterdam's main commercial rival, Antwerp. Second, war facilitated merchant hegemony within Holland. The revolt against Spain in 1572 was accompanied by a purge of pro-Habsburg Catholic and noble officeholders from town and provincial governing bodies, most drastically in Amsterdam.[1] Popular and elite reaction against Catholic allies of the Habsburgs eliminated Catholics from the polity of the United Provinces by the 1580s. The ferocity of the Spanish terror against Protestants in the south led to a flight of Protestants and of Protestant capital to the north in the same decades. The post-1572 ruling elite was almost uniformly Protestant, removing religion as a basis for division within the governing bodies of the Republic and its provinces.

Finally, the cohesion of Amsterdam's ruling elite gave it the capacity to raise large sums of governmental revenue and investment capital quickly and consistently and to apply those monies to take advantage of the geopolitical opening created with the oscillating imposition and suspension of Spain's embargo against the rebellious United Provinces from the 1590s to the final peace in 1648. Similarly, elite unity within Holland, and Holland's wartime dominance over the other provinces, allowed the Dutch state to force a merger of the eight companies engaged in trade with the East Indies into the VOC in 1601.[2]

The consolidated company could afford to send enough armed ships to Asia to determine the outcome of conflicts among Europeans and with local rulers in Asia. The VOC's main tactic was to make deals with local rulers for monopoly access to commodities in return for Dutch (mainly VOC) protection from Portugal and from rival local

---

1   Ibid., 337–41.
2   Ibid., 318–27.

rulers.[1] VOC's goal was not to send settlers to create colonies. Rather, VOC sought to control trade routes and create settlements only to the extent that they were needed to project military power, and to procure, store, and ship the commodities that were the predominant source of VOC profits.

The VOC was chartered with a rigid structure that ensured that all families and factions of the Dutch merchant elite would have an interest in preserving the VOC's monopoly and would share in the obligation to inject capital and then share proportionally in the joy of reaping profits. The VOC had six chambers, represented by seventeen directors, chosen according to quotas for particular localities[2] that had been set to entice the participants in the previous eight East India companies to merge into VOC. That structure also ensured the VOC directors in Amsterdam could exert rigid control over their agents in Asia by preventing the creation of autonomous links between particular Dutch merchants in the metropole and their own agents in the colonies. This central control initially was an advantage in the Netherlands' colonial and commercial competition with European rivals, but, as we will see later, undermined the VOC in its competition with the British East India Company in the eighteenth century.

Similarly, the Dutch West India Company (hereafter WIC) was structured to incorporate the interests of key Dutch merchant families and factions. It had nineteen directors in five chambers. However, the WIC's main structural difference from the VOC and its greatest weakness was that private WIC shareholders had the right to claim personal trading rights in the Americas in return for a fee paid to the WIC.[3] This fatally undermined the WIC directors' capacity to control trade in the Americas, making it impossible to regulate prices paid for commodities in the WIC colonies or to confine exports to WIC ships.

The lack of complex native polities (because they had been exterminated by genocide and disease) prevented WIC from using the VOC strategy of negotiating with and coopting local rulers to secure

------

1    Van Zanden, *Rise and Decline of Holland's Economy*, 67–87; Nierstrasz, *In the Shadow of the Company*, chapter 3.
2    Adams, "Trading States, Trading Places," 332–6.
3    De Vries and van der Woude, *The First Modern Economy*, 396–402.

commodities. Instead, WIC followed the path of other European powers in the Americas, constructing colonies and using slaves to grow commodities, and in North America encouraging immigrants who could people colonies and farm and hunt in areas where slave plantations were not feasible. WIC sought to profit by overcharging settlers in Brazil for supplies,[1] and tried to reduce settlers in North America to the status of tenant farmers. This strategy yielded short-term profits but antagonized the settlers who did not defend WIC when Catholics revolted, opening the way for the Portuguese to take Brazil. Similarly, the exploited Dutch settlers in New Amsterdam did not fight the British.

The Dutch, through WIC, dominated the transatlantic slave trade,[2] creating the crucial African leg of the Atlantic triangular trade. The Dutch profited as well from funneling Spanish American silver to northern Europe. Wallerstein, in describing the Netherlands' role in developing the triangular trade, points out that

> the initial "social investment" was heavy and time consuming and, in bookkeeping terms, borne by the Dutch, with the profit just ready to be reaped after the end of Dutch hegemony in the 1670s by the subsequently productively more efficient English (and to some extent by the French).[3]

However, the Dutch gave up the chance to profit from their initial investment in large part because WIC had lost Brazil because of its shortsighted exploitation of its colonists. After the loss of Brazil, WIC was reorganized as primarily a trading company that became highly profitable,[4] even as it became secondary to British merchants and contributed almost nothing to the Dutch economy besides dividends for its shareholders.

Unity within the WIC and VOC directorships had allowed the rapid mobilization of resources to achieve dominance in Asia and the

---

1   Adams, "Trading States, Trading Places," 337–42.
2   Israel, *Dutch Republic*, 934–56.
3   Wallerstein, *Modern World-System*, volume 2, 51.
4   Israel, *Dutch Republic*, 934–56.

Atlantic. However, differences among the merchants who backed the two companies prevented cohesive military strategies by the Netherlands as a state that could have allowed those two Dutch firms, and through them Amsterdam, to preserve hegemony over international commerce. We need to look at the development of elite conflicts in the Netherlands in the second half of the seventeenth and eighteenth centuries to explain the loss of Dutch hegemony.

## THE SOURCES OF ELITE STASIS AND DUTCH RIGIDITY

### i. Taxes and State Debt

The Amsterdam merchant elite and the less prosperous and powerful elites from elsewhere in Holland and the other Dutch provinces were all able to build protections for their political and economic interests into the structures of the Dutch state, military, and colonial enterprises. Julia Adams[1] shows that Dutch merchant families (and their counterparts elsewhere in Western Europe) were concerned above all with preserving their families' privileges and powers over generations more than advancing their individual careers and wealth. They accomplished that dynastic feat by legitimizing their claims to offices, property, and authority in terms of their paternal authority within families and the claims rulers and lesser officials made to be the political fathers of their subjects (and priests and ministers made to be the fathers of their spiritual flocks).

Along with carefully constructing and repeatedly reasserting and living their ideological claims to patrimonial authority, Dutch elites embedded their assertions legally and organizationally. Adams[2] shows how Dutch merchant families wrote "Contracts of Correspondence," legal documents that created a system for rotating offices and dividing the profits from trade routes and merchant companies among elite families, thereby preserving those powers and income rights as

---

1   Julia Adams, *The Familial State: Ruling Families and Merchant Capitalism in Early Modern Europe* (Ithaca: Cornell University Press, 2005).

2   Adams, *Familial State*; "Trading States, Trading Places"; "The Familial State: Elite Family Practices and State-Making in the Early Modern Netherlands," *Theory and Society* 23 (1994).

patrimonial property. The system also prevented the sort of competition among multiple elites that was rife in France, as we saw in the previous chapter. Elite unity served to forestall significant challenges from Dutch non-elites and prevented the Dutch stadtholder from augmenting his power at the expense of the provinces.[1]

During the Dutch rise to hegemony, Contracts of Correspondence provided a mechanism for merchants and landowners to join together and pool their resources to fight the Spanish, control Baltic sea lanes and fisheries, and send ships and armed men to the Mediterranean and then the Americas and Asia. Contracts of Correspondence also ensured that participating families would, through their guaranteed control over offices, be able to veto governmental and chartered company policies that could undermine their abilities to protect their wealth or that could marginalize their roles in the Dutch polity. Similarly, the application of Contracts of Correspondence to the merger of eight competing Dutch trading companies into the VOC ensured that merchants would be willing to convert their existing investments and access to Asian markets, trade routes, and officials into company shares, secure in the knowledge that the Contracts would guarantee their access to opportunities to actively engage in Asian commerce as well as passively receive a share of the VOC's company profits as shareholders. Overall, the Contracts of Correspondence created the framework that ensured the vast revenues realized from the formal and informal Dutch empire flowed to the families that had invested their capital and political power in the creation of the Dutch state and in Dutch military and economic conquests throughout the world.

Contracts of Correspondence prevented elite conflicts[2] and allowed for the consolidation and mobilization of merchant wealth and power because they contained "written succession rules, which laid out systems by which all eligible elite families would take turns getting mayoralties, East Indies Company directorships, and other corporate privileges."[3] The Contracts of Correspondence existed

---

1   Israel, *Dutch Republic*, 595–609 and passim.
2   Ibid., 837–8.
3   Adams, "Familial State," 516.

within a larger constitutional system that set relations among the towns of Holland and between Holland and the other, poorer and less populous, provinces. The United Provinces' institutional structure was fixed in 1609 and remained unchanged until the fall of the Republic in 1795,[1] long after the Netherlands had been supplanted as the hegemon by Britain.

The Dutch fiscal system was designed, like the Contracts of Correspondence, to entice multiple elites to enter into a single polity by protecting, seemingly in perpetuity, each province and town's ability to block policies that would impose new fiscal burdens they did not want to assume. Each province had one vote in the States General of the United Provinces, and any province could veto increases in the total tax burden.[2] Each province's contribution to the national budget was set as a share of the total, adapted from the provincial quota system devised by the Habsburgs, and which remained unchanged from 1616 to 1792. Holland paid 58 percent. Only customs duties and some minor levies were directly assessed, and those taxes contributed only 20 percent of the national budget. The provinces met their quotas for the remaining 80 percent mainly with excise taxes in Holland and land taxes in the other more rural provinces.[3]

In essence, the Dutch constitutional structure and the organizations of the VOC and WIC created "veto points" that gave each province and town, and the major merchant families included in the Contracts of Correspondence, the ability to block any reforms or adjustments that would have undermined their particular familial and financial interests, even at the cost of preventing investments or policy changes that were needed to extend or preserve Dutch hegemony. If Dutch institutions were designed to create early unity and mobilize the resources that allowed the United Provinces, in Giovanni Arrighi's words, "to catch 'the wind actually blowing,'"[4] then those same

---

1   Israel, *Dutch Republic*, 276–84.
2   Ibid., 291–306.
3   De Vries and van der Woude, *The First Modern Economy*, 96–113; Marjolein 't Hart, "The Merits of a Financial Revolution: Public Finance, 1550–1700," in *A Financial History of the Netherlands*; Israel, *Dutch Republic*, 285–91.
4   Arrighi, *Long Twentieth Century*, 133.

institutions prevented the Dutch from changing course or reconditioning the ship of state to catch the winds that blew in different directions and with much greater force once Britain built the capacity to compete in manufacture, trade, war, and finance.

The Dutch fiscal system worked well in the first decades of the seventeenth century, since the poorer provinces shared Holland's desire for an aggressive military stance against the Habsburgs, and Holland was paying the majority of the cost of military ventures all the provinces endorsed. However, once the Spanish retreated and seemed to accept the northern Netherlands' autonomy, the Amsterdam merchants, eager for a truce with Spain and the wealth that would flow from renewed trade, were willing to settle for a status short of full independence. In contrast, rural Dutch elites profited from the high food prices brought on by the Spanish embargo and so gained from continued war. Similarly, Leiden and Haarlem, the centers of the Dutch textile industry, benefited from "high wartime customs duties" that kept textiles from rival producers in the southern Netherlands out of the United Provinces and therefore those two towns "were mostly the core of the war party."[1] In addition, Amsterdam and the rural provinces were divided over religion. Amsterdam was mainly Remonstrant (less orthodox Protestants who were not committed to spreading rigid Calvinism beyond the northern Netherlands), while the rural provinces were allied to William II, the stadtholder who wanted to keep fighting.[2]

The growing economic divergence between Holland and the other provinces also undermined unity over increasing the state budget. The excise taxes that Holland used to meet its quota of the state budget were borne mainly by middle-class consumers and therefore would not have significantly impacted rich merchants, while the land taxes in the other provinces fell mostly on wealthy landowners.[3] As yields on land investments fell with peace and a decline in food prices and rents after 1667, the burden of land taxes became relatively heavier. In response to the falling returns from

---

1   't Hart, *Making of a Bourgeois State*, 46.
2   Israel, *Dutch Republic*, 421–609.
3   't Hart, "Merits of a Financial Revolution."

investments in land, urban merchants dumped much of their land holdings[1] so that the Amsterdam elite was ever less affected by any potential rise in land taxes. In addition, Amsterdam and Rotterdam became wealthier relative to the other provinces,[2] so an increase in the state budget, and hence in each province's quota, would hit the other provinces and their landowning elites much harder than the Amsterdam merchants.

The Dutch constitutional system gave veto power to the declining landowner class outside Holland since those landowners named the men who served as representatives of their provinces in the States General and set tax quotas. The poorer provinces blocked increases in the total tax, and Holland was unwilling to increase its quota to relieve the poorer provinces.[3] The result was stalemate and a stagnant budget. Revenue peaked in the 1670s and declined, controlling for inflation, 25 percent by the 1720s.[4] Two of the principal methods— selling offices and coining (and debasing) currency—that other European governments used to raise revenue were closed to the Dutch. Existing officials guarded their control over offices, guaranteed through Contracts of Correspondence, by blocking any attempts to create venal offices.[5] Local governments minted coins and prevented the central government from competing in that realm. Local officials were pressured consistently and successfully by merchants to never debase their currencies since merchants needed a stable currency for international trade and, in the eighteenth century, to attract foreign capital.[6]

Elite veto points in the administrative and fiscal arenas, while motivated solely by self-interest, did have the effect of making the Dutch state administration more rational (in Weber's sense of the

1   De Vries and van der Woude, *The First Modern Economy*, 217–18, 673–5.
2   Marjolein 't Hart, "The Dutch Republic: The Urban Impact upon Politics," in *A Miracle Mirrored: The Dutch Republic in European Perspective*, eds. Karel Davids and Jan Lucassen (Cambridge: Cambridge University Press, 1995), 76–83.
3   't Hart, *Making of a Bourgeois State*, 141–4.
4   Table 3.1, on page 89.
5   't Hart, "Dutch Republic."
6   Dehing and 't Hart, "Linking the Fortune;" Wantje Fritschy and René van der Voort, "From Fragmentation to Unification: Public Finance, 1700–1914," in *A Financial History of the Netherlands*; 't Hart, *Making of a Bourgeois State*, 90–117.

word) and furthering Dutch merchants' goal of dominating international trade and finance. Venal offices that could have competed
administratively and financially with the Dutch military and civilian
administrations were never created. Therefore, the state's zones of
inefficiency and paralysis were the result of elites' collective abilities to
veto policies rather than individual actors' capacities to appropriate
governmental powers and resources for their personal interests. The
stability of the various local Dutch currencies facilitated the floating of
bonds by the central, provincial, and local governments as well as the
development of the Dutch Bourse and of Amsterdam as the banking
center of Europe.

Dutch elites, for whom government bonds became an ever-greater
share of their wealth, rising from 24 percent of their estates in 1650–
74 to 61 percent in the eighteenth century,[1] used their political power
to ensure that interest payments were the first priority in the central
and provincial budgets, even at the cost of military expenditures. This
created a fiscal virtuous cycle, but a geopolitical vicious cycle, for the
United Provinces.

As tax revenues stagnated, debt increased first to meet extraordinary war costs and then to close deficits in the regular budgets of the
central government and even more in the provincial budgets.[2]
However, the fiscal burden of rising debt was limited by the extremely
low interest rates Dutch state organs had to pay. Holland, which
borrowed by far the most and which was the richest Dutch province,
paid less than 5 percent interest on bonds in the mid-seventeenth
century, and that rate fell to less than 3 percent by the 1690s and was
2.5 percent for the entire eighteenth century.[3] In comparison, the
British government, as we will see in the next chapter, paid 8 to 10
percent in the first half of the seventeenth century and 4 to 6 percent

---

1   De Vries and van der Woude, *The First Modern Economy*, 591–2.
2   't Hart, *Making of a Bourgeois State*, 158–72.
3   L. van der Ent, W. Fritschy, E. Horlings, and R. Liesker, "Public Finance in
the United Provinces of the Netherlands in the Seventeenth and Eighteenth
Centuries," in *Crises, Revolutions and Self-Sustained Growth: Essays in European
Fiscal History, 1130–1830*, eds. W. M. Ormrod, Margaret Bonney, and Richard
Bonney (Stamford: Shaun Tyas, 1999), 267; Bruce Carruthers, *City of Capital: Politics
and Markets in the English Financial Revolution* (Princeton: Princeton University
Press, 1996), 82.

in the second half of the seventeenth century, while other governments paid substantially higher rates.[1]

Interest rates were low because, until 1688 (when British state debt
was guaranteed by excise taxes and so became safe from default),
Dutch government bonds were the safest investment available in
Europe.[2] Low interest rates kept annual payments low. Low rates on
government bonds kept interest rates in the private sector lower than
in other countries, making it cheaper for Dutch firms to borrow and
giving them an advantage over foreign competitors.

'T Hart[3] shows that debt service, as a percentage of the entire
budget of the Dutch Republic, rose from 4 percent in 1641 to 41
percent in 1801, when it almost equaled military expenditures.
Nevertheless, thanks to low interest rates, this burden could be borne
without threat of bankruptcy, default, or restructuring of debt. The
increasing share of the budget devoted to debt service also reflected
the slow rate of increase in tax revenues.

Provincial debt was far greater than that of the Republic. The province of Holland's debt rose from almost nothing in 1599 to 50 million
guilders in 1632, 200 million in 1700, and 300 million in 1720.[4] In
part, the increase in debt was the result of a deal in which the national
government's debt was assumed by Holland in return for other provinces accepting slightly higher shares of the national tax quota, when
the national debt had ballooned from 13 million in 1648 to 61 million
by 1715. The transfer allowed the national debt to decline to 21 million
by 1786.[5]

Holland agreed to the deal since its richest merchants were the
ones who stood to lose the most if the national government suspended
payments or sought to renegotiate the debt. As debt payments
consumed ever more of the budget, and interest on government
bonds became the main source of income for the Amsterdam elite,
state policy, in the absence of a mechanism to increase taxes overall,

---

1   Sidney Homer and Richard Sylla, *A History of Interest Rates*, 4th ed. (New
York: Wiley, 2005), table 11; see also 't Hart, "United Provinces," figure 9.3.
2   De Vries and van der Woude, *The First Modern Economy*, 141–58.
3   't Hart, "United Provinces," 312.
4   Ibid., 314.
5   Ibid., 313.

became focused on minimizing military expenses so that there would be no danger of a default on debt. Amsterdam thus pushed to reduce the size of the army after 1648, a position that overwhelmed the militarist desires of the other provinces after the death of stadtholder William II in 1650.[1] Amsterdam demanded and achieved significant reductions in military spending. This allowed Holland's provincial debt to decline to 295 million in 1740. It rose with the United Provinces' involvement in the War of the Spanish Succession to 360 million in 1756 and then, with the Republic neutral in the Seven Years' War, fell to 320 million in 1780, which was the equivalent of a drop in debt service from 70 percent to 60 percent of Holland's annual revenue.[2] The central and provincial states' fiscal rectitude, which reflected their overriding concern for merchant bondholders, had geopolitical consequences that were fatal for Dutch hegemony, as we will see below.

## ii. VOC and WIC

Initially, the armed men and merchants of the VOC and WIC were able to capture trade routes and win access to lands that produced valuable commodities because they only had to fight less-well-armed Asians and Native Americans. Similarly, it took only limited armed force to capture Africans and transport them as slaves to the Americas.[3] As we discussed above, the Dutch advantage was due to the institutional mechanisms that united traders into single chartered companies for Asia and the Americas. That unity, in turn, created a disciplined structure for transporting and holding commodities so that they could be released onto European markets in volumes and with timing designed to "achieve a stable medium-term optimum rather than a short-term maximization."[4]

--------

1    't Hart, *Making of a Bourgeois State*, 43–50.

2    Fritschy and van der Voort, "From Fragmentation to Unification: Public Finance," 64–93.

3    While the Dutch had to share the slave trade with other Europeans, there was little direct competition since each colonial power for the most part supplied the slaves for their own colonies, and in Africa there were more than enough men and women who could be easily captured.

4    De Vries and van der Woude, *The First Modern Economy*, 431.

By the mid-seventeenth century, other European powers had established chartered companies, most significantly the British East India Company (EIC), and sent armed ships to Asia and the Americas to compete with the Dutch commercially and militarily. Similarly, in Europe, the declining economy of the mid-seventeenth century prompted protectionist measures by Britain and France, which led to a contraction of Dutch industry, since the domestic market was too small to sustain Dutch manufacture.[1] Most significantly, the Navigation Act of 1651 required goods shipped within the empire to be carried on British ships. That act severely reduced demand for Dutch ships and stimulated the British shipping industry. The French state also favored its own ships by imposing high fees on goods brought to France on Dutch vessels beginning in 1649 and further handicapped Dutch merchants by raising the duties in later years.[2] Dutch merchants responded to limits on their access to Britain, France, and their colonies by ceasing to invest capital in shipbuilding in the Netherlands. Instead, Dutch merchants invested their money in, and sold their technical know-how to, the British shipbuilding industry, and within the Netherlands moved their capital to other sectors. By the end of the seventeenth century, British and French shipbuilders had surpassed the Dutch in their technological level.[3]

The Netherlands' loss of dominance in manufacturing and shipping meant that Dutch control of international commerce and commodities and of finance loomed ever larger in determining the United Provinces' position in the global economy and, of course, became an ever more significant source of national income and of Dutch elites' wealth. The Netherlands' remaining advantage was its vast and unrivaled store of capital, which increased from 10–12 million guilders in 1500 to 1,750 million guilders by 1790.[4] However, the particular organizations of the WIC and VOC combined with the United Provinces' political structure to prevent the investment of that capital, including to expand and deploy an army and navy, in ways

1   Ibid., 341–2.
2   Ibid., 409–12.
3   Ibid., 298–300.
4   Dehing and 't Hart, "Linking the Fortune," 37.

that could have allowed the Dutch to retain commercial and financial hegemony even after they lost manufacturing hegemony to Britain.

The WIC, as we saw above, differed from the VOC in that it empowered its shareholders to trade individually for their own accounts: at first in supplying settlers, and then, after Brazil fell to the Portuguese, in the even more lucrative slave trade. WIC merchants maximized their profits by limiting the number of slaves they imported to the Dutch American colonies. This created a slave shortage that drove up labor costs and restricted sugar production. WIC shareholders were able to block efforts to repeal their monopoly on the slave trade in the Dutch empire until 1730.[1] After the slave trade was opened to competition, more slaves were brought to the Dutch Caribbean, which allowed a significant expansion in sugar, coffee, cocoa, and cotton. However, that reform came too late; by that time, Dutch plantation owners faced competition from the British and French and therefore were never able to control trade in those commodities. Nor was the United Provinces willing at any point to pay for military forces to attempt to seize more Caribbean colonies, retake Brazil, or disrupt rival European shopping networks. WIC shareholders and Dutch Caribbean plantations owners were marginalized politically in Holland, and the richer and more politically central Amsterdam merchants who were invested in the VOC never supported WIC requests for spending on Atlantic military ventures.[2]

The decline in the scope and volume of WIC's commodity business did not mean that its privileged shareholders lost income.

Ironically, this progressive marginalization of the Dutch position in the Atlantic economy made them the preferred suppliers of slaves and commercial services to the Spanish colonies. The WIC and its Curaçao trade center, its teeth having been drawn by British and French protectionism [and the unwillingness of the Dutch state to intervene militarily] prospered in the 1680s and '90s as the holder of

1  Van Zanden, *Rise and Decline of Holland's Economy*, 88–102.
2  De Vries and van der Woude, *The First Modern Economy*, 396–402; Israel, *Dutch Republic*, 934–6.

the Spanish . . . slave supply contract, and as tolerated purveyor of manufactured goods and shipping services.[1]

For the WIC shareholders who had the lucrative Spanish concession, their nation's geopolitical weakness in the Atlantic made them a more desirable business partner than British or French merchants who could have called on their governments' military might to subordinate Spanish colonies to their more robust commercial networks, which the British managed to do in the eighteenth century.

Dutch ship owners reacted to the lack of diplomatic and military support from their government by shifting vessels from West Africa and the Americas to Asia and to the speculative and ultimately unprofitable whaling industry.[2] However, the VOC also came under competitive commercial and geopolitical pressures in the late seventeenth century from the EIC, which, like the VOC, mobilized its own armed forces to control territory and trade networks. The VOC lost the competition to the EIC for two reasons: First, its rigid organizational structure could not be adapted to the new competitive situation because the merchants who controlled VOC high offices in perpetuity and could exercise veto power over VOC policies, thanks to the Contracts of Correspondence, blocked any reforms that would have lessened their share of VOC profits. Second, the military forces the VOC was able to field with its own resources were never augmented by the Dutch state, while the EIC was able to call on the British navy in key battles. Dutch fiscal restraint was fatal to the Netherlands' overall geopolitical situation (as we will see in the next section), and that further narrowed the VOC's commercial opportunities.

The VOC attracted more investment as manufacturing in the United Provinces and opportunities in the Americas contracted, and as the total pool of Dutch capital increased. The VOC issued long-term bonds in the 1680s and '90s, and used the proceeds to invest in

---

1   De Vries and van der Woude, *The First Modern Economy*, 467.
2   Maddison, *World Economy*, volume 1, 79; de Vries and van der Woude, *The First Modern Economy*, 676–81.

expanding markets such as calicoes, silks, porcelain, coffee, sugar, and tea [even though] the Company directors recognized that they were shifting from [spices] over which the VOC had substantial market power to goods traded—in both Asia and Europe—in competitive markets.[1]

The VOC confined its Asian trade to company ships that were required to bring their commodities to Batavia, where they then would be sent on VOC ships to warehouses in Amsterdam, giving the VOC total control over supply and pricing. This organizational structure had three defects once the VOC faced competition from the British. First, the effort to keep all commerce within VOC ships and warehouses prevented the company's agents from expanding their trading networks. The VOC system worked well for a few high-priced commodities that were produced in relatively small geographic areas that the VOC could control with military force and/or through alliance with local rulers. However, when the VOC sought to enter into other lines of trade that could not be monopolized, it found itself at a fundamental disadvantage to the EIC. Emily Erikson[2] shows that the EIC expanded its Asian trade networks beyond company-controlled territories because it was *unable* to control its captains' private dealings. EIC captains established ties to, and gained knowledge of, products and markets that allowed them to enrich themselves while making use of EIC ships. However, in the long run these self-dealing captains brought new products and producers into the EIC orbit. Each captain had only small amounts of personal capital to use in their personal trade, and so the new markets could be maintained only when the captains brought the EIC in as the senior partner. In this way the EIC outflanked the VOC in markets for products beyond the few spices that had first enriched the Dutch. Heavy VOC investments in markets for other Asian goods were "speculative," and "rarely succeeded in . . . earning a profit;" this was an "era . . . of profitless growth."[3] The VOC

1   De Vries and van der Woude, *The First Modern Economy*, 678.
2   Emily Erikson, *Between Monopoly and Free Trade: The English East India Company, 1600–1757* (Princeton: Princeton University Press, 2014).
3   De Vries and van der Woude, *The First Modern Economy*, 678.

could not earn a profit in these new lines of commerce because they lacked the information about the new markets that the EIC got from its captains.

Second, the Contracts of Correspondence ensured that the old merchant families that controlled company offices would determine the future direction of the VOC. As the VOC profit rate fell, due to declining European demand and greater competition from the British, the VOC offered less of a return than alternative investments, above all state bonds. The controlling families insisted that the dividend be maintained and that the offices they controlled continued to be lucrative. The result of those preferences was that all the VOC profit was paid out in dividends and the company's trading capital declined and had to be supplemented with money borrowed from outside investors who, ignorant of the workings of the VOC, made what became a poor bet. From 1730 to 1780, the dividend yield on VOC stock averaged 2.9 percent, but considering that the stock lost half its value in those decades, the actual return was 1.9 percent. For those who held onto VOC stock until 1795, when its value fell to zero, the annual return was 0.9 percent.[1]

Third, the already existing rigidity of the Contracts of Correspondence, which blocked entry of any new families into the elite, combined with economic stagnation in the eighteenth century to convince a growing number of colonial agents to remain in Asia. These agents engaged in corrupt practices: trading on their own accounts, skimming commodities from VOC plantations and warehouses, and selling lesser offices they controlled.[2] To avoid detection by the VOC, corrupt agents conducted much of their illicit trade and repatriated corrupt profits through the EIC, which strengthened the EIC's trade network.

Dutch elites, by the eighteenth century, were reduced largely to rentier status, with more and more of their income coming from passive investments outside of the Netherlands and the Dutch empire. The incomes of the Dutch rich increasingly came to depend on the prosperity of British industries and the creditworthiness of the British

---

1   Ibid., 463–4.
2   Nierstrasz, *In the Shadow of the Company*, 167–85.

state since British stocks and state bonds made up growing portions of their portfolios, although Dutch government bonds remained their largest assets and hence elite pressure for fiscal restraint was unstinting up to the end of the Dutch Republic. Both pillars of Dutch wealth were threatened by warfare between the United Provinces and Britain: During wartime, when the central and provincial Dutch governments took on more debt, it became harder to pay the interest due unless taxes were increased. The same dynamic threatened the British bonds held by Dutch elites. Similarly, British openness to Dutch investment was lost in wartime. These financial considerations sapped Dutch elites' support for military efforts by the Netherlands to push back against British geopolitical expansion.

## GEOPOLITICS: THE UNITED PROVINCES VS. BRITAIN IN EUROPE AND ASIA[1]

The Netherlands fought three wars with Britain in 1652–54, 1665–67, and 1672–74. A fourth war occurred a century after the other three and well after Britain had clearly achieved hegemony at the Netherlands' expense, so it need not concern us here.[2] These wars, like the other early modern wars we analyzed in chapter 2, for the most part ended inconclusively with treaties that returned most of the lands seized in battle to their former rulers. Nevertheless, by the end of the three Anglo-Dutch Wars and the longer Franco-Dutch War of 1672–78, "the Dutch suddenly became a secondary [military] factor despite continuing Dutch economic strength."[3] Although the Dutch fought those wars with a number of objectives, they did not achieve the ones most important for their contest with Britain for hegemony: undermining Britain's Navigation Act and controlling colonies and trade routes in Asia and the Americas. Why did the Dutch fail to realize their objectives by military means?

--------------------------------

1   This section relies on Israel, *Dutch Republic*, for narratives of the course of the wars the Dutch fought from 1652 to 1678 and for accounts of the internal Dutch politics about finance and strategy, both military and diplomatic, for those wars.

2   The Fourth Anglo-Dutch War of 1780–84 gave Britain control over the Netherlands' Indian colonies and commercial access to the Dutch East Indies, most importantly to Batavia (present-day Indonesia).

3   Wallerstein, *Modern World-System*, volume 2, 80.

Wallerstein believes Dutch decline was because that polity was too small to pay the rising costs of naval and land wars.

> By the end of the seventeenth century, the demographic conse-quences of the partition of the Burgundian state [into the United Provinces and the southern Netherlands, the future Belgium] had begun to take their military toll. The United Provinces, despite its wealth, was too small to carry indefinitely the insupportable burden of military and naval defence they had to bear.[1]

In fact, the Dutch enjoyed an overwhelming financial advantage, with state revenues more than triple those of Britain throughout the years of the first three Anglo-Dutch Wars.[2] In the first two wars Britain had no allies, and in the second war France, then the strongest land power in Europe, provided massive and decisive military assis-tance to the Netherlands. In the Third Anglo-Dutch War (1672–74) France was allied with Britain, but when the Netherlands was on the verge of defeat, Britain, fearing French hegemony on the Continent, made a quick peace with the Dutch and, in the later years of what then became the Franco-Dutch War (1672–78), Spain and other countries fought on the side of the Netherlands against France. Thus, allies made no difference in the first war, favored the Dutch in the second, and in the third at first harmed the Netherlands but then, after Britain's withdrawal, the Dutch had a more powerful coalition than did France.

Despite their fiscal advantage, and, in the second war, a stronger set of allies, the Dutch were unable to prevent Britain from enforcing its Navigation Act and thereby shifting commercial hegemony from the Netherlands to Britain. While neither Britain nor the Netherlands gained territory in Europe, Britain won control over key Dutch colo-nial territories, ports, and trade routes. The end result of the first three wars was a decisive shift of land and trade routes from Dutch to British control in the Americas, Africa, and Asia. Again, why were the Dutch unable to translate fiscal advantage into military success?

--------------------------------

1   Ibid., 80.
2   See table 2.1, on page 89.

Two factors explain the incongruity between the Netherlands' fiscal strength and its failure to effectively harness military power to protect its geopolitical interests. First, elites disagreed with one another over their objectives for Dutch foreign policy. Second, those elites had the institutional power to withhold funding, and the ships and armed men they controlled, from foreign ventures they opposed. Thus, the total state budget and "Dutch" naval ships were not under the control of a head of state or central government that could deploy those assets. Instead, there were five separate Dutch navies, each financed by customs duties and excise taxes raised from within the territory controlled by the town or province to which the navy belonged. In addition, the WIC and the VOC had their own fleets and armed forces as well. All efforts to consolidate the five admiralties, or even to place them under a genuine central command, foundered.[1] Attempts to control WIC and VOC forces through the stadtholder or any other appointee of the States General repeatedly failed. The stadtholder's nominal control over all land armies was undermined by the fact that each company was financed by a specific province and by the willingness of Holland especially to disband its troops when the stadtholder's foreign policy became too aggressive or otherwise did not conform to the desires and interests of the Amsterdam regents.

All elites, and indeed the population at large, shared in their determination to maintain Dutch independence and to preserve the territorial integrity of the United Provinces. Dutch financial and military power were unified and effectively mobilized behind that particular goal. When French forces invaded the Netherlands in 1672 at the outset of the Third Anglo-Dutch War and the British sought to blockade the Dutch ports and capture VOC fleets arriving from Asia, provincial elites united, in part because of popular pressure and the threat of mass violence being turned on them, and mobilized enough ships and armed men (and agreed to breach dikes to flood farmlands to halt the French army's advance). This ensured that Britain

---

1  Modelski and Thompson's (*Leading Sectors and Global Politics*) exhaustive analysis of the number and relative share of warships floated by each European power makes no mention at all of the fact that "Dutch" warships were under multiple autonomous commands.

withdrew from its alliance with France and made a separate peace with the Dutch. Dutch provincial armies remained united, and the provinces continued to appropriate enough money to push the French out of the United Provinces and to ensure that French conquests in the later years of the Anglo-French War would remain limited to the southern Netherlands.

Dutch elites were divided over their objectives beyond Europe. Polities can pursue various and often conflicting objectives in war. Since the United Provinces, like every other polity in the seventeenth century (and indeed like every polity throughout human history), lacked the military resources to advance all of its interests, the Anglo-Dutch and Franco-Dutch wars reveal the priorities that mattered most to the United Provinces government in this era. Or, to be more precise, the wars highlight the political capacities of various elites to make the government pursue *their* particular priorities.

The elites of Holland, above all the Amsterdam merchants, were most concerned with asserting their demand for free shipping rights everywhere, including to Britain and its colonies, and with maintaining control over trade routes and colonies. Elites in the other provinces did not gain much direct financial benefit from commerce and colonies and were less willing to pay for naval vessels and hiring and equipping armed men. Amsterdam merchants were divided between those who invested in the VOC and those who financed the WIC. As we saw when we tracked the history of the WIC, those merchants were an isolated faction and were unable to mobilize state resources to defend their interests in the Americas against rival European powers and those nations' chartered companies and privateers. In the absence of support from the provinces, WIC ships were overwhelmed by rival European powers in the Americas, while the richer VOC was able to float a larger navy and pay for armed companies that controlled its colonies and trade routes through the seventeenth century—but then was overwhelmed by the more powerful EIC and British fleets early in the eighteenth century.

Amsterdam merchants' commercial interests, and their short-term calculations, prevented the Netherlands from preserving the geopolitical advantage it had gained from its victory over Britain in the Second Anglo-Dutch War. The French-Dutch alliance that had won that war could have acted as a long-term check on British naval and commercial domination of the North Sea. However, Amsterdam quickly split from other Dutch elites at the end of the war to advocate for an alliance with their former Spanish rulers against France. Amsterdam merchants had three reasons for wanting to break the alliance with France. First, French expansionism in the Caribbean threatened Dutch colonial interests in the Americas. Amsterdam merchants thought they were not threatened by Spain's weaker military presence in the Americas and that, in any case, they could profit from trade with Spanish American colonies. Second, Amsterdam merchants feared their exports would be limited by French mercantilism. Finally, Amsterdam merchants feared that if the United Provinces and France forced the Habsburgs out of the southern Netherlands, Antwerp would revive and prosper in the absence of Spanish control and then pose a commercial challenge to Amsterdam.

The Amsterdam merchants were able to force their diplomatic preferences on the other provinces, successfully antagonizing France by imposing a ban on French imports and using WIC to attack French shipping in the Caribbean. Amsterdam's preferred Dutch-Spanish alliance backfired in the short-term, pushing France to ally with Britain and bring the United Provinces to the brink of total defeat and conquest with the French-British joint attack at the outset of the Third Anglo-Dutch and Franco-Dutch War in 1672. Holland's strategy was a disaster over the long term, because the Amsterdam merchants misjudged the source of its biggest economic challenge. It was not the potential revival of Antwerp, or French mercantilism, or French expansion in the Americas. Rather, the British, whom Amsterdam merchants regarded as challengers only in the North Sea, mounted their main challenge in the Americas and Asia and served to destroy the WIC and progressively weaken the VOC.

The elite of Holland already had underestimated the threat from Britain as they negotiated an end to the First Anglo-Dutch War. The *Staatsgezinde* faction, which was composed mainly of elites from Holland, joined with the British in demanding that the treaty include a secret annex obliging the United Provinces to pass an Act of Seclusion that would forever ban any member of the House of Orange from becoming stadtholder. Other provinces opposed this provision but were unable to overcome the combined power of Britain and Holland. Holland got what it wanted, a permanent weakening of the central government. However, Holland won this advantage in internal Dutch politics and government at the cost of having to agree that Britain could maintain the Navigation Act, which had drastic long-run effects on the Netherlands' position in European commerce. And, of course, the permanent weakening of the Dutch state through the Act of Seclusion made it impossible for the elite of Holland to build up a military powerful enough to challenge the British in later decades, when such a military became essential to any efforts to preserve Dutch hegemony from British challenge.

In the absence of a strong central state, there was no mechanism to challenge the Amsterdam merchants' narrow self-interest or its repeated geopolitical misjudgments. As we discussed earlier, the national budget was divided among provinces, and within each province, among towns. If any one province refused or reduced its share of the assessment, all the other provinces would reduce their payments in proportion. Thus, tax increases for war required consensus among all the provinces. Amsterdam controlled Holland and Holland withheld or cut its contribution when it decided that negotiations with France, Spain, or Britain were better for those merchants' short- or long-term interests and plans than continued fighting. The division of Dutch land and sea forces into multiple navies and armed forces allowed any province to withhold its men and weapons, undermining the war effort and forcing an end to efforts to defeat rivals in Europe or in Asia and the Americas.

Provincial autonomy undermined preparation for war as well as the fight during wartime. Naval warfare was even more vulnerable to elite dissention than land-based war since it required high up-front expenditures on ships. Thus, efforts to build up Dutch naval power required years of consensus among provinces, or at least within Holland, to finance a sustained warship-building program. Britain and the Netherlands, as we saw earlier in examining its merchant fleet, were at the forefront of marine technology. They engaged in a naval arms race with each other, attempting to build larger and faster ships with more firepower than those of their enemies. This caused a rapid escalation in costs and reinforced the need for sustained spending in peacetime to prepare for war.

The Dutch were at an additional disadvantage to Britain in that they did not use press gangs to recruit (or more accurately to kidnap) sailors for their warships. Few Dutch were willing to volunteer or even to fight for pay in the army. In the 1590s, only 17 out of 132 army companies fielded by the Dutch republic were made up of Dutch fighters; the rest were foreign mercenaries,[1] and the United Provinces continued to rely on mercenaries in its later wars with France and England, although the Dutch did contribute to defensive efforts, most notably during the opening of the dikes to prevent a French advance in 1673. Mercenaries everywhere in Europe were expensive and would quit if not paid.[2] The Netherlands' wealth and unparalleled access to credit gave it an advantage in recruiting and keeping mercenaries in battle, but the Dutch army could and did quickly unravel if any province refused to pay its share of the tax quota and other provinces then followed suit and reduced the government's war budget. The resources that could have allowed the Netherlands to build an army and navy capable of overwhelming Britain, or at least of preventing the British from excluding the Dutch from a widening sphere of European and world commerce, remained decentralized in provinces and chartered companies. Dutch wealth was locked up by institutional paralysis.

## LOST HEGEMONY AND THE PRESERVATION OF ELITE PRIVILEGE

A single elite, the Amsterdam merchants, preserved multiple veto points in the Dutch polity. No matter how far those merchants' interests diverged from those of other elites, nor how badly that single elite misjudged its own long-term interests as well as those of the nation as a whole, no political force or combination of forces within the Netherlands and its empire could loosen the merchants' capacity to guard what it considered its rightful privileges.

This chapter has focused on the contingent chain of conflicts and institutional formations that first allowed the Dutch to achieve hegemony and then prevented the steps needed to preserve that hegemony.

---

1   Kennedy, *Rise and Fall of the Great Powers*, 67.
2   Lachmann, "Mercenary, Citizen, Victim."

In chapter 1, I argued that the Netherlands was the first polity (followed by Britain and the United States) that lacked any of the four factors that precluded previous and rival polities from attaining hegemony: (1) a high level of elite conflict in the metropole, (2) a high level of colonial elite autonomy from the metropole, (3) a unitary elite dominant in the metropole, and (4) the lack of infrastructural capacity to impose economic hegemony. Dutch elites came together to fight against Habsburg rule and to gain commercial dominance in the North Sea, creating elite unity (removing factor number one), while developing a political system that prevented the Amsterdam merchants from eliminating or subordinating the other elites in the Netherlands (blocking factor number three). The way in which the WIC and VOC were financed and organized ensured that company agents in the Americas and Asia lacked autonomy (removing factor number two). And we have seen how the Dutch built the infrastructural capacity in commerce, manufacture, finance, and military organization to assert hegemony under those favorable social structural conditions.

How were the conditions that facilitated Dutch hegemony undermined? In chapter 1, I hypothesized that hegemony itself must have re-created one or more of the four factors that blocked hegemony for other empires. I suggested that hegemony affected the first factor, that it disrupted stable elite relations and heightened elite conflict in the metropole. That, as we have seen in this chapter, is indeed what happened in the Netherlands in the late seventeenth century. Amsterdam elites used the wealth they amassed from their hegemonic control over global markets to buy enough armed force to pursue their own military and foreign policy in Asia and the Americas and to determine Dutch policy toward Britain and France in Europe. In this way, elite accord became conflict and, while the Amsterdam merchants did not become a single unitary elite in the metropole, they did attain the power to block the central state from pursuing any policy that they opposed. The Amsterdam merchants' shortsightedness degraded Dutch military infrastructure. The system that elites of Holland used to control the VOC and WIC gave colonial elites in the Americas a degree of autonomy that crippled the WIC's capacity to defend itself against rival European powers. In Asia, metropolitan elites maintained their hard control over colonial agents in the VOC, but that system, which had allowed the Dutch to get the jump on rival European powers, could not be maintained once the British attained a significant presence in Asia through the EIC.

The Netherlands' loss of hegemony was thus internally generated, the consequence of a structure that once had facilitated elite harmony and the mobilization of resources for shared goals. However, that structure allowed any dissenting elite to block collective action at the state level. Amsterdam elites came to have an interest in, and a capacity to, oppose other Dutch elites because of the wealth they accrued from their colonial ventures. It was in this way that colonial elites had influence on the metropole. Not by direct investment or lobbying, but by transforming the Amsterdam merchant elite that they served. At the same time, the Amsterdam merchants maintained rigid control over their agents in the colonies.

The elite structure of the Dutch polity and of its larger empire blocked reform. Various writers in the late seventeenth and eighteenth centuries recognized the need for change and identified reforms that could have preserved Dutch dominance or at least slowed decline. Self-interested elites in other provinces, but also some Amsterdam officials who saw the need for larger and more consistent revenues for the central government, proposed changes in provincial tax quotas or a shift to nationally assessed taxes that would circumvent provincial quotas entirely or at least provide another stream of revenue that provinces could not limit or block.[1] However, the majorities of Amsterdam elites opposed such reforms and were able to veto both changes to provincial tax quotas and the imposition of new national taxes.

Nor was it possible to reform the structures of either the WIC or the VOC. The latter especially was stultified by the rigid Contracts of Correspondence that prevented any organizational changes to respond to competition from the EIC or to the opportunities the EIC created for VOC agents in Asia to engage in self-dealing. The low level of autonomy enjoyed by VOC agents and the high degree of autonomy for WIC plantation owners both had facilitated Dutch dominance

---

1   't Hart, "Dutch Republic," "Merits of a Financial Revolution"; de Vries and van der Woude, *The First Modern Economy*, 681–3.

during the years of colonization but later underlined Dutch power in Asia and the Americas.

The absence of a strong central authority also made it impossible to stem the flow of Dutch capital abroad. The Netherlands' massive store of capital, the ultimate basis of a financial hegemony that lasted after the Dutch had lost manufacturing and commercial supremacy to the British, became instead the source of rentier income, increasingly derived from abroad, for Dutch elites whose familial interests therefore diverged sharply from that of their nation by the mid-eighteenth century.[1]

The Dutch did not lose hegemony and decline because of a lack of awareness of the nature of competition from the British. Nor was there a lack of understanding of how the structures of the Dutch state and of the WIC and VOC prevented needed adaptation. Rather, elites maintained their unassailable power to protect their particular interests even at the cost of their collective futures. We now must see whether British and US elites built similar structural protections for their privileges, and analyze how those privileges shaped British and American responses to economic and geopolitical challenges.

1   De Vries and van der Woude, *The First Modern Economy*, 681–3; 't Hart, Jonker, and van Zanden, *A Financial History of the Netherlands*; Bas van Bavel, *The Invisible Hand? How Market Economies Have Emerged and Declined Since AD 500* (Oxford: Oxford University Press, 2016), chapter 4.

# 5

# Britain: Exceptional Reform

Britain began to create its empire during an era of heightened domestic elite conflict. It achieved hegemony after those conflicts were resolved in a stable structure of multiple elites. Britain was exceptional in the durability of its hegemony, which lasted from the late eighteenth to late nineteenth centuries,[1] and, above all, in its capacity to enact reforms that maintained British hegemony through the Industrial Revolution.

My goal in this chapter is to track and explain the chains of contingent change, propelled by elite conflicts and alliances, that first formed the British Empire, culminated in a century of British dominance, and then ended in the loss of that primacy decades before the achievement of US hegemony. This chapter proceeds chronologically. I begin by tracing elite conflict in Britain from the sixteenth to the seventeenth century and show how those conflicts produced a stable structure of multiple elites in the wake of the Civil War and the Glorious Revolution. I then explain how domestic elite structure shaped state policies and

---

1   Wallerstein ("Three Instances of Hegemony," 256) and Giovanni Arrighi (*Long Twentieth Century*, table 3.4) both identify a shorter span, 1815 to 1873, as the era of British hegemony, although Wallerstein elsewhere (*Modern World-System*, volume 2, xxiii) gives "from 1815 to 1848, perhaps a little longer" as the years of British hegemony. Michael Mann, defining hegemony by the "two-power standard" (*Sources of Social Power*, volume 2, 264), i.e., as possessing more than the next two powers, argues that while Britain was hegemonic in naval power throughout the nineteenth century, its economy never met that standard for hegemony, although it did achieve hegemony in manufacturing briefly between 1860 and 1880 and "entered diplomatic arrangements whereby Britain ceded Continental in return for naval global dominance" (265). Modelski, *Long Cycles in World Politics*, as we noted in chapter 1, argued that Britain achieved hegemony twice, with an era of decline dividing its eighteenth- and nineteenth-century peaks. I will try to justify my longer time span as more accurate in the body of this chapter.

capacities and the forms of British colonialism and trade during the "First Empire,"[1] the period from the conquest and settlement of Britain's first colonies up through the American Revolution and Napoleonic Wars. I contrast the distinct dynamics of the settler and dependent colonies and their varying effects on British political economy.

This chapter then focuses on the era of British hegemony in the nineteenth century. I identify the colonial elites of Britain's "Second Empire," the period from the end of the Napoleonic Wars until World War I, and analyze their interactions with existing domestic elites and with the rising financial elite. Following the structural template presented in table 1.2, I specify the degree of colonial elites' autonomy from metropolitan officials, and colonial elites' influence over Britain's domestic economy and politics. As I suggested in chapter 1, we will see a sharp contrast between the pattern of Britain's settler colonies and that of India and the other dependent colonies.

British historians, most famously Cain and Hopkins, found that the landed elite and City financiers maintained a close alliance throughout the nineteenth century, and argue those ties shaped and stabilized British imperial policy. Cain and Hopkins's interpretation remains dominant, but they do not explain why that alliance endured.[2] As a result, they are unable to explain what forces, domestic or from colonial elites, ultimately disrupted that alliance or made it less effective for sustaining British dominance. That lacuna in their analysis, in turn, undermines efforts to explain the decline of British hegemony.

--------

1   My periodization of a first and second empire follows those of John Darwin, "A Third British Empire? The Dominion Idea in Imperial Politics," in *The Oxford History of the British Empire, Volume IV: The Twentieth Century*, ed. Judith M. Brown (Oxford: Oxford University Press, 1999), and Lance E. Davis and Robert A. Huttenback, *Mammon and the Pursuit of Empire: The Political Economy of British Imperialism, 1860–1912* (Cambridge: Cambridge University Press, 1986). Darwin also describes what he characterizes as a largely unsucessful effort to reconstitute a third British Empire in the interwar years.

2   I am grateful to Vivek Chibber for pointing out the strengths and limitations of Cain and Hopkins's work. See also Martin Daunton, "Creating Legitimacy: Administering Taxation in Britain, 1815–1914," in *Paying for the Liberal State: The Rise of Public Finance in Nineteenth-Century Europe*, eds. José Luís Cardoso and Pedro Lains (Cambridge: Cambridge University Press, 2010) for an excellent review and critique of various authors who make this sort of argument.

As we will see, most existing work attributes British decline to the *dei ex machina* of imperial overexpansion, the rise of US or German economic power, or the costs of World War I.

My focus on the dynamics of domestic and imperial elite relations provides the basis, in the last sections of this chapter, to explain both Britain's uniquely long hegemony and its demise in the last decades of the nineteenth century, well before the United States or Germany became significant rivals, before Britain was weighed down with the costs of World War I, and before the world wars "emboldened demobilized soldiers who joined teachers, lawyers, trade unionists, and civil servants to form nationalist movements in the colonies" that unraveled the British Empire.[1]

Elite analysis will also allow us to understand the sources of the "financialization" of the British metropolitan and imperial economy, and to identify the ways in which finance, and the political power of financiers, contributed to and then undermined British hegemony. This chapter, and indeed this book, can be read as an effort to understand the central role of politics in the rise and demise of empires and hegemons. In so doing, we are taking up Arrighi's invitation, which he attributes to Braudel, to "follow the possessor of money into another hidden abode, where admittance is only on business but which is one floor above, rather than one floor below the marketplace. Here, the possessor of money meets the possessor, not of labor-power, but of political power."[2] We will find that it is the interactions among elites, inhabiting different institutions and wielding different forms of power, that creates the geopolitical and capitalist dynamic that made Britain dominant and then undid its hegemony.

## FROM FEUDALISM TO CAPITALISM AND COLONIALISM

England prior to the Reformation was characterized by a tripartite elite structure. Kings, lay landlords, and the clergy each controlled manors at the local level, while the crown and church also controlled

---

1   Mann, *Sources of Social Power*, volume 3, 55.
2   Arrighi, *Long Twentieth Century*, 26.

judicial systems that regulated land tenure on all manors. All three elites had the capacity to extract revenues and labor from peasants. Both kings and lay landlords wielded armed force, while the clergy was linked to the transnational Catholic Church.[1] Relations among elites, and with peasants, changed little over centuries of feudalism, justifying Weber's description of it as "a chronic condition."[2]

The Reformation almost entirely eliminated the Catholic Church as a distinct institution in England. Yet the Henrician Reformation did not simply allow the tiny royal government to absorb all the Catholic clergy's powers and properties. The crown, with only a few dozen officials directly under its control, had used clerics to carry out administrative functions. With the elimination of much of the clergy and (often justified) doubts about the loyalty of the remainder, the crown, already dependent on nobles to collect taxes and provide armed men, was forced to collaborate with lay landlords in expropriating the property and powers of the Catholic Church. Most monastic properties, and also benefices (the right to appoint ministers) and clerical rights to collect tithes, ended up in the hands of the lay elite. This transformed the previous tripartite elite structure of crown, lay landlords, and clerics into a dual elite structure in which the crown was unchallenged at the national level while the gentry gained full control over land, peasant labor, and county and local politics. Henry VIII and his successors were able to use their national-level hegemony to break the military and political power of the landed magnates, creating a monopoly on the legitimate use of armed force in England and later in all of Britain. In this way, the English dual elite structure diverged from that of Spain, which we discussed in chapter 3. The Reformation gave the English crown the resources to break the magnates and devolve landlord power down to the local level, in contrast to Spain, where the lack of a Reformation meant that the Habsburgs had to reach a settlement with each province's aristocracy as a bloc (a bloc that in most provinces was controlled from the

1  For a fuller analysis of the dynamics of feudalism and the sources for my argument about the consequences of the Reformation, see Lachmann, *Capitalists in Spite of Themselves*, chapters 2 and 4.

2  Max Weber, *Economy and Society*, eds. Guenther Roth and Claus Wittich (Berkeley and Los Angeles: University of California Press, [1922] 1978), 1086.

top by magnates), foreclosing the possibility of challenging the greatest Spanish nobles.

English kings, despite their safety from national-level military or political challenges, were never able to escape from their dependence upon lay landlords. Monarchs lacked the resources to create a bureaucracy, since they had alienated most of the seized monastic properties to meet war expenses or to buy the loyalty of lay elites, and had to win parliamentary approval for taxes. Kings therefore continued to rely on largely unpaid local officeholders who served their own private interests and were controlled by county political blocs. Unable to play clergy and laity against one another in Parliament after most clerics were purged from their seats, the crown found it increasingly hard to control the county blocs, which by the eighteenth century had coalesced into two national parties. The fiscal crisis brought on by Charles I's eleven-year attempt (1629–40) to rule without calling Parliament, and the outcomes of the Civil War (1642–51) and the Glorious Revolution (1688), demonstrated the limits of royal power and kings' narrow room for autonomous action. All royal initiatives, whether to increase taxes, pass legislation, or fight wars, required consent from the Members of Parliament who represented the interests of the dominant elite of county-based landowners and later also of merchants organized into guilds and chartered companies and represented through city governments.

At the same time as relations between the crown and landowners were restructured in the aftermath of the Henrician Reformation, the crown lost control over an ever larger and more prosperous faction of merchants who then allied with the landed elite that benefited from the Reformation and emerged victorious in the Civil War. Let us examine how sixteenth- and seventeenth-century elite conflicts affected the crown's ability to control traders and colonial elites and settlers.

Robert Brenner, in his massive and magnificent study *Merchants and Revolution*,[1] finds that there were three largely distinct groups of

---

1   Robert Brenner, *Merchants and Revolution: Commercial Change, Political Conflict, and London's Overseas Traders, 1550–1653* (Princeton: Princeton University Press, 1993).

merchants in seventeenth-century England: (1) the Merchant Adventurers, (2) the traders of the Levant, East India, Russia, and other chartered companies, and (3) the colonial interloper merchants. The first two groups waxed and waned relative to each other as the crown traded favors for revenues from increased customs duties and for political support during the Civil War and then after the Restoration. At the same time, both groups were buffeted by transnational economic forces: The Merchant Adventurers were harmed by declining continental European demand for the cloths that they exported, while the rapidly growing home market for imported luxuries delivered great wealth to the investors in the geographically defined trading companies. Nevertheless, the Merchant Adventurers and Levant–East India traders both benefited from royal efforts to shield them from competition. The crown eliminated foreign cloth merchants from England, ensuring that the Merchant Adventurers would be able to monopolize a shrinking market; in that way foreigners, not English investors, bore the brunt of declining demand for cloth. The company traders benefited from royal monopolies that restricted entrants into their markets and, as Brenner emphasizes, from the even more important royal prohibition of artisans and retailers from foreign trade. This latter limit ensured that traders could demand a uniform and high markup on imported goods, preventing domestic merchants and retailers from undercutting their prices.

Brenner certainly demonstrates that the Merchant Adventurers and Levant–East India traders' profits were politically derived from royal concessions. While the crown repeatedly demanded increased customs duties in return for those concessions, and at times (especially in 1624–25) alienated the company merchants with unprecedented demands or outrageous antics, the two groups of chartered merchants remained dependent on the crown for their livelihoods.

The third group of merchants, the colonial interlopers, was quite different. They were excluded from the great chartered companies because of the double handicap of limited capital and unimpressive social origins. Most were sons of lesser gentry, shopkeepers and manufacturers in London, or involved as ship captains or traders with the American colonies. For a time, in the early seventeenth century, the traders involved with the Americas were able to operate with little interference from the chartered merchants. Trade with the Americas depended upon the establishment and growth of permanent colonies, which, in turn, required the long-term investment of capital. The great merchants and landed elite had safer and quicker opportunities for profitable investment in eastern trade and by improving landed estates at home. American plantations were built by the lesser strata who became rich by selling provisions and slaves to American settlers and importing American tobacco and furs to Britain.

Only this third group of merchants was capitalist in Marxist terms or even in Weber's sense of economically oriented capitalism. Their prosperity depended upon the free import of American products to Britain outside the monopoly system of the chartered companies. These colonial merchants also desired government help in excluding foreign traders, especially the Dutch, and in forcing the colonial settlers to buy only British provisions. Of course, slaves were vital to the "triangular trade" with the colonies and provided the labor for tobacco, and later sugar and cotton, plantations.

The colonial merchants were unable to get Stuart monarchs to defend their interests against the established merchants, or even against foreign rivals. Later, when colonial shippers became interlopers in the East India trade, the crown attempted, albeit with little effect, to guard the East India Company's monopoly. The colonial interloper merchants did receive a more sympathetic hearing from Parliament. A majority in Parliament represented interests opposed to the company merchants: the outports that had been decimated by the chartered merchants' centralization of trade in London, and manufacturers and growers, especially of wool, who sought wider markets for their products than were provided by the merchant adventurers and chartered companies. The colonial-interloper merchants were also linked by business and ideological ties to the subset of great landlords who invested in and guided the Puritan colonies in the Americas.

The business and political links between colonial-interloper merchants and great Puritan landlords with American interests endured from the 1620s through all the conflicts of the 1640s. Indeed, they are central to Brenner's analysis of the Civil War. His study of merchants allows him to explain why the colonial interlopers were stalwarts of the parliamentary cause (their economic interests depended upon defeat of the crown and a reversal of royal commercial and foreign policies), and why the company merchants generally were spurned by Parliament even though the crown's inconsistent and exploitative relations with its chartered merchants gave those merchants reasons to join the opposition (company merchants demanded policies that were costly to important parliamentary constituencies, leading Parliament to reject the basis upon which company merchants could have split from the crown and forcing those merchants back into the arms of a monarch who cared about them only as pliable sources of revenue). In any case, long-standing business, political, religious, and personal ties between Puritan colonizing landowners and the colonial interloper merchants gave the landowner-parliamentarians confidence in 1641 that they could rely upon and control the London popular forces whom the colonial interloper merchants mobilized against the crown. This alliance was further reinforced because the landowners and capitalist merchants (though not the popular forces, which were increasingly marginalized after they had served their purpose and helped Parliament win the Civil War) had a common interest in an anti-Catholic militaristic foreign policy and a shared desire for state stimulation of foreign trade and the domestic economy. Both elites demanded a Presbyterian or an independent religious settlement that would guard landowners and merchants' control over former church properties and over the ministers in their congregations.

The elites who won the Civil War and dominated the Rump Parliament of 1648–53 rewarded their colonial interloper merchant allies. The Rump created a permanent blue-water British navy, which ensured consistent and more effective protection for merchants' foreign investments than had the privateers the crown previously used for that purpose, although privateers continued to be allowed to harass Dutch ships and those of other enemy countries.[1] The Commonwealth adopted an aggressive foreign policy designed to seize Portuguese and Dutch colonies in the Americas and to roll back rival European powers' control

---

1  John Brewer, *The Sinews of Power: War, Money and the English State, 1688–1783* (New York: Knopf, 1989), 10–12.

over transatlantic trade routes. Parliament accommodated merchants' desires and created free trade zones that allowed for the reexport of goods without duties that would have eaten into or eliminated Britons' competitive edge over Dutch and other commercial rivals. The Rump established the Commission of Trade, which provided permanent support for free trade ports. While Parliament reauthorized the East India Company's charter, it gave interloper merchants control over the EIC's board. The 1651 and subsequent Navigation Acts required all British and colonial goods to be carried on British ships, freezing out the Dutch merchant fleet and tying the colonies tightly to merchants based in Britain.[1] These policies all continued even after the Restoration, except that Charles II and James II sought to ally with Catholic France. However, while the religious aspects of that alliance were repulsive to interloper merchants, France posed less of an economic threat to merchant interests in Europe or the Americas than did the Dutch.

The alliance of landed and financial elites, which Cain and Hopkins[2] argue endured from the Glorious Revolution of 1688 until World War I, was an artifact of the contingent series of elite conflicts outlined above. The elimination of the clergy as a national elite, and the crown's consequent inability to reach down to the local level, left locally based elites in firm control of each county and town government. Crown weakness allowed interloper merchants to take advantage of openings in the world economy and in Britain's growing empire. Landowners and interloper merchants allied to defeat the crown and its chartered company supporters in the Civil War. We will trace the shifts in the makeup and interests of this enduring alliance in the rest of this chapter. However, the alliance itself was formed in response both to crown threats and to the contingent opportunities first created by the Henrician Reformation. The British state then became, and remained into the twentieth century, an amalgam of elites, each with its own institutional base for wielding economic and political power, and with strong ideological legitimacy.

--------

1   Brenner, *Merchants and Revolution*, chapter 12; H. V. Bowen, *Elites, Enterprise and the Making of the British Overseas Empire 1688–1775* (Houndmills: Macmillan, 1996), 32–6.
2   P. J. Cain and A. G. Hopkins, *British Imperialism: Innovation and Expansion 1688–1914* (London: Longman, 1993).

DOMESTIC STABILITY AND IMPERIAL DYNAMICS, 1688–1815

The resolution of the conflicts between the crown and the landed elite and among different sorts of merchants shaped British imperialism in three ways. First, as we noted above, the victors of the Glorious Revolution recast British foreign policy and set in train dynamics that (often unintentionally) created constituencies for that new imperialist policy. Second, the dominant landed and commercial elites increased state administrative and military capacity to realize their foreign policy aims. Third, the political gains by colonial interloper merchants and the Puritan landlords who had invested, financially and ideologically, in the North American colonies in essence served to institutionalize a bifurcated empire in the century after the Glorious Revolution. Let us examine each of these consequences in turn and see how imperial goals, capacities, and structure affected one another in the long century from the Glorious Revolution to the end of the Napoleonic Wars.

*i. Foreign Policy Goals and Their Supporters*
The British crown, like monarchs elsewhere in Europe, sought to play and win the great power game. Britain was handicapped in this pursuit by its relatively small population and, until the eighteenth century, its relatively weak fiscal capacity.[1] Britain's location at the periphery of the Continent protected it from frequent invasions, even as it at times sent armed forces onto the Continent. Monarchs and/or parliaments varied in the efforts they made to gain territory within Europe or take colonies elsewhere in the world. As we saw in chapters 3 and 4, the Habsburgs, French kings, and the Dutch stadtholder in collaboration with States General and the assemblies of the seven United Provinces selected foreign policy goals opportunistically, based on where they had realistic opportunities to add to their home territories or to accrue colonies, and defensively, in response to attacks from rival powers. However, when multiple opportunities opened up, rulers were constrained by the interests of domestic elites, who in the sixteenth through eighteenth centuries still provided the armed men and

---

1   See tables 2.1 and 2.2.

resources for war. Rulers thus selected military targets that met domestic elites' interests in and capacities for procuring trade routes or new landed domains in border regions, further afield in Europe, or in the rest of the world. Once colonies were taken, the elites who controlled them became a new lobby for and constraint on rulers' foreign policy objectives. We saw how interactions between rulers and a varying number of elites produced foreign policies in Spain, France, and the Netherlands in the previous two chapters. Now we will conduct the same analysis for Britain, beginning in this section by showing how the outcome of the Civil War and the Glorious Revolution combined with Britain's initial colonial conquests to transform foreign policy.

Tudor and Stuart rulers went to war to (1) maintain or expand a territorial presence on the Continent, (2) to block rival powers from interfering in crown efforts to gain control of Scotland and Ireland, and (3) to take and hold trade routes and colonies beyond Europe. They pursued those objectives at times in alliance with Catholic monarchs, and even allied with Catholics against Huguenots (French Protestants) and Protestant Netherlands. The first two objectives took precedence in crown decisions of where to fight and with whom to ally over non-European goals. Those priorities reflected the high degree of pre–Civil War royal autonomy in war making that was made possible by the Henrician Reformation, which provided a source of revenues (the sale of former monastic properties) beyond Parliamentary control, and furthered by the crown and great nobles' joint interests in and capacities for procuring lands in nearby Scotland and Ireland. Merchants and lesser landowners lacked the weight in Parliament to demand that foreign policy respond to their interests in long-distance trade and colonial acquisitions. Favored merchants, as we saw above, were able to procure charters allowing them to mobilize resources to act on their own in the Americas or in Asia. The crown's failure to suppress interloper merchants was a sign of the crown's inability or unwillingness to commit significant resources far from England.

Once monastic lands had been sold off, the crown's freedom to commit the state to war was restricted, a limit confirmed by the outcome of the Civil War. Thereafter, any British war had to be funded, and therefore supported, by Parliament. Britain continued to involve itself in continental wars in the period from the Civil War to Waterloo. However, the interests Parliament sought to protect when they funded those wars changed from those that animated the Tudors and Stuarts. England had finally lost all of its French holdings in 1559. Thereafter, English nobles were unwilling to fight to regain those properties or for any other continental lands. Landlords looking for new profitable domains had easier pickings in Ireland and in the new American and Asian colonies. In the subsequent centuries, the only continental lands Britain secured were Gibraltar and Menorca in 1714, and those tiny properties were taken and were of value only to guard British naval and trade access to the Mediterranean.

Scotland and Ireland remained a focus of English wars in the seventeenth century. The Commonwealth solidified England's military and economic position in Scotland and Ireland. England successfully fought off French efforts to interfere in those lands and to disrupt William of Orange's claim to the English throne, a result confirmed in the Nine Years' War (1688–97, aka the War of the League of Augsburg), and guaranteed French non-interference in the 1697 Treaty of Ryswick that ended the war. Thereafter, except for a small and unsuccessful French effort to intervene in the 1798 Irish Rebellion, Britain was secure from external attack.

Britain's safety from invasion and its lack of territorial ambitions on the continent allowed it to pioneer a new method for influencing the balance of power in Europe, in which it remained interested. Britain used its growing fiscal resources to pay for mercenaries who fought under British commanders and subsidized allied armies in various continental wars,[1] intervening with its own forces infrequently and often only at the climax of a war, once the other combatants had exhausted themselves.[2] Britain had fewer than 200,000 personnel in its army and navy during the Nine Years' War, War of the Spanish Succession, War of the Austrian Succession, Seven Years' War, and

---

1  Kennedy, *Rise and Fall of the Great Powers*, 124–31.
2  Mann, *Sources of Social Power*, volume 2, 276; Wallerstein, "Three Instances of Hegemony," 257–8; David Chandler, "The Great Captain-General 1702–1714," in *The Oxford History of the British Army*, eds. David Chandler and Ian Beckett (Oxford: Oxford University Press, 1994), 67–91; Alan Guy, "The Army of the Georges 1714–1783," in *The Oxford History of the British Army*, 92–111.

American War.[1] In 1709, at the height of the War of the Spanish Succession, foreign troops "accounted for 81,000 out of 150,000 in the field."[2] After each war, the British army was largely demobilized. "The regular army expanded in the course of the French Revolutionary and Napoleonic Wars from some 40,000 in 1793 to a peak of over 250,000 personnel in 1813 [plus] 140,000" in the navy.[3]

British spending on wars increased 62 percent in real terms, controlling for inflation, through the eighteenth century, from an average of £3.64 million per annum in the Nine Years' War of 1689–97 to £12.15 million per annum during the American War of 1775–84, and then exploded during the Napoleonic Wars to £55.1 million per annum, a real increase of 250 percent since the American War.[4] However, the major change in the 1688–1815 era was that Britain committed armed forces and funds to military ventures beyond Europe. As we saw in table 2B, Britain seized vast lands in the Americas and Asia, and smaller holdings in Africa from the non-Europeans who lived there, and then in the late seventeenth and eighteenth centuries from other European powers. This was partly opportunism, a way Britain could strike a blow against rival powers at a much cheaper cost than was needed to win victories on the Continent. However, increasingly, the focus on colonies reflected the interests of domestic elites who aspired to attain or increase the size or number of their colonial plantations and concessions, or who sought protection for the trade routes they used. As with the Americas and India, interloper merchants successfully used their influence in Parliament to challenge the charter company monopolies in Africa, winning legal recognition for their position in 1697.[5]

----

1    Brewer, *Sinews of Power*, 30.

2    David Chandler, "The Army in Marlborough's Day," in *History of the British Army*, eds. Peter Young and J. P. Lawford (New York: Putnam, 1970), 25–32.

3    David Gates, "The Transformation of the Army 1783–1815," in *The Oxford History of the British Army*, 132.

4    Brewer, *Sinews of Power*, 30; Patrick K. O'Brien, "The Impact of the Revolutionary and Napoleonic Wars, 1793–1815 on the Long-Run Growth of the British Economy," *Review* 12 (1989), 341; inflation index from Allen, "Great Divergence in European Wages and Prices," table 4.

5    William Robert Scott, *The Constitution and Finance of English, Scottish, and Irish Joint-Stock Companies to 1720. Volume 2: Companies for Foreign Trade, Colonization, Fishing and Mining* (Bristol: Thoemmes, [1910–12] 1993), 22–3.

As Britain took more territories beyond Europe, the British economy became increasingly reliant on trade with colonies and informal dependencies for growth. British overseas trade quadrupled from 1759 to 1790 and then doubled again in the 1790s.[1] "[B]etween 1700 and 1773 the trade to America and Africa multiplied 7.75 times while that to continental Europe increase only 1.13 times."[2] By 1772–74, the share of British exports to North America exceeded those to Europe,[3] and were double the value of Asia and the Near East by 1785. North America was also, by far, the biggest source of Britain's trade surpluses in that century.[4] Legislation ensured that the benefits from this growing market would accrue to British elites. The Navigation Acts served to create a huge British merchant marine and made sterling the sole currency of a vast market.[5]

The growing British economy and empire created openings for new groups of merchants and for settlers, investors, administrators, and soldiers in the colonies. Following the 1707 Act of Union, Scots, Welsh, and Irish became increasingly active and prominent in London trade and finance, as did foreigners. "By 1763 around three-quarters of London's merchants were of foreign origin or descent."[6] The Whig politicians who dominated London city government in the eighteenth century were largely dissenters. Huguenots, Jews, and Dutch moved into Anglo-Dutch trade in the early eighteenth century, allowing (or forcing) English merchants to shift capital from the North Sea to the Atlantic trade.

British imperialism created opportunities for non-English Britons, religious dissenters, and immigrants to prosper and to build economic and political links with each other and with English elites. Increasingly,

---

1   Stanley Chapman, *Merchant Enterprise in Britain* (Cambridge: Cambridge University Press, 1992), table 1.7; Javier Cuenca Esteban, "Comparative Patterns of Colonial Trade: Britain and Its Rivals," in *Exceptionalism and Industrialisation: Britain and Its European Rivals, 1688–1815*, ed. Leandro Prados de la Escosura (Cambridge: Cambridge University Press, 2004).

2   Chapman, *Merchant Enterprise in Britain*, 5.

3   Bowen, *Elites, Enterprise and the Making of the British Overseas Empire*, 34.

4   Chapman, *Merchant Enterprise in Britain*, 6.

5   Bowen, *Elites, Enterprise and the Making of the British Overseas Empire*, 32–6.

6   Ibid., 150.

it was Scots, Irish, and Welsh rather than English who settled in the colonies and who staffed government, military, and EIC offices abroad. Scots were a plurality of immigrants to North America and Caribbean colonies in the first half of the eighteenth century and were dispropor-tionately represented among colonial officials both in London and abroad. This created another basis for ties between metropole and colonies and between merchants and settlers. Dissenter merchants linked their churches at home with brethren in colonies, such as the Quakers in Pennsylvania.[1] A third of merchants in eighteenth-century Britain were foreigners: Huguenots, Jews, (mainly from Portugal), and Dutch, although some of the Dutch may have been returning Dissenters or descendants of English exiles.[2]

Rich Britons, and over the course of the eighteenth century a growing fraction of the middle class, had direct or indirect invest-ments in the Americas and India and/or had family members who had settled in the colonies.[3] The amount of capital needed to enter trade fell through the eighteenth century, bottoming out at £3–4,000 before inflation at the end of the century raised that to £10,000.[4] Settler colonies became sites for highly profitable investments by British merchants, nobles, and gentry landowners looking for places to deploy their surplus capital, and by financiers who loaned money (both theirs and funds from the landed elite) to settlers in North American colo-nies and the owners of Caribbean slave plantations and to the merchants who traded with both.[5]

Joint ventures and shared interests in the colonies linked once-sep-arate elites, building on the ties between colonial interloper merchants and Puritan landlords identified by Brenner. Military officers, who often were younger sons of the gentry or great aristocrats,[6] served in

---

1    Ibid., 149–70.

2    Chapman, *Merchant Enterprise in Britain*, 30.

3    Cain and Hopkins, *British Imperialism*, 84–104; Bowen, *Elites, Enterprise and the Making of the British Overseas Empire*, 79–100, 108–10.

4    Chapman, *Merchant Enterprise in Britain*, 26.

5    Bowen, *Elites, Enterprise and the Making of the British Overseas Empire*, 47–78.

6    N. A. M. Rodger, *The Wooden World: An Anatomy of the Georgian Navy* (New York: Norton, 1986), 252–72; Brewer, *Sinews of Power*; Gwyn Harries-Jenkins, *The Army in Victorian Society* (London: Routledge & Kegan Paul, 1977).

the American colonies and were given land grants at the end of their terms of service to encourage them to remain in America,[1] turning those retired military men into bridges between the British landed families of their origin, the merchants who financed their American enterprises, and the merchants with whom they did business. There was also intermarriage between North America and Caribbean settlers and the (usually younger) children of landowners and merchants in Britain.[2]

The links forged by commerce and colonial settlement between old and newly expanding elites had the effect of unifying elites throughout Great Britain around an aggressive colonial policy. Interests and policies reinforced each other. As foreign policy increasingly focused on colonies, more and more Britons were able to invest or live in the empire, and they then provided ever more political support for a foreign policy that protected their interests.

## ii. State Capacity

The desires by various elites for an aggressive foreign policy, and for measures that fostered and protected commerce and private investments abroad, depended on a state with the capacity to project military power and to administer the Empire's growing territories. The alliance among landed and commercial elites that was institutionalized and confirmed in the Glorious Revolution enhanced the ability of Parliament to act through the state administration to limit self-serving behavior by individual elites both in the metropolitan state and in the colonies, increasing state capacity in the fiscal, administrative, and military realms.

Revenue is the first measure of state capacity. As we saw in chapter 2, British revenue rose dramatically following the Glorious Revolution, up 257 percent from the 1670s to the 1720s, 1,972 percent from the 1670s to the 1790s, and another 86 percent from the 1790s to 1815, the peak year of the Napoleonic Wars. This is even greater than the increase in the Netherlands, which was 1,110 percent from the 1580s

---

1   Bowen, *Elites, Enterprise and the Making of the British Overseas Empire,* 39–44.
2   Ibid., 108–10.

to the 1670s, at which point it remained stagnant until the Netherlands were absorbed into Napoleon's empire in 1806. The comparison is even more favorable to Britain on a per capita basis. British revenue increased 2,300 percent per capita from the 1600s to 1805, while per capita Dutch revenue was up 292 percent in those same two centuries.[1]

Governmental tax revenues rose from 3–4 percent of national income under James II (1685–88) right before the Glorious Revolution to 9 percent in 1715.[2] In another calculation, O'Brien shows that taxes collected as a share of national income was 6.7 percent in 1693–97, stayed in a range of 9.1–11.7 percent from 1703 to 1782, and then jumped to 18.2 percent in 1812–15.[3] Since the poor in England, and almost everyone in Ireland and Scotland, paid little tax, that meant that for the remaining population of England the effective tax rate rose from 15 percent in 1700 to 30 percent in 1810.[4]

Britain's increasing revenue was a political as well as a bureaucratic achievement. Not only did the state figure out how to collect taxes, it also adopted policies that minimized opposition to the growing tax burden. First, because the British state was able to borrow as much as it needed at rates that declined over the course of the eighteenth century, from 8 percent in 1710 to 3 percent by 1735, the state was able to greatly reduce the need for short-term tax increases during wartimes. This eliminated the opposition that had been created in earlier centuries and was still evoked in other countries by sudden and sharp increases in the tax burden. Interest rates popped up to 5 percent in the early 1780s, then fell below 4 percent and again briefly rose to over 6 percent in the mid-1790s before the imposition of an income

---

1  Data from tables 2.1 and 2.2.

2  Patrick K. O'Brien, "Inseparable Connections: Trade, Economy, Fiscal State, and the Expansion of Empire, 1688–1815," in *The Oxford History of the British Empire, Volume II: The Eighteenth Century*, ed. P. J. Marshall (Oxford: Oxford University Press, 1998), 64.

3  O'Brien, "Impact of the Revolutionary and Napoleonic Wars," 342.

4  Patrick K. O'Brien, "The Political Economy of British Taxation, 1660–1815," *Economic History Review* 41, no. 1, new series (1988): 6; Mann, *Sources of Social Power*, volume 2, table 11.3 calculates that central government expenditure was 27–31 percent of national income in 1810, but if local government is included it climbs to a range of 37–43 percent of national income.

tax lifted government revenues and caused rates to fall back below 4 percent.[1] In addition, eighteenth-century governments tolerated tax avoidance by Scots and Irish (unlike their error of trying to tax American colonists).

> Realistically, ministers also chose to ignore demands for reform to the anomalous valuations of land and other types of wealth assessed for taxation in different counties[2] [and] Compassion, or perhaps a prudent anticipation of potential outbreak of disorder, restrained Chancellors from pushing the incidence of indirect taxes too far in a blatantly inequitable direction.[3]

Public debt became increasingly widely held and made up a growing fraction of the income and assets of the wealthy and then of the middle class.[4] Britons either held government bonds directly or invested in joint stock companies that then "loaned the money to the government. The companies received interest on their loans and paid this to shareholders in the form of dividends."[5] This gave the growing number of bondholders an interest in the government's ability to collect enough taxes to repay the loans, or at least to pay interest on the loans. As we will see below, direct and indirect bondholders became a lobby for restraint in government spending in the nineteenth century, but in the 1689–1815 period they expressed their interests as bondholders by supporting parliamentary primacy in fiscal and budgetary matters. David Stasavage[6] finds that bondholders

---

1   Homer and Sylla, *History of Interest Rates*, 152–8.

2   Eighteenth-century British officials' political wisdom was not shared by California politicians in the 1960s, whose scheme to reassess properties to equalize valuations sparked a tax revolt that culminated in 1978 with Proposition 13, which reduced property taxes in California and served as a model for similar efforts in other states and by Reagan and later Republicans at the national level. Isaac Martin, *The Permanent Tax Revolt: How the Property Tax Transformed American Politics* (Stanford: Stanford University Press, 2008).

3   O'Brien, "Inseparable Connections," 68, 69, and passim.

4   Bowen, *Elites, Enterprise and the Making of the British Overseas Empire*, 79–100.

5   Carruthers, *City of Capital*, 87 and passim.

6   David Stasavage, *Public Debt and the Birth of the Democratic State: France and Great Britain, 1688–1789* (Cambridge: Cambridge University Press, 2003).

were crucial allies of the Whig Party, providing votes to keep or bring the Whigs to power in return for Whig commitments to pay bond interest. Interest rates went up when Conservatives won parliamentary elections in the 1689–1815 period.

Political considerations also shaped the extent to which tax collection was bureaucratized. The level of bureaucracy varied among the types of taxes and reflected British governments' pragmatic decisions to respect elite power and to avoid provoking opposition. Parliament either exempted or set low excise rates on "many of the rapidly growing sectors of industry, transportation, internal distribution and finance."[1] For items on which Parliament did agree to impose an excise, the revenues were collected by Commissioners of Excise who ran an efficient, bureaucratized department, staffed with officials recruited from the lower middle class who were hired and promoted on merit, trained on the job, and paid good salaries and pensions.[2] The customs agency was less professionalized, and smugglers cut into tariff revenues until the Napoleonic Wars, when increased navy patrols of the waters around Britain and the government's determination to raise revenues led to dramatic increases in customs in both absolute and relative terms, rising from 24 percent of governmental revenues in 1785 to 35 percent by 1805.[3]

The land tax remained low throughout the eighteenth century, and even during the Napoleonic Wars.[4] Volunteer officials, drawn from the landed elite, collected it. Continuing a medieval practice, these officials ensured that their own lands paid virtually no tax. Taxes on the rich increased and became significant only when an income tax was imposed in 1799 during the Napoleonic Wars at a moment when bond prices were falling in response to fears of a default, and soldiers and sailors mutinied to demand the money that they were owed and the government lacked the funds to pay.[5]

Even more important than the revenue total, which remained less than that of the Netherlands and Spain until the 1720s, and less than

1   O'Brien, "Political Economy of British Taxation," 16 and passim.
2   Ibid., 28; Brewer, *Sinews of Power*, 64–85.
3   O'Brien, "Political Economy of British Taxation," 9.
4   Brewer, *Sinews of Power*, 88–134.
5   O'Brien, "Political Economy of British Taxation," 17–28.

France until the last years of the Napoleonic Wars, was the fact that Parliament gained full control over the national budget after the Glorious Revolution: During the Tudor and early Stuart era, 75 percent of revenues were not under parliamentary control since they came from crown lands, profits from the royal mint, and sales of monastic lands. After the Glorious Revolution, such non-parliamentary revenues were only 3 percent of the state budget;[1] the rest were taxes and customs duties voted by and therefore controlled by Parliament. The Triennial Act of 1694 guaranteed that Parliament would meet annually (with elections at least every three years), preventing the king from ruling on his own. That act, combined with precisely written annual appropriation bills that spelled out in detail how state revenues would be spent,[2] ensured that control over state funds passed permanently into parliamentary hands.

The growing number of revenue officials, which increased 295 percent for all fiscal departments and 405 percent for the excise commission from 1690 to 1782,[3] became increasingly professionalized and invulnerable to royal and partisan political pressure as they carried out their duties (even as the policies they were hired to enforce continued to be set politically). During the eighteenth century, tax collection was by far the largest and most bureaucratized branch of government: "By 1782 there were almost 8,300 full-time tax collection employees . . . The Board of Trade had only 122 employees in 1782," and other departments were even smaller.[4]

The professional tax bureaucracy replaced tax farmers. The customs tax farm was abolished in 1671, the excise farm in 1683, and the hearth tax farm in 1684; none were ever revived.[5] By the early eighteenth century, tax and other administrative officials were no longer dismissed when parliamentary control shifted parties or when

---

1   Ron Harris, "Government and the Economy, 1688–1850," in *The Cambridge Economic History of Modern Britain, Volume 1: Industrialisation, 1700–1860*, eds. Roderick Floud and Paul Johnson (Cambridge: Cambridge University Press, 2004), 215.

2   Brenner, *Merchants and Revolution*, 709–16; Brewer, *Sinews of Power*, 137–61.

3   Brewer, *Sinews of Power*, 67.

4   Harris, "Government and the Economy," 207.

5   Brewer, *Sinews of Power*, 93.

new factions gained sway over the monarch, who in any case had ever less control over the "royal" government.[1] While many positions were filled through "influence," once those men took office they were part of a bureaucracy that limited their abilities to enrich themselves or to do favors for those who had arranged their appointments.

British military success outpaced state revenue growth, as we saw in chapter 2. Britain's outsized colonial gains, and its ability to defeat rival powers Spain, France, and the Netherlands when each of those three had larger budgets than that of Britain, were possible because Britain reformed its army and especially its navy sooner and more thoroughly than the other powers. The British army, and more so the navy, increasingly came under central control in the century after the Glorious Revolution. The navy had been largely private in the sixteenth century. "Only 34 of the 197 vessels which sailed in 1588 to stop the Armada were crown ships."[2] Private ships, as we saw with the navies of the VOC in chapter 4 and with French and Spanish ships in chapter 3, did not necessarily follow the orders or pursue the aims of commanders appointed by the crown, nor did they always even show up for battle. The same lack of coordination and commitment weakened the efficacy of private armies under noble control.[3]

Appropriations for the three naval wars against the Dutch in the seventeenth century served to build up the Royal Navy,[4] leading to a rapid decline in the number and significance of armed ships under private control, at the same time as the Navigation Acts funneled commercial demand to a growing British merchant marine and thereby built a constituency for a strong navy. In the eighteenth century, authority over the navy was centralized under the Admiralty Board. The board took control over and used a staff of professional officers to manage the hiring and promotion of personnel, the building of ships in naval yards owned and operated by the navy, and the purchase of food and supplies. By the time of the Seven Years' War, the British navy was the largest organization in Europe.[5]

---

1   Ibid., 64–85.
2   Ibid., 10–11.
3   Lachmann, "Mercenary, Citizen, Victim," 46.
4   Brewer, *Sinews of Power*, 10–12.
5   Rodger, *Wooden World*, 29–36.

The navy was better able than any other state military entity in seventeenth- and eighteenth-century Europe to assert and maintain its autonomy from outside interests. While private merchants got rich provisioning army bases and selling supplies to the navy,[1] the navy was able to keep the construction of ships under its own control. The navy in general and the yards in particular gained political leverage from the fact that the navy controlled ten parliamentary seats.[2]

The Admiralty kept control over promotions, ignoring recommendations from civilian politicians that would have weakened the navy's authority over its own officers and disrupted the "followings," the patronage networks that high officers created for themselves.[3] Officers built followings by recommending junior officers to the Admiralty for promotion. Senior officers ultimately advanced their careers, and put themselves in positions to have their promotion recommendations heeded, through military success (theirs and that of their followers), so they rarely risked picking well-connected but incompetent men for promotion.

Captains and admirals sought to be stationed abroad because empire widened opportunities for them to advance their careers in several ways. First, deaths and injuries in battle or from disease were more frequent abroad and created new openings and upward mobility for junior officers. Gentlemen in the navy were mainly younger sons who were willing to risk their lives (as they also were in the colonies) for the chance to get rich.[4] Second, ships captured in battle needed captains, so battle victories created new officer positions. Third, overseas commanders-in-chief were allowed to promote junior officers on their own, subject to the Admiralty's usually granted approval.[5] Thus, it was easier for a high-level officer to create a following while stationed abroad than it was back in Britain.

There were openings for corruption and abuse of trust in the navy, mainly because captains and crews that captured enemy ships got

---

1  Brewer, *Sinews of Power*, 206–10.
2  Rodger, *Wooden World*, 328–31.
3  Ibid., 331–43.
4  Ibid., 252–72.
5  Ibid., 273–303.

prize money (i.e., a share of the value of the ship and cargo seized). This had the potential to distort battle tactics as captains vied to chase enemy ships even if that was detrimental to overall victory in battle. That "tragedy of the commons" was solved through agreements among commanders to share prize money from a battle equally among all the ships involved. Captains also engaged in private deals to carry private specie or cargo on navy ships in return for payments to the captain. Some captains listed ghost employees, members of their family who did not sail and whose pay the captain could pocket. However, both sorts of private dealing were limited by Admiralty supervision and by the lure of promotion, which depended on military success that could be undermined by ships weighed down with private cargo or insufficient crews due to the diversion of pay to ghost employees. The Admiralty was more concerned with abuses that affected performance than with those that cost money,[1] and had the resources and autonomy to create long-term career incentives that oriented captains toward military success over private dealing.

The flow of influence went mainly from the navy to the civilian sector, as the Admirals who controlled the navy's parliamentary seats used that leverage, and their allocation of civilian contracts and decisions to protect shipping routes and colonial outposts, to win support from civilian politicians and interests. By insulating naval promotions from outside influence and allowing high officers to construct followings that gave them leverage over junior officers and their civilian families, the navy became a highly autonomous organization within the British state and empire. Naval autonomy made possible a highly meritocratic promotion system for officers. The navy was the only professional career that did not require a cash investment for education, as did the law and clergy, or to buy an office, as the army still did. Sailors on merchant ships needed to invest in the ship if they wanted to rise above the rank of mate.[2] Thus, the navy drew from the middle class and tradesmen, which widened the navy's talent pool and built support for the navy among Britons who either were voters or who had indirect influence on electors.

---

1   Ibid., 314–27.
2   Ibid., 252–72.

The army was less autonomous and less professionalized than the navy in the eighteenth century.[1] Nevertheless, significant reforms weakened the power of officers who had inherited or purchased their positions. A growing fraction of army officer vacancies were not filled by purchase, and even those who bought offices had to demonstrate competence. Proprietary soldiering, where officers were given an allotment to pay for troops and supplies, and therefore had an incentive to underpay troops and skimp on weaponry, was largely ended in the eighteenth century.[2] The Napoleonic Wars created a demand for many new officers to command the enlarged army. Many of those posts were sold to wealthy young men to raise revenue for war expenses, while commanders, most notably the Duke of York, sought to commission and promote officers on merit. The British army officer corps remained divided between rich dilettantes and professionals throughout the Napoleonic Wars.[3] In the half century from Waterloo to the end of the Crimean War, "officers continued to be drawn from a narrow segment of society, principally from the landed aristocracy and gentry, often from families with military traditions."[4] The purchase of commissions was abolished only in 1870.[5]

The growing efficiency of the Treasury and the navy cannot be understood merely or even largely as the working out of a Weberian logic of bureaucratic rationality. Those two organizations' capacities did not extend to other governmental entities, as we saw above. The land tax was collected inconsistently and corruptly in response to landowners' political powers and recognition of the dangers of provoking gentry anger in Scotland and Ireland. The army remained a bastion

---

1   William S. Maltby, "The Origins of a Global Strategy: England from 1558 to 1713," in *The Making of Strategy: Rulers, States, and War*, eds. Williamson Murray, MacGregor Knox, and Alvin Bernstein (Cambridge: Cambridge University Press, 1994).

2   Brewer, *Sinews of Power*, 10–12, 55–60; Harries-Jenkins, *Army in Victorian Society*.

3   Gates, "Transformation of the Army."

4   Peter Burroughs, "An Unreformed Army? 1815–1868," in *The Oxford History of the British Army*, 170.

5   Philip Warner, "Peacetime Economy and the Crimean War 1815–56," in *History of the British Army*.

of nepotism and amateurism for more than a century after those practices had been isolated and minimized in the navy.

The Treasury and the navy benefited from the political realignment produced by the Civil War and the Glorious Revolution. The landed and financial elites who emerged victorious from those conflicts created and sustained an alliance over the following centuries because each needed the other to gain policies and resources at the national level that they could not take for themselves without broader political support. Parliament became the primary locus of national power, the site at which property rights and political authority were allocated and protected, and the only institution through which elites could work out compromises on issues of national or foreign policy that they were not able to resolve unilaterally within counties or towns.

The dominant elites' shared interest in empire led them to grant immense resources to the navy and to allow that institution's leadership to undermine the vested privileges of narrow elites in order to fulfill its mission of protecting the broader elite's colonial and trade interests. Similarly, the relative weight of, and methods for collecting, tariffs, duties, and land taxes responded to a combination of national and local elites' weight in Parliament, capacity for tax resistance and avoidance at the local level, and ability to place the burden of each tax on non-elites. That complex political calculus yielded a bureaucratized Treasury to collect tariffs and duties and sustained an archaic land tax under the control of local landed elites.

### iii. A Bifurcated Empire

The political gains by colonial interloper merchants and the Puritan landlords who had invested, financially and ideologically, in the North American colonies in essence served to institutionalize a bifurcated empire in the century after the Glorious Revolution. The chartered companies, albeit with the addition of some interloper merchants, retained control over the expanding British domain in India, and over other Asian colonies and trading posts that Britain added to its portfolio in the eighteenth century.[1] In such "dependent colonies,"

--------------------------------

1   Bernard Porter, *Empire and Superempire: Britain, America and the World* (New Haven: Yale University Press, 2006), 17–22.

chartered companies bargained directly with the royal state and elites within Britain over the terms of their charters. Chartered companies were authorized by the state to use armed force to protect their colonial possessions and at times to seize new territories, although often companies undertook expansionist military ventures on their own initiative, most famously when the EIC bribed (mainly) and fought (slightly) its way to control over Bengal in 1757.[1] Companies' autonomy and share of the spoils extracted from colonies and from international trade waxed and waned as their relationship with British elites changed.[2] We will examine, in the section on India below, the trajectory of company-state relations and identify the elites who were spawned by and who benefited from the companies' presence in dependent colonies.

In contrast, "settler colonies," peopled with emigrants from Britain who exterminated the indigenous populations and, where profitable, brought in slaves from Africa, were increasingly run by the settlers themselves, even as they depended on royal armed force for protection from other colonial powers and for help in subduing and killing indigenous peoples.[3] No single British entity or elite was able to control any of the settler colonies and, as a result, those territories became increasingly open to trade and investment by English landlords and smaller interloper merchants.[4] The growing economic weakness and ultimate political defeat of the chartered company merchants in the Civil War eliminated the main advocates back in Britain for strong central control over the American colonies.[5] This left the interloper merchants as the main lobbyists on policy in the Americas. These

---

1   Bowen, *Elites, Enterprise and the Making of the British Overseas Empire*, 23–31; Bowen, "British India, 1765–1813: The Metropolitan Context," in *The Oxford History of the British Empire, Volume II*; Nicholas B. Dirks, *The Scandal of Empire: India and the Creation of Imperial Britain* (Cambridge: Harvard University Press, 2006).

2   C. A. Bayly, "The British Military-Fiscal State and Indigenous Resistance, India 1750–1820," in *An Imperial State at War: Britain from 1689 to 1815*, ed. Lawrence Stone (London: Routledge, 1994).

3   Bowen, *Elites, Enterprise and the Making of the British Overseas Empire*, 23–31.

4   Chapman, *Merchant Enterprise in Britain*, chapter 1.

5   Brenner, *Merchants and Revolution*, chapter 3.

merchants had relatively little capital to invest in creating American plantations. Thus, they came to favor giving land to settlers, who the merchants then could profit from by supplying inputs and exporting their agricultural products to Britain and elsewhere in Europe. White settlers demanded autonomy (as we will see in the next section), but they were pushing against an open door since the politically dominant interloper merchant faction after 1648 had adopted, by necessity, a business model based on trade with autonomous settlers rather than collecting political rents or exploiting conquered natives. Any possibility of an alternate colonial system in British America was extinguished by the interloper merchants' victory over the chartered company merchants in the Civil War.

Once the die was cast with the outcome of the English Civil War, an America with access to free land for white settlers became enticing to emigrating Britons. Certainly, there were factors (poverty, overpopulation, lack of mobility) pushing Britons abroad, but the post–Civil War political settlement created conditions in North America (and later in South Africa, Australia, and New Zealand) that pulled emigrants to those colonies. The next section examines how settler colonies won increasing autonomy and how that autonomy affected elite relations and the economy within Britain and in the empire in its entirety.

## SETTLER COLONIES FROM THE GLORIOUS REVOLUTION TO AMERICAN INDEPENDENCE

The American colonies, despite (and in part because of) the myriad tight links between settlers and their families, co-religionists, and financial backers in Britain, became sites of contestation between the royal government in London, appointed and elected officials in the colonies, settlers, and various interest groups in Britain that stood to gain or lose profits depending on the outcomes of those struggles for colonial power.

Britain's colonial policy became ever more central to the wealth and income of a growing fraction of the metropolitan population. Until the late eighteenth century, British manufacturing technology was similar to that of France and the Netherlands. Britain's advantage over rivals for most of the eighteenth century was commercial, not technological, and in turn derived from its political structure. As we discussed above, parliamentary legislation, most notably the Navigation Acts, funneled the benefits from the empire's growing market to British elites and deepened the financial, political, and familial links among colonists and merchants in the metropole. These ties served to integrate the economies of the colonies with Britain and with one another, and built a constituency for a large and capable navy. This made it easier for British merchants and investors to penetrate the economies of the parts of the Americas colonized by other European powers, and after 1783 to maintain a strong commercial presence in the United States.[1]

The settler elites of the colonies were able to use their business and familial ties to merchants and landowners in Britain to win royal favors in the forms of colonial land grants and offices and then to press for greater autonomy from the crown. The crown and, increasingly after 1689, Parliament were the sites at which colonial officials and settlers pushed against each other, as governors sought to claim the power to collect taxes and grant lands and privileges on their own, and to appoint lesser officials. Settlers sought to protect their lands and incomes from taxation and to assert the right to self-government.

Colonial governors and ultimately the crown were the long-term losers in the struggle with settlers. Settlers' advantage was partly because

> the colonies were three thousand miles from the mother country, with considerable logistic autonomy and therefore de facto civil and political freedoms. Under eighteenth century communications conditions, America could not be run from London . . . Sailing ships took at least four months to complete the round trip, virtually an entire campaigning or agricultural season.[2]

Yet we should not exaggerate the value of frequent communications. Fundamental conditions did not change quickly, and supervision

---

1   Cuenca Esteban, "Comparative Patterns of Colonial Trade."
2   Mann, *Sources of Social Power*, volume 2, 137–8.

could work when and where loyal and capable agents could be placed in office. In some colonies, slow communication empowered governors rather than colonists[1] because governors could act before colonists could appeal to their allies in London. The Thirteen Colonies won independence even while the other colonies, which were just as distant, did not. As we will see below, Canada, Australia, and New Zealand won greater autonomy in the nineteenth century, and Britons in Africa acted without London's permission, just when steamships and then the telegraph greatly speeded communications and it became possible for London to be in almost immediate and constant contact with their colonial agents. In neither the eighteenth nor nineteenth centuries did speed of communication determine the degree of central control over colonies.

Ultimately, American colonists won autonomy because they had more leverage in Parliament than did the governors since the settlers had more links to investors, business partners, and relatives in parliamentary districts throughout Britain. The governors, as we noted above, lost powerful allies when the chartered company merchants ended up on the losing side in the Civil War. This left the interloper merchants as the main lobbyists on policy in the Americas. As the population of settlers grew, and the number and value of their commercial ties to Britain increased, colonists had more avenues of influence in parliamentary politics. Colonists also gained autonomy because they were on the front lines of what had become, by the middle of the eighteenth century, a global war between France and Britain. The British government needed settlers' support in the Seven Years' War and had to offer greater autonomy to get it. As a result, the crown acceded to settler demands that it abandon plans to centralize crown control of the American colonies by empowering governors.[2]

Despite the mutually lucrative political and trade relationship between Britain and the American colonies, points of tension arose

1   Peter Burroughs, "Imperial Institutions and the Government of Empire," in *The Oxford History of the British Empire, Volume III: The Nineteenth Century*, ed. Andrew Porter (Oxford: Oxford University Press, 1999).

2   Ian K. Steele, "The Anointed, the Appointed, and the Elected: Governance of the British Empire, 1689–1784," in *The Oxford History of the British Empire, Volume II*, 119–21.

and deepened in the course of the eighteenth century, especially after Britain's 1763 victory over France and Spain in the Seven Years' War removed those rival powers from the lands west of the Thirteen Colonies. "The military threat to the colonies was virtually over ... The colonies now barely needed British protection or rule."[1] With foreign attack (though not native raids or slave rebellions) unlikely, British governments focused on minimizing the costs of protecting North American and Caribbean colonies and adopted policies designed to achieve that aim.

Britain attempted to restrict westward settlement in North America after 1763 as a way of limiting the costs of defending far-flung settlements and also to reduce the attraction of America to potential emigrant Britons by limiting the amount of new land open to settlement; British politicians, like their French counterparts, acted on the mercantilist doctrine that a large domestic population was a source of economic strength. Those efforts were thwarted by Britons who were invested in America and benefited from increases in the number of settlers with whom they could trade. In addition, rich colonists saw new settlements as opportunities for themselves to engage in land speculation and commerce (e.g., George Washington's career, before he became commander of the revolutionary army, was surveyor/land speculator), while poorer colonists saw the West as a place where upward mobility was possible. Thus, even though efforts to limit westward settlement were largely ineffective, they angered colonists.[2] Most fatefully, Britain sought to recoup the costs of the Seven Years' War in America by taxing colonists, which provoked boycotts of British goods[3] and armed resistance, and culminated in a successful revolution.

Settlers elsewhere in the Americas were in a weaker position in the eighteenth century than were the residents of the Thirteen Colonies. Canada was sparsely settled and remained more dependent on British troops to suppress indigenous peoples than the colonies to the south.

--------

1   Mann, *Sources of Social Power*, volume 2, 144.
2   Bowen, *Elites, Enterprise and the Making of the British Overseas Empire*, 185–93.
3   Breen, *Marketplace of Revolution*.

In the Caribbean, whites remained dependent on Britain to protect them from the danger of slave rebellions, and Britain, in an effort to avoid the cost of having to commit troops to suppress slaves, sought to restrict white settlers' opportunities to provoke racial rebellion by limiting local white rule.[1] Whites in the Caribbean were much less likely to settle permanently than their counterparts in North America,[2] and therefore did not develop the dense ties nor develop the sense of themselves as Americans with distinct interests that propelled the American Revolution.

American independence and the Napoleonic Wars both served to concentrate wealth and control over international trade in the hands of the richest merchants. Smaller merchants were less able to repatriate their investments in the American colonies and on continental Europe than were bankers and traders with greater and more diversified investments. Thus, when the national and state governments and local vigilantes in the newly independent United States expropriated British property in the areas under their control,[3] numerous merchants were bankrupted. Similarly, merchants whose capital was trapped on the Continent suffered when Napoleon seized their assets.[4] Nevertheless, the United States remained dependent on British capital and the trade networks controlled by British merchants through much of the nineteenth century,[5] which provided continuing opportunities for larger and better-capitalized merchants.

Despite American independence and the beginnings of autonomy in other settler colonies, British merchants remained able to secure policies and investments from their government that allowed them to profit from commerce with the remaining settler colonies as well as with the United States and the growing number of other non-European lands that were part of British commercial networks. We

1   Porter, *Lion's Share*, 1–26.
2   Bowen, *Elites, Enterprise and the Making of the British Overseas Empire*, 103–24.
3   Mann, *Sources of Social Power*, volume 2, 150; Noam Chomsky and Edward S. Herman, *After the Cataclysm: Postwar Indochina and the Reconstruction of Imperial Ideology* (Boston: South End Press, 1979), 41–6.
4   Bowen, *Elites, Enterprise and the Making of the British Overseas Empire*, 79–100; Chapman, *Merchant Enterprise in Britain*, 51–78.
5   Mann, *Sources of Social Power*, volume 2, 269.

will trace the effects of those profits, and the influence of the merchants who secured them, on British politics below, but first we need to examine the dynamics of the dependent colonies and see how the men who controlled that part of the empire interacted with the political economy of the metropole.

## INDIA AND THE DEPENDENT EMPIRE FROM 1600 TO 1858

The British holdings and concessions in India until 1858 belonged not to the royal government but to the chartered East India Company. Throughout the two and a half centuries, from the EIC's first voyages to and establishment of trading posts in India at the turn of the seventeenth century until the government nationalized all the EIC's powers and holdings in 1858, the company and the government maneuvered against each other to increase their relative share of the wealth extracted from the subcontinent. The government had the ultimate advantage since the EIC's presence in India was legalized by a royal charter, which had to be renewed periodically by Parliament. The royal government used each renewal to extract payments or loans from the EIC, and would expand the scope of the company's charter in return for additional payments. Thus, each gain in EIC privileges was bought with payments and loans.

A similar dynamic of selling charter rights for money marked the government's relationship with the other chartered companies, most notably the Bank of England, during the seventeenth century. The government pushed the Bank of England, the EIC, and other companies to renew charters years before their expiration as a way to extract low-interest loans that allowed the government to reduce interest costs on loans amassed to pay war costs.[1] The crown's frequent need for quick infusions of cash during wartime, and the political necessity of reducing interest costs after wars had ended, gave the EIC and other chartered companies leverage that mitigated their total dependence on government charters

---

1   J. Lawrence Broz and Richard S. Grossman, "Paying for Privilege: The Political Economy of Bank of England Charters, 1694–1844," *Explorations in Economic History* 41, no. 1 (2004).

for their legal existence. The EIC took advantage of a fiscal crisis in 1688 to gain greater autonomy in return for giving the Treasury a cash infusion.[1] In 1709, in return for a loan of £3.2 million to the Treasury, the EIC won permission to merge with and absorb the rival "new" East India Company (formally the English Company Trading to the East Indies) and thereby reassert its monopoly on the East India trade. The British government also agreed to guarantee EIC bonds.[2]

It would be a mistake to see either the British state or the EIC as unified entities with singular interests. The upward trajectory of greater EIC autonomy and ever-higher payments by the EIC to the Treasury was confounded and ultimately destroyed by the ability of actors within the EIC to pursue their own interests and by opposition from elites within Britain who were harmed by the growing wealth and power of the EIC. Let us examine, in turn, the bases of autonomy and decentralization within the EIC, the sources of opposition to the EIC in Britain, and the development of government policy toward the EIC, which culminated in its nationalization. Then we will see how British India and the rest of the dependent empire became part of a stable imperial polity in the mid-nineteenth century.

### i. EIC Decentralization and the Autonomy of Its Agents

The EIC, unlike the VOC examined in chapter 4, was unable to exert full control over its agents in Asia. The captains who commanded EIC ships and the officials who administered EIC forts and factories in India found ways to enrich themselves, although such self-serving enterprise in some instances ultimately increased rather than diminished EIC profits. Captains engaged in private trade with Indians, with local merchants throughout South and East Asia, and with other Europeans, trade that had the unanticipated effect of expanding the EIC's network of commercial relations and increasing the company's profitability and the volume of trade between Britain and Asia.[3]

The EIC's conquest of Bengal and of other Asian territories was for the most part planned by company officials in India on their own

1    Bayly, "British Military-Fiscal State."
2    Ibid.; Dirks, *Scandal of Empire*, 38.
3    Erikson, *Between Monopoly and Free Trade*.

initiative and for their own profit, realized from looting and exploiting conquered lands and from accepting payoffs from local Indian rulers for deploying EIC troops against rival Indian forces.[1] Conquests diverted military resources from what the EIC directors back in London regarded as their highest priority: fending off French efforts to seize Indian territories and trade.[2]

The British state was unable to prevent further efforts by EIC agents to conquer parts of India despite stratagems like sending a government plenipotentiary to India in 1769 to try to take over negotiations with local rulers from the EIC.[3] Agents' autonomy was fostered by the EIC's high degree of decentralization, with separate "presidencies" that administered each region under EIC control. Erikson[4] shows how the EIC organizational structure combined with opportunities created by the presence of powerful local elites and Asian merchants with whom EIC ship captains and officials could partner. Parliament in 1785 gave a governor-general, appointed by the crown rather than the EIC's "Court of Directors, their nominal employers,"[5] full authority over the presidencies and all their officials. Yet, even after 1785, EIC administrators continued to develop revenue collection systems in each presidency that reflected the administrators' particular conceptions of Indian society.[6]

The company was also limited in its ability to prevent EIC officials from enriching themselves, even after Governor-General Cornwallis's 1786 reform of the EIC civil service.[7] In the nineteenth century, the

1   Dirks, *Scandal of Empire*; H. V. Bowen, *The Business Empire: The East India Company and Imperial Britain, 1756–1833* (Cambridge: Cambridge University Press, 2006).

2   P. J. Marshall, "The British in Asia: Trade to Dominion, 1700–1765" in *The Oxford History of the British Empire, Volume II*.

3   Bowen, *Elites, Enterprise and the Making of the British Overseas Empire*, 183–5; Wallerstein, *Modern World-System*, volume 3, 180–2.

4   Erikson, *Between Monopoly and Free Trade*.

5   Kanta Rajat Ray, "Indian Society and the Establishment of British Supremacy, 1765–1818" in *The Oxford History of the British Empire, Volume II*, 51 and passim.

6   Nicholas Hoover Wilson, "From Reflection to Refraction: State Administration in British India, circa 1770–1855," *American Journal of Sociology* 116, no. 5 (2011).

7   John Darwin, *Unfinished Empire: The Global Expansion of Britain* (New York: Bloomsbury Press, 2012), 54–9; Ray, "Indian Society and the Establishment of British Supremacy."

EIC began paying high salaries to company men in a partly successful effort to reduce personal corruption. However, company officials still used their positions to steer contracts to their family firms and to ensure that their sons got into Haileybury school, where EIC men were trained in England, providing a way to indirectly pass on offices, contacts, and contracts to their scions.[1]

## ii. Beneficiaries and Opponents of the EIC in Britain

Opposition to the EIC's trade monopoly and other privileges, and to its close and mutually enriching relationship with the government, came from merchants, especially those in British outports, who were excluded from the monopoly. In the nineteenth century, landed elites felt threatened by the EIC's growing political power and saw the inducements the EIC offered to MPs as a threat to British liberty and governance.[2] However, for the seventeenth and much of the eighteenth century, those oppositional forces were overwhelmed by the lure of EIC payments and loans to the state and by pressure from EIC shareholders, traders, and current and retired company employees who lobbied and bribed Members of Parliament to ensure that the company's charter was renewed on favorable terms,[3] and to fend off parliamentary inquiries into the malfeasance of the EIC and its officials.[4]

The immense amounts of money that flowed from India through the EIC into Britain distorted parliamentary politics and ultimately created divisions among EIC beneficiaries. As more and more rich Britons held EIC shares or profited from business with the EIC, they came to have an interest in protecting the EIC from increasing Treasury demands for revenues and from laws and investigations

---

1    D. A. Washbrook, "India, 1818–1860: The Two Faces of Colonialism," in *The Oxford History of the British Empire, Volume III*.

2    Bowen, "British India;" Nicholas Hoover Wilson, " 'A State in Disguise of a Merchant?' The English East India Company as a Strategic Action Field, ca. 1763–1834," in *Chartering Capitalism: Organizing Markets, States, and Publics*, ed. Emily Erikson (Bingley: Emerald, 2015).

3    Dirks, *Scandal of Empire*, 37–85; Wilson, " 'A State in Disguise of a Merchant?' "

4    Philip Lawson, "Parliament and the First East India Inquiry, 1767," in *Parliamentary History Yearbook I* (1983), 99–114.

that could undermine either company profits or the ability of merchants to enrich themselves through side deals with the EIC. Blocs of EIC merchants and the Britons with whom they did business lobbied for special favors against the interests of the EIC as a whole. Thus, when Parliament passed the first bill limiting EIC autonomy, the 1773 Regulating Act, it exempted EIC merchants in southern India who had established strong ties to a parliamentary bloc.[1]

Opponents of EIC privileges gained strength in the latter half of the eighteenth century. Internal divisions among EIC merchants, and the ability of captains and traders in India to engage in private ventures outside the company's control, created groups of merchants in Britain with interests antagonistic to those of the EIC, while opening new opportunities for EIC officials and other merchants to make money from plantations and internal trade within India and to other parts of Asia that were not dependent on the EIC's trade monopoly. Furthermore, happenstance weakened the EIC politically in the last decades of the eighteenth century. In 1769, false reports of British defeats in India led to a crash of EIC stock, which had become the object of a speculative bubble, wiping out some of the biggest British investors.[2] The panic points to the overwhelming role of EIC stock in British financial markets during the eighteenth century and the political risk the company faced when it proved unable to deliver steadily rising profits to its shareholders and growing payments to the Treasury.

The EIC was further tarnished and its leverage in Parliament undermined by the charges of corruption made by Edmund Burke at the impeachment trial of Warren Hastings, the governor-general of Bengal, and by reports of the millions of Bengals who died in the 1769–73 famine that was brought on by EIC taxes and agricultural policies. Another force beyond the EIC's control was the American Revolution. Colonists' boycotts of British tea left the EIC with supplies in their warehouses and on ships sailing from India that it

---

1  Dirks, *Scandal of Empire*, 59.
2  Bowen, *Elites, Enterprise and the Making of the British Overseas Empire*, 171–8.

was no longer able to sell. The EIC then suspended payments to the Treasury, thereby undermining its main base of support in the government.

Parliament, reflecting the shifting balance of power and interest among British elites, passed a series of bills that limited EIC autonomy and gradually undid the EIC's trade monopoly. Liverpool merchants, who displaced their London rivals and came to dominate the cotton trade, mobilized to gain direct access to Indian markets rather than having to trade through the EIC. The EIC was able to keep its monopoly in 1792, but in 1813 the company was forced to share the India trade with "licensed private traders shipping to Bombay, Madras, Calcutta and Penang."[1] "The gradual build-up of pressure from the provinces had served to undermine the defences that had long protected the Company's privileged position."[2] Within the EIC, shareholders and others who felt that the company's, and their personal, opportunities for profit were inhibited by those who gained from their longstanding control over EIC shipping joined the opposition to renewing the EIC monopoly in 1813.[3] While Parliament continued the monopoly, it cut back on EIC privileges. Over the following decades, actual control over trade and profit opportunities in India shifted from EIC to agency houses, firms that began as agents for domestic manufacturers but then traded on their own accounts, invested abroad, including in India, and then became conduits for EIC officials and other expatriates seeking ways to repatriate their foreign profits.[4]

As the agency houses became wealthier, established their own connections with Britons in India, and deepened their political influence in the metropole, they transformed the Indian economy, supplanting indigenous Indian businessmen as well as the EIC. Those

---

1    Chapman, *Merchant Enterprise in Britain*, 83; see also John Darwin, *The Empire Project: The Rise and Fall of the British World-System, 1830–1970* (Cambridge: Cambridge University Press, 2009), 37.

2    Bowen, "British India," 549.

3    Anthony Webster, *The Twilight of the British East India Company: The Evolution of Anglo-Asian Commerce and Politics, 1790–1860* (Woodbridge: Boydell, 2009).

4    Ray, "Indian Society and the Establishment of British Supremacy."

firms were able to extract favors from the British colonial administration and from dependent Indian rulers. By the 1830s,

> British business houses now came to enjoy, if sometimes informally, privileged access to loans from state treasuries and banks, to licenses from state monopolies, to contracts for government supplies, and to powers over land and agricultural production in order to found plantations.[1]

The agency houses' success at winning contracts and privileges within India was a marker of the company's declining ability to ensure that it, or even its employees, were the exclusive beneficiaries of deals with Indian rulers. The non-EIC community of expatriate British businessmen became a lobby opposed to renewal of the company's privileges.[2] Over time, British businessmen in India and the agency houses with whom they collaborated parlayed their privileged access to British markets and capital to supplant indigenous Indian businessmen as well as the EIC in Asian markets. The EIC's decline as a political and economic power opened markets in India, the rest of Asia, and beyond to British financial and commercial interests that, as we will see below, became the essential advocates of free trade and political reform.

### iii. From Regulation to Nationalization

Parliament sought to limit EIC autonomy in a series of bills that were only partly effective. The Regulating Act of 1773 asserted the government's right to supervise all aspects of EIC activities.[3] In 1784, the East India Company Act created a Board of Control appointed from the Cabinet and Privy Council and established the office of governor-general, who was de facto ruler of EIC territories, but these measures had only limited success in preventing EIC officials from engaging in self-dealing.[4] These and later parliamentary interventions sought

---

1    Washbrook, "India, 1818–1860," 411.
2    Webster, *Twilight of the British East India Company*.
3    Bowen, *Elites, Enterprise and the Making of the British Overseas Empire*, 183–5.
4    Ray, "Indian Society and the Establishment of British Supremacy;" Ferguson, *Empire*, 55–6.

above all to ensure the EIC was capable of making regular payments and loans to the Treasury while attempting to balance the demands of EIC shareholders and traders against the growing interests of outport merchants excluded from the EIC's monopoly system.

The British government's continuing and overriding interest in India was to realize revenues, and later to defray costs by building up an Indian army (financed by the EIC and then under direct British rule by taxes on Indians) that could be used along with, or, even better, in lieu of British forces to take and hold other colonies and to fight European rivals. The crown, Cabinet, and navy worried that EIC initiatives to take more lands in India would divert British military assets from their primary task of countering European rivals, both in Asia and in Europe. Expansion of the EIC was not encouraged by the British state; instead, conquest was spurred by EIC civil and military officials' desires for "jobs, plunder and perquisites."[1] Thus, the British/EIC Indian army conquered lands elsewhere in South and Southeast Asia, and then in the 1840s took Punjab.[2] EIC officials were able to use the company's army to further their opportunities for profit ahead of any strategic considerations determined in London.

Parliament attempted to tailor a trade policy that maximized state revenues, either through tariffs or by allowing the EIC to generate profits that could be rebated to the Treasury. The general interests of British industrialists, to the extent that those could be determined, were not a significant factor in parliamentary changes in trade policy toward the EIC.[3] However, as we noted above, the particular interests of provincial business interests to gain their own access to Indian trade were allowed to undermine EIC profits and thus the amount the company could give to the Treasury. Parliament sought to compensate fiscally from the EIC's decline by ending the company's trade monopoly with China in 1833 in an effort to increase Indian trade with China and thereby boost tariff revenues. Thereafter, Britain raised and lowered tariffs on India's trade depending on the EIC's, and then the

1   Darwin, *Empire Project*, 53.
2   Washbrook, "India, 1818–1860."
3   Cain and Hopkins, *British Imperialism*, 316–50.

British Indian government's, ability to raise revenues from other sources and on British India's military costs.

Despite the inroads of non-EIC merchants and firms and the loss of its trade monopoly, the EIC was bolstered in the 1840s by the conquest of the Punjab and other Indian lands. In the early 1850s, the EIC had revenues of £30 million a year, about half that of the British state. The EIC used its income to hire 250,000 Indians for its company army and to pay the British Treasury £1 million p.a. for the 20–30,000 British troops stationed on the subcontinent. However, those payments went straight to the Treasury rather than to support the army. "The reward for Britain's taxpayers was great; the strain on the army unremitting."[1]

The 1857 Indian Rebellion (or Mutiny) exposed the inherent conflict between EIC interests, or more often the interests of EIC officials in India, and those of the British imperial government. The government was concerned above all with excluding rival European powers from India and thus saw EIC weakness as a fundamental strategic problem for Britain, and worried that an EIC bankruptcy would be a disaster for state revenues and for the overall British economy.[2] The rebellion itself was interpreted by the British government, most notably by Disraeli, as the result of misguided efforts by EIC officials to reform Indian society that upset existing land tenure systems and disrupted local elites. EIC-directed reforms came to an end, although many of the changes in land tenure arrangements were irreversible by 1857. Missionaries and some in the India Office still advocated for further reforms of land tenure arrangements and of other aspects of Indian society,[3] but their proposals were rejected by the British state officials and civil servants who ruled India after 1857.

The 1858 Government of India Act dissolved the company and put the British government in direct control of India, with a Cabinet official, the secretary of state, at the head of a new Indian Civil Service that replaced company officials. Opportunities for civil servants to profit from their offices were sharply curtailed, and the far less

--------

1   Darwin, *Empire Project*, 55.
2   Darwin, *Unfinished Empire*, 77–9.
3   Porter, *Lion's Share*, 28–47.

lucrative civil service positions attracted a different sort of recruit than had the EIC. At first, a majority of those who entered the Indian Civil Service were Oxbridge graduates, but as the size of the civil service expanded and their activities were more tightly controlled from above, the Oxbridge graduates turned to different, more profitable careers elsewhere.

> Between 1860 and 1874 three-quarters of the recruits came from professional, middle-class backgrounds, over a quarter from the clergy, a tenth each from government service and the medical profession, and 15 per cent from mercantile or legal families. Many did not have degrees. Most, having no Indian connections, signed on for a career of which they could know little.[1]

The broadening of the pool of men who served in and profited from India had the effect of blurring the line between Britons in India and the broader landowning and commercial elites in the metropole. Former Indian Civil Service officials and their relatives resided throughout Britain, and businessmen throughout the nation profited directly or indirectly from Indian ventures. Instead of an insular and self-perpetuating elite, viewed as corrupt by those excluded from opportunities to share in Asian loot, the post-EIC India was (accurately) seen as a source of revenue and armed force for the state and a contributor to the overall British and imperial economy.

> Considerable sectors of British society depended, however, upon posts in the civil and military hierarchies of the Indian Empire . . . the effect on the British public mind of the presence in society of quite large numbers of influential persons whose active life had been spent in India, and who carried from that experience a bias perceptible in their reaction to many major issues of foreign policy or defence [generated support for imperialism in general].[2]

--------

1   Robin J. Moore, "Imperial India, 1858–1914," in *The Oxford History of the British Empire, Volume III*, 429.
2   Max Beloff, *Britain's Liberal Empire: 1897–1914* (London: Macmillan, 1987), 32.

## Colonial Elites and Domestic British Politics:
## A Stable Imperial Polity

The fate of the East India Company demonstrated the limits of elite autarky in nineteenth-century Britain.[1] Despite access to vast sources of revenue and an army of its own that was able to protect and expand its territories against both rival European powers and indigenous rulers, the EIC lost the capacity to shape the British state's policies as they affected the company and ultimately was unable to block its nationalization. Why was the EIC vulnerable to outside forces in ways that the VOC or French and Spanish colonists were not? The EIC was less dependent on its home government than were colonists from the other major European powers, or even than British colonists elsewhere in the world. The EIC was self-financing and militarily autonomous: Only the Spanish American colonists (analyzed in chapter 3) were similarly self-sufficient, and they sustained their positions without challenge from the metropole and were the beneficiaries if not always the instigators of independence from Spain. Chartered companies everywhere depended on royal and/or legislative approval for their continued legal existence, but only the EIC lost its charter while still profitable, unlike its French counterparts (discussed in chapter 3) or the British companies in Africa, Russia, or the Americas, which lost charters only when they fell into financial difficulties.[2] We are left with the question: What changed for the EIC in the decades from the last renewal of its full monopoly in 1792 to its nationalization in 1858?

What changed was British politics. The restrictions on the EIC and then its nationalization were political decisions. We need to explain how the balance of power in Britain shifted. In essence, the EIC lost its charter because the British state and the structure of elite relations in Britain and throughout the Empire were transformed in the first half of the nineteenth century. The winners of the Civil War and the Glorious Revolution, the mainly English lay landowners and financiers, were challenged by rising elites: manufacturers from northern

1  Elite autarky can be defined as the ability to appropriate resources from and to exercise authority over non-elites and to legitimate one's position of authority without any need for assistance or support from other elites.

2  Scott, *Constitution and Finance of English, Scottish, and Irish Joint-Stock Companies*.

England, Wales, and Scotland, and men who increasingly combined commerce with manufacture. These new men became rich in large part as a result of imperial and trade policies that the established elites had pushed forward with the power they gained from the Civil War and the Glorious Revolution. Thus, the growing empire, with the EIC as its greatest source of wealth, created new opportunities for elite careers and investments.

The wealth gained from Britain's growing domestic economy and formal and informal empire did more than create new cohorts of rich men. It is a mistake to view the old and new elites as separate groups with consistently opposed interests. Rather, old and new elites increasingly came together to make money and to press government to enact policies favorable to them all. "Incumbents did not have to beat the new sectors, they could join them fairly easily by investing in turnpikes, canals, cotton mills, and later railroads."[1] World events led British businessmen to diversify their investments, while the inability of agriculture to absorb more capital investment, since increased profits in the mid-nineteenth century were due entirely to rising rents rather than gains in efficiency, pushed landowners to invest in commerce, blurring the lines between landed and commercial elites, and between London and the provinces, and over time fostering an increase in the scale of British firms.

MPs and judges, whose positions remained largely out of reach for merchants and their sons in the first half of the nineteenth century, became passive investors in bonds and stocks[2] and thereby reduced their political difference, at least on issues of tariffs and trade, with manufacturers. The abolition of slavery weakened old mercantile interests.[3] The expropriation of British assets in the newly independent United States, and Napoleon's conquests and the British embargo of France and French-controlled territories, combined to bankrupt primarily smaller merchants and pushed British businessmen to shift

---

1   Joel Mokyr, *The Enlightened Economy: An Economic History of Britain, 1700–1850* (New Haven: Yale University Press, 2009), 76.

2   Ron Harris, *Industrializing English Law: Entrepreneurship and Business Organization, 1720–1844* (Cambridge: Cambridge University Press, 2000), 231–3, 253–4.

3   Darwin, *Empire Project*, 57–63.

their focus to opportunities in Asia, the Americas, and Africa. At the same time, other merchants got rich supplying war matériel. Opportunities for war profiteering flowed mainly to those with already substantial assets, causing an increase in the scale of British firms and a shift in the locus of wealth from the North West manufacturing centers to London and the surrounding counties.[1]

Commerce rather than manufacture or plantations became the main mechanism through which profit was extracted from both the settler and dependent empires, from Britain's commanding position in global commerce, and from the fact that sterling was the global reserve currency between 1815 and 1900. The City merchants who were bankrupted in the 1847–48 financial crisis were the ones who had made heavy and illiquid investments in West and East Indies plantations.[2] Their bankruptcy, at just the moment when repeal of the Corn Law and Navigation Acts was being decided, eliminated the strongest supporters of those legislative restrictions on trade.

In the second half of the eighteenth century, so much money flowed from India to Britain that "Indian plunder became a substitute for Dutch money." Britain's debts to the Netherlands were extinguished, and by the early nineteenth century British investors became the primary suppliers of capital in the world.[3]

> Until 1905, the City's "invisible earnings" from banking, insurance, and shipping exceeded its income from foreign investments. And both far exceeded income from domestic manufacturing industry ... The City and the treasury began to cement the alliance that has dominated British political economy ever since. Investment went through country and city banks, discount houses, bill brokers, and solicitors to banks that lent to industry, usually over the short term, or more commonly to manufacturers' merchant suppliers and commercial distributors ... [At the same time] petty bourgeois

---

1  Chapman, *Merchant Enterprise in Britain*, 2, 51–78.

2  A. C. Howe, "Free Trade and the City of London: c. 1820–1870" in *History* 77 (1992).

3  Giovanni Arrighi et al., "Geopolitics and High Finance," in *Chaos and Governance in the Modern World System*, 37–96 and passim.

savings went through solicitors and insurance companies into land-owners' consumption and investments [through land mortgages].[1]

Growth in the size of firms and in the volume of capital flowing through Britain created links between formerly separate elites. Landowners and the petite bourgeoisie came to share an interest in the profitability and market access of the commercial firms in which they directly or indirectly were invested. Power followed profits. Liverpool overtook London as the center of the cotton trade in the first half of the nineteenth century, and Liverpudlian and other provincial merchants were central in opposing the EIC monopoly and in demanding other policies that facilitated their ability to profit from international trade.[2] Those policies undermined special privileges and fostered "free trade." The political and financial successes of the biggest firms—the ones that had the resources to diversify and ride out wars, expropriations, and depressions—were possible because they were embedded within an international commercial system centered on Britain, and as the links among bankers, merchants, and manufacturers deepened, they magnified merchant-financiers' political sway.

The old elites' need to accommodate the growing power of provincial interests and of the ever richer and more numerous commercial men (who often were their business partners) led to a series of reforms that undermined the ability of narrow groups to claim a share of state revenues and offices, to protect their special privileges, or to block new policies. The nationalization of the EIC was the culmination of a series of reforms that reversed the policies of the early nineteenth century when the fiscal pressures of the Napoleonic Wars combined with the entrenched power of the landed elite and London financiers to pass the 1815 Corn Law and to restore the gold standard in 1819.[3]

The most significant indicator of a shift in the balance of power was the 1831 election,[4] which the Whigs won in a landslide after

1   Mann, *Sources of Social Power*, volume 2, 127.
2   Chapman, *Merchant Enterprise in Britain*, 81–106.
3   Cain and Hopkins, *British Imperialism*, 53–84.
4   Earlier indicators were the 1828 repeals of the 1661 Corporation Act that restricted membership in town corporations to Church of England members and of the 1673 Test Act that imposed the same requirement on holders of civil and military

campaigning in favor of electoral reform and against the Old Corruption, the offices and privileges given to parliamentary and country allies of the royal government and scions of old families. The 1832 Reform Act added "300,000 men . . . to the electorate of 500,000. The elimination of 140 rotten boroughs was the death knell for royal and ministerial patronage over the Commons."[1] Economic growth and ever-denser commercial links gave merchants more leverage over landowners through their economic relationship and shared interests with the petite bourgeoisie who "were 'virtually represented' by partic-ipating in long-established segmental patron-client networks."[2]

Electoral reform combined with the 1836 Established Church Bill, designed to eliminate corruption within the Church of England, were rapidly and highly effective in reducing the Old Corruption, in essence removing opportunities for what Weber[3] labeled political capitalism from domestic though not imperial British politics, thus ensuring that British elites after 1832 would gain wealth within Britain almost exclu-sively from land and commerce. The change was profound: Prior to the reform, one hundred MPs in Commons were "members of the court and treasury party—civil servants, courtiers, merchants, lawyers, and military officers seeking preferment, sinecures, or honors."[4] William Rubinstein finds that income from the Old Corruption

in 1831 . . . may well have been equal to, or even exceeded, the entire agricultural income which the Tory aristocracy derived from its rent-rolls at the time . . . To be sure, there remained colonial admin-istration, the army and navy, even the church, and eventually busi-ness directorships, but one must conclude that had the period between 1837 and 1879 not fortuitously been one of agricultural prosperity, much of the decline of the lesser aristocracy and gentry,

office. The Catholic Emancipation Act was enacted in 1829 (Andrew Porter, "Religion, Missionary Enthusiasm, and Empire" in *The Oxford History of the British Empire, Volume III*; Jews got similar rights only in 1890). These reforms opened offices, though at first only lower-level ones, to dissenter and Catholic businessmen.

1   Mann, *Sources of Social Power*, volume 2, 125.
2   Ibid., 110.
3   Weber, *Economy and Society*, 166.
4   Mann, *Sources of Social Power*, volume 2, 114.

so notable after 1879, would have occurred long before. Similarly, although the military and the empire doubtless absorbed many an aristocratic relative after 1832, its rewards could simply not be compared with those possible in the past; for many minor aristocrats one cannot help feeling that the Reform Bill marked the end of a way of life and the beginning of an era of diminished opportunities.[1]

The City bankers, and the Bank of England above all, were the first beneficiaries of the new parliamentary balance of power. The Bank Charter Act of 1844 gave the Bank of England exclusive power to buy and sell gold, allowing it to manipulate the money supply and interest rates for its own profit at the expense of smaller banks that previously had the ability to issue their own notes. Although this was in fact a form of rent-seeking, industrialists backed this policy in the belief that it would reduce deficits and taxes and weaken the beneficiaries of the Old Corruption, who depended both on government sinecures and on their ability to borrow from smaller banks. The industrialists' political calculations were correct, even though the Bank of England's interest rate manipulations harmed those firms' profits in the long term.[2]

The tariffs that protected British farmers (and ultimately and primarily landowners) from foreign competition, and the system of protected trade with colonies and preferences for British shippers, were abolished with the respective 1848 repeal of the Corn Law and the 1849 repeal of the Navigation Acts. Pressure for those legislative changes came from provincial interests that were harmed by the trade preferences and that did not own enough land to gain from the Corn Laws,[3] and were facilitated, as noted above, by the bankruptcy of anti-free trade City bankers in the 1847–48 financial crisis, and supported by those landowners whose wealth was moving into commercial ventures.[4] Yet the parliamentary votes of the 1840s cannot be understood in terms of the balance of interests within Britain alone.

--------

1   William D. Rubinstein, "The End of 'Old Corruption' in Britain, 1780–1860," *Past and Present* 101 (1983), 77, 79.
2   Cain and Hopkins, *British Imperialism*, 141–60.
3   Daunton, "Creating Legitimacy."
4   Mokyr, *Enlightened Economy*, 76.

Commercial interests in Canada and the West Indies also objected to the continuation of the Navigation Acts, especially after earlier tariff cuts undermined the advantage enjoyed by traders within the Empire.[1] As the Empire became better integrated commercially, the wealthiest settlers became an ever more powerful political force within Britain, exerting indirect influence through their ties to British merchants and landowners and also with their ability to shift commerce to the United States or rival European powers, which brought British businessmen to their side.

The British state differed from those of the Netherlands, Spain, and France in its capacity to revoke the privileges of autarkic elites. The electoral reform, nationalization of the EIC, repeal of the Corn Laws and Navigation Acts, and the drastic cutbacks in Old Corruption were the outstanding signs of elites' inability to sustain autarkic privileges. Autarkic elites, for the most part, did not suffer absolute declines in their capacities and resources, although, as we saw above, financial crises and bankruptcies removed some merchants from the political equation, just as the Indian Mutiny changed the government's strategic calculus and stance toward the EIC. Rather, the overall structure of elite relations within Britain and the Empire were transformed in the first half of the nineteenth century by the growing links between old and new elites. Empire was essential to that restructuring, as the flow of resources from, and investment opportunities in, the dependent and settler colonies and the informal empire created new elites and enticed old elites to invest in new enterprises that supplemented and increasingly overwhelmed income from land and Old Corruption. As a result, the number of men who paid a significant price in wealth and income from the proposed reforms declined until it became possible in the 1830s and '40s to pass the legislation and implement the policies that undid autarkic monopolies, offices, and privileges.

The reform policies sustained themselves politically because the financial returns from the "free trade" system made possible by abolition of the EIC, the repeal of the Corn Law and Navigation Acts, and reductions in tariffs so quickly enriched both old and new elites. The

---

1   P. J. Cain, "Economics and Empire: The Metropolitan Context," in *The Oxford History of the British Empire, Volume III,* 38–41.

top 0.5 percent of Britons tripled their share of the nation's wealth from 11 percent in 1688 to 31 percent by the turn of the twentieth century. The next 6 percent held 40 percent of the nation's wealth in 1895–1903.[1] This increase in the concentration of wealth was not achieved by impoverishing average Britons. Wages, which in 1800–09 were the same as in 1680–89, rose rapidly after the end of the Napoleonic Wars, more than tripling in the century from 1800–09 to 1900–09.[2] In fact, the era of rapid and sustained increases in wages and per capita GDP began in Britain in the early nineteenth century, at the same time as the rich became so much richer. Britain's empire and commanding position in the world economy made most Britons better off, but the vastly disproportionate benefits enjoyed by the elites ensured that the top 0.5 percent and the next 6 percent pulled far head of the rest of the nation.

The unified and relatively open elite of mid-nineteenth-century Britain had the power to create an imperial system that generated unprecedented profits. The nationalization of the EIC allowed the increasingly professionalized government officials who administered India and the other dependent colonies[3] to impose taxes on Indians that sucked resources out of the subcontinent and increasingly from other parts of Asia to subsidize Britain's military and domestic spending, while organizing Asian trade in ways that enriched Britons rather than Indians.

## FINANCIAL ELITES IN THE TRIUMPH AND DECLINE OF BRITISH HEGEMONY

Free trade and the declining share of resources tied up in land, sinecures, and other forms of politically derived profit meant that Britons

---

1   Gregory King, "Natural and Political Observations and Conclusions upon the State and Condition of England," in *Two Tracts* (Baltimore: Johns Hopkins University Press, [1696] 1936), 31; Statistical Abstract for the United Kingdom #50 (London: His Majesty's Stationery Office, 1903).

2   Gregory Clark, "The Condition of the Working Class in England, 1209–2004," *Journal of Political Economy* 113 (2005), table A2.

3   Moore, "Imperial India;" Anthony Kirk-Greene, *On Crown Service: A History of HM Colonial and Overseas Civil Services, 1837–1997* (London: I. B. Tauris, 1999).

incurred few costs, financial or political, as they shifted assets across sectors and around the world in search of higher rates of return. The financialization of the British economy, analyzed so clearly by Arrighi,[1] was spurred by the fact that British elites did not endanger their political and social positions or their network ties by moving their money out of land and industry into finance, or from Britain abroad, or even out of the empire entirely. In fact, elites strengthened their mutual interests and deepened their political ties as they invested with one another beyond the sectors in which they originally made their wealth.

The vast scale of British foreign investment "fertilized a growing service sector in South-East England which, with the City of London's financial and commercial businesses at its centre, became the most dynamic and innovative part of the British economy after 1850."[2] Indeed, in 1859–60, by far the highest percentage of Britons rich enough to owe income tax were in London, indicating that finance rather than manufacture was the main source of wealth, even at the height of the Industrial Revolution.[3]

Financialization, i.e., the shift of capital into financial assets, was the result of both push and pull factors. Money was pushed out of agriculture, as the repeal of the Corn Laws reduced the profitability of farming and made investment in British land less lucrative than North American farms.[4] Similarly, the end of British shipping privileges codified in the Navigation Acts pushed investment away from ships. The end of Old Corruption pushed money away from government. When elites could no longer get rich from offices or from trading in government bonds with inside knowledge, they shifted to a consensus in favor of low government spending and low taxes,[5] freeing up more money for private investment. At the same time, the profitability of

---

1   Arrighi, *Long Twentieth Century*; Arrighi et al., "Geopolitics and High Finance."

2   Cain, "Economics and Empire," 47–8.

3   William D. Rubinstein, *Capitalism, Culture and Decline in Britain, 1750–1990* (London: Routledge, 1993), 30 and passim.

4   Cain and Hopkins, *British Imperialism*, 107–40.

5   Cain, "Economics and Empire;" O'Brien, "Security of the Realm and the Growth of the Economy."

finance increased due to the position of sterling as the global reserve currency, a position that was the result of conscious government policy, above all the gold standard, which weakened the competitive advantage of British manufacturing, pushing capital out of British industrial firms and into the Empire.[1] Britain's resulting low interest rates, and the higher interest rates in other countries with weaker currencies, pulled investment abroad. The share of money raised in London that went to domestic British firms fell from 47 percent in 1865–69 to 20 percent in 1909–13.[2] Money was pulled abroad by opportunities in the growing empire, both in settler and dependent colonies, but also pushed by "the steady decline in returns on safe British investments like government paper and railways which forced gentlemanly investors to look abroad after 1870."[3] British fiscal and foreign policies created conditions that pulled capital into financial instruments throughout the world. Britain imposed free trade on India and the rest of the dependent empire and protected investors from nationalization or defaults by local governments, even in locales not part of the formal British empire.[4]

The structure, size, and membership of British investment firms changed over the course of the nineteenth century, drawing new entrepreneurs from increasingly diverse backgrounds and capital from Britain and abroad into the financial sector. British investment firms grew in size in the second half of the nineteenth century. Agency houses, which had played a central role in allowing British merchants to circumvent the EIC monopoly, became mechanisms through which Britons in the metropole as well as those abroad could invest capital in multiple foreign markets. While the agency houses, and home trade and international houses, began by specializing in a single commodity or manufactured good and often trading with a single country, they diversified over the course of the nineteenth century by investing in multiple sectors and countries. Most investors in Britain had little

1   Davis and Huttenback, *Mammon and the Pursuit of Empire*, 195–220; Cain and Hopkins, *British Imperialism*, 141–60, 181–201.
2   Cain and Hopkins, *British Imperialism*, 191.
3   Cain, "Economics and Empire," 49.
4   Darwin, *Empire Project*, 124–41; Chapman, *Merchant Enterprise in Britain*, 262–83.

knowledge of foreign markets in which they sought to invest in search of higher yields and so relied on the reputation of well-known firms. This gave established British firms an advantage in attracting capital from Britons and also from investors in "India, China, Russia and some of the Latin American republics."[1]

Investment firms remained under family control throughout the nineteenth century yet were able to attract investors as a result of the prestige of their named partners (even when those partners were long dead and the firms were directed by less able scions). At the same time, those investment firms relied on smaller trading firms, often run by immigrants (Germans who were largely Jews, Irish Americans, and Greeks), to actually engage in trade or to run the plantations and manufacturers which they had bought in other countries.[2] Chapman argues that investment firms achieved economies of scale by outsourcing trading, manufacturing, and management functions to other firms, and that the mix of British and foreign entrepreneurs, and the frequent bankruptcies of inefficient or just unlucky firms, created dynamism in British finance.

The domestic banking sector was less dynamic and became much more concentrated than the investment sector. Britain's two-tier banking system, with provincial banks that had long-term relationships with, and made loans to, firms of their particular local industries, and big banks that focused on international finance,[3] was transformed in the last decades of the nineteenth century. The regulatory power the Bank of England was granted in the 1844 Bank Charter Act combined with repeal of the Joint Stock Banking Act in 1857 and the subsequent rise of checking to undermine small banks' ability to issue their own still profitable banknotes.[4] This encouraged mergers.[5] "The number of independent banks fell to 60 by 1901 and to 40 by 1917, by which time

---

1    Chapman, *Merchant Enterprise in Britain*, 249 and passim.
2    Ibid.
3    Michael H. Best and Jane Humphries, "The City and Industrial Decline," in *The Decline of the British Economy*, eds. Bernard Elbaum and William Lazonick (Oxford: Clarendon, 1986).
4    Cain and Hopkins, *British Imperialism*, 141–60.
5    Richard S. Grossman, *Unsettled Account: The Evolution of Banking in the Industrialized World Since 1800* (Princeton: Princeton University Press, 2010).

the five major clearing banks controlled two-thirds of the system's resources."[1] As a result, smaller British firms were increasingly unable to access capital from the ever fewer small banks that once had provided them with long-term loans.

Britons' international investments, and the ease with which British investment firms facilitated the transfer of capital around the world, helped firms in other countries borrow the money needed for industrialization.[2] This led to a boom in industrial production worldwide, but a decline in profits, which hit the less efficient older British firms harder than newer, technologically advanced and vertically integrated American and German corporations.[3] Mann, who defines hegemony as exceeding "the next two Powers combined," finds that Britain met that standard for "industrial production between 1860 and 1880." On a per capita basis, its industrial production was more than double the next two powers "from the 1830s to the 1880s. Britain still retained first rank in 1900, falling behind the United States by 1913," by which time total US industrial production was 250 percent of Britain's, and Germany had surpassed Britain.[4] Britain accounted for a third of world industrial output in 1870, and a seventh in 1913. It produced a third of world steel in the late 1870s, and a tenth in 1909–13, when Germany produced twice as much and the United States quadrupled Britain's output.[5] Chronic trade deficits were clear indicators of Britain's declining position in the world economy.

By the late 1890s Britain was regularly recording import figures 50 per cent above her exports. Those massive deficits were bridged partly by the interest on her capital investments abroad ... The empire did something to help the situation, but not much.[6]

1   Best and Humphries, "City and Industrial Decline," 228.
2   Porter, Lion's Share, 1–26.
3   Arrighi, Long Twentieth Century, chapter 3; Scott Lash and John Urry, The End of Organized Capitalism (Cambridge: Polity, 1987), 42–55.
4   Mann, Sources of Social Power, volume 2, 263–5.
5   Cain and Hopkins, British Imperialism, 113.
6   Porter, Lion's Share, 121.

EMPIRE WITHOUT HEGEMONY: THE FAILURE OF
REFORM IN PRE–WORLD WAR I BRITAIN

Foreign investment in itself did not undermine Britain's position at the apex of the world economy. Large British firms and the state were able to attract all the capital they needed, as evidenced by the very low and falling interest rates they paid for loans in the second half of the nineteenth century. Rather, the British state and British firms failed to adopt reforms that could have allowed Britain to counter the growing power of its economic and military rivals: France, Germany, and the United States. British elites continued to share an interest in, and voiced strong support for, low taxes, free trade, and the gold standard. However, the coherence of shared interests, derived from British elites' joint investments and ventures in the metropole and the Empire, were distorted by the growing weight financiers, settler colonies, and investors in fringe areas were able to assert over governmental policy.

In essence, it became easier for the state to preserve relations with increasingly self-interested settler colonies and to expand the Empire into marginal areas, and for financiers to invest in more successful foreign firms, than to undertake the policy reforms needed to sustain British industrial as opposed to financial hegemony.[1] Similarly, the budgetary and policy costs of maintaining British military and geopolitical dominance were not paid since that would have required tax increases, the imposition of a draft, or transforming Britain's relationship with the settler colonies in ways that would have cost British elites

---

1   John Gallagher and Ronald Robinson, in their classic article "The Imperialism of Free Trade," *Economic History Review*, 2nd series, VI, no. 1 (1953), argued that decisions to expand both the formal and informal British empire in the second half of the nineteenth century were made to keep the world open to British trade, investment, and the extraction of raw materials. They see that strategy as most successful where economic penetration preceded political control. Where the British merely sought to exert political dominance or where a British invasion destroyed the local government, as in Egypt in the 1880s, then British political control was weak or unsteady. While Gallagher and Robinson offer a fair description of the effects of British imperialism, their schematic analysis leaves out the actors who pushed those policies and the obstacles they overcame to achieve their goals, and therefore cannot explain why British imperialists used different ratios or temporal sequences of economic or political power.

money and undermined their relationships with the lands where they invested and potentially provoked the lower classes at home.

As British investments flowed abroad and were increasingly kept in highly liquid form, and therefore were ever more vulnerable to speculative fluctuations,[1] wealthy Britons demanded policies that (1) fostered their abilities to protect their foreign investments, (2) maintained the value of sterling, the currency they used to attract foreign capital and to invest abroad, and (3) minimized taxes on their incomes. Ultimately, these three objectives came into conflict with one another, and even more with the settler colonies' demands, the initiatives of the new imperialists seeking to expand the Empire in Africa, and above all with the rapidly rising costs of maintaining geopolitical preeminence. Thus, even though late-nineteenth-century British elites, with the exception of some of those who sought to create new colonies in Africa, were unable to establish autarkic privileges, they were able to preserve governmental policies at home and in the Empire that enriched them in the short and middle term but doomed British hegemony by blocking reforms that could have allowed Britain to revitalize its economy and reassert its geopolitical mastery. Let us look at the stasis of British financial and industrial firms, fiscal policy and its effects on military and foreign policy, and finally the metropole's evolving relationship with the settler colonies and the imperialists who initiated imperial expansion in Africa. We want to understand how those policies were set in ways that undermined British hegemony and why they were not reformed.

### i. Stasis and Decline in British Firms

The disappearance of the small provincial banks in waves of bankruptcies and mergers in the second half of the nineteenth century, which were results of the broader process of financialization, starved many British industrial firms of access to the capital needed to modernize, expand, or merge. (In chapter 8, we will examine how bank mergers in the United States affected the American economy and politics.) The surviving big banks preferred to invest abroad and offered mainly

---

1 Arrighi, *Long Twentieth Century*; Arrighi et al., "Geopolitics and High Finance."

short-term loans to both large and small British firms. The share of money raised in London that went to domestic firms declined from 47 percent in 1865–69 to 20 percent in 1909–13.[1] "London did not finance the factories and mines of the north . . . London's own economic base, as always, led to the outside world, to finance and commerce abroad and overseas."[2] Large banks' short time horizon also meant that they did not make the effort of their American or German counterparts to reorganize industries to create oligopolies. British firms therefore were subjected to more domestic competition and had lower profits than US or German firms, making it difficult to attract new investors or to pay for modernization with retained earnings.[3] This problem was compounded by the fact that British firms did not enjoy the tariff protections of their German or American competitors. Nor did British industrial firms merge or buy up competitors to achieve the economies of scale that American and German firms did.[4] Revealingly, merger activity was largely confined to banking and finance rather than industry in Britain in the decades before World War I. The few large industrial firms formed through mergers were "holding companies which were loosely organized as federations of firms, with small central headquarters, little co-ordination or integration, and with operating decisions left to the constituent companies. In most cases, owners and their families continued to control and mange both at the holding company and subsidiary level."[5] While these loose federations were competitive within Britain, and would have been profitable in a closed empire, they were ever less able to compete with the more tightly integrated and growing German and US corporations.

Cain and Hopkins argue that British firms, both large and small, did not seek long-term financing from banks because they did not want to endanger family control.[6] External financing was limited

---

1   Cain and Hopkins, *British Imperialism*, 191.

2   Rubinstein, *Capitalism, Culture and Decline in Britain*, 146.

3   Best and Humphries, "City and Industrial Decline."

4   Lash and Urry, *End of Organized Capitalism*, 43–6.

5   Howard F. Gospel, *Markets, Firms and the Management of Labour in Britain* (Cambridge: Cambridge University Press, 1992), 17.

6   Cain and Hopkins, *British Imperialism*, 181–201. James Foreman-Peck and Leslie Hannah, "Extreme Divorce: The Managerial Revolution in UK Companies before 1914," *The Economic History Review* 65, no. 4 (2012): 25, find that in 1911,

because "British companies . . . appear to have been consistently more secretive than American and German companies, and obviously without information there was great disincentive to invest."[1] Chapman finds that investment groups as well as industrial firms gave priority "to maintain[ing] the wealth and power of the family (or families) that controlled the particular business,"[2] rather than to maximizing control of a market or profits. Those priorities were facilitated by British corporate law, which allowed firms' founding families to maintain control by limiting new capital to bonds or preferred shares.[3]

British firms, in seeking senior and junior employees and potential partners who were socially compatible with the scions who owned and ran the firms,

> recruited staff whose family backgrounds and education prepared them for careers in the civil service, armed services, Church and law, and only a few technical men like jute mill managers and mining engineers were recruited to subordinate positions for their technical expertise.[4]

It became increasingly difficult for British firms with technically ignorant managers to compete with US and German firms that looked to

---

"Fewer than 3,000 men served as directors of [British corporations with share capital of more than £1 million], but they collectively owned only 3.4 per cent (£65 million) of the total share capital (£1,926 million)." Foreman-Peck and Hannah take that as conclusive evidence for a separation of ownership and management in late Victorian Britain (decades before a similar development in the United States, which was the subject of Berle and Means's famous 1932 book). However, they also acknowledge that British firms were less innovative in this period than their American and German competitors. They have nothing to say about why "outside" directors would support inefficient and slow-moving family managers, a reality best explained by the broader British elite's shared interests and culture that spanned individual firms, interests that were fostered by director interlocks and firms' reliance on elites to buy debentures (which Foreman-Peck and Hannah mention but don't analyze). Furthermore, family leverage over directors was aided by the small size of corporate boards: "An average of 9.6 directors, these British boards were generally smaller than their German and US counterparts."

1   Lash and Urry, *End of Organized Capitalism*, 50.
2   Chapman, *Merchant Enterprise in Britain*, 249 and passim.
3   Patrick K. O'Brien, "The Costs and Benefits of British Imperialism," *Past and Present* 120 (1988), 182–6.
4   Chapman, *Merchant Enterprise in Britain*, 302.

engineers for leadership. The familial and cultural commonalities among the landed elite, government officials, bankers, merchants, and manufacturers that facilitated the development of policy consensus in the eighteenth and nineteenth centuries then held back the recruitment of men with the sorts of education and experiences necessary to compete against the large corporations that formed to invent, produce, and market advanced machines and consumer goods in the late nineteenth century.

## ii. British Budgets, Military Strategy, and Foreign Policy

British elites were able to keep taxes low throughout the century from the end of the Napoleonic Wars until the start of World War I. Elites were able to protect their interests against efforts during the Crimean and South African (Boer) wars to raise land taxes or reimpose tariffs.[1] Instead, the Treasury paid for the wars with bonds that then were paid down in peacetime by keeping government civilian and military expenses low.[2]

The overall budget of the national government fell from 23 percent of GDP in the final year of the Napoleonic Wars to a range of 12–13 percent in the 1830s and '40s. The budget was 13 percent of GDP in 1855, the peak year of spending during the Crimean War. The budget fell into the 6–7 percent of GDP range from the 1870s to '90s, and rose only to 11 percent in 1902, the peak year of spending during the South African War. In 1913, as Britain prepared to counter a militarized Germany, spending was just 8 percent of GDP.[3]

British military spending as a percentage of GDP from 1870 to 1913 was "78 percent that of the French, 67 percent that of the Russian, and 41 percent that of the Japanese" and comparable to that of Italy, Germany, and Austria.[4] However, since those other countries used

1   Cain and Hopkins, *British Imperialism*, 202–25.

2   Aaron L. Friedberg, *The Weary Titan: Britain and the Experience of Relative Decline* (Princeton: Princeton University Press, 1988), 89–134; Darwin, *Unfinished Empire*, 328–30; Andrew S. Thompson, *Imperial Britain: The Empire in British Politics c. 1880–1932* (Harlow: Longman, 2000).

3   B. R. Mitchell, *International Historical Statistics: Europe 1750–2000*, 5th ed. (Houndmills: Palgrave, 2003), 816–21, 905–13.

4   John M. Hobson, "The Military-Extraction Gap and the Wary Titan: The Fiscal-Sociology of British Defence Policy 1870–1913," *The Journal of European Economic History* 22 (1993): 480–1; see also O'Brien, "Security of the Realm and the Growth of the Economy," who concurs in Hobson's findings.

conscription, and Britain had to pay salaries to its soldiers, all of whom were volunteers, the data understate the gap between Britain and all the other great powers, except for the United States, the only power that spent less than Britain (and also relied exclusively on volunteers). Nevertheless, to "Victorian statesmen," the expenses were "onerous and deplorable."[1]

The British government justified low military spending by redefining its strategic needs. After viewing the United States as more of a threat than Japan in the last decades of the nineteenth century, Britain abandoned competition with the United States in the Americas and signed a 1901 treaty ceding rights to build the Panama Canal to the United States. Britain's decision to treat the United States as an ally and junior partner rather than a strategic rival provided justification for abandoning the goal of maintaining a fleet equal to that of all the other powers combined, and instead adopting the more modest standard of trying to equal the combined French and Russian fleets.[2] Throughout the last decades of the nineteenth century, Britain remained focused on threats to its empire from France, Russia, or the United States rather than from Germany on the Continent.[3]

The weight of interests and sources of income for British elites, their allies in the Empire, and the Treasury justified the attention to Empire over Europe. Elites were able to maintain the low taxes they desired as long as the military was focused on the cheaper task of holding and expanding the Empire rather than the far more expensive goal of countering Germany, France, or Russia in Europe. This approach worked as long as the Empire was profitable and there was peace in Europe. The Empire was cheap to maintain and expand because of the Indian army, a force that did much of Britain's dirty work in the nineteenth century. Trained in European combat techniques and led by British officers, India supplied the bulk of troops for nineteenth-century fighting in Abyssinia, China, Burma, Afghanistan, and the Persian Gulf.[4]

---

1   O'Brien, "Security of the Realm and the Growth of the Economy," 69.
2   Friedberg, *Weary Titan*, 135–208.
3   O'Brien, "Security of the Realm and the Growth of the Economy."
4   Tarak Barkawi, *Globalization and War* (Lanham: Rowman & Littlefield, 2006), chapter 3.

Most of Britain's nineteenth-century colonial wars were cheap in monetary terms and in British, though not in non-European, lives. Singer and J. David/Melvin Small identify five wars in the 1816–1913 period from the end of the Napoleonic Wars until the start of World War I in which more than 10,000 "British" soldiers died: the Anglo-Burmese War of 1823–26 (15,000 dead), the British-Afghan War of 1838–42 (20,000 dead), the Crimean War of 1854–56 (22,000 dead), the Mahdist War in Egypt of 1882–85 (20,000 dead), and the South African War of 1899–1902 (22,000 dead).[1] The Anglo-Burmese and Mahdist wars provoked little debate or dissention in Britain, in part because they were successful in securing Burma and Egypt for British control and because almost all the "British" dead in fact were Indian soldiers in the case of Burma[2] and were Egyptians fighting for Britain rather than Britons in the Mahdist war.[3]

The British-Afghan War was fought mainly with Indian troops.[4] The 4,500 "British" troops who were massacred in 1842 in one of the worst defeats in British military history included fewer than 700 Britons; the rest were Indians.[5] Britons evidenced no concern at all with the deaths of these Indian soldiers; however, there was opposition to the monetary cost of the war, especially since plans for the war were drawn up in secrecy and the war's reasons and objectives were kept opaque by the government. The newly victorious Tories, who replaced the Whig government in 1841, midway through the war, contributed to Britain's defeat: The Tory government instructed British commanders in Afghanistan to reduce costs. They did so by cutting their subsidies (bribes) to the Ghilzais, who then stopped protecting British troops, making the 1842 massacre possible.[6] The massacre of the mainly Indian

1    J. David Singer and Melvin Small, *The Wages of War, 1816–1965: A Statistical Handbook* (New York: John Wiley, 1972).

2    John F. Cady, *A History of Modern Burma* (Ithaca: Cornell University Press, 1958), 73–6.

3    Singer and Small, *Wages of War*, 392.

4    T. A. Heathcote, *The Afghan Wars: 1839–1919* (London: Osprey, 1980), 67–83; John W. Fortescue, *History of the British Army*, volume 11 (London: Macmillan, 1923), 269–352.

5    Patrick Macrory, *Signal Catastrophe: The Story of the Disastrous Retreat from Kabul, 1842* (London: Hodder & Stoughton, 1966), 207.

6    Diana Preston, *The Dark Defile: Britain's Catastrophic Invasion of Afghanistan, 1838–1842* (New York: Walker, 2012), 135–41; Heathcote, *Afghan Wars*, 52.

troops in Afghanistan "unleashed a torrent of criticism in the press in India,"[1] while the British press focused on the financial costs of the war. The *Times* was typical: "This nation spent £15 million on a less than profitable effort after self-aggrandizement in Afghanistan."[2]

The other two of Britain's major wars in the years between 1815 and 1914 were longer and more costly in money and British lives than the military commanders or Cabinet Ministers expected. Britain's difficulty, despite the help of its French and Ottoman allies, in winning a decisive victory against Russia in the Crimean War sparked debates over the causes of British military weakness as well as demands that the British army give an honest accounting of the number of war casualties. The Crimean War's strategic blunders and the lack of supplies and of medical facilities for wounded troops were reported by newspaper war correspondents, reporting from the battlefield for the first time in Crimea. Public outrage led to the resignation of the prime minister and the war minister.

After the Crimean War, limited reforms were made in the army. The government took over provision of troops, ending profiteering by officers. The organization of the army was simplified and centralized, eliminating autonomous departments outside the chain of command. Military schools were expanded to allow for in-service training of officers, though little was done to train ordinary troops.[3] Most effort was put into fighting small colonial wars, at which the British excelled and were almost uniformly successful.[4]

--------------------

1   Ibid., 22.

2   Quoted in Preston, *Dark Defile*, 22.

3   Warner, "Peacetime Economy and the Crimean War;" Brian Bond, "Colonial Wars and Punitive Expeditions 1856–99," in *History of the British Army*.

4   Bond, "Colonial Wars and Punitive Expeditions." Antoinette Burton, in *The Trouble with Empire: Challenges to Modern British Imperialism* (New York: Oxford University Press, 2015), catalogues many instances of resistance by the colonized to British rule, which in her view demonstrate the precariousness of the Empire. However, most of her case studies occurred after Britain had been decisively weakened in World War I. Nevertheless, despite the military, civil, and ideological challenges, Britain maintained its Empire, and profits continued to flow to the metropole. Britain never, even as the Empire unraveled after World War II, failed to profit from its colonies or lost many British lives fighting its non-European subjects. We must look to the British (both those located at home and abroad), rather than those they ruled, to explain the loss of British hegemony.

The British army, which as we saw earlier in this chapter had not reformed its officer corps as decisively as had the navy in the eighteenth century, made little further progress in the second half of the nineteenth century. Unlike the Germans, who forced officers to attend military schools that focused on technical training (an approach the French and Americans emulated after the Prussian victory over France in 1870), British officers continued to be drawn from the ranks of gentlemen who received a very different sort of education that was virtually worthless in preparing to fight modern wars with rapidly improving weaponry. Gentlemen had a virtual lock on officer positions in the army because, until 1871, they were allowed to purchase their commissions, and then afterward were promoted based on social background and education rather than attendance at military academies.[1]

> The social composition of the officer corps proved resistant to change, too. Abolishing purchase [of officer rank in 1870] had little effect, as the low rates of pay, the high cost of living, and the expensive uniforms and regimental traditions ensured that officers came from broadly the same classes in 1914 as they had done in 1870.[2]

The characteristics the British army used to select for their officers throughout the nineteenth (and previous) centuries were not entirely irrational. The army, after Waterloo, was used in colonial rather than European wars, and for the most part officers were charged with the tasks of administering the native soldiers in colonial and neo-colonial states' armies. They also, in many cases, were the main administrators in the territories where they were based. Thus, selecting officers for political skills and connections rather than military ability made sense for Britain as an empire, even though it weakened the army's ability to fight against European rivals.

The contradiction *between* Britain's needs as an empire and as a European power underlay the disaster of the Crimean War.

---

1   Harries-Jenkins, *Army in Victorian Society*.
2   Edward Spiers, "The Late Victorian Army 1868–1914," in *The Oxford History of the British Army*, 190.

Contradictions *within* the Empire, between the ability of politically well-connected freebooters, most notably Cecil Rhodes, and the overall needs and limited resources of the state, caused Britain's other costly foreign intervention in the century from 1815 to 1914: the South African War, which was sparked by Rhodes, who, after he was granted a British charter in 1889, took unilateral actions that antagonized the Boer Republic. Rhodes was able to buy parliamentary support and newspaper coverage with shares in his firms and outright bribes.[1]

At first, the South African War was popular; "the government was returned with a convincing majority at the 'khaki' election in 1900."[2] However, the war took much longer to win than expected, "required the services of 448,435 British and colonial troops and had cost the British taxpayer some £201 million. In all, 5774 men had been killed in action and another 16,168 had died of disease or wounds."[3] British public opinion turned against the war. Opposition focused on the costs in money and British soldiers' lives. (In chapter 7, we will track similar and even more intense reaction against the death toll of one's own soldiers in the United States during Vietnam and later wars.) There was virtually no attention given to the effects of the South African, or any other British, war on the inhabitants of the countries in which they were fought, although after 1870 the British public, spurred on by activists and newspapers reports, did voice outrage at atrocities committed by other European powers, most strongly against mass killings and torture by the Belgians in the Congo[4] and "opposing the Portuguese at the time of the Anglo-Portuguese Treaty of 1884."[5]

The difficult victory in the South African War led to further retrenchments in British strategic goals rather than increased

---

1    Darwin, *Empire Project*, 217–54.

2    Christopher Saunders and Iain R. Smith, "Southern Africa, 1795–1914: The Two Faces of Colonialism," in *The Oxford History of the British Empire, Volume III*, 618.

3    Spiers, "Late Victorian Army," 201.

4    Adam Hochschild, *King Leopold's Ghost: A Story of Greed, Terror, and Heroism in Colonial Africa* (New York: Houghton, Mifflin, 1998).

5    Andrew Porter, "Trusteeship, Anti-Slavery, and Humanitarianism," in *The Oxford History of the British Empire, Volume III*, 220.

investment in the military. Defense focused on India, and the army's main planning was to prepare for war against Russia in Afghanistan,[1] a war that could be fought mainly with Indian troops whose deaths would be of no concern to the British public. Britain was unable to settle on a global strategy, in part because authority for decisions was fragmented among the army, navy, and various ministries.[2] However, even if the government had been able to decide on a plan of action, implementing any plausible grand strategy would have required imposing significantly higher taxes, which both elites and voters would have resisted. Indeed, after the South African War, the main concern was the increase in state debt caused by military expenditures. This led to cuts in spending on social programs and opposition to expanding the size of the army.[3] Elites retained the political sway to block narrowly focused taxes, such as tariffs on specific industries or commodities,[4] banking taxes, or the land transfer tax proposed in 1909 by the Liberal Party.

When taxes finally were increased in 1910 with the passage of the Liberals' People's Budget after a year-long stalemate and new elections, the income tax rate on the wealthiest Britons was doubled, albeit to a still-miserly 7.5 percent, while a proposed tax on land sales opposed by the landed interests that still dominated the House of Lords had been dropped. Those new revenues were enough for only limited social spending and totally inadequate for a significant increase in military spending, which was not attempted. The Parliament Act of 1911 did permanently limit the Lords' ability to block tax and spending bills. However, the removal of that veto point did not lead to significant peacetime increases in taxes or to social programs until after World War II. Nor did British social movements, which were focused mainly around expansion of the franchise, demand such redistributionist policies. Liberal reforms were in part an effort to

---

1   Friedberg, *Weary Titan*, 209–78.
2   Ibid., 279–91.
3   Geoffrey Searle, " 'National Efficiency' and the 'Lessons' of the War," in *The Impact of the South African War*, eds. David Omissi and Andrew Thompson (Houndmills: Palgrave, 2002).
4   Friedberg, *Weary Titan*, 89–134.

coopt that mobilization,[1] while opposition to increased taxes and social spending by Conservatives and some Liberals preceded and outlasted voting rights agitation before and after World War I.

With India already supplying 250,000 troops, which was the limit of what the revenues Britain extracted from that colony could support (and perhaps was the limit of the number of "loyal" Indians Britain could recruit), any further troops needed to fight land wars in Europe or Asia would require that Britain emulate the Continental powers and impose a draft. Britain did enjoy some success in getting volunteers from settler colonies to fight in the South African War to make up for the government's unwillingness to accept non-white soldiers from India to fight whites in Africa,[2] but the 30,000 troops from Canada, Australia, and New Zealand who fought in that war were less than a tenth of the total soldiers Britain fielded,[3] and would have been (as they proved to be in World War I) a marginal element in a major land war.[4]

The South African War was an instance where, contra Michael Mann, British racism weakened empire: First, Britain's unwillingness to send non-white Indian soldiers to fight white Boer rebels means that more white Britons had to be sent to fight and die than if Britain had been able to overcome its racist queasiness at the thought of whites dying at the hands of non-whites. Second, Britons, while cruel to their Boer enemies, were not as brutal and hence less effective than they were in wars against non-whites, where there were no compunctions about employing extreme violence.

British elites never considered imposing conscription. Indeed, Britain fought the first two years of World War I with an army of volunteer and colonial troops and only resorted to the draft after its

---

1   Searle, " 'National Efficiency.' "

2   Thompson, *Imperial Britain*, 157–8.

3   Peter Burroughs, "Defence and Imperial Disunity," in *The Oxford History of the British Empire, Volume III*.

4   The number of troops who served overseas and died, respectively, in World War I included 458,218 and 56,639 from Canada, 331,814 and 59,330 from Australia, 112,223 and 16,711 from New Zealand, and 1,019,013 and 65,056 from India (Thompson, *Imperial Britain*, 158). The contributions of the four polities constituted 22 percent of both the number of troops who served and of those who died for Britain in that war.

army had been decimated in bone-headed assaults on German trenches. The difficulty of imposing conscription during World War I gives retrospective support for the political impossibility of using conscripts to sustain empire or impose hegemony in Europe. The British masses were as unwilling to sacrifice their lives as the elites were their money to the cause of British military power. Even though Britain's wealth from commerce depended on divisions among its European rivals and ultimately on its ability to prevent those other powers from going to war, except against colonial subjects,[1] it lacked the ability to mobilize its existing fiscal and human resources to sustain geopolitical dominance.

### iii. Settler Colonies and the Costs of Empire

"The mid-Victorians had solved the problem of Imperial cohesion by a bold set of pragmatic compromises . . . [creating a] tripartite world system" of settler colonies with increasing autonomy, India, and a dependent empire controlled with a combination of military coercion and cooption of local elites, and an informal empire managed by "private enterprise or an erratic combination of diplomacy and force."[2] That stability was undermined in the late nineteenth century as British imperial policy developed in two contradictory directions in response to the demands of domestic and colonial elites. The government sought to reduce its costs in the existing empire, especially in the settler colonies,[3] while at the same time moving to add new colonies in Africa and concessions in China.

The colonial additions partly reflected a geopolitical calculation that if Britain did not take those lands, other European powers or the United States would do so.[4] Porter sees British expansionism as grounded in "pessimism . . . The suggestion now being made was that Britain had to expand in order to stay alive."[5] However, the specific decisions to intervene in Africa or China came at the behest of particular British entrepreneur-adventurers or firms seeking to exploit

---

1   Darwin, *Empire Project*, 263–72, 284–301.
2   Ibid., 65.
3   Porter, *Lion's Share*, 47–58.
4   Beloff, *Britain's Liberal Empire*, 39–46.
5   Porter, *Lion's Share*, 82.

foreign territories. Financialization, and the increasing urgency with which British investors and firms sought new opportunities to realize higher returns as profits from land and older businesses at home fell, made it easy for entrepreneurs to round up funding for ventures in Africa that then created a presence that drew in governmental assistance. We need to remember, as John Darwin so aptly puts it, " 'Empire' is a grand word. But behind its façade (in every place and time) stood a mass of individuals, a network of lobbies, a mountain of hopes: for careers, fortunes, religious salvation or just physical safety."[1]

Despite the desire for economy, Britain did intervene when its interests, or more accurately, the interests of politically influential elites, were threatened and the cost of military action seemed to be low. City firms with growing investments in Africa demanded and got British diplomatic and military intervention in those lands.[2] Britain invaded Egypt in 1875 to put a new ruler in power who would honor Egypt's debt to Britain. Britain, as we noted above, fought the Afrikaner Republic, largely at the behest of Cecil Rhodes, to protect British control over newly discovered gold and diamonds.[3]

In tropical Africa, colonization was pushed by Foreign and Colonial Office officials for geopolitical reasons, for personal and organizational self-aggrandizement, and by "a mass of overlapping mini-empires of traders, investors, migrants, missionaries, railway companies, shipping companies, mining ventures, banks, botanists and geographers"[4] who stood to gain financially and/or in career advancement if the areas where they invested became formal British colonies.[5] Missionaries for the most part were from modest backgrounds—artisans, tradesmen, craftsmen, or the sons of such[6]— and found their work in distant colonies more lucrative and prestigious than the careers open to them at home. "Commercial companies, religious dissidents, planters, and adventurers were at least as

---

1   Darwin, *Unfinished Empire*, xi.
2   Chapman, *Merchant Enterprise in Britain*, 252–3.
3   Porter, *Lion's Share*, 90–101; John Darwin, *After Tamerlane: The Global History of Empire since 1405* (London: Allen Lane, 2007), 304–18.
4   Darwin, *Empire Project*, 97.
5   Cain and Hopkins, *British Imperialism*, 351–96.
6   Darwin, *Unfinished Empire*, 281–2.

important in extending the bounds of Empire as the soldiers and sailors of the monarch."[1] Parliament and the voting public endorsed the taking of new colonies provided there was no cost to the Treasury and the lands could be won without war. Advocates for taking new colonies built public support by planting articles in the *Times* and other newspapers, and by eliciting endorsements from emigrants, retired civil servants, and military men.[2]

In chapter 2 we heard from Niall Ferguson, who compared contemporary Americans with "their British counterparts of a century ago, who left elite British universities with an overtly imperial ethos."[3] Now, having examined British colonialism and colonists from the sixteenth through nineteenth centuries, we can conclude that any imperial ethos was overlaid with the continuing reality that it was easier to get rich in the colonies, and especially in lands that were "unexplored" and "uncivilized," than it was back home. Missionaries often did have an imperial ethos; however, their views were never determinative, and at times their behavior in the colonies and advocacy at home undercut the policies fostered by capitalists and the Foreign Office.[4]

To the extent that Britons at home supported imperialism, it was the result, as we just noted, of campaigns by self-interested investors and adventurers to orchestrate public pressure on the government to send troops. As we saw in the previous section, whenever the costs and casualties mounted, public support melted away and was replaced with anger and retribution over the "needless" sacrifice of British lives. Ferguson misreads the history of an era of which he supposedly is expert, viewing it through a miasma of Churchillian rhetoric, nostalgia for the jingoism of the early days of World War I, and the real devotion and sacrifice of World War II.[5]

--------

1  Davis and Huttenback, *Mammon and the Pursuit of Empire*, 9.
2  Darwin, *Empire Project*, 83–106.
3  Ferguson, *Colossus*, 204.
4  Porter, *Empire and Superempire*, 56–61, 175.
5  Burton, in *Trouble with Empire*, shows that Churchill himself was tireless (and dishonest) in his efforts, during his long career in various Cabinet offices charged with maintaining the Empire, to present British attempts to suppress colonial resistance as effortlessly and inexpensively successful while also serving to further natives' well-being and progress.

At the same time as the empire was expanding, the British government faced repeated challenge to its rule in the settler colonies. Beginning with the 1837 Canadian rebellion, which, while small, raised fears of US intervention,[1] Britain responded with offers of ever-greater autonomy, which then failed to prevent demands from colonists for further concessions. The policy was a success in that it made the settler colonies self-supporting, although they contributed virtually nothing to Britain's defense of their territories or to general imperial military expenses.[2] Britain, then and afterward, was unwilling to pay the costs of sending enough troops to its settler colonies to bolster local elites or to sustain direct rule. British elites, rather than raise taxes or impose a draft, instead took the only remaining option: Establish local governments in the settler colonies that would remain within the Empire but also raise the funds needed for their own administration and self-defense. Thus, Britain withdrew most of its troops from Canada in the 1850s and '60s. It did send troops in 1860 to suppress a Maori rebellion in New Zealand, but then quickly withdrew most of them to keep costs down.[3]

Elected governments in the settler colonies, not surprisingly, served the interests of their electorate, or at least of local elites. In 1859, Britain allowed "responsible governments" in settler colonies to impose tariffs, and they all used that new authority to raise revenues and to protect local industries from British and other foreign competition.[4] Despite repeated lobbying by business groups in Britain against tariffs,[5] Britain never challenged the settler colonies as they raised those taxes. It was easier politically to minimize expenses in, and the potential for a rupture with, the settler colonies[6] than it would have been to confront the colonists and try to reverse their demands for autonomy and pursuit of economic self-interest by resuming direct rule, which also would have required Britain to pay the cost of those territories' defense. In any case, the various

1   Burroughs, "Imperial Institutions and the Government of Empire."
2   Davis and Huttenback, *Mammon and the Pursuit of Empire*, 11–12.
3   Burroughs, "Defence and Imperial Disunity."
4   Darwin, *Empire Project*, 51; Cain, "Economics and Empire," 42.
5   Davis and Huttenback, *Mammon and the Pursuit of Empire*, 253–61.
6   O'Brien, "Security of the Realm and the Growth of the Economy."

colonial departments were all understaffed and under constant pressure from white settlers and from lobbies for the white colonists in
the dependent colonies[1] and were unable to formulate a new, more
assertive strategy.

In addition, the British government had offered loan guarantees
for the notes issued by both dependent and settler colonies,[2] so to
avoid having to pay for defaults Britain allowed those colonies to
protect their industries while the "home market [was] kept open and
unprotected, in part to assist the nation's competitors to service their
debt to British investors."[3] The interests of British industrialists harmed
by the settler colonies' tariffs were overwhelmed by these larger fiscal
and geopolitical considerations, and by the power of financiers to
make repayment of their bonds a top priority in foreign and imperial
policy. The question of how long the Empire remained profitable for
Britain is a complex problem that has yet to be resolved. However,
what is beyond dispute is that it remained profitable for "the interlocking elites of government, finance, landownership, commerce, and the
professions in the south east of the country."[4]

## iv. Conclusion

How did the changing relationship of settler colonies to metropole
matter? Think back to table 1.1. Colonial elites in India and the dependent colonies were located in the quadrant with a low level of autonomy from metropolitan officials and a high degree of influence on the
metropole's economy and/or politics. That classification, as we have
seen in this chapter, is justified by the nationalization of the EIC and
the British state's continuing ability to appropriate Indian resources
for the Treasury and Indian soldiers to fight battles to preserve British
geopolitical supremacy. However, elites in the settler colonies occupied the opposite quadrant, with a high level of autonomy from metropolitan officials and a high degree of influence on the metropole's

---

1   Andrew Porter, "Introduction: Britain and the Empire in the Nineteenth
Century," in *The Oxford History of the British Empire, Volume III*, 15–19.

2   Davis and Huttenback, *Mammon and the Pursuit of Empire*, 166–94.

3   O'Brien, "Costs and Benefits of British Imperialism," 184.

4   Avner Offer, "The British Empire, 1870–1914: A Waste of Money?" *The
Economic History Review*, new series, 46, no. 2 (1993): 232.

economy and/or politics. We have seen the high level of autonomy in the successful American Revolution and in the growing ability of the remaining settler colonies to achieve self-rule and use their political powers to adopt policies, like tariffs, that benefited the colonies even as they harmed the metropole. Settler colonial elites leveraged their interlocking economic relations with the metropole to influence British politics and foster policies that undermined Britain's ability to sustain its dominance in manufacturing and shifted the balance of power, both economically and politically, toward the financial elite.

In essence, Britain in the late nineteenth century lost one of the four essential attributes for achieving and sustaining hegemony identified in the Boolean truth table of table 1.3: The settler colonies' increasing autonomy, and their growing ability to influence policy in metropolitan Britain, came to outweigh or at least to counterbalance India's lack of autonomy and contributions to British fiscal and military power. Thus, to understand the rise, sustainability, and demise of British hegemony, we needed to analyze the Empire and its elites as a whole, to track the interactions among metropolitan and colonial elites, and to weigh the relative effects of autonomous and dependent colonial elites on metropolitan political economy. I hypothesized in chapter 1 that hegemony disrupted stable elite relations and heightened elite conflict in the metropole. That turns out not to have been true for Britain. Rather, settler elites found a path to greater autonomy within British hegemony. In the case of Britain, it was greater elite autonomy in settler colonies rather than heightened elite conflict in the metropole that fatally weakened British hegemony.

British imperialism created new elites, both at home and in the colonies, altering the overall structure of relations among elites. Financialization was the product of British imperialism and of the double dynamic of metropolitan and colonial elite formation it engendered. Britain's monetary and financial hegemony, the windfalls from colonies and commerce, and the demands from colonial elites for both autonomy and protection, made the financial elite the keystone that united the material interests and political goals of other landed, colonial, commercial, manufacturing, and governmental elites, creating an unalterable consensus behind low taxes and a strong currency. Those policies ensured that finance remained the most profitable form of investment, and in turn blocked the reorganization of British industry and the domestic investments needed to counter competition from American and German firms. Low taxes prevented the level of military spending necessary to overwhelm the other European powers, above all Germany, and thereby prevent the great power rivalry that doomed British commercial and colonial hegemony. Britain's unusually long hegemony, which spanned the Industrial Revolution, was undermined uniquely without the formation of autarkic elites. Rather, consensus among interlocking elites allowed an enduring imperial and fiscal policy that actually was able to serve all those elites' self-perceived interests but that blocked reforms vital to countering the rise of economic and military rivals.

# II.  Hegemony Present

# 6

# From Consensus to Paralysis in the United States, 1960–2016

Most of us are conditioned for many years to have a political viewpoint, Republican or Democrat, liberal, conservative, moderate. The fact of the matter is that most of the problems, or at least many of them that we now face, are technical problems, are administrative problems. They are very sophisticated judgments which do not lend themselves to the great sort of "passionate movements" which have stirred this country so often in the past. Now they deal with questions which are beyond the comprehension of most men.

President John F. Kennedy, 1962[1]

From our vantage point a half century later, President Kennedy's confidence in experts' capacity to solve problems with their technical

1    Quoted in Stephen W. Rousseas and James Farganis, "American Politics and the End of Ideology," *The British Journal of Sociology*, 14 (1963): 358–9. In another speech that year, President Kennedy developed this line of thinking further: "Today . . . the central domestic problems of our time are more subtle and less simple. They do not relate to basic clashes of philosophy and ideology, but to ways and means of reaching common goals—to search for sophisticated solutions to complex and obstinate issues. What is at stake in our economic decisions today is not some grand warfare of rival ideologies which will sweep the country with passion but the practical management of a modern economy. What we need are not labels and clichés but more basic discussion of the sophisticated and technical questions involved in keeping a great economic machinery moving ahead . . . Political labels and ideological approaches are irrelevant to the solutions . . . The problems of . . . the Sixties as opposed to the kinds of problems we faced in the Thirties demand subtle challenges for which technical answers not political answers must be provided" (quoted in Rousseas and Farganis, "American Politics and the End of Ideology," 359). Though there is no evidence he read it, Kennedy's views paralleled those of Daniel Bell in *The End of Ideology: On the Exhaustion of Political Ideas in the Fifties* (New York: Free Press, 1960).

knowledge seems both touching and misplaced. Yet what appears most unrealistic, to those of us who spent the first decades of the twenty-first century in the United States, is his belief that elites or citizens more broadly could be convinced by expert judgment to abandon their ideological positions or to subordinate their particular interests to policies that would advance general prosperity and the common good.

At the time Kennedy spoke, though, there were good reasons for his confidence that ideological convictions were giving way to expert consensus. What Kennedy described in another speech as "the practical management of a modern economy" enjoyed bipartisan support. Leaders of both parties in Congress endorsed Keynesian strategies of tax cuts and government spending,[1] as did the "corporate moderates" who headed most of the largest US firms.[2] The consensus extended to foreign policy in the early 1960s, with agreement on an aggressive approach to armament and to counter-insurgency in the Third World. Leaders of both parties agreed not only on the broad goals of economic growth, reduction of poverty, and the containment of Communism; they also believed in the efficacy of the strategies formulated by experts in government. (Mort Sahl mocked this consensus when he summarized the 1956 presidential campaign: "Eisenhower stands for 'gradualism.' Stevenson stands for 'moderation.' Between these two extremes, the people must choose.")[3]

--------

1   The bipartisan faith in Keynesian "fine-tuning" of the economy encompassed tax increases as well as cuts. The Revenue and Expenditure Control Act of 1968, which added a 10 percent surcharge to the federal personal and corporate income tax, was approved 64–16 in the Senate, with thirty-one Republicans voting yes (govtrack.us/congress/vote.xpd?vote=s1968-468), and 268–150 in the House, with 114 Republicans voting yes (govtrack.us/congress/vote .xpd?vote=h1968-357). The most prominent votes against the surcharge came from opponents of the Vietnam War, like Senator George McGovern, who otherwise favored more generous social programs financed through higher taxes.

2   G. William Domhoff, *The Myth of Liberal Ascendancy: Corporate Domination from the Great Depression to the Great Recession* (Boulder: Paradigm, 2013); Kotz, *Rise and Fall of Neoliberal Capitalism*.

3   Quoted in Jeffrey Frank, *Ike and Dick: Portrait of a Strange Political Marriage* (New York: Simon & Schuster, 2013), 142.

At the same time, there was little effective opposition to these policies from outside government in the United States. On the left, the peace movement was weak and focused mainly on ending nuclear tests, while slighting US military intervention around the world.[1] Unions endorsed the government's macroeconomic policies and limited their demands to wage and benefit increases that tracked the rise in productivity and corporate profits. The influence, in national politics, of what was then labeled "the lunatic fringe" was becoming marginalized as the Republican Party led by Eisenhower and Nixon embraced an internationalist foreign policy, government management of macroeconomic growth, and modest efforts to gradually ameliorate poverty. Outside the South, both parties supported the gradual extension of civil rights to blacks.

Capitalists, at least those who headed the largest industrial and financial firms, were supportive of or, more often, resigned to government social programs, economic regulation, progressive taxation, even as they tried to block or slow new governmental initiatives. This acceptance, like the regulatory regimes and social programs themselves, were pragmatic responses to the massive upsurge of labor and farmer militancy in the 1930s and to radical electoral politics within (and potentially beyond) the Democratic Party exemplified by Huey Long.

The American rich, like their counterparts in Europe, saw no choice but to accept historically unprecedented low levels of inequality in income and wealth.[2] The seventy-six wealthiest Americans (those with fortunes of more than $75 million) portrayed in a 1957 *Fortune* article "think it's a little immoral for their children to live on money they didn't earn." However, even those who wanted their children to inherit their fortunes felt resigned to high tax rates. "A cut in

1   Charles DeBenedetti and Charles Chatfield, *An American Ordeal: The Antiwar Movement of the Vietnam Era* (Syracuse: Syracuse University Press, 1990), 9–78; Lawrence Wittner, *The Struggle Against the Bomb*, 3 volumes (Stanford: Stanford University Press, 1993–2003); Penny Lewis, *Hardhats, Hippies, and Hawks: The Vietnam Antiwar Movement as Myth and Memory* (Ithaca: Cornell University Press, 2013), 58.
2   Thomas Piketty, *Capital in the Twenty-First Century* (Cambridge: Harvard University Press, 2014).

the 90 percent inheritance tax is politically impossible without a general reduction in taxes. Yet even if real tax relief is impossible, the situation of the Very Rich could hardly be called desperate."[1]

Businessmen's support for US foreign policy was greased by the US government's diplomatic, financial, and military protection of their foreign investments, and by the outsized profits they earned from contracts for weapons that flowed not only to large firms but to subcontractors that were located in virtually every congressional district. Unions, treasuring the well-paying and stable jobs their members held at defense firms, supported the foreign policy that made the weapons their members built necessary.

Bipartisan agreement on the goals of foreign and much domestic policy, and on the methods for achieving those goals through governmental management, was built upon a high degree of cohesion among elites. Firms were linked together by director interlocks, centered on the largest banks. The ability of corporate managers to pursue their own interests, rather than act as fiduciaries of their shareholders and workers, was hemmed in by their dependence on banks for financing and by a web of government regulations that stymied their capacities to alter the shares of income that went to owners, managers, and workers. Firms were constrained by unions' ability and willingness to strike in the era from the 1930s to the 1970s. Non-union industrial firms outside the South faced the threat of unionization if their wages and benefits fell significantly behind those won by unionized workers. The government's share of national income had grown significantly in the 1950s and increased again in the 1960s in the absence of effective opposition to military spending, and as both political parties were committed to maintaining New Deal social programs and differed mainly on which of those programs should be expanded and at what cost.

Conflict along ideological, class, or other lines was limited, above all, by the United States' commanding position in the world economy and geopolitics, which provided the resources to accommodate multiple interests and priorities. Tax revenues made new social programs

1   Richard Austin Smith, "The Fifty-Million-Dollar Man," *Fortune* (November 1957): 233, 238.

affordable at the state and local as well as national levels. Public sector construction, which had expanded drastically with New Deal programs, continued in the quarter century after World War II with the main focus on schools, universities, hospitals, and roads. University enrollment, which had risen gradually in the first half of the twentieth century, immediately doubled after the end of World War II and more than quadrupled by the end of the twentieth century.[1] US military dominance was financed by a Pentagon budget that consumed 7–10 percent of GDP in the two decades from the end of the Korean War to the end of the Vietnam War,[2] and supplemented by foreign aid, which totaled 1–2 percent of GDP.[3] Productivity, wages, corporate profits, and GDP all grew rapidly and in tandem in the 1950s and 1960s, and the S&P stock index increased 527 percent from 1945 to its peak in 1969.[4]

The elite consensus around foreign and domestic policy was reflected in bipartisan support for presidents Kennedy and Johnson's commitment of troops in Vietnam, and in the heavy bipartisan majorities in favor of many of Johnson's Great Society and civil rights bills. The Eighty-Ninth Congress of 1965–66, in which the Democrats had their largest majorities in both the House and Senate since 1937–38, enacted a wave of legislation in civil rights; the Hart-Celler Immigration and Nationality Act, which abolished national quotas favoring Europeans; anti-poverty programs; environmental protection, including the Endangered Species Act; public broadcasting; created the National Endowments for the Arts and Humanities; and established Medicare and Medicaid, which were the largest social programs since Social Security. Many of these programs enjoyed support from significant blocs of Republicans in Congress.

---

1   US Census Bureau, *The 2010 Statistical Abstract* (2010), table HS-21; National Center for Educational Statistics, *120 Years of American Education: A Statistical Portrait* (Washington, DC: US Department of Education, 1993), figure 2.

2   See table 7.2 on page 309.

3   Curt Tarnoff and Larry Nowels, "Foreign Aid: An Introductory Overview of US Programs and Policy," Congressional Research Service (2005), 16.

4   US Census Bureau, *2010 Statistical Abstract*, table HS-38.

## THE EXCEPTION

The major exception to (large) capitalists' acquiescence in Keynesian economics and government social programs was their continuing opposition to, and desire to weaken, labor unions. Employers had been helpless to stop the waves of unionization before and after the passage of the Wagner Act and during World War II, and only after decades of concerted efforts were they able to diminish unions' scope and power. Employers' first and most far-reaching victory over unions, the Taft-Hartley Act of 1947, was achieved opportunistically, during one of the only two congressional sessions between 1932 and 1994 in which Republicans had majorities in both the House and Senate, and follow-ing the wave of strikes and price inflation immediately after the end of World War II. Yet the congressional coalition of Republicans and south-ern Democrats that enacted Taft-Hartley over President Truman's veto[1] was the same coalition that pushed through the Landrum-Griffin Act in 1959, a year in which Democrats had large majorities in the House and Senate, which further hobbled unions, and which has successfully blocked every single effort to counter employers' growing ability to thwart union organizing drives by easing the path to National Labor Relations Board (NLRB) recognition of unions.

The employers who lobbied for Taft-Hartley did not anticipate the dramatic long-term effects that legislation would have in hampering unions. Indeed, Kotz argues that

> a critical mass of corporate leaders concluded the time [after the passage of Taft-Hartley] was right to make a deal with a labor lead-ership that was now more moderate and hemmed in by Taft-Hartley ... Had the elimination of unions been a possibility, it is likely that few, if any, of the big corporations would have signed onto this deal, but the option of continuing the effort to drive out unions was an unrealistic one

---

1   Benjamin C. Waterhouse, *Lobbying America: The Politics of Business from Nixon to NAFTA* (Princeton: Princeton University Press, 2014), 53–4.

in the 1940s, '50s and '60s.[1] The provisions that allowed individual states to create "right-to-work" laws that ban closed shops, i.e., the requirement that all employees in a unionized workplace belong to and pay dues to the union that represents them, were intended to maintain the South as union-free. No one foresaw the extent to which firms would move facilities to the South, creating leverage they could use against employees in the rest of the country. Also unexpected was the ability of capitalists to muscle through right-to-work laws in the Southwest as well as the South in the 1940s and '50s, and then in Michigan, Indiana, and Wisconsin in the twenty-first century. Finally, the Taft-Hartley Act of 1947 made it possible for firms to sue unions for damages from losses during wildcat strikes. This gave national unions a powerful incentive to discipline and control locals, which over decades sapped locals' autonomy and weakened militancy among members.[2]

Unions inevitably lose members as firms and industries they have organized decline. Only if unions are able to organize emerging businesses and sectors can membership remain steady or increase. Thus, the ways in which Taft-Hartley, Landrum-Griffin, and NLRB rulings during Republican administrations have reinforced one another to hobble union organizing have been reflected in a decades-long decline in membership, both in absolute numbers and especially as a percentage of the workforce. Union density, as a percentage of the non-agricultural workforce, peaked at 33.3 percent in 1954 (the same as the earlier 1945 peak), declined to 28.6 percent by 1960, declined only to 26.6 percent in 1972, but then fell at an accelerating pace: to 23.9 percent in 1981, 18.2 percent in 1991, 14.8 percent in 2001, and 13.0 percent in 2011.[3]

American unions have been weakened by a combination of factors that have endured from the postwar decades to the present. First, the sorts of divisions among capitalists along dimensions of industry, size, locality, or ideology that created openings for social welfare legislation

---

1   Kotz, *Rise and Fall of Neoliberal Capitalism*, 58.
2   David R. Roediger and Philip S. Foner, *Our Own Time: A History of American Labor and the Working Day* (New York: Greenwood Press, 1989), 266–7.
3   Barry Eidlin, *Labor and the Class Idea in the US and Canada* (Cambridge: Cambridge University Press, 2018), table A1.1.

and regulation in other policy realms never extended to unions. Employers were always unified in opposition to unions,[1] so it was impossible for unions to find allies or to strike deals with capitalists or the federal government in the absence of massive strike waves or the need to quell labor unrest during wartimes.

Second, unions were divided by racism and so made little effort to organize in the South, the bastion of the anti-union congressional majority and the region to which unionized firms relocated factories before they exported facilities and jobs to other countries. While racism divided unions and their liberal allies,[2] it united southern Democrats and Republicans in Congress and repeatedly allowed Republicans to appeal to voters who otherwise would have been antagonized by conservative economic policies.[3] Gregory Hooks and Brian McQueen find that the congressional districts that the Republicans picked up in 1946, and which provided them with the majority that passed Taft-Hartley over Truman's veto, were the sites of aircraft manufacturing plants that experienced significant in-migration of non-whites during World War II.[4] Racism also provided an opening, as we discuss below, for Nixon to use the issue of affirmative action to split trade unions away from their northern Democratic allies who were committed to civil rights.

Third, unions were divided over communism, leading to purges that removed the most dedicated and successful organizers, leaving unions headed by increasingly passive and bureaucratic officials.[5]

---

1  G. William Domhoff, "Is the Corporate Elite Fractured, or Is There Continuing Corporate Dominance? Two Contrasting Views," *Class, Race and Corporate Power* 3, no. 1, article 1 (2014); *Myth of Liberal Ascendancy*.

2  Reuel Schiller, "Singing 'The Right-to-Work Blues': The Politics of Race in the Campaign for 'Voluntary Unionism' in Postwar California," in *The Right and Labor in America: Politics, Ideology, and Imagination*, ed. Nelson Lichtenstein and Elizabeth Tandy Shermer (Philadelphia: University of Pennsylvania Press, 2012).

3  Tami J. Friedman, "Capital Flight, 'States' Rights,' and the Anti-Labor Offensive after World War II," in *The Right and Labor in America*; Elizabeth Tandy Shermer, " 'Is Freedom of the Individual Un-American?' Right-to-Work Campaigns and Anti-Union Conservatism, 1943–1958," in *The Right and Labor in America*.

4  Gregory Hooks and Brian McQueen, "American Exceptionalism Revisited: The Military-Industrial Complex, Racial Tension, and the Underdeveloped Welfare State," *American Sociological Review* 75 (2010).

5  Judith Stepan-Norris and Maurice Zeitlin, *Left Out: Reds and America's Industrial Unions* (Cambridge: Cambridge University Press, 2003).

Thus, a corporate strategy designed in the years following World War II to limit the expansion and growing power of unions had the long-term effect of weakening unions and isolating them politically to an extent no one foresaw when Taft-Hartley and Landrum-Griffin were enacted. Finally, the string of Republican and conservative Democratic presidencies from 1969 through 2008 shifted the membership and rulings of the NLRB in ways that hampered union organizing and allowed employers to use union-busting methods devised by firms like Modern Management Methods in the 1970s.[1] The turn toward intensified efforts to fight union organizing accompanied the wave of mergers (discussed later) that removed the divisions between (primarily northern) formerly union-accommodating corporations and (primarily southern) firms that previously stood out for their vehement opposition to unions.

## THE GREAT U-TURN

The American economy and public policy changed abruptly after the 1960s. Individual wages, family incomes, labor productivity, corporate profits, and government revenues, which all had risen rapidly since the end of World War II, stagnated in the 1970s. As bad as the 1970s were in comparison to the boom of the 1950s and '60s, the rate of growth in GDP (both in total and per capita), labor productivity, and real compensation per employee fell off in each subsequent decade, reversed only by the 1995–2000 expansion that was sparked and sustained mainly by a financial bubble that was punctured with the 2000 stock market crash.[2]

US labor productivity, which grew an average of 2.5 percent per annum from 1950 to 1973, grew only 1 percent from 1973 to 1984.[3]

---

1   Kim Phillips-Fein, *Invisible Hands: The Making of the Conservative Movement from the New Deal to Reagan* (New York: Norton, 2009), 206–7.

2   Robert Brenner, *The Boom and the Bubble: The US in the World Economy* (London: Verso, 2003).

3   Angus Maddison, "Growth and Slowdown in Advanced Capitalist Economies: Techniques of Quantitative Assessment," *Journal of Economic Literature* 25 (1987): 650.

Real wages, which rose at 10 percent per annum in the 1960s, increased only 2.7 percent per year in the 1970s, which itself was more than double the rate in any subsequent decade.[1] The rate of profit for non-financial business firms, "which fluctuates sharply over the business cycle," had peaks of 9.2 percent in 1982, 12.6 percent in 1997, and 11.7 percent in 2006, which compared poorly with peaks of 16 percent in the 1950s and 17.3 percent in 1966. In addition, the peaks lasted longer, and the declines were shorter and less severe in the 1950s and '60s than in any subsequent decades, including the 1990s.[2]

Workers captured only a small share of productivity growth after 1973. From 1948 to 1973, productivity increased 96.7 percent and average hourly compensation of production/nonsupervisory workers in the private sector 91.3 percent. From 1973 to 2014, productivity grew 72.2 percent while wages increased only 9.2 percent.[3]

Income inequality, which fell under every president from FDR to LBJ except Eisenhower, under whom it remained stable, has risen under every president from Nixon through Bush, including Clinton. It fell slightly under Obama. Wealth inequality has widened even more rapidly since the 1970s, reaching a peak under Bush in 2007 that exceeded the peak previously set in 1929.[4] The top 1 percent's share of total national income was in 23.9 percent in 1928, fell to 10 percent in 1979, rose again to 23.5 percent in 2007, and had fallen slightly to 20.1 percent in 2013.[5] Expressed another way,

1  Brenner, *Boom and the Bubble*, 47.

2  Kotz, *Rise and Fall of Neoliberal Capitalism*, 87, 63.

3  Josh Bivens and Lawrence Mishel, "Understanding the Historic Divergence Between Productivity and a Typical Worker's Pay: Why It Matters and Why It's Real," *Economic Policy Institute*, Policy Briefing Paper no. 406 (2015), figure A.

4  Thomas Piketty and Emmanuel Saez, "Income Inequality in the United States, 1913–2002," in *Top Incomes over the Twentieth Century: A Contrast Between European and English Speaking Countries*, ed. Anthony B. Atkinson and Thomas Piketty (Oxford: Oxford University Press, 2007), table A1. This shift was first documented by Barry Bluestone and Bennett Harrison, *The Great U-Turn: Corporate Restructuring and the Polarizing of America* (New York: Basic, 1988), who coined the term "the Great U-Turn" in the title of their book.

5  Estelle Sommeiller, Mark Price, and Ellis Wazeter, "Income Inequality in the US by State, Metropolitan Area, and County," *Economic Policy Institute* (2016), table 10.

The top 1% used to earn 11% of national income in the late 1960s and now gets slightly over 20%; the bottom 50% used to get slightly over 20% and now captures 12%. Eight points of national income have been transferred from the bottom 50% to the top 1%. The top 1% income share has made gains large enough to more than compensate the fall in the bottom 50% share, a group demographically 50 times larger. While average pre-tax income has stagnated since 1980 at around $16,000 for the bottom 50%, it has been multiplied by three for the top 1% to about $1,300,000 in 2014. As a result, while top 1% adults earned 27 times more income than bottom 50% adults on average in 1980, they earn 81 times more today.[1]

From 1949 to 1979, the top 1 percent captured 10 percent of total income growth during years of economic expansion, in line with or a bit less than their share of national income, while from 1981 to 2013 the top 1 percent captured 58.9 percent of the growth, far outpacing and adding to their share of national income.[2] "US CEOs of major companies earned 20 times more than a typical worker in 1965; this ratio grew to 29.9-to-1 in 1978 and 58.7-to-1 by 1989, and then it surged in the 1990s to hit 376.1-to-1 by the end of the 1990s recovery in 2000." CEO compensation fell with the 2000–01 stock market decline and with the 2008–09 financial crisis, but quickly recovered in both instances: "the CEO-to-worker compensation ratio in 2014 had recovered to 303.4-to-1."[3]

Government policy also made a dramatic turn in the 1970s. The only significant expansion of the federal government's regulatory or social welfare role came in the early years of the Nixon administration with the establishment of the Environmental Protection Agency in 1970, enactment of the Clean Air Act of 1970 and the Clean Water Act of 1972, and passage of the Occupational Safety and Health Act of

---

1   Thomas Piketty, Emmanuel Saez, and Gabriel Zucman, "Distributional National Accounts: Methods and Estimates for the United States," National Bureau of Economic Research (2016), 21–2.

2   Sommeiller, Price, and Wazeter, "Income Inequality in the US," table 9.

3   Lawrence Mishel and Alyssa Davis, "Top CEOs Make 300 Times More than Typical Workers," *Economic Policy Institute*, Issue Brief no. 399 (2015).

1970.[1] Since then, no significant environmental laws have been passed in the United States.

Efforts to further expand social benefits were blocked again and again in the four decades since the Great Society. Most famously, plans to guarantee health care to all Americans were defeated in the Nixon, Carter, and Clinton administrations. All three defeats occurred when the Democrats controlled Congress, in the case of Carter with majorities in 1977–78 that were almost as large as those Johnson enjoyed in 1965–66. The plans proposed by those three presidents were each more comprehensive than the one that became law under Obama in 2010.

The only civil rights legislation to pass since the Johnson years was the Americans with Disabilities Act of 1990, and a series of modest bills designed to reverse Supreme Court decisions that undercut existing laws protecting African Americans and women from discrimination. Even when groups won court cases that expanded their civil rights, they failed to gain enhanced social benefits. American women won legal equality in many realms since the 1960s while failing to achieve the government-funded maternity leave and childcare benefits that are the right of women in every other wealthy nation.[2] The overall poverty rate at the end of Obama's presidency was higher than in 1973 at the end of the first Nixon administration, still the lowest level ever recorded.[3]

---

1   The Occupational Safety and Health Act of 1970 passed Congress in 1970 after business interests defeated a stronger bill proposed by the Johnson administration in 1968. Unions thought that an independent Occupational Safety and Health Administration (OSHA) would be more vulnerable to business pressure than if its regulatory powers were lodged in the Department of Labor, as Johnson had proposed. Those fears have proven justified in the subsequent half century. Nevertheless, the act's passage was possible because unions in 1970 still had a level of political power that forced business interests to compromise by supporting Nixon's OSHA bill.

2   Sally Cohen, in *Championing Child Care* (New York: Columbia University Press, 2001), details the repeated defeat in the 1970s of legislation guaranteeing childcare; see also Kimberly J. Morgan, "A Child of the Sixties: The Great Society, the New Right, and the Politics of Federal Child Care," *Journal of Policy History* 13 (2001).

3   US Census Bureau, *Historical Poverty Tables* (2017), Table 2 census.gov/data/tables/time-series/demo/income-poverty/historical-poverty-people.html. Retrieved January 14, 2019.

The most consequential governmental initiative toward African Americans since the 1970s, joined by officials at the federal, state, and local levels and during both Democratic and Republican administrations, has been the extraordinary increase in black imprisonment, which rose from 3 percent of all black men aged 18 to 65 in 1980 to 7.9 percent in 2000.[1] This has affected more African Americans, with far more profound consequences, than have tepid affirmative action programs by employers or universities.[2]

The history of US governmental policy since 1968 is not only a story of the total absence of significant new programs until Obama's Patient Protection and Affordable Care Act in 2010, but also of a government taking affirmative steps to weaken protections for workers and consumers while altering regulations and tax policies in ways that increased inequality and left citizens far more vulnerable to the depredations of large corporations. All the strides of the New Deal and Great Society in reducing inequality were reversed in the three decades from Reagan's election to Obama's as the United States returned in the first decade of the twenty-first century to 1920s levels of inequality in wealth. The United States also returned to the 1920s in terms of state control of capitalism. New Deal laws regulating banking and finance were almost entirely repealed in the 1990s. Thomas Volscho and Nathan Kelly find that declines in union density have the greatest and longest-lasting effect on the top 1 percent's share of income, followed by asset bubbles in stocks and real estate, Republican's share of Congressional seats, and then the top marginal tax rate. All four measures shifted in the period from the late 1970s to the present in the direction that enhanced the income and wealth of the top 1 percent.[3] Bruce Western and Jake Rosenfeld find "the decline of organized labor explains a fifth to a

---

1   Bruce Western, *Punishment and Inequality in America* (New York: Russell Sage Foundation, 2006), 17.

2   Western, *Punishment and Inequality*, 29, shows the full effect of the prison boom on the cohort of black men born from 1965 to 1969. In 1999, 22.4 percent of those men had been imprisoned, while only 12.5 percent had received bachelor's degrees.

3   Thomas W. Volscho and Nathan J. Kelly, "The Rise of the Super-Rich: Power Resources, Taxes, Financial Markets, and the Dynamics of the Top 1 Percent, 1949–2008," *American Sociological Review* 77 (2012).

third of the growth in inequality—an effect comparable to the growing stratification of wages by education."[1]

We already noted the drastic increase in income and wealth
inequality from 1970 to 2008. That increase was due in part to changes
in the tax code. The top income tax rate fell from 77 percent at the end
of the Johnson administration to 28 percent under Reagan. In 2009–
10, Congress, with Democratic majorities in both houses, debated
whether to leave the top rate at the 35 percent it was under Bush or
return it to the 39.6 percent of the Clinton years, a debate that was
settled with a bipartisan deal brokered by Vice President Biden and
Republican Senate Minority Leader Mitch McConnell to continue the
Bush levels through 2012. The Clinton rate became permanent again
with legislation passed in 2013. The restoration of the 39.6 percent
rate, along with a tax surcharge on investment income to help fund
Obamacare, combined with "tax cuts on the middle-class and poor . . .
reduced incomes for the highest-earning 1% by an average of 5% per
household and increased incomes for the lowest earning tenth of
households by an average of 9.7% . . . Obama had moved the needle
against income inequality."[2] The 2017 tax cut bill dropped the top rate
to 37 percent, and it is unclear when conditions will allow for a new
reduction in inequality.

Along with the rate cuts, the federal government has acquiesced in
wealthy Americans' use of an increasing array of techniques for shel-
tering income, stratagems that will be expanded by the 2017 tax legislation. Aided by lawyers, accountants, and offshore bankers from the
"income defense industry,"[3] the four hundred Americans with the
highest incomes paid only half of the nominal 35 percent top rate in
2007, down from 85 percent of the nominal rate of 31 percent in 1992.
Such tax avoidance schemes reduce federal tax revenues by $70 billion
a year. President Obama, in 2009, proposed measures to crack down
on "tax cheats" and "shut down overseas tax havens." Those measures,
which would have recovered only $8.7 billion of the $700 billion that

---

1   Bruce Western and Jake Rosenfeld, "Unions, Norms, and the Rise in US
Wage Inequality," *American Sociological Review* 76 (2011), 513.

2   Jonathan Chait, *Audacity: How Barack Obama Defined His Critics and
Created a Legacy That Will Prevail* (New York: Custom House, 2017), 70.

3   Jeffrey Winters, *Oligarchy* (Cambridge: Cambridge University Press, 2011).

would be lost to tax avoidance by high-income taxpayers over the next decade, were rejected by the Democratic Congress.[1] The release in 2016 of the Panama Papers, files leaked from Mossack Fonseca, a Panama City–based law firm that specialized in helping rich people create offshore shell companies, gave insight into the continuing scale of this form of tax avoidance. The United States and Britain have for the most part refused to participate in EU and OECD efforts to force disclosure of the true owners of these assets and thereby collect taxes from them.[2]

Corporate income tax receipts have also declined dramatically, from 23 percent of federal revenues in 1967 to 12 percent in 2008, mainly because Congress has voted into law a growing array of tax credits and deductions, and administrations from both parties have ignored firms' use of corporate tax shelters that are similar to those used by rich individuals to hide money in foreign tax havens.[3] The share of federal revenues from estate and gift taxes, paid only by the richest 2 percent of Americans, and mainly by the wealthiest tenth of 1 percent, dropped in half between 1967 and 2008.[4]

The two main pillars of governmental support for the poor have been carved away over the past four decades. The minimum wage,

------

1   Jeffrey Winters, "America's Income Defense Industry," *Huffington Post*, October 22, 2010.

2   Richard Murphy, *Dirty Secrets: How Tax Havens Destroy the Economy* (London: Verso, 2017). J. C. Sharman, in *Havens in a Storm: The Struggle for Global Tax Regulation* (Ithaca: Cornell University Press, 2006), traces the failure of OECD efforts to force tax havens "to adopt a standard package of tax, financial, and banking regulations in order to tame this competitive dynamic and avert a 'race to the bottom' in tax rates" (1). Sharman argues that tax havens were able to fend off strict sanctions against their practices by winning a rhetorical war against big states. Sharman, without offering any serious analysis, discounts the role of rich people and banks in the United States or European countries in stemming more strenuous efforts by their governments to crack down on parking money abroad in tax havens. Nevertheless, his book offers a clear history of the rise and persistence of tax havens and of the history and consequences, though not the causes, of US and EU failures to use the powers they possessed and still possess to shut down tax havens.

3   Matthew Gardner, Robert S. McIntyre, and Richard Phillips, "The 35 Percent Corporate Tax Myth: Corporate Tax Avoidance by Fortune 500 Companies, 2008 to 2015" (Washington, DC: Institute on Taxation and Economic Policy, 2017). itep.org.

4   Office of Management and Budget, *Historical Tables*, tables 2.2 and 2.5.

which raises incomes not only for those paid at that rate, but for the entire lower half of the work force, whose wages are set in relation to that minimum, has been eroded by inflation. The minimum wage, controlling for inflation, peaked in 1968 when a full-time worker at that wage earned 90 percent of the poverty-level income for a family of four. That declined to little more than half the poverty level by the late 1980s, and even less in the mid-2000s. The three-part increase in the minimum wage in 2007–09 brought it up to two-thirds of the poverty level.[1] "Had the minimum wage risen in line with productivity since 1968, it would be over $18."[2]

Aid to Families with Dependent Children (AFDC), the federal welfare program created in the New Deal and drastically expanded under the Great Society, was also undermined by a lack of benefit increases to make up for inflation in the 1970s and 1980s. The program was abolished in 1996 and replaced with Temporary Assistance for Needy Families (TANF). TANF fulfilled Clinton's campaign pledge "to end welfare as we know it." The effects of the end of AFDC and the decline in the minimum wage were masked in the 1990s by a general expansion in the availability of low-wage jobs and partly cushioned by an increase in the Earned Income Tax Credit. The recession that began in 2008 produced levels of hunger, homelessness, and extreme poverty not seen since the years before the Great Society.

Finally, the federal government has retreated in the extent to which it regulates corporations on behalf of workers and consumers. Deregulation in most sectors has been accomplished by rule changes or lack of enforcement of existing regulations rather than through outright abolition of regulatory agencies. Antitrust laws remain on the books, but federal authorities have approved virtually every merger since the Nixon era.[3] Television and radio stations, which are given free licenses to profit from bands of publicly owned airwaves, had their obligations to provide public service programming and to offer

---

1    US Census Bureau, *2010 Statistical Abstract*, table 636.
2    Economic Policy Institute, "The Top Charts of 2015" (2015), epi.org, chart 4.
3    Lina Khan and Sandeep Vaheesan, in "Market Power and Inequality: The Antitrust Counterrevolution and Its Discontents," *Harvard Law and Policy Review* 11 (2017), trace the evolution of antitrust doctrine in a far more permissive direction by the Justice Department and among federal judges from the Reagan era to the present.

equitable coverage to political candidates and controversial issues eliminated by the Federal Communications Commission in 1987 when it revoked the fairness doctrine. Various agencies, such as the Environmental Protection Agency and the Occupational Safety and Health Administration, have become far less effective as they fall ever further behind in developing new regulations to limit or ban unsafe chemicals, machines, and work practices that have been developed since the initial spate of environmental and work safety regulations those agencies promulgated in the 1970s when they were founded. This is partly the result of "policy drift," the inability of existing laws and regulatory agencies to keep up with new technologies and organizational forms, and partly due to conscious decisions by Republican and, to a lesser but real extent, Democratic administrations to reject new regulations that they view as too burdensome on business and as not justifiable by market-based calculations.

The NLRB has become increasingly lax since the 1970s in preventing firms from using intimidation and other illegal tactics to undermine unionization efforts.[1] Efforts by the Carter, Clinton, and Obama administrations to reform labor law to strengthen the NLRB and unions against such employer tactics were defeated in Congress (in 1977, the Labor Law Reform Act came within one vote of overcoming a Senate filibuster and being enacted). As a result, unions are increasingly helpless against employer efforts to break strikes and block organizing with both legal and illegal methods, and unionization rates, as we noted above, have steadily declined as existing unions are ever less effective in protecting their members' wages, benefits, and working conditions.

Marc Linder traces efforts by large construction and industrial firms to weaken construction worker unions, which they perceived as the source of demands for large wage increases that cut profits and, by encouraging other unions to imitate construction workers' contract successes, spurred inflation.[2] Linder shows that the Business Roundtable

---

1   James A. Gross, *Broken Promise: The Subversion of US Labor Relations Policy 1947–1994* (Philadelphia: Temple University Press, 1995).

2   Marc Linder, *Wars of Attrition: Vietnam, the Business Roundtable, and the Decline of Construction Unions*, 2nd ed. (Iowa City: Fanpihua, 2000).

was formed initially to lobby the federal government to undermine construction worker unions. The Johnson administration largely spurned businessmen's entreaties, but under Nixon the NLRB issued rulings that made it harder for construction worker unions to challenge the growth of non-union construction firms. Later court decisions and NLRB rulings made it possible for construction firms to establish non-union subsidiaries that could share contracts with and bid against the firms' divisions that were unionized. The campaign against construction workers was the opening wedge in a broader effort by a unified national corporate elite to progressively weaken unions in the 1970s and subsequent decades,[1] thereby creating a political opening for that elite to move to the right and enact a range of policies, now labeled "neoliberal," that further undermined non-elite political influence and shifted income and authority to that elite.

Most fatefully, the banking and financial sector was deregulated in a series of administrative decisions and legislative acts,[2] culminating in the Gramm-Leach-Bliley Act of 1999, a collaborative effort of a Republican Congress and the Clinton administration that repealed the 1933 Glass-Steagall Act, and in the Commodity Futures Modernization Act of 2000 (CFMA, also signed by President Clinton), which ended most regulation of derivatives. The deregulation of the financial sector allowed the sorts of speculative practices and outright fraud that produced the 2008 financial crisis.[3]

## WHAT KILLED THE POSTWAR ELITE CONSENSUS IN AMERICA?

How can we explain the post-1960s shift in public policy, whose contours we have just outlined? Why did the narrow range of political

---

1  Domhoff, *The Myth of Liberal Ascendancy*; Waterhouse, *Lobbying America*.

2  Greta Krippner, *Capitalizing on Crisis: The Political Origins of the Rise of Finance* (Cambridge, MA: Harvard University Press, 2011).

3  The CFMA had provisions, later nicknamed the "Enron loopholes," that ended all regulation under the 1936 Commodity Exchange Act of energy futures. This exemption allowed Enron to engage in fraudulent transactions that culminated in its bankruptcy in 2001. Congress passed a "Close the Enron Loophole Act" in 2008 over President George W. Bush's veto.

debate, and more importantly of structural opportunities to challenge the balance of power among state and civil society, capitalists and workers, military and civilians, elites and masses, open in varied and dramatic ways in the decades after Kennedy's speech? Today, we are still debating the reasons why the stasis of the early 1960s was disrupted, and who benefited from the political flux that followed. Five main culprits appear, alone or in combination, in almost all explanations for the disorganization of American politics and the weakening of the US state. These five are not contemporaneous, and so in some explanations the factors build upon, or undermine, one another.

The five factors are: (1) US economic decline since the 1970s, caused by the rise of economic competitors and/or general globalization, which rendered the state unable to finance further expansion of social programs and heightened social conflict as groups fought over a shrinking or stagnant economic pie; (2) America's loss of geopolitical hegemony, variously timed from the 1960s to the 2000s, which caused a crisis in the world capitalist system and forced firms and the state to adopt neoliberal strategies, i.e., to reduce social expenditures to meet international competition and the demands of world financial markets; (3) the end of the Cold War, which meant, in Margaret Thatcher's words, "there is no alternative," and therefore corporations and capitalists no longer had to restrain their pursuit of profit to avoid making American capitalism appear less desirable than the socialist alternative; (4) mobilization from the left in the 1960s and after by African Americans, women, students, and other "new social movements;" and (5) mobilization, beginning in a few accounts in the late 1960s or '70s, and more commonly in the 1980s, from the right by business interests or populist forces, reacting to liberal state policies, leftist movements, and/or a crisis of falling profits.

These five explanations are helpful in identifying forces that disrupted the balance of power and undermined the bases for progressive social reform. They are not so useful in accounting for the specific policies that both Democratic and Republican administrations furthered since the 1970s and for the uneven decline in state capacity that were the intended and unintended consequences of the post-1960s political realignment and policy changes.

Let us examine each of the five sorts of explanations in turn and identify the strengths and limits of each. We then will see that the forces and interests identified in these explanations had their greatest impact indirectly. We cannot understand the changes in the US state from 1970 to 2010 as merely a successful adaptation to new geopolitical or global capitalist conditions. Rather, the actions of social movements on the left and right, and of self-interested elites, had the effect of weakening the federal government's capacities, and occurred at the same time as deregulation set in train processes of intra- and inter-firm restructuring that disorganized economic elites in the United States. Once we understand the new structure of elite relations that emerged at the end of the twentieth century, we will be able to explain the geopolitical, economic, and social policies adopted by the US state in recent decades, and the strategies of profit-seeking and wealth accumulation adopted by firms and wealthy Americans in those years.

## AMERICA, INTERNATIONAL COMPETITION, AND THE CRISIS OF PROFITS

Perhaps US decline and a resulting pullback in social spending were unavoidable. The overwhelming advantage the United States enjoyed as the only major power whose homeland and industrial capacity emerged unscathed (indeed vastly strengthened) by World War II narrowed as other countries rebuilt their economies (in part with US aid). Competition, facilitated by the widening of world trade and the globalization of finance, led to a falling rate of profit. When that happened, the postwar practices of sharing productivity gains with unionized workers and expanding social benefits became untenable. American firms responded by demanding givebacks from their workers and tax cuts from the federal and state governments.

Robert Brenner,[1] who offers the most sophisticated and empirically grounded version of this argument, accurately points out that the US government managed to cushion and postpone the crisis for decades, beginning with Nixon's policies of economic stimulus and de facto dollar devaluation, thereby shielding US workers and firms from

---

1   Brenner, *Boom and the Bubble*.

the consequences of their declining competitive position at the expense of their Japanese and German rivals. Ultimately, those interventions deepened the crisis since they allowed firms to maintain production in sectors that never could be competitive absent government manipulations and subsidies. Brenner does not identify the interests that led firms to cling to declining sectors, nor the political forces that enabled workers and firms to extract benefits from the state in the 1970s. Brenner has even less to say about the political shifts that led the hidebound firms of the 1970s to restructure themselves in the 1980s and '90s, nor does he attempt to explain why the Reagan administration and its successors were able to favor financial firms at the expense of industrial firms as well as workers. The shifts from a low to a high dollar and back to a low dollar under Reagan, and then a renewed high dollar under Clinton, are described but not explained. Brenner's is a Marxist analysis with virtually no politics.

Brenner's inattention to politics, and his focus on competition among capitalists rather than conflict with workers,[1] means he is unable to account for changes in policy that do not match the temporal rhythms he identifies in the overall US or world capitalist economy. Most seriously, he is unable to account for intra-class differences: Why did some capitalists gain state subsidies and protections while others did not? Why did some workers and mass groups make extraordinary gains in the 1960s or '70s while others did not?

There are two problems with Brenner's sort of argument. First, it assumes that US capitalists in the quarter century after 1945 were willing to leave potential profits in the hands of workers and the state as long as their rate of profit and share of national income remained steady, and only confronted workers and demanded tax cuts and regulatory rollbacks when profits fell below some unspecified level. In fact, capitalists always seek to increase profits; this is one of Marx's fundamental claims. If workers or the state are able to take a steady or increasing share of productivity gains, it is because they have the power to make those demands of capitalists. Capitalists' success after 1970 in forcing wage and benefit cuts on their workers and tax cuts

--------

1   Giovanni Arrighi, "The Social and Political Economy of Global Turbulence," *New Left Review* II, no. 20 (2003).

and regulatory rollbacks on the state reflects a shift in the balance of power, not new desires or fears on the part of capitalists.

Second, this interpretation of history assumes that all capitalists everywhere react to a crisis of profits by squeezing workers and the state. In reality, capitalists in each country, and in different industries and firms within countries, have pursued particular strategies of advantage. Some seek to drive down costs to undercut competitors; others are willing to pay relatively high wages to produce better quality goods and services that can then be sold at a premium. Capitalists and their firms do not make these decisions on their own: Governments and other institutions offer incentives and impose costs that create path-dependent "varieties of capitalism," directing investments along channels that sustain "liberal" or "coordinated market economies."[1]

Generalizations about varieties of capitalism, or Esping-Andersen's typology of the "worlds of welfare capitalism,"[2] are most useful in showing that capitalists and countries vary in their capacity to insulate themselves from competition and from the pressures of globalization. These theories are a powerful antidote to policy prescriptions, such as those of Thomas Friedman,[3] who believes all states including the United States are incapable of controlling the heightened global competition unleashed by technologies that facilitate the flow of goods, people, and capital, and to the assumptions that undergird the demands the International Monetary Fund (IMF) has imposed upon debt-ridden countries to open their economies to foreign competition in return for loans. For the United States, the IMF's prescriptions remain purely rhetorical, since America remains able to attract all the funds it needs to finance its deficits at low interest rates, even after the 2011 downgrade of the federal government's credit rating by Standard

--------

1    Peter Hall and David Soskice, eds., *Varieties of Capitalism: The Institutional Foundations of Comparative Advantage* (Oxford: Oxford University Press, 2001), offer the best overview of this approach; see Fred Block, "Understanding the Diverging Trajectories of the United States and Western Europe: A Neo-Polanyian Analysis," *Politics and Society* 35 (2007), fn. 2, for other key works from this perspective.

2    Gøsta Esping-Andersen, *The Three Worlds of Welfare Capitalism* (Princeton: Princeton University Press, 1990).

3    Thomas L. Friedman, *The World Is Flat: A Brief History of the Twenty-First Century* (New York: Farrar, Straus and Giroux, 2005).

& Poor's. Hall and Soskice and Esping-Andersen's path-dependent explanations of national differences in welfare states or capitalist strategies are less helpful in accounting for reversals of policy within countries, whether in specific areas where neoliberalism was implemented or the broad U-turn US policy took in the 1970s. Such models also ignore the ways in which US firms still draw subsidies from the state and rely upon governmental coordination to provide benefits for their employees.[1] We need to understand these firm-state interactions if we hope to explain the uneven changes in state policies and capacities over the decades since the 1960s.

## NEOLIBERALISM AND THE END OF AMERICAN CAPITALIST HEGEMONY

The United States is different from other capitalist countries, and was affected by and responded to the global crisis of capitalism differently, because it is still the hegemon of the world capitalist system. World dominance in any realm (economic, technological, military, or geopolitical) confers vast benefits on its holder, and dominant powers therefore respond to crises differently from other polities when they adopt strategies designed to maintain their hegemony. This is the great insight of world-systems theory.[2] Hegemony, in Arrighi's analysis, means that the United States is more than just another, albeit especially large and rich, competitor in the world economy. Hegemons are able to respond to crises caused by "the accumulation of capital over and above what can be reinvested in the purchase and sale of commodities without drastically reducing profit margins"[3] with what Arrighi, citing David Harvey, calls a "spatial fix."

Geographic expansion, of the hegemon's home polity and also in imperialist control over trade routes, colonies, and dependent nations, opens new spaces for profitable investment. However, the expanding scope of capitalist investment and production spurs "uneven

---

1   Block, "Understanding the Diverging Trajectories," 13–14.
2   Wallerstein, *Modern World-System*; Arrighi, *Long Twentieth Century*; *Adam Smith in Beijing*; Arrighi and Silver, *Chaos and Governance*.
3   Arrighi, *Adam Smith in Beijing*, 232.

development" (this is the process at the center of Brenner's analysis of the profits crisis) as backward territories take advantage of lower labor costs and newer facilities to undercut and outcompete the hegemon. "At this point, capitalist agencies tend to invade one another's spheres of operation; the division of labor that previously defined the terms of their mutual cooperation breaks down; and competition becomes increasingly vicious." Capitalists respond by keeping their resources liquid and loaning their capital to governments, firms, and individuals in financial crisis. For a few decades, financialization seems to create a new boom, as it did during Britain's Belle Époque of 1896–1914 and for the United States from the 1980s to 2008. But the relief is temporary and the prosperity highly concentrated as "the underlying over-accumulation crisis" intensifies and "exacerbates economic competition, social conflicts, and interstate rivalries to levels that it was beyond the incumbent centers' power to control."[1]

While the crises are inevitable, the responses by capitalists, states, and popular forces are highly variable across space and between each historical epoch. Here is where Arrighi moves well beyond Brenner's economistic argument or the path-dependent analysis of varieties of capitalism and types of welfare states. His focus on the interactions among classes and states, which he uses to explain hegemons' foreign policy decisions, above all the extent to which they go to war to stymie rising rivals' ambitions, can be employed as well to explain internal policy decisions. Arrighi reminds us that elites and classes within polities derive resources and have goals that extend beyond their home countries. Their interactions with the world beyond can only be understood in terms of the world-system as a whole, one whose dynamics cannot be reduced to the competition among leading economies traced by Brenner, or described in terms of unfettered markets as claimed by Friedman (Thomas or Milton), or assumed in IMF prescriptions.

Arrighi's model needs to be twinned with an analysis of political dynamics internal to hegemons, such as that offered by Monica Prasad[2]

---

1   Ibid., 232.

2   Monica Prasad, *The Politics of Free Markets: The Rise of Neoliberal Economic Policies in Britain, France, Germany, and the United States* (Chicago: University of Chicago Press, 2006).

in her comparison of the diverse forms of neoliberalism. She finds that the US, British, French, and German governments differed in the neoliberal policies they were actually able to implement. Firms were privatized in France under Chirac and in Britain under Thatcher, as were the government-owned Council Houses where 30 percent of Britons lived, but there was virtually no privatization in Germany or the United States. The main neoliberal policy in the United States was tax cuts, of which there were some in Britain and almost none in Germany and France. Social benefits were cut for the poor in the United States under Reagan, but not for the middle class, and social programs remained largely intact in the other three. Deregulation was confined mainly to the United States and to the financial sector in Britain.

For Prasad, this variability points to the necessity of analyzing the specific policy-making processes in each country. To do that, we must pay attention to changes in political dynamics internal to each country as well as to global capitalist cycles. These diverse policies may all be justified in terms of market fundamentalism, an "ideology [that] insists that the private sector is efficient and dynamic while the state is wasteful and unproductive,"[1] but they are implemented by actors constrained by domestic as well as international politics. Neoliberalism's particular and variable successes can only be explained if we combine world-system analysis with an understanding of domestic political dynamics within hegemons. That is our task in this book because, while elites and classes are disciplined by and derive resources from a global economy and engage in geopolitics, they are organized and act through institutions that still remain national, above all the nation-state.

## THE END OF THE COLD WAR AND THE SOCIALIST ALTERNATIVE

One force that might have compelled capitalists to forgo profits, and to give their workers better treatment than the balance of class or market forces would have indicated, was fear of the Soviet Union. However far-fetched it now seems in retrospect to imagine Soviet

---

1   Fred Block, "Swimming Against the Current: The Rise of a Hidden Developmental State in the United States," *Politics and Society* 36 (2008), 15.

communism as a viable alternative to US capitalism, American elites did fear the appeal of communism or at least of socialism to their workers as the Soviet Union matched and, in some years, exceeded the US growth rate in the first two decades after 1945[1] and demonstrated technological prowess with Sputnik in 1957. Beyond the United States, "there were many intelligent and idealistic people outside the Soviet Union in the 1950s, and even 1960s, to whom [Khrushchev's] faith [in socialism's superiority to capitalism] did not seem incredible."[2]

Capitalists did not decide on their own to forgo profits or to treat their workers with dignity in order to score propaganda victories against the Soviet Union. Indeed, a significant minority of US capitalists thought even the most modest demands for and governmental concessions on civil rights and social benefits were signs of existing communist power in the United States rather than antidotes to its appeal. (The John Birch Society was the most extreme manifestation of this view.) Rather, geopolitical competition affected domestic policy through the efforts of presidents and members of Congress whose offices spanned the foreign and domestic policy realms.

The cohesive elites that set US foreign policy in the postwar decades definitely did see the US and Soviet systems in competition for the loyalties of publics in Europe and the Third World. In large part, the US government fought for the support of foreign peoples with economic aid, most notably in the Marshall Plan, but also sought to portray the United States in a favorable light. Fear of what Soviet propagandists could do with the dark side of American reality prompted reform measures.[3] Supreme Court justices and members of

---

1   Gur Ofer, "Soviet Economic Growth: 1928–1985," *Journal of Economic Literature* 25 (1987).

2   Dominic Lieven, *Empire: The Russian Empire and Its Rivals* (New Haven: Yale University Press, 2000), 67.

3   Mary L. Dudziak, *Cold War Civil Rights: Race and the Image of American Democracy* (Princeton: Princeton University Press, 2000); Azza Salama Layton, *International Politics and Civil Rights Policies in the United States, 1941–1960* (Cambridge: Cambridge University Press, 2000); John Skrentny, "The Effect of the Cold War on African-American Civil Rights: America and the World Audience, 1945–1968," *Theory and Society* 27 (1998); Joshua Bloom, "The Dynamics of Opportunity and Insurgent Practice: How Black Anti-Colonialists Compelled Truman to Advocate Civil Rights," *American Sociological Review* 80 (2015), 392; James Baldwin, *The Fire Next Time* (New York: Dial, 1963), 85.

Congress alike discussed civil rights as a way to counter (accurate) Soviet depictions of American racism,[1] as did Vice President Nixon, who in 1954, a few months after the *Brown v. Board of Education* decision, asserted:

> There are six hundred million people in this world who hold the balance of power, and who are not white. They are trying to determine whether they should be on the Communist side or on our side . . . One of the factors that would be tremendously helpful is for us here in the United States to show by example, by word and deed that the dream of equality—equality of opportunity, of education, and of employment and the like—is coming true.[2]

President Kennedy as well, in his first and only major speech about civil rights on June 11, 1963, stated:

> We preach freedom around the world, and we mean it, and we cherish our freedom here at home, but are we to say to the world, and much more importantly, to each other that this is the land of the free except for the Negroes; that we have no second-class citizens except Negroes; that we have no class or caste system, no ghettoes, no master race except with respect to Negroes?

Similarly, US labor unions and their rights and their members' benefits were held up as a contrast to the state-controlled unions and low living standards of the Soviet bloc. American social benefits, from Social Security old-age pensions to the high levels of college attendance, were justified by their political sponsors in comparison to those offered by socialist governments, and anti-poverty programs were seen as a way to eliminate yet another source of anti-American Soviet propaganda.

The collapse of the Soviet Union removed the need to present an egalitarian or socially progressive American reality, or at least image,

---

1   Richard Kluger, *Simple Justice: The History of Brown v. Board of Education and Black America's Struggle for Equality* (New York: Knopf, 1976).
2   Quoted in Frank, *Ike and Dick*, 99.

to the rest of the world. The end of ideological competition on a world scale allowed Margaret Thatcher to contend, "There is no alternative." Yet it is not clear how that ideological shift has affected public policy in the United States. The end of new social legislation, and the U-turn away from the redistribution of wealth and income and the alleviation of poverty that began with the New Deal, can be dated, as we noted above, to the early 1970s, almost two decades before the collapse of the Soviet Union. While the rhetorical rejection of social legislation and egalitarianism intensified and encountered very little challenge after 1989, elites developed their capacities to institute policies that achieved those ends earlier, even while an ideological alternative existed.

The collapse of communism mattered little for US ideological debates since, despite the paranoid fears of a right-wing fringe that spanned the twentieth century from A. Mitchell Palmer to Joseph McCarthy to Robert Welch to Phyllis Schlafly, American ideological arguments on both the left and right drew almost exclusively upon domestic cultural traditions and engaged hardly at all with ideas and actors from the rest of the world. The fall of the Soviet Union affected domestic US debates indirectly. No longer did American domestic or foreign policy need to be restrained by the concern that prejudice and inequality at home or rapacious capitalism abroad would make the United States appear less appealing in comparison to a rival power. Under those conditions of American ideological hegemony, foreign policy elites could and did withdraw from championing liberal social and economic policies.

Most consequentially, the end of communism allowed the US government and firms to press for market fundamentalism in international agencies and in Third World countries whose own governments could no longer play two superpowers against each other. The United States' capacity to impose the "Washington Consensus" restructured United States as well as world capitalism, reorganizing elites within the United States in ways that we will examine later in this chapter and in chapter 8, and facilitating those elites' efforts to block domestic social legislation while furthering measures that redistributed wealth and power in their favor.

CHALLENGE FROM THE LEFT

C. Wright Mills, in *The Power Elite*, identified the bases of elite hegemony and then in his later writings identified sources of challenge to
elite rule. Mills argued that the quiet of the 1950s and early 1960s
was bought with the exclusion of most Americans from the sites
where actual decisions to allocate resources and set policies were
made. Mills identified the top officers of major corporations, federal
agencies, and the military as the only men (and they all were men
then) with true power to set domestic and foreign policy and to
make the investments that determined the future of the national
economy. The men of those elites, in Mills's view, had two advantages over all other Americans: First, the organizations they headed
had so many more resources, including technical expertise, than
every other public and private entity. Second, those elites used
personal and organizational ties to harmonize their interests, allowing them to reach decisions without having to submit them to public
view or approval.

Elite power and consensus, Mills argued, could survive only because
of the demise after the New Deal of "voluntary associations ... the
working class ... parties and unions" as effective agents of historical
change. Yet, in 1960, only four years after he analyzed the decline of the
American public into an apathetic and demobilized mass, Mills heralded
the emergence "all over the world" of the "young intelligentsia ... even
in our own pleasant Southland, Negro and white students are—but let
us keep that quiet: it really *is* disgraceful."[1] Mills, who died two years
later in 1962 (the same year in which Kennedy gave his speeches on the
end of ideology), did not get the chance to evaluate the efficacy of the
mobilizations whose beginnings he recognized.

Later authors[2] celebrated an array of "new social movements" and

--------

1    C. Wright Mills, "Letter to the New Left" in *New Left Review* I, no. 5 (1960),
22–3.
2    Ernesto Laclau and Chantal Mouffe, in *Hegemony and Socialist Strategy:
Towards a Radical Democratic Politics* (London: Verso, 1985), were the first to
develop a full-fledged theory of how and why class conflict has largely given way
since the 1960s to new social movements whose participants are drawn together by
their shared gender, racial, ethnic, sexual, or generational identity, or by their shared

asserted that African Americans, women, gays, immigrants, students, environmentalists, and others would be able to replace the working class as effective challengers to elected officials. (These authors are much more modest, if not silent, about the capacity of new social movements to challenge capitalists and other private interests.) In the realm of personal rights, those movements achieved notable successes, as citizens who identified themselves in terms of race, gender, and sexual orientation achieved real advances in civil rights and moved

---

concern for non-class issues such as the environment and human rights. Claus Offe (see "New Social Movements: Challenging the Boundaries of Institutional Politics," *Social Research* 52 [1985] for a concise statement) and Ulrich Beck (e.g., *Power in the Global Age: A New Global Political Economy* [Cambridge: Polity, 2006]) produced a seemingly endless outpouring of books and articles that make sweeping and confident claims for the transformative power of new social movements based on impenetrable theoretical carapaces rather than any serious and sustained empirical research. Nelson Pichardo ("New Social Movements: A Critical Review," *Annual Review of Sociology*, 23 [1997]) offers a summary and critique of the new-social-movement literature.

Revealingly, Western European studies of new social movements, such as those by Alberto Melucci (*Nomads of the Present: Social Movements and Individual Needs in Contemporary Society* [Philadelphia: Temple University Press, 1989]) and Hanspeter Kriesi et al. (*New Social Movements in Western Europe: A Comparative Analysis* [Minneapolis: University of Minnesota Press, 1995]), are written with a self-confident tone reflecting the authors' double certainty that those movements are replacing earlier class-based organizations that focus their efforts on the state and workplace and that the new movements will be able to supercede the transformative accomplishments of unions and parties.

In contrast, American authors more often temper their hopes with realistic appraisals of the limited achievements of new social movements in the United States and clear analyses of the structural and cultural forces in the United States that can block future gains. Dan Clawson enumerates many of the obstacles to a "fusion" in the United States of labor unions with movements based on race and gender. However, he does contend that those new movements have more potential to invigorate labor than do the existing unions themselves, and therefore believes there is a real possibility of a sudden "upsurge, leading to a period where labor's numbers and power triple or quadruple in a short period" (*The Next Upsurge: Labor and the New Social Movements* [Ithaca: Cornell University Press, 2003]).

Christine A. Kelly notes that "broader systemic imperatives . . . combine with American ideological traditions and institutional constraints in such a way as to particularly handicap the new forms in the United States" (*Tangled Up in Red, White and Blue: New Social Movements in America* [Lanham, MD: Rowman & Littlefield, 2001], 5). Kelly outlines ways in which new social movements could overcome those constraints, although, like Clawson, she is less clear on the conditions that would allow for a movement upsurge today on the scale of old social movements' successes in the 1930s and '60s.

toward formal legal equality. Those gains were achieved largely through a combination of mass mobilization and court challenges.

The movements have been far more limited in their abilities to make material demands on economic elites or on government at any level, achieving success in those realms only in brief periods. The civil rights movement in the 1960s enjoyed support from labor unions (though much less so from union members, as we noted earlier) and became engaged in electoral politics, providing crucial political support for the anti-poverty programs of the Great Society. Yet almost all that legislation was enacted during a single two-year period, the Eighty-Ninth Congress of 1965–66. Since then, virtually no social legislation has been enacted in the United States, even as minority groups and women have gained enhanced legal rights.

The environmental movement stands out as the only progressive force that was able to enact significant legislation after the Great Society, if only for a few years, adding to the environmental laws passed under Johnson with landmark legislative acts and the establishment of the EPA under Nixon. It is especially notable that environmentalists succeeded in forcing legislation that imposed regulations and costs on private firms as well as creating new governmental programs. Since then, no significant environmental laws have been passed in the United States.

Why did the long-lasting civil rights and environmental social movements produce only concentrated bursts of legislation, and the upsurge of worker militancy in the 1960s yielded little besides wage increases that were reversed in later decades? How can we explain the sudden, and decades-long, inability of any US social movement to extract benefits from government? Social movement theories, which were formulated to explain how those movements recruit supporters and sustain their commitment, are not so helpful in explaining when and how activists succeed in winning enduring concessions from government. Social movement scholars have yet to produce the equivalent for the 1960s and '70s of Theda Skocpol's *Protecting Soldiers and Mothers*,[1] which shows how movements, in her cases of veterans and

---

1   Theda Skocpol, *Protecting Soldiers and Mothers: The Political Origins of Social Policy in the United States* (Cambridge, MA: Harvard University Press, 1992).

mothers, found openings within the then patronage-based two-party political system that allowed them to win significant benefits, and also how changes in US politics (partly caused by those movements) blocked further expansions of social benefits.[1]

Similarly, we have a far better understanding of how activists came together to oppose nuclear weapons, the Vietnam War, and other US interventions abroad than we do of the short- or long-term effects of their mobilization. It is difficult to disentangle the effectiveness of the peace and anti-war movements from the brute fact of US defeat in Vietnam at the hands of Vietnamese willing to endure massive casualties over many years. To do so requires considering two counterfactuals: If there had been no anti-war movement, could the United States have continued to maintain the war for years longer? And if the United States had "won" the Vietnam War, would the draft have been abolished and would Americans have been more willing to fight other wars in the years after Vietnam?

Even if we will never be able to answer those questions (and we examine the effects of Vietnam on the US military in the next chapter), we can identify the combined consequences of opposition to and defeat in the Vietnam War. The draft was ended, never to be revived. Military spending fell drastically under Nixon, from 45 percent of federal outlays in 1969 to 26 percent in 1975,[2] and the nuclear arms race with the Soviet Union was restricted by a series of treaties. The United States switched to a strategy of foreign intervention that relied upon proxies. We will examine in the next chapter the effectiveness of the US military as it operated under those limitations in the subsequent decades.

--------------------

1    Frances Fox Piven and Richard A. Cloward, in *Regulating the Poor: the Functions of Public Welfare* (New York: Pantheon Books, 1971) and *Poor People's Movements: Why They Succeed, How They Fail* (New York: Pantheon Books, 1977), identify ways in which the civil rights movement, urban riots, and the welfare rights movement of the 1960s all led to voting rights and increased welfare benefits. Unfortunately, they have almost nothing to say about how popular mobilizations affected, for better or worse, future prospects for progressive politics and reform. Indeed, they look to future protests and disorder as the sole significant predictor of further political and social gains for African Americans and the poor.

2    Office of Management and Budget, *Historical Tables*, table 3.1.

In contrast, the peace movement and America's defeat in Vietnam left only a limited legacy at home. The "peace dividends" that followed both the end of the Vietnam War and the disintegration of the Soviet Union were not used to pay for any new social programs. Vietnam mainly affected American politics by weakening and discrediting presidents Johnson and Nixon and isolating the liberal wings of both parties, preventing them from building political coalitions that could have provided support for further social programs and governmental investments in economic restructuring. Vietnam War spending sparked inflation that could have been restrained had Johnson either increased taxes earlier than he finally did in 1968 or imposed wage and price controls. Instead, inflation became a political issue that unfairly discredited Keynesian economics and opened the way for financialization and neoliberalism.[1]

Block,[2] as we will see in the next section, argues that Johnson and Nixon's policy failures in Vietnam and on the economy, and their inability to contain dissent, undermined business support for liberal policies. The failure to manage dissent also weakened mass electoral support for the Great Society and for the Democratic Party. Support for Johnson, the Democratic Party, and the Great Society fell dramatically following the 1965 Watts and 1967 Newark and Detroit riots, and steadily in reaction to anti-war protests.[3]

Johnson was fully aware of the political costs of Watts and Vietnam. As Johnson put it in his inimitable way, "that bitch of a war" took money and attention away from "the woman I really loved," the Great Society.[4] Johnson was correct; in the absence of the war, and the splits it opened in the Democratic coalition, he certainly could

--------

1    Colin Crouch, *The Strange Non-Death of Neoliberalism* (Cambridge: Polity, 2011).

2    Block, "Understanding the Diverging Trajectories."

3    Gallup, "Presidential Job Approval Center" (2011); Thomas Byrne Edsall, *Chain Reaction: The Impact of Race, Rights, and Taxes on American Politics* (New York: Norton, 1991), 47–64; Bruce E. Altschuler, *LBJ and the Polls* (Gainesville, FL: University of Florida Press, 1990), 38–60; John E. Mueller, *War, Presidents and Public Opinion* (Lanham, MD: University Press of America, 1985).

4    Robert Mann, *The Walls of Jericho: Lyndon Johnson, Hubert Humphrey, Richard Russell, and the Struggle for Civil Rights* (New York: Harcourt Brace, 1996), 487.

have further expanded the Great Society and better financed the myriad programs that were established and almost certainly won a second term as president in 1968, allowing him to consolidate the Great Society and to ensure liberal control of the Supreme Court for decades. Johnson also asserted, following the 1967 Newark and Detroit riots: "It's [the riots] knocked our polls down 15 percent— more than Vietnam [and] inflation . . . Every white man says he doesn't want his car turned over, [he] doesn't want his neighbor throwing bricks at him."[1] The riots, even in the absence of the Vietnam War, would have damaged Johnson politically but, in combination with Vietnam, were fatal to the Great Society and to liberalism for the next forty years.

We cannot study leftist social movements in isolation. Indeed, the dominant explanation for the now four-decade-long drought of legislative achievements for progressive social movements is the rise of countervailing pressures from populist and/or corporate groups on the right.

## THE RISE OF THE RIGHT

The postwar liberal consensus was challenged from the right as well as the left, by the privileged as well as the impoverished and disenfranchised. Recent historical research has uncovered the ways in which backlash politics was framed, organized, and legitimated by well-funded organizations that became, by the end of the 1970s, the dominant shapers of Republican Party politics and designers of the Reagan administration's policies.[2] Those organizations, in turn,

---

1   Quoted in Nick Kotz, *Judgment Days: Lyndon Baines Johnson, Martin Luther King Jr., and the Laws That Changed America* (New York: Houghton Mifflin, 2005).

2   Lisa McGirr, *Suburban Warriors: The Origins of the New American Right* (Princeton: Princeton University Press, 2001); Rick Perlstein, *Before the Storm: Barry Goldwater and the Unmaking of the American Consensus* (New York: Hill and Wang, 2001); *Nixonland: The Rise of a President and the Fracturing of America* (New York: Scribner, 2008); Matthew Lassiter, *The Silent Majority: Suburban Politics in the Sunbelt South* (Princeton: Princeton University Press, 2005); Hacker and Pierson, *American Amnesia*. Phillips-Fein, *Invisible Hands*, 321–31, offers the best overview of scholarly literature about the right.

were financed by and embodied the concerted interests of much of the economic elite, which had decisively broken from their acceptance of government regulation, Keynesianism, and social reform. Domhoff shows how the Committee for Economic Development, which represented the interests of and organized policy proposals on behalf of the "corporate moderates" who ran many of the largest US firms, lost influence to harder right organizations, such as the Business Roundtable, in the 1970s.[1] Domhoff traces the effect of that shift in business elite organization and sentiments on federal policy and legislation. The Business Roundtable, in turn, lost influence in the 1990s as the US Chamber of Commerce became by far the largest lobbying organization in the nation and allied directly with the Republican Party, eschewing bipartisanship to push for an agenda of deep cuts in social programs, deregulation, and tax cuts for the rich.[2]

The literature on conservative movements presents the move to the right, on the part of business elites and both the Democratic and Republican parties, as mainly a matter of desire and resources. Conservative businessmen, in some tellings aided by social conservatives, decided they wanted to reverse the New Deal and later reforms. They then invested the resources necessary to sustain a long-term strategy of creating foundations and media outlets to develop and propagate conservative ideas.[3]

The problem with this analysis, as Domhoff demonstrates,[4] is that right-wing opposition to the New Deal existed since FDR's election, just as businessmen had opposed the reforms of the Progressive Era. We cannot explain the post-1960s triumph of the right in terms of the desires or farsightedness of rich businessmen. There have always been enough businessmen who opposed redistributive and social welfare programs to fund politicians and organizations capable of mounting a challenge to progressive government. What needs explanation is how businessmen's desires, and the efforts those desires

1   Domhoff, *The Myth of Liberal Ascendancy*.
2   Hacker and Pierson, *American Amnesia*, chapter 7.
3   Hacker and Pierson, *American Amnesia*, and Waterhouse, *Lobbying America*, are recent, well-documented, and clearly argued exemplars of this view.
4   Domhoff, *The Myth of Liberal Ascendancy*; "Is the Corporate Elite Fractured."

produced, yielded success since the 1970s that they failed to produce in previous decades.

One possible explanation can be found in Fred Block's contention that business elites turned against expansive government programs because the Johnson and Nixon administrations failed to win or end the Vietnam War, manage political dissent, and formulate policies that could address economic decline.

> It is difficult to exaggerate the cumulative impact on business of the political missteps by Johnson and Nixon between 1964 and 1974. The fact that neither of these two highly skilled and centrist politicians was able to make headway against the multiple problems that the United States faced led to an agonizing reassessment of their assumptions about US politics. They decided, in short, that the "vital center" could not hold and that they needed to move away from their support for big-government politicians of both parties.[1]

Block argues that, up through the 1960s, a large faction of big business supported Keynesian policies and social programs. This faction, in alliance with unions and self-aggrandizing state officials, was enough to defeat right-wing objections to new social programs. Block's description of the 1960s tracks the picture of elite consensus we drew earlier in this chapter. However, his explanation for the shift away from "corporate liberalism" is mainly focused on elite perceptions and ideology: Big business was disillusioned by dissention and governmental failures in the 1960s and '70s and therefore fell for the blandishments of market fundamentalism.

There are two problems with Block's analysis and similar arguments that attribute the fall of liberalism to its policy failures in the 1960s. First, he cannot explain why a strengthened right wing produced the uneven accomplishments of neoliberalism that we noted above. Elsewhere, Block[2] accurately describes the continuing role of the US state in regulating and subsidizing business and offering

---

1   Block, "Understanding the Diverging Trajectories," 18.
2   Block, "Swimming Against the Current."

benefits to the middle class, but he offers no mechanism to explain how government drew back in some realms but not others.

Second, we should be careful not to exaggerate the policy short-comings of the 1960s. Civil rights legislation, court decisions, and Great Society social programs did succeed in their stated aims of elim-inating legal segregation and reducing poverty, which fell from 22 percent of the US population in 1960 to 12 percent in 1969.[1] In actu-ality, dissatisfaction with governmental domestic policy during the Johnson and Nixon administrations came mainly from popular forces on the left and right rather than from elites. Significant sectors of the population, but not corporate elites, regarded those administrations' egalitarian and reformist measures as ideological choices rather than objective applications of legal rules or expert knowledge; when so framed by political opportunists on the right, including Nixon himself, despite his administration's efforts to desegregate schools in the South and establish affirmative action,[2] the measures aroused broader and more sustained, if less intense, opposition on the right than did the Vietnam War on the left.

Nixon was brilliant at adopting policies that had the effect of divid-ing Democratic constituencies, as when his administration forced construction unions to adopt affirmative action plans, sparking anger on the part of working-class whites against African Americans while widening the pool of construction workers in ways that ultimately undermined union control over construction jobs in northern cities.[3] (Mayor John Lindsay's transfer of control over schools in New York City to community-elected boards also sparked conflict between liberal, heavily Jewish, unionized school teachers and African Americans, although Lindsay, unlike Nixon, was not Machiavellian, just very foolish.)

Backlash politics combined various elements, and different authors have highlighted particular aspects. To some, including Martin Luther

---

1   US Census Bureau, *Historical Poverty Tables*, table 2.

2   Tom Wicker, *One of Us: Richard Nixon and the American Dream* (New York: Random House, 1991).

3   Linder, *Wars of Attrition*; Allen. J. Matusow, *Nixon's Economy: Booms, Busts, Dollars, and Votes* (Lawrence: University Press of Kansas, 1998), 28–9; Domhoff, *The Myth of Liberal Ascendancy*.

King, Jr., the backlash was a sign "that the roots of racism are very deep in America," in the North as well as South.[1] Others view it as a spontaneous reaction to student radicals' arrogance and cultural obtuseness,[2] or a challenge to what Donald Warren[3] believes were the radicals' liberal allies in government. Others focus on its anti-feminist[4] or religious fundamentalist elements.[5] Phillips-Fein[6] finds that the 1978 IRS ruling denying tax exemption to segregated Christian schools (the so-called "seg academies") brought the religious right into an alliance with business against the IRS. This contingent event strengthened and popularized anti-tax ideology, and in widening the coalition for tax cuts paved the way for Reagan and Republicans in Congress to push for the Kemp-Roth individual income tax cuts over business tax cuts in 1981.

Hacker and Pierson combine these and other elements into a comprehensive explanation of how the Republican Party has been transformed into an extreme right party since the 1990s. They ask, "Why would the GOP want to move so far to the right? Second, and equally puzzling, why can it move to the right without paying an unacceptable electoral price"[7] since most Americans still favor progressive

---

1 Quoted in Taylor Branch, *At Canaan's Edge: America in the King Years, 1965–68* (New York: Simon & Schuster, 2006), 554.

2 Edsall, *Chain Reaction*; Todd Gitlin, *The Intellectuals and the Flag* (New York: Columbia University Press, 2007).

3 Donald I. Warren, *The Radical Center: Middle Americans and the Politics of Alienation* (Notre Dame: University of Notre Dame Press, 1976).

4 Barbara Ehrenreich, *The Hearts of Men: American Dreams and the Flight from Commitment* (New York: Anchor, 1983); Susan Faludi, *Backlash: The Undeclared War Against American Women* (New York: Crown, 1991).

5 Daniel Williams, in *God's Own Party: The Making of the Christian Right* (Oxford: Oxford University Press, 2010), argues that the Christian right gained power in politics by identifying issues that could bridge divisions between northern and southern churches, and between evangelicals and fundamentalists: first, anti-communism in the 1950s and '60s, and then social issues. In Williams's history, Nixon emerges as the key figure in the rise of the Christian right and its position in the Republican Party. Nixon's focus on "law and order" in his 1968 presidential campaign provided a way to focus on social issues in a way that appealed to religious conservatives, who previously had been divided on civil rights and on religious doctrine, and provided the basis for their concord even after the end of the Cold War eliminated anti-communism as a unifying issue.

6 Phillips-Fein, *Invisible Hands*, 232–4.

7 Hacker and Pierson, *American Amnesia*, 249.

taxes, enhancing rather than reducing social benefits, universal health care, and stronger regulation of banks? Hacker and Pierson note that the GOP has the motive and means for its rightward shift in a base that reliably votes Republican in elections at all levels and has been pushed ever further to the right by three forces: "Christian conservatism, polarizing right-wing media, and growing efforts by business and the wealthy to backstop and bankroll Republican politics."[1]

Christian conservatives give "the GOP a substantial base of middle-income voters who side with the party for mostly noneconomic reasons"[2] but go along with the party's shift to the right on economic issues. Hacker and Pierson note that the Civil Rights Act of 1964 pushed the nation's most conservative voters, southern racists, out of the Democratic Party. As we noted above, Nixon used law and order to pull northern and southern Christians into the GOP, uniting them around the social issues Hacker and Pierson see as the main motivator of their party loyalty. The base is further spurred to vote by right-wing media, most notably Fox News and talk radio. The money to finance Republicans' electoral campaigns and to discipline Republicans in Congress and intimidate Democrats is provided by superrich donors who also finance their own electoral organizations and lobbying groups. Thus, Hacker and Pierson believe a racist/religious base, excited and mobilized by right-wing media, and unlimited funding are the motivators for Republican politicians to adopt ever more extreme positions.

However, if the majority of voters are moderate, how does an extreme party win elections and get away with pursuing extreme policies once in office? The Republicans have controlled the House for all but four years and the Senate for all but eight years of the twenty-four years from 1994 to 2018. The GOP as of 2017 controlled two-thirds of state governments (holding the governorships and majorities in both legislative houses). Only at the presidential level have the Republicans not dominated, losing the popular vote in six of the seven elections from 1992 to 2016 (but, thanks to the electoral vote, winning the presidency in three of those seven elections). Conservative Republican

---

1   Ibid., 251.
2   Ibid., 252.

majorities have controlled the Supreme Court ever since Nixon appointed four justices in his first term.

Hacker and Pierson note that low turnout of Democratic voters in midterm elections, the concentration of Democrats in urban areas combined with gerrymandered House and state legislative districts, and voter suppression (with ever more blatant measures condoned by the Supreme Court) mean that Republicans are more likely to show up at the polls and to have their votes actually counted, and their votes carry more weight in districts as they are drawn and in the Senate where small rural states get the same two senators as urbanized states with far greater populations.[1]

In addition, Republicans, beginning with Newt Gingrich's elevation to Speaker of the House following the Republicans' 1994 victory, have adopted a scorched-earth policy of opposing virtually every initiative proposed by Democratic presidents, capped by the use of the once rare Senate filibuster to require sixty votes for almost every bill. This had the effect of making Clinton and Obama appear to be ineffective presidents[2] and making Democratic candidates' promises of new programs appear unbelievable.

----

1   Gerrymandering was fostered by a devil's bargain between the George H. W. Bush administration and a few career African American southern politicians following the 1990 census. Until then the 1965 Voting Rights Act was understood to ban practices that diluted African American voting strength, including "packing" black voters into a few districts. The Bush Justice Department proffered a new interpretation: that African Americans could only have representation in Congress and state legislatures if they were represented by black politicians rather than officials of various races who owed their election to black voters. This interpretation was accepted by federal judges, a majority of whom by then had been appointed by Republican presidents, and blacks were packed into a few districts, thereby pulling out black voters who had provided the margins of victory for numerous white legislators throughout the South while elevating a few African American state legislators into safe congressional seats. This was the turning point that sharply reduced Democrats in southern state legislatures and made possible the Republican takeover of the House in the 1994 election.

2   Chait, *Audacity*, 224, observes that "self-identified centrists in Washington tend to assume that the sensible position lies halfway between whatever the two parties are saying at any given moment" even if the Republicans have moved far to the right while Democrats have maintained a moderate position. "They conclude, as a matter of course, that if the two parties cannot agree, they are equally to blame." When Obama adopted, while Republicans refused to even consider, the compromises urged by "moderate opinion leaders" in the media, those pundits refused to acknowledge the Republicans' intransigence. "After all, if they sided with one of the parties, they wouldn't be 'nonpartisan' anymore!"

Josh Pacewicz, in a study of politics in two Iowa cities, finds that mergers and deindustrialization undermined the local business and union elites that organized municipal politics and acted as intermediaries between their constituents and state- and federal-level officeholders. In addition to this large structural shift,

> subsequent reforms of federal social service and urban development funding transformed the large, discretionary transfers of the Keynesian era into a complex system of small, targeted, hyper-competitive grants controlled by a shifting mix of federal agencies, state agencies, and middle-men nonprofits.[1]

Party politicians representing long-standing but weakening local business or labor groups generally were incapable of creating the "broad-based, shifting, and flexible partnerships [that] could make the city appear as all things to all people," or at least to outside grant bestowers.[2] Instead, local planning entrepreneurs, whom Pacewicz labels "partners," eschewed partisan politics, which they accurately saw as impediments to developing the plans that could win outside grants or entice national corporations to their locales. This left the field of politics to "partisans" who, Pacewicz argues, get most of their ideas about which issues to care about from national and increasingly ideological media rather than from interactions with citizens in their localities who are ever less likely to be organized into clear interest groups like unions or business networks.[3]

---

1   Josh Pacewicz, *Partisans and Partners: The Politics of the Post-Keynesian Society* (Chicago: University of Chicago Press, 2016), 280.

2   Ibid., 280.

3   Pacewicz notes that despite the rise in contributions to the national Democratic and Republican parties in 2012, "the operating budget of all Republican and Democratic committees was roughly $1.2 billion, which is comparable to the national advertising budget of Coca-Cola and Pepsi . . . In fact, the parties spent most of their money on TV advertising, leaving them incapable of building a national bureaucratic structure. Effectively, party leaders are still akin to a few figureheads in a room; the only difference is that these figureheads now have a substantial advertising budget . . . In effect, parties and PACs are national organizations in name only; really, they are glorified advertising agencies" (*Partisans and Partners*, 199).

Pacewicz shows that partners' local-level divorce from partisan politics, and partisans' focus on externally generated social issues, undermines elected politicians' abilities to develop programs at the national or state levels because at those higher levels politics remains a matter of allocating scarce resources, not winning grants from above. As Pacewicz reminds us, there is no higher level to which the federal government can appeal for resources. Therefore, attempts to replicate a post-political grant-getting consensus that works in a few successful localities at the national level are doomed to fail. Such failures will not be reversed unless local-level partners engage in partisan politics and are able to displace partisan ideologues. Thus,

> This utopian celebration of the antipolitical is problematic firstly because it is self-reinforcing . . . People see the latest crackpot to be elected governor and exclaim that reasonable people should stay out of politics. But their governor, who was championed by otherwise politically marginal activists [marginal because they embody tropes created by national media rather than represent actual local constituencies], was elected precisely because community leaders desire to be reasonable and avoid partisan politics.[1]

Pacewicz identifies structural forces that leave the field of politics to ideologues, allowing right-wing extremists to win state and then national elections. Pacewicz's book anticipates that Obama, who presented himself as postpartisan and who in office championed programs that rewarded nonpartisan "partners" over class-based politicians, would enable "those with a real axe to grind [to] eventually take over political institutions."[2]

Finally, the increasing harshness and vulgarity of election campaigns and of Republican legislators once in office has repelled many voters.[3] Conservative true believers and racists, motivated by right-wing media, still turn out to vote. Indeed, after years of failing to get substantive benefits from government, such voters will find racist

---

1  Ibid., 300.
2  Ibid., 301.
3  Ibid., 248 and passim.

showmen like Trump more attractive and worthy of the effort of voting than sober right-wing technocrats like Romney. For such diehard Republican voters, the bluster and bigotry are features, not bugs. But more moderate voters and even committed Democrats are less likely to vote after such harsh campaigns and with the prospect that public policy will not change even if Democrats win smashing victories as they did in 2008. Trump's openly bigoted and vicious campaign was a culmination of past trends, not a break with past Republican campaign practices.

The vast expansion since the 1980s in the number of lobbyists, and in the number of firms and trade associations that hire full-time Washington lobbyists, further deepens voters' cynicism and alienation from politics. The growth of corporate spending on lobbying has created a highly lucrative career path that entices

> more and more experienced and talented government staffers [to] become lobbyists, drawing policy expertise and political know-how out of the public sector and into the private sector. The increasing complexity and specialization of policy makes this public-private gap in expertise all the more consequential, as inexperienced staffers come to need to rely on experienced lobbyists to make sense of policy. [Corporations that can afford to hire the most knowledgeable and best-connected lobbyists] gain from policy complexity, both because it gives them more opportunities to insert narrow provisions with limited public scrutiny and because they are more capable of supplying expertise to overworked staffers.[1]

Lobbyists, as they provide or coordinate campaign contributions, constantly monitor the progress of legislation and often propose the actual language of bills and amendments tailored to their corporate clients' desires for tax breaks, regulatory preferences, or appropriations. While lobbyists most often succeed merely in preventing adverse legislative and regulatory changes, "One key advantage for corporate

---

1   Lee Drutman, *The Business of America Is Lobbying: How Corporations Became Politicized and Politics Became More Corporate* (Oxford: Oxford University Press, 2015), 3–4.

America in having a network of savvy lobbyists is its ability to capital-
ize quickly on unexpected developments . . . propitious circumstances
[that] can arise out of the blue."[1]

Lobbyists' specific achievements remain invisible to most voters,
and few unions or nonprofit and citizen organizations can afford to
match the focus and expertise of corporate lobbyists. Voters have
limited attention spans and so it is difficult to mobilize them to oppose
insider dealing except in rare circumstances. Even when voters
become engaged, they usually lack the time for the unending grind of
monitoring legislation and pressuring their elected representatives. In
contrast, time and money are what lobbyists have in abundance.
Voters do have some awareness of the aggregate effect of lobbying in
creating an unfair tax system and directing federal funds to rich and
privileged insiders. Yet, as the 2016 presidential election made obvious, voters are unable to identify the principal culprits or to evaluate
which remedies or politicians could be effective rather than counter-
productive in "draining the swamp" or even just minimizing future
unfairness. The perception that Washington is incurably corrupt
contributes to voter cynicism and further reduces participation in
elections.

Hacker and Pierson, along with kindred scholars, offer a convincing explanation for why Republicans win elections with increasingly
extreme positions. However, Hacker and Pierson make clear that
Republican politicians and their core supporters had no commitment
to specific economic policies even as they were stalwart in their
demands for conservative social policies and for pushing back against
civil rights. Rather, Republicans are presented as passive acceptors of
the economic policies large firms and wealthy individuals ask them to
support. Thus, we are still left with the question of why elites rejected
the postwar consensus and pushed for more extreme policies beginning in the 1970s. If the more moderate policies elites supported
during the decades of consensus were not what they really wanted,
why did it take until the 1970s for them to begin to create the conditions for enacting a much more conservative agenda? After all, those
elites had the resources to build alternate media and to back

---

1  Thomas Byrne Edsall, "Kill Bill," *New York Times*, May 22, 2013.

right-wing candidates (and some elites did so) in the 1950s and '60s. What and who held them back during the decades of consensus?

## THE TRANSFORMATION OF AMERICAN POLITICS

If we want to understand what changed and what did not, we must trace the decline of support for progressive government. That decline can be found in a combination of three sources: (1) the movement of business interests that had supported or acquiesced in liberal policies from the 1930s through the 1960s to alliance with their counterparts who had always been in opposition, (2) the decline of mass organizations, above all labor unions, capable of mobilizing supporters of existing and proposed progressive governmental policies, and (3) a loss of capacity by the government to implement public investment and social welfare programs still supported by the majority of voters. In other words, the right-wing victories from the 1970s into the twenty-first century were not the fruition of strategies set in motion in earlier decades, or the product of a sudden and complete disillusionment on the part of corporate moderates, but consequences of a realignment and restructuring of elites and classes that first transformed politics and degraded government in the 1970s and, in turn, made possible further shifts in the capacities of American political actors in both the state and civil society.

Political actors are motivated by ideas and interests, but political accomplishments arrive at particular moments because opponents have been weakened, alliances strengthened, and structural impediments cleared away. If we can trace the sources and course of political transformation in the United States since the 1960s, we will be able to understand why the right has been able to block further expansion of the state. We will also be able to specify why certain governmental programs have been vulnerable to efforts to roll them back while others have been maintained or even expanded in the decades since the Great Society.

## THE STRUCTURE OF ELITE POLITICAL ACTION

The United States was characterized during the postwar decades of consensus by a dual elite structure, which, like the similar structure in Britain after its Civil War, ensured that local and national elites could limit each other's attempts to appropriate state powers and offices.[1] National firms, linked together by director interlocks centered on the biggest commercial banks,[2] and which devised joint positions on government policy through policy-discussion/lobbying groups,[3] coexisted with regional and local banks and firms that were shielded from competition with bigger rivals thanks to federal and state regulations that local elites had the political muscle to sustain through influence on their congressional delegations and in their state governments.

That structure of elite relations has been transformed in recent decades by waves of mergers in sectors such as banking, telecommunications, media, utilities, retail sales, and agriculture,[4] and by the declining capacity of national banks to control firms. US antitrust policy first shifted under Nixon, but the overall process needs to be seen as having a ratcheting effect. Each merger eliminated a firm that

---

1    Mann, in *Sources of Social Power*, volume 3, 72–3, notes that in the late nineteenth and early twentieth centuries, the Republican and Democratic parties represented regional rather than class interests. In one sense both were capitalist parties, but they each protected the particular interests of certain sorts of, largely regionally based, capitalists.

2    Mark S. Mizruchi, *The Fracturing of the American Corporate Elite* (Cambridge, MA: Harvard University Press, 2013); "Berle and Means Revisited: The Governance and Power of Large US Corporations," *Theory and Society* 33 (2004); Gerald F. Davis and Mark S. Mizruchi, "The Money Center Cannot Hold: Commercial Banks in the US System of Corporate Governance," *Administrative Science Quarterly* 44 (1999); Harland Prechel, *Big Business and the State: Historical Transitions and Corporate Transformation, 1880s–1990s* (Albany: SUNY Press, 2000).

3    Domhoff, *The Myth of Liberal Ascendancy.*

4    Khan and Vaheesan, "Market Power and Inequality;" Gregor Andrade, Mark Mitchell, and Erik Stafford, "New Evidence and Perspectives on Mergers," *Journal of Economic Perspectives* 15 (2001); Charles W. Calomiris and Jason Karceski, "Is the Bank Merger Wave of the 1990s Efficient? Lessons from Nine Case Studies," in *Mergers and Productivity*, ed. Steven N. Kaplan (Chicago: University of Chicago Press, 2000); Linda Brewster Stearns and Kenneth D. Allan, "Economic Behavior in Institutional Environments: The Corporate Merger Wave of the 1980s," *American Sociological Review* 61 (1996).

had an interest, and a degree of political sway, to block further mergers or regulatory changes that would allow national firms to encroach
on local firms' privileges and markets. As smaller and locally based
firms disappeared, intra-industry differences in various sectors over
government policy were reduced, creating unified voices that pushed
legislative changes to enactment.[1] The banking and telecommunications "reform" acts of the 1990s had failed to pass Congress in earlier
decades due to counter-lobbying by sectors of those industries with
opposed interests. Mergers resolved those disagreements as secondary sectors were brought within larger firms (or merged themselves to
form new large firms) and so came to share the most general interest
of their industries. Deregulation then opened the way to further waves
of mergers and acquisitions,[2] intensifying elite consolidation within
major industries.

Just as banks were the central actors in the director interlocks that
set corporate and governmental policy toward business practices in
the 1945–1968 era, so their consolidation and the interacting changes
in US financial regulation and legislation epitomized and guided the
overall changes in the structure of US capitalism. Bank mergers were
not just, or even primarily, a process of national banks buying out
smaller local banks. Rather, the Nixon and Reagan administrations
catered to their business supporters, who were for the most part
outside the New York and Chicago banking centers, by allowing
regional banks to merge and buy out rivals. Reagan's base in the southern and western states easily explains this tilt. For Nixon, who began
this shift, the orientation was somewhat contingent, created by his

---

1    Sandra Suarez and Robin Kolodny, in "Paving the Road to 'Too Big to Fail':
Business Interests and the Politics of Financial Deregulation in the United States,"
*Politics and Society* 39 (2011), trace the shift of small banks in favor of deregulation,
but they credit "incremental policy changes" rather than mergers as the ratchet that
led to unified support among bankers of all sorts for repeal of Glass-Steagall.
2    Gerald F. Davis, *Managed by the Markets: How Finance Reshaped America*
(Oxford: Oxford University Press, 2009), 116–21; Donald Tomaskovic-Devey and
Ken-Hou Lin, "Income Dynamics, Economic Rents, and the Financialization of the
US Economy," *American Sociological Review* 76 (2011); Krippner, *Capitalizing on
Crisis*; Jeff Madrick, *Age of Greed: The Triumph of Finance and the Decline of America,
1970 to the Present* (New York: Knopf, 2011); Andrade, Mitchell, and Stafford, "New
Evidence and Perspectives on Mergers."

rival in presidential politics, Nelson Rockefeller's stranglehold over support from New York bankers, and by the political opportunities in the South opened by Democrats' visible shift toward civil rights in the 1960s.

The formerly dominant national banks faced increasing competition in the 1980s and 1990s from the rise of new regional behemoths created by the merger of smaller competitors. That competition and the relaxation of federal regulations,[1] which both the national and large regional banks demanded, led national banks to focus their resources on more lucrative investment banking, further removing them from active involvement in the management of industrial firms.[2] Non-banking firms had a widening range of financial firms to which they could turn for financing, epitomized by the rise of "junk bonds" in the 1980s and hedge funds in the 1990s. Bankers thus lost the capacity to manage firms in other sectors, just as federal deregulation gave bankers the interest and capacity to focus on more lucrative financial engineering and speculation instead.

Consolidation within sectors facilitated the capture of government agencies and powers by those elites, narrowing the room for state actors to exercise autonomy, which further reduced "the limited institutionally available means of political mobilization and communication open to a US president or allied policy promoters in the 1990s."[3] A weakened state, combined with the decline of labor unions, undermined

> two of the key forces that had disciplined the business community . . . The consequence of [the commercial banks' decline] was a paradoxical situation in which business appeared to lack any kind of unifying institution that would be the source of long-term perspective, while at the same time its power seemed virtually unchallenged. This unchecked power, combined with the absence of disciplinary forces, either internal (the banks) or external (labor

---

1   I discuss changes in regulation in more detail in chapter 8.
2   Davis and Mizruchi, "Money Center Cannot Hold."
3   Theda Skocpol, *Boomerang: Clinton's Health Security Effort and the Turn Against Government in US Politics* (New York: W. W. Norton, 1996), 83.

or the state), may have contributed to the excesses of the late-1990s and early-2000s.[1]

Johan Chu and Gerald Davis are more emphatic, finding a sharp drop after 2000 in director interlocks. They show that firms with few or no interlocks contribute less money and personnel to civic organizations and most significantly give just to Republican or Democratic candidates rather than splitting contributions between the two parties.[2]

Facing such weak state and class actors, elites are able to block new social programs that threaten their hold over existing budget items or their capacities to profit by providing services such as health care, education, credit, and retirement benefits that could be offered through government but instead are left to the private sector. Elites' leverage over government has been strengthened further by their growing unity as moderate conservative business leaders joined with right-wingers to formulate and lobby for NAFTA and other "free" trade treaties, deregulation, and tax cuts,[3] and with a decisive shift in campaign donations to Republicans, including ultraconservative challengers, over Democrats beginning with the 1980 election.[4]

President Obama recognized this reality when he designed his health care legislation. His plan protects the interests and profit opportunities of every private industry involved in selling health insurance and medical services and supplies. Indeed, his recognition of insurance firms' power led Obama to include the mandate that all Americans buy private health insurance (except those who qualify for government programs). In essence, Obama accepted a mandate that quickly

1   Mizruchi, "Berle and Means Revisited," 607–8.
2   Johan S. G. Chu and Gerald F. Davis, "Who Killed the Inner Circle? The Decline of the American Corporate Interlock Network," *American Journal of Sociology* 122 (2016).
3   Domhoff, "Is the Corporate Elite Fractured."
4   Dan Clawson and Alan Neustadtl, "Interlocks, PACs, and Corporate Conservatism," *American Journal of Sociology* 94 (1989); Dan Clawson, Alan Neustadtl, and Mark Weller, *Dollars and Votes: How Business Campaign Contributions Subvert Democracy* (Philadelphia: Temple University Press, 1998); Thomas Ferguson and Joel Rogers, *Right Turn: The Decline of the Democrats and the Future of American Politics* (New York: Hill & Wang, 1986); Hacker and Pierson, *American Amnesia*, chapter 7.

aroused popular revulsion (with ample prompting from the Republican Party and right-wing media outlets, above all Fox News) in return for the insurance firms' support. Without that deal, Congress never would have enacted the legislation.

United States fiscal policy and budget priorities are increasingly set by such deals, which reflect the power of consolidated corporate elites over politics and policy. This is different from the unified national elites of the 1945–68 period, described by Mills, Domhoff, and others. The contemporary elites do not use their financial and organizational muscle to push for broad national policies, with the exceptions of anti-labor legislation, discussed earlier, and trade agreements, to be discussed in more detail in chapter 8. Rather, they use their leverage over legislators and regulators to win privileges that can best be described as autarkic. Their goal is not to shape the overall economy or to formulate programs and policies with national reach. Instead, they seek to appropriate resources from the federal, and state and local, governments, and to secure laws and regulations that protect their particular interests and profit opportunities from competitors, both foreign and domestic, and to undermine the rights of their customers, clients, and employees.

As a result, a continually growing portion of the federal budget is allocated to the long-standing claims of existing elites who also enjoy the right to shelter portions of their incomes and assets from taxation. Current examples include:

(1) Subsidies, water rights, and access to federal lands for the over-production of agricultural commodities that then can be sold abroad thanks to provisions US negotiators placed in trade treaties;

(2) The commitment of a sector of the federal budget to a Medicare drug plan that pays prices significantly higher than anywhere else in the world for drugs developed mainly in federal or university labs or for copycat drugs designed to extend patents with no medical advantage over older generic drugs.[1] "Product hopping"—small, clinically

1   Matt Richtel and Andrew Pollack, "Harnessing the US Taxpayer to Fight Cancer and Make Profits," *New York Times*, December 19, 2016; Charles Ornstein and Ryann Grochowski Jones, "The Drugs that Companies Promote to Doctors Are Rarely Breakthroughs," *New York Times*, January 7, 2015; Michele Boldrin and David K. Levine, *Against Intellectual Property* (Cambridge: Cambridge University Press,

insignificant changes in drug formulations—allows pharmaceutical firms to renew patents. The firms then use their marketing muscle to convince and/or pay off physicians to prescribe the patented drugs instead of equally effective and far cheaper generics. Drug companies employ such maneuvers without legal challenge to increase their profits at the expense of Medicare and Medicaid and of private consumers through increased insurance premiums and higher out-of-pocket expenses.[1]

Drug firms' profits are not for the most part invested in research. Indeed,

> from 2003 through 2012, Pfizer [one of the largest pharmaceutical firms] funneled an amount equal to 71% of its profits into [stock] buybacks, and an amount equal to 75% of its profits into dividends. In other words, it spent more on buybacks and dividends than it earned and tapped its capital reserves to help fund them. The reality is, Americans pay high drug prices so that major pharmaceutical companies can boost their stock prices and pad executive pay,[2]

not for research, which is left largely to the federal and nonprofit sectors;

(3) Free access to federal lands for mining, ranching, and logging with no obligation to pay for environmental effects, which are then borne by public funds and health;

(4) Federal tax and direct subsidies for the export of technology and capital to foreign subsidiaries and customers;[3] and

---

2008), chapter 9; Iain Cockburn and Rebecca Henderson, "Public-Private Interaction and the Productivity of Pharmaceutical Research," Working Paper 6018 (Cambridge, MA: National Bureau of Economic Research, 1999); Donald Drake and Marian Uhlman, *Making Medicine, Making Money* (Kansas City, MO: Andrews McMeel, 1993); Skocpol, *Boomerang*.

1   Khan and Vaheesan, "Market Power and Inequality," 252–4.

2   William Lazonick, "Profits Without Prosperity," *Harvard Business Review* 92 (2014), 55.

3   Beverly J. Silver and Giovanni Arrighi, "Polanyi's 'Double Movement': The *Belle Époques* of British and US Hegemony Compared," *Politics and Society* 31 (2003), 347–9.

(5) The growing share of federal student loans that are channeled to for-profit colleges and trade schools even as they fail to graduate most of their students, charge much more than state schools, and account for almost half of all student loan defaults despite enrolling less than a tenth of post-secondary students.[1]

Together, these claims and immunities ensure either growing deficits or, even in times of fiscal stability as in the late 1990s, an inability to finance new public projects for either infrastructure or the development of human capital. The new structure of elite autarky also allows individuals to loot their own firms as well as the state, as we will discuss in further detail in chapter 8. Managers took some of their firms private and increased their share of publicly traded firms through stock options, which amounted to "one fifth of non-financial corporate profits (net of interest) [in 1999] . . . Whereas in 1992, corporate CEOs held 2 per cent of all equity outstanding of US corporations, by 2002 they owned 12 percent."[2]

## MASS ORGANIZATIONS

Mass membership organizations in the United States underwent a transformation that was almost the structural inverse of the one that made American elites decentralized and autarkic. In contrast, mass membership organizations and unions lost efficacy as they became highly centralized and their local chapters lost autonomy.

Skocpol[3] finds that, prior to World War II, the largest US membership organizations were cross-class in membership and had local chapters from which leaders were elected and could rise in a national hierarchy. At the local level, the organizations "combined social or

---

1   Suzanne Mettler, *Degrees of Inequality: How the Politics of Higher Education Sabotaged the American Dream* (New York: Basic, 2014).
2   Brenner, *Boom and the Bubble*, 299.
3   Theda Skocpol, *Diminished Democracy: From Membership to Management in American Civic Life* (Norman: University of Oklahoma Press, 2003); "Government Activism and the Reorganization of American Civic Democracy," in *The Transformation of American Politics: Activist Government and the Rise of Conservatism*, ed. Paul Pierson and Theda Skocpol (Princeton: Princeton University Press, 2007).

ritual activities with community service, mutual aid, and involvement in national affairs. National patriotism was a leitmotif."[1]

Such organizations were highly effective at mobilizing members across the nation to lobby for government programs that addressed concerns that members raised at the local level. A prime example is the Servicemen's Readjustment Act of 1944 or GI Bill, which provided subsidized home mortgages, unemployment benefits, and free university educations for returning veterans. This bill was the first significant piece of social legislation since 1937 and came long after the New Deal coalition lost control of Congress. It was pushed primarily by the American Legion, a veterans' group that became notorious during the Vietnam War for its ultra-reactionary political positions. The plans that Congress proposed to address the millions of soldiers who would be demobilized and thrown onto the housing and job markets with the end of the war were regarded as inadequate by the veterans who had suffered the consequences of a similarly weak program at the end of World War I. Those veterans, who met at American Legion halls to socialize, discussed the issues and formulated a stronger program. Veterans' organized presence in every congressional district allowed them to pressure Congress to approve the bill. This was legislation from the bottom up,[2] albeit amended by southern congressmen to ensure that the states rather than the federal government administered most GI Bill programs to ensure that African Americans would be excluded, at least in the South, from opportunities to escape agricultural labor.[3]

The mass membership organizations lost potency in the second half of the twentieth century as women went to work, sex-segregated social activities lost favor, and the number of veterans declined. They were supplanted by new sorts of organizations staffed by professionals and reliant upon contributions solicited through the mail (and today

---

1 Theda Skocpol, "Advocates Without Members: The Recent Transformation of American Civic Life," in *Civic Engagement in American Democracy*, ed. Theda Skocpol and Morris P. Fiorina (Washington, DC: Brookings Institution Press and Russell Sage Foundation, 1999), 465.

2 Suzanne Mettler, *Soldiers to Citizens: The G.I. Bill and the Making of the Greatest Generation* (New York: Oxford University Press, 2005), chapter 1.

3 Domhoff, *The Myth of Liberal Ascendancy*, 50–3.

on the internet). Those organizations do not call on members for anything but money, and so their proposals have little resonance with their members. Since the members are not mobilized, elected officials feel free to ignore them and instead cater to the desires of their largest financial contributors, who, in the United States, are mainly investors in and officers of large corporations.

A similar process occurred in labor unions. Locals, which were the site of organizing drives, strikes, slowdowns, and other actions against employers, and mobilizations for political campaigns, increasingly lost autonomy to the national unions into which they were amalgamated. Locals lost power for a number of reasons. Some were the same that affected mass membership organizations: the professionalization of leadership, the decline of ties among members based on race, ethnicity, and residency in homogeneous neighborhoods and communities, and the weakening of sex segregation and male solidarity. In addition, as we noted above, Taft-Hartley further encouraged national-level union officials to control and weaken locals, sapping them of their organizing strength and initiative, since under Taft-Hartley national unions became liable for damages to firms from wildcat strikes.

All of this matters, not because we pine for a lost world in which cohesive ethnic groups could practice bigotry and women were confined to the role of helpmate, but because US politics is constitutionally structured to reward localized power. Members of Congress are elected from districts or states, and they respond to those who hold power within a state or district or to entities that have a significant economic or organizational presence across a number of districts. From Henry Jackson of Washington State, who served in the 1950s and '60s as the "Senator from Boeing," to Lloyd Bentsen of Texas, who ran against George H. W. Bush for the Senate in 1970 in a race to become "errand boy for the oil companies," to Charles Schumer of New York, who ran interference for banks and hedge funds from the moment he arrived in the Senate in 1999 (and for two decades before that as a representative), industries based in locales have had their congressional champions and lackeys. When and where unions were strong, they had their particular advocates, such as the Michigan delegation's advocacy for auto unions or New York's for garment workers' unions. As unions and membership organizations lost the capacity to mobilize supporters in localities, they lost their leverage over representatives and senators (as well as over state legislators).

Elites, whether organized through banks and interlocking directorships, or in autarkic firms, have leverage at the local level, and that leverage is magnified as they face ever-weaker worker and popular organizations. Business has always contributed far more money to congressional campaigns than have unions and liberal organizations. The advantage that liberal groups, and especially unions, have is in providing campaign workers. As local organizations lose resources and surrender initiative to national headquarters, they are less able to mobilize their members to pressure legislators between elections when laws and regulations affecting them are under consideration, even as unions retain the resources and organizational capacity to mobilize members to work on campaigns.[1] It is in the ongoing work of lobbying that elites, who can marshal contributions and who pay attention on a continuing basis, have the advantage.

When elites and popular forces were more evenly balanced in the attention they brought to government and in their ability to mobilize supporters, members of Congress also had to balance their votes and the pressures they placed on executive agencies to satisfy both elite and popular constituents. As popular organizations have lost the capacity to educate and mobilize their members, elites have achieved close to a monopoly of influence in Congress and within the executive branch.

## GOVERNMENTAL CAPACITY

Citizens who turn out to vote once every two years at best, and whose votes for one party or the other are open to myriad interpretations, lose influence over governmental policy in the absence of popular

---

1   I have not been able to locate any research that compares over time US unions' capacities to mobilize members or other voters at election time for Democratic candidates, nor that compares unions with church and other conservative groups. This would be a worthy topic of research for a social movements or labor scholar.

mobilization or continuing organizational presence and pressure on their members of Congress at the local level.

Larry Bartels[1] argues that elections are still decisive because the Democratic and Republican parties have diverged ever more sharply on key economic issues such as the minimum wage and the inheritance tax. Hacker and Pierson[2] concur with Bartels, but emphasize that the divergence is due to the Republicans' sharp move to the right over the past forty years, not to a significant move by the Democrats to the left. Bartels makes two major arguments. First, voters focus on the incumbent party's economic record in the year before a presidential election rather than over the whole four-year term. This favors Republicans because they attempt to concentrate growth in the pre-election year. (Bartels is unable to determine if this represents a higher capacity on the part of Republicans at economic manipulation for electoral ends,[3] or if this is a natural outgrowth of the two parties' divergent policy preferences, which leads Democrats to push for growth from the start to provide jobs and rising incomes for their mass base but is hard to sustain at a high level for four years, vs. the GOP's interest in curbing inflation, which leads to recession early in their term and then recovery at the end.)[4] Regardless, this favors Republicans and allows them to win more presidential elections than they would if voters focused on the whole four years, a time frame over which Democrats have consistently produced better results. Bartels's second argument is about the policy consequences of voters' (mistaken) preference for Republicans. He argues that inequality, which he measures as "the ratio of incomes at the 80th percentile of the income distribution to those at the 20th percentile," has gone up

................................

1   Larry Bartels, *Unequal Democracy: The Political Economy of the New Gilded Age* (Princeton: Princeton University Press, 2008).

2   Hacker and Pierson, *American Amnesia*.

3   Matusow, in *Nixon's Economy*, demonstrates that Nixon, who believed he had lost the presidency to Kennedy because the Federal Reserve failed to stimulate the economy in 1960, worked tirelessly and successfully to ensure that both fiscal and monetary policy would produce an economic boom for his 1972 reelection.

4   Voters' focus on the last year of a four-year presidential term benefited Obama in 2012, since he came into office at the depths of the deepest postwar recession, and the recovery accelerated only in 2012, enabling him to run for reelection in a year of relatively high growth.

under each Republican president since 1945 but has remained stable under each Democrat except for Carter.[1]

If Bartels is correct, then the decline of unions and membership organizations, and the transformation of the structure of elite relations in the United States, matter little to the outcomes of elections. Nor do those structural changes explain policy outcomes, which for Bartels reflect deep-seated and increasingly polarized preferences by professional politicians in the two parties. A similar logic propels Thomas Frank's argument in *What's the Matter with Kansas? How Conservatives Won the Heart of America.*[2] Frank contends that Republicans win elections not because voters misperceive the two parties' economic performance, but because religiously-addled fundamentalist Christians vote against their self-interest in an effort to ban abortion or to strike back at "elites" whom they define as graduates of prestigious universities or practioners of decadent lifestyles, rather than the economic elites who are looting Kansas and the rest of the United States. Block[3] sees religious conservatives as playing a secondary role in the Republican's rise to power since 1980 but argues that the religious right plays an increasingly decisive role in setting policy, although Block's only examples are Supreme Court appointments and support for Bush's decision to invade Iraq, neither of which are incompatible with the economic elite's interests and agenda that we highlighted earlier.

The Great U-Turn then appears in Bartels's (and Frank's) analyses as a result of voter misperceptions that turned elections. However, Bartels's argument is unable to explain other data that he presents. He shows that incomes in all percentiles rose almost equally (except for

---

1   Bartels, *Unequal Democracy*, 35. Jacob S. Hacker and Paul Pierson, in "Winner-Take-All Politics: Public Policy, Political Organization, and the Precipitous Rise of Top Incomes in the United States," *Politics and Society* 38 (2010): 162–4, correctly subject Bartels to critique for focusing on the 80:20 ratio rather than the far more polarized 99:1 ratio. As a result, Bartels is able to argue that party matters because Democrats do more for the poor than Republicans while he ignores "the issue of why growth has been so skewed toward the very top since the late 1970s" (*American Amnesia*, 163).

2   Thomas Frank, *What's the Matter with Kansas? How Conservatives Won the Heart of America* (New York: Holt, 2004).

3   Block, "Understanding the Diverging Trajectories."

the top 5 percent, whose incomes rose more slowly) from 1947 to 1974, a period that includes Republican presidents Eisenhower and Nixon. After 1974, incomes were stagnant for the bottom half of the population and only grew substantially for the very top percentiles.[1] These data align closely with the pathbreaking work of Piketty and Saez, who find that the share of national income received by the top 0.1 percent was stable from 1960 to 1980 and rose continuously since then, with the sharpest increases under Clinton.[2] That top group's tax rate declined mainly under Carter and Reagan.[3] These data allow us to conclude that, even if the Democrats had won more presidential elections after 1974, it would not have had a substantial effect on the dramatic increase of income and wealth inequality since then. Nor does Bartels offer any evidence that Democratic victories would have produced significant advances in social benefits, since the years when Democrats controlled both the presidency and Congress, 1977–80 and 1993–94, yielded no new social programs, not a single one.

The most recent episode of Democratic control of the presidency and Congress, 2009–10, resulted in passage of the Affordable Care Act, the first major piece of social legislation since the 1960s. Unfortunately, Obamacare, in contrast to the Great Society programs, was not part of a spate of legislation that addressed a range of problems and constituencies. The hopes that the worst economic crisis since the Great Depression and the debacles of Afghanistan and Iraq would create a significant progressive opening were not realized. Obamacare was sui generis, both in that it was not accompanied by other redistributionist measures or by checks on corporate power, and that its enactment required massive subsidies and concessions to the for-profit entities that control the US health care system.

The Democratic Congress of 2009–10 rejected proposals from Obama that would have fostered unionization, controlled global warming, and liberalized immigration; executive measures on those issues have been modest in their effects. The Dodd-Frank Wall Street

---

1 Bartels, *Unequal Democracy*, 9.
2 Piketty and Saez, "Income Inequality in the United States," figure 2.
3 Piketty and Saez, "How Progressive Is the US Federal Tax System? A Historical and International Perspective," *Journal of Economic Perspectives* 21 (2007), table 2.

Reform and Consumer Protection Act of 2010 has so far been limited in its effect on the financial sector. Its ultimate effect will be determined by regulations that were not yet fully written six years after the law's enactment, and which will have to be enforced by executive agencies that under Obama, as under previous presidents, exhibited little appetite for confronting Wall Street (and under Trump are committed to undermining if not revoking these rules)—as evidenced most notoriously by the almost total lack of prosecutions against financiers whose fraud brought on the 2008 collapse.[1] As James K. Galbraith observed, "nothing [was] done about bankers' pay, with obviously disastrous political consequences as bonus reports came in. No one can say that the administration handled this matter with an eye on public opinion."[2]

It is a mistake to attribute Obama's shortcomings, as so many journalists and political rivals have done, to his supposed lack of assertiveness, or his aloofness, or a deep psychological need to find compromise, or too much faith in the judgment of highly credentialed advisors. In fact, even a more aggressive and assertive president could not have accomplished significantly more than he did, neither in his first two years with a Democratic Congress, and certainly not after that, with Republican control of first the House and then the Senate as well. Obama had to work within narrow political limits, created by the processes I analyzed above, and which were not overcome by the 2008 election or subsequent events.[3]

Any explanation that focuses on elections and differences between the two parties masks the dramatic shift of both parties after the early

---

1   Jesse Eisinger, *The Chickenshit Club: Why the Justice Department Fails to Prosecute Executives* (New York: Simon & Schuster, 2017).

2   James K. Galbraith, "The Great Crisis and the Financial Sector: What We Might Have Learned," in *Aftermath: A New Global Economic Order?*, ed. Craig Calhoun and Georgi Derluguian (New York: NYU Press, 2011), 23.

3   These limits became ever more apparent to Theda Skocpol and her collaborators. Compare the hopefulness of Skocpol and Larry Jacobs in *Reaching for a New Deal: Ambitious Governance, Economic Meltdown, and Polarized Politics in Obama's First Two Years* (New York: Russell Sage Foundation, 2011) with Skocpol's *Obama and America's Political Future* (Cambridge: Harvard University Press, 2012) to see how even a most sympathetic social scientist had to acknowledge the narrowness of the 2008 opening.

1970s away from policies designed to maintain each stratum's share of national income, which included high tax rates on the rich, and a commitment to expanding social programs. Only the sort of structural analysis we offered above can account for (1) the capacity of elites to appropriate resources from publicly held corporations as well as from the state, (2) the dramatic decrease in regulation of firms, (3) declining investment of public funds in education and infrastructure, and (4) the inability to legislate new social programs on any terms but ones that allow private firms to maintain or increase their claims on public resources (as demonstrated in both Bush's Medicare Part D for pharmaceuticals and in Obama's health reform).

Thus, if we look at the long sweep of US history from 1945 to 2016, we see a transition from one era of political stasis to another. The first, the liberal consensus expressed by President Kennedy, was institutionalized in a structure of state regulation, relations among business firms and with government and unions, and commitments to maintaining the power of the national government to sustain global geopolitical dominance and to foster economic growth and social progress at home within circumscribed limits. After the political and policy failures (and successes) of those who sought and held office in the federal government in the 1960s, and the structural shifts in the United States' world position, which we examine in the following two chapters, sparked challenges from many directions, the consensus was disrupted. The ideological debates opened in those years remain unresolved and animate the two parties' platforms as well as the agendas of social movements and professionally directed membership organizations focused on identity and environmental issues on the left, and on religion and other "social" issues on the right. Yet, during those decades of unresolved debate, a new stasis emerged. Elite relations were restructured and mass organizations, especially unions, lost much of their capacity to challenge elite initiatives. The state itself lost the capacity to enact new legislation or to implement regulations and policies that challenged elite interests. The new stasis was challenged only modestly and reversed even more slightly by the Obama administration.

Our task in the coming chapters is to see how the domestic transformation we just traced combined with changes in the United States' capacity to exert military, geopolitical, and economic power abroad. We will then be in a position to trace the course of US decline and determine how the loss of world dominance will further narrow the possibilities for future political action and affect American social well-being in the coming years.

# 7

# The American Military: Without Rival and Without Victory

"You don't know the connection? You don't know that every privilege in your life and every thought in your mind depends on the ability of the two great powers to hang a threat over the planet?"

"That's an amazing thing to say."

"And you don't know that once this threat begins to fade?"

"What?'

"You're the lost man of history."

Don DeLillo, *Underworld*

The United States, we are told, is the most powerful nation in world history, the sole superpower, winner of the Cold War, the "indispensable nation," a "hyperpower" that has achieved "full spectrum dominance" and "command of the commons"[1] over all other military forces on Earth. Yet, as we noted in the introduction, the United States failed to achieve its objectives in Iraq and Afghanistan, was defeated outright in Vietnam, and since World War II won clear victories only in the first Gulf War of 1991 and in smaller "police actions" in the Dominican Republic in 1965, Grenada in 1983, and Panama in 1989. How can we explain this dichotomy between unparalleled military advantage over all rival powers and a virtually unblemished record of military defeat since the end of the Cold War? And how has the strange mix of great military capacity and

---

1  Barry R. Posen, "Command of the Commons: The Military Foundation of US Hegemony," *International Security* 28 (2003).

inability to utilize that power to attain military victories affected America's ability to maintain geopolitical hegemony?

We explained in chapters 2 through 5 why the European polity with the largest budget did not necessarily win wars or take colonies from poorer rivals. We examined why Spain and France were unable to parlay their military dominance within Europe into economic or geopolitical hegemony, and why the era of Dutch hegemony was so brief, while Britain was able to build the dominant global empire and maintain hegemony for far longer than any other polity over the five centuries of global capitalism. We identified five factors that caused disjunctures between military resources and the outcomes of wars: (1) lack of central control over the military, (2) high levels of autonomy for military officers, (3) divisions among branches of the armed forces, (4) self-serving weapons suppliers, and (5) lack of innovation in strategy. We will see that all five factors are present in the US military in recent decades with the addition of two new factors: a dramatic decline in the willingness of Americans to risk their lives (or to allow professional and volunteer US troops to lose their lives) in combat, and US efforts to impose neoliberal policies in countries it invades.

The first part of this chapter follows the trajectory of US military spending in relation to its geopolitical rivals from World War II to the present. I then examine the organization of the US military, its relation to private contractors, and its war-fighting and counterinsurgency strategies. My goal is to examine how the five factors that weakened the militaries of previous great powers manifested themselves in the US military, determine the extent to which they are strengthened by interaction effects, and track the particular American dynamics that in the past mitigated those factors but no longer do so. The next section of the chapter traces the decline in casualty tolerance in the United States since the Vietnam War. I then look at the switch by the United States in its goals for the countries it dominates/invades, from developmentalism to neoliberalism, and how that shift affects America's capacity to win wars and to dominate other countries. This chapter concludes by explaining how, despite its loss of military efficacy, the United States retains (at least for the moment) a degree of geopolitical hegemony.

## THE TRAJECTORY OF US MILITARY SPENDING

Champions of US global dominance have an easy and clear explanation for America's military setbacks. The problem, in their view, is that Americans are unwilling to pay the financial or human cost of maintaining their empire or, when they bother to express it in more palatable terms, to uphold democracy and the rule of law in the world. I will address American attitudes toward casualties below, but in terms of spending there is no evidence to support this claim by twenty-first-century imperialists. The United States, in fact, has easily maintained, and since the end of the Cold War vastly expanded, its edge over the budgets of geopolitical rivals. Indeed, the US advantage in military spending and technology is unprecedented in recorded history.

As we see in table 7.1, the United States spent more than the Soviet Union throughout the Cold War, and America's NATO allies spent six to eight times as much as the USSR's Warsaw Pact allies, widening the margin. In 1954, at the peak of American power and after the end of the Korean War, the United States and NATO spent more than twice as much as the USSR, Warsaw Pact allies, and China combined. In 2016, the United States and NATO spent three times as much as Russia and China combined. Much of the spending by the "rest of the world" is from US allies in the Middle East and Asia, which widens the margin of the US bloc over any potential enemies.

Throughout the twenty-first century, the United States has spent as much as the next ten biggest spenders and in most years as much as the next fourteen, a majority of whom are allies.[1] This is a margin far greater than that enjoyed by any of the dominant powers in Europe, as we saw in chapters 2 through 5, and appears to be the greatest margin ever.[2]

--------

1   Stockholm International Peace Research Institute, 1976–2017.
2   Two other trends in table 7.1 deserve mention. One is the rapid increase in military spending by the "rest of the world" (everywhere except the United States, the Soviet bloc, and China) in the early 1970s. That increase had two causes. First, OPEC's drastic increase of oil prices in 1973 gave oil-exporting countries, mainly in the Middle East, the wherewithal to buy weapons and expand their armies, and made possible a second upsurge in spending around the turn of the twenty-first century. Second, the Nixon Doctrine sought to lessen America's burden of countering the Soviet bloc in the Third World by offering advanced American weapons for

**Table 7.1:  Military Spending as a Percentage of World Spending¹**

|                    | 1954 | 1964 | 1974 | 1984 | 2010 | 2016 |
|--------------------|------|------|------|------|------|------|
| United States      | 49   | 40   | 32   | 31   | 43   | 36   |
| Other NATO         | 16   | 16   | 18   | 19   | 16   | 15   |
| USSR/Russia        | 24   | 29   | 23   | 22   | 04   | 04   |
| Other Warsaw Pact  | 02   | 02   | 03   | 02   | –    | –    |
| China              | 03   | 05   | 06   | 06   | 07   | 13   |
| Rest of world      | 06   | 08   | 18   | 20   | 30   | 35   |

sale to regional proxies (most famously to Iran under the shah). This encouraged newly rich oil-exporting nations, and also increasingly prosperous East Asian countries, to increase their military spending. Nixon's scheme had an ambiguous effect on America's geopolitical position, but it definitely benefited US defense firms while lowering US trade deficits and offsetting some of the costs of developing new weapon systems, albeit with the inevitable risk that some purchasers would become enemies over the decades during which advanced weapon systems are developed and sold by the United States (Martin van Creveld, *The Transformation of War* [New York: Free Press, 1991]). Again, Iran is the key example, while Saddam Hussein's Iraq was a lesser proxy and purchaser of US and NATO weaponry up to the very day it invaded Kuwait.

The other trend of note is the slow increase in Chinese military spending, which supports Arrighi's assertion in *Adam Smith in Beijing* that China is not attempting to compete militarily in the way past rising powers in the West sought to do. China's military spending in 2016 was only 36 percent of America's (table 7.1). While that amount may be enough to allow China to challenge the United States, at least in its sphere of influence in East Asia (as lesser powers with smaller budgets were able to challenge greater powers in previous centuries, as we saw in the historical chapters, and as middle-level powers such as Saudi Arabia, Israel, Iran, and Brazil seek to build regional dominance today), it is not enough to give China the global reach the Soviet Union once enjoyed and which would be necessary if China hopes to actually rival or supplant the United States' geopolitical hegemony.

1    Stockholm International Peace Research Institute (SIPRI) is the source for all the data in table 7.1. Sources: for 1954–74, *SIPRI Yearbook* 1976, pp. 150–1; for 1984, *SIPRI Yearbook* 1985, p. 270; for 2010, *SIPRI Yearbook* 2011, p. 183; for 2016, "Military Expenditure," https://www.sipri.org/research/armament-and-disarmament/arms-transfers-and-military-spending/military-expenditure, SIPRI 2017. SIPRI data rely on market exchange rates instead of purchasing power parity to compare nations' military budgets. SIPRI prefers MER to PPP because the latter requires subjective judgments, and in SIPRI's view it is problematic to apply PPP ratios that are constructed from comparisons of the prices of civilian goods and apply them to military budgets that go in large part for arms purchased on world markets. SIPRI's figures also exclude legacy costs of past wars reflected in state debt payments or veterans' benefits. SIPRI's results are similar to those of the US Arms Control and Disarmament Agency, *World Military Expenditures and Arms Transfers* (1966–98), http://www.state.gov/t/avc/rls/rpt/wmeat/index.htm for the 1960s and '70s, though not for the 1980s when the Reagan-appointed director of the agency cooked the data to exaggerate Soviet and Warsaw Pact military spending.

The United States has been able to enjoy this unprecedented advantage even as its military spending as a percentage of GDP has declined drastically from war to war. The military budget in 1968, the peak year of Vietnam War spending, was, as a percentage of GDP, two-thirds that of spending during the Korean War. And the burden of the 1968 military budget was the same as that of 1961, the peak year of Kennedy's Pentagon budget, which itself was a decline from the Eisenhower peacetime military budgets of 1955–59. Reagan's peak military budget of 1986 imposed only two-thirds the burden of the Vietnam and Kennedy Cold War budgets. Reagan's military budgets were never burdened by any real wars. Yet the peak George W. Bush military budget of 2008 was only 70 percent of the Reagan peak (as a percentage of GDP), despite the costs of two wars.

**Table 7.2:  US Military Spending as a Percentage of GDP[1]**

| Year(s) | Percentage of GDP |
|---|---|
| 1943–45 (World War II) | 37–38% |
| 1952–54 (Korean War) | 13–14% |
| 1955–59 (Eisenhower post-Korea) | 10–11% |
| 1961 (Kennedy peak spending) | 9.4% |
| 1968 (Vietnam peak spending) | 9.4% |
| 1978–79 (post-Vietnam trough) | 4.7% |
| 1986 (Reagan peak spending) | 6.2% |
| 1999–2000 (post-Reagan trough) | 3.0% |
| 2008 (G. W. Bush peak spending) | 4.3% |

The United States' ability to lessen the burden of military spending so greatly while maintaining and enhancing its edge over both allies and opponents is the exact opposite of Paul Kennedy's prediction that the United States would follow previous great powers in overspending on war to an extent that would sap economic growth. Similarly, America's success in accumulating and holding a set of allies that was far richer than the Soviet satellites, and therefore far more capable of contributing to the US-directed military bloc, is at odds with Paul Kennedy's

----

1    Source: Office of Management and Budget, *Historical Tables*, table 6.1. Where a percentage is given for multiple years, e.g., 1952–54, the percentages are the range of spending in those years.

thesis that leading powers are brought down by alliances among lesser powers (just as we saw in chapter 5 that Britain gained enormously from its ability to tap the fiscal and manpower resources of India and the Commonwealth). Thus, Paul Kennedy is utterly unable to account for either the fiscal or geopolitical bases of America's continuing and deepening military advantages.

## THE CONFLICTING REQUIREMENTS OF THE MILITARY-INDUSTRIAL COMPLEX AND OF WINNING WARS IN THE EARLY TWENTY-FIRST CENTURY

The US military command occupies a central place in determining when and how American wars will be fought. Once the decision to go to war has been made, or is in the process of being made, the top generals play a decisive role in decisions about how to fight it. They do not have absolute authority, but it is very difficult for the civilian leadership to defy their advice. This is in part because any move to oppose the generals' recommendations opens politicians to the charge of weakness in defending America and of failing to give the troops "the tools they need."

The generals' views of how to fight wars and what weaponry they need are shaped, indeed determined, by the ways in which their careers and those of lesser officers are structured. They advance by commanding expensive and technically complex weapons. Success in winning appropriations for those weapons systems ensures long careers for the ever-expanding corps of generals. These career and organizational imperatives mesh perfectly with defense firms' interest in selling advanced weapons systems, which consistently yield the largest profits. Thus, advanced weapons continue to absorb the lion's share of the Pentagon budget, even though those weapons are fundamentally ill suited for the actual wars the United States fights in the twenty-first century.

### The Structure of the US Military
The United States military differs from those of earlier great powers in fundamental ways: Officers are professionals who are recruited and promoted on merit. They are not able to purchase or inherit their positions and, instead, are bureaucrats in Weber's sense of that term.

The US military depends on the federal government for all of its funding; it does not have its own income-producing assets, nor is it able to raise revenues on its own. (The hybrid venture capital funds that the Pentagon has created since the 1960s are designed to foster technological innovation that is useful to the military, and almost all profits from the firms spun off from those funds are allowed to accrue to private investors. The Pentagon's interest in those investments is technological. They are not intended to subsidize other portions of the military budget, and the profits the Pentagon retains are plowed back into new high-tech enterprises).[1] Yet, despite the US military's "modernity," it suffers from debilitating structural handicaps that in some ways parallel those of early modern armed forces and account for the paradoxical coexistence of American strategic defeats along with an unprecedented technological and fiscal edge over all rivals.

The US military is highly autonomous from the rest of the federal government.[2] At the same time, the military is itself divided among four service branches: Army, Navy, Air Force, and Marine Corps, and each has an interest in maintaining its own organizational autonomy, in large part because (as we will discuss in detail below) officers make their careers in a single branch and career advancement depends on having men and especially weapons to command. Each branch maintains its own academy that trains junior officers and awards undergraduate degrees, as well as war colleges for advanced postgraduate training that helps officers advance in rank and influence. These separate educational and training institutions foster distinct "personalities" in each service branch: Officers learn to prize particular weapons and develop strategies for warfighting based on their control over

---

1   Linda Weiss, *America Inc.? Innovation and Enterprise in the National Security State* (Ithaca: Cornell University Press, 2014).

2   C. Wright Mills, in *Power Elite*, recognized this autonomy at the height of the Cold War when he distinguished between the military and political elites, noting that they headed distinct bureaucratic organizations and followed different paths of education and career advancement even if, late in their careers after retiring from the armed forces, military men were able to assume positions in the economic or political elites. The military, six decades after Mills wrote, has achieved an even higher degree of autonomy over both the allocation of its overall budget and strategies for deploying and using weapons and men.

those weapons systems.[1] These preferences and career interests in turn, as we will see in the next section, drive each branch to fight to maintain its share of the overall Defense Department budget and of sophisticated weapons. Thus, the Navy and Marines as well as the Air Force buy and fly planes, and the Navy, Air Force, and Army each purchase and command nuclear weapons.[2]

The Defense Department, since World War II, has cultivated direct relations with their military counterparts elsewhere in the world, as has the Central Intelligence Agency,[3] both agencies going far beyond the level of coordination with allies that existed during the two world wars. In addition, the military and CIA sustain independent relations with civilian officials of many foreign governments.[4] More broadly, the Pentagon has created "commands" for each region of the world, headed by senior generals or admirals, who negotiate directly with both military and civilian officials in the countries of those regions about policy matters that extend far beyond military cooperation.[5] These commands endure across presidential administrations and thus provide more continuity in US strategic policies and in relations with

--------------------

1    Carl H. Builder, *The Masks of War: American Military Styles in Strategy and Analysis* (Baltimore: Johns Hopkins University Press, 1989).

2    Ann Markusen and Joel Yudken, *Dismantling the Cold War Economy* (New York: Basic, 1992), chapter 2.

3    Michael V. Hayden, *Playing to the Edge: American Intelligence in the Age of Terror* (New York: Penguin, 2016).

4    Oftentimes, differences between the State Department's professed support for democratic civilian governments and the Pentagon and/or CIA's training and cultivation of officers who then staged military coups were merely cosmetic, and in fact all departments of the US government were supportive of such coups and the brutal repressive measures that were implemented in their wakes (Tim Weiner, *Legacy of Ashes: The History of the CIA* [New York: Anchor, 2008]; Stephen Kinzer, *Overthrow: America's Century of Regime Change from Hawaii to Iraq* [New York: Times Books, 2006]). The 1975 reports of the Church Committee (United States Senate Select Committee to Study Governmental Operations with Respect to Intelligence Activities, chaired by Idaho senator Frank Church), the most comprehensive examination of US government covert activities, can be accessed at aarclibrary.org.

5    Robert Killebrew, "Strategy, Counterinsurgency, and the Army," in *Lessons for a Long War: How America Can Win on New Battlefields*, ed. Thomas Donnelly and Frederick W. Kagan (Washington: AEI Press, 2010); James Carroll, *House of War: The Pentagon and the Disastrous Rise of American Power* (Boston: Houghton Mifflin, 2006).

foreign governments than do the civilian side of the US government. These commands override service rivalries at the level of strategy (although service differences still impede military missions within these commands). However, these commands are yet another source of independent bailiwicks that prevent unity within the military, and they also create policies that civilian officials find difficult to reverse in the rare instances when they might wish to do so.

Military officers increasingly receive postgraduate degrees, often in foreign affairs and public policy, at elite universities and "thus possess proconsul skills that far exceed those necessary to command men in battle."[1] Those academic credentials, beyond any knowledge and wisdom actually conveyed through study at places like Harvard's Kennedy School or Princeton's Wilson School, add to senior officers' claims of prestige and auras of expertise in their dealings with presidents and their aides, members of Congress, and journalists who display added deference to officers with advanced degrees even though (or perhaps especially when) those politicians and journalists attended elite schools themselves. In addition, there has been a drastic decline in the fraction of politicians and journalists, even more so than in the general population, who have served in the armed forces and thus have direct experience of any sort with military matters. By 1949, as World War II veterans were elected to office, 65 percent of senators were veterans. More than two-thirds of senators were veterans until 1993. By 2012, only 16 percent of senators were veterans.[2]

--------------------------------

1   Hanson, *Father of Us All*, 199; although Paul Yingling, in "A Failure in Generalship," *Armed Forces Journal* (2007), points out that "a survey of Army three- and four-star generals shows that only 25 percent hold advanced degrees from civilian institutions in the social sciences or humanities."

2   Micah Cohen, "Lautenberg's Death Continues Sharp Decrease in Military Veterans in Senate," *New York Times*, June 3, 2013. Of course, most senators and indeed most veterans did not experience combat, since in any military a large majority of soldiers are support personnel. Nevertheless, military experience at least gives veterans the prestige to comment on and challenge (or more often to uncritically support) military commanders' claims, even if that service consisted of making propaganda films in Hollywood and later falsely claiming he helped liberate Auschwitz (Ronald Reagan), taking a single flight as an observer for which he was awarded the Army's Silver Star Medal by General Douglas MacArthur (Lyndon Johnson), claiming his nickname was Tail-Gunner Joe and that he had been wounded in battle even though he never flew a combat mission and was injured in an onboard

Civilian officials in the US government, including presidents, find it politically risky to deny military commanders' requests for troops once wars have been initiated. President Truman's dismissal of General Douglas MacArthur was a rare instance of a president who rejected a military strategy (in that case, a direct armed confrontation with China) and backed that decision by replacing the commander in the field. Truman and congressional Democrats paid a high political price for their opposition to MacArthur, although the price was reduced by the rare unwillingness of the rest of the military high command to support MacArthur and his strategic proposals after his dismissal.[1]

The Vietnam War was propelled forward by presidents' fear of denying generals' demands for more troops. Historians still debate why the United States government launched itself into a war in Vietnam that at its peak committed 550,000 US soldiers and ultimately resulted in 58,220 US military deaths and those of perhaps 2 million Vietnamese. Porter argues that the Vietnam war was prosecuted by a US military convinced that it enjoyed such an overwhelming strategic edge over the Soviet Union and China that it could roll back communism in Vietnam without having to fear a significant pushback from any communist power. Gareth Porter contends that the Soviets, Chinese, and North Vietnamese concurred in that view and were ready to stand aside as the United States crushed the southern insurgency, but that the three governments were pushed into

---

party crossing the Equator (Joseph McCarthy), or supervising the loading and unloading of cargo planes while spending most of his time playing poker and winning enough to finance his first congressional campaign (Richard Nixon). Conversely, George McGovern, who flew thirty-five missions as a bomber pilot during World War II and received the Distinguished Flying Cross and the Air Medal for genuinely heroic actions (Thomas J. Knock, *The Rise of a Prairie Statesman: The Life and Times of George McGovern* [Princeton: Princeton University Press, 2016], chapter 4), rarely mentioned his military record in public. McGovern was the rare presidential candidate who was *successful* in combat, in contrast to John F. Kennedy (ship sunk), George H. W. Bush and John McCain (shot down), or Bob Dole (ambushed).

1  Committee on Armed Services and the Committee on Foreign Relations, United States Senate, Eighty-Second Congress, First Session, "To Conduct an Inquiry into the Military Situation in the Far East and the Facts Surrounding the Relief of General of the Army Douglas MacArthur from His Assignments in that Area" (Washington, DC: Government Printing Office, 1951); Robert. A. Caro, *Master of the Senate: The Years of Lyndon Johnson* (New York: Knopf, 2002), chapter 16.

countering the United States by the autonomous decision of South Vietnamese communists (the Viet Cong) to successfully fight the Americans and their puppet government.[1]

Frank Logevall finds that Johnson and some of his advisors already in 1964–65 were highly pessimistic of the chances of winning the war, and that American allies and some in Congress and the media were willing to endorse withdrawal even if it led to communist control in all of Vietnam. Logevall sees Johnson's macho unwillingness to preside over the "first" American "defeat" as the main cause of the decision to escalate rather than withdraw.[2] H. R. McMaster argues that the Joint Chiefs knew early on that Johnson and McNamara's strategy was inadequate to win the war but that they failed to confront the civilian officials both because generals accepted their constitutional subservience to presidents and because interservice rivalries allowed the far more politically skillful Johnson and secretary of defense Robert McNamara to divide and stymie the generals. Nevertheless, McMaster's book is based on the premise that, with the right strategy, the United States could have defeated the communists, echoing Porter's rendition of the generals' view thirty years earlier.[3]

In an analysis of an unpublished memoir by McGeorge Bundy, one of Johnson's key pro-war advisors, Goldstein finds that Rusk and Bundy were concerned mainly with preserving US credibility with its allies, and both aides thought that was reason enough to fight in Vietnam, even if the war could not be won. American credibility also became Nixon's reason for not negotiating a settlement of the war that would lead to a unified communist Vietnam, although Nixon was

---

1   Gareth Porter, *Perils of Dominance: Imbalance of Power and the Road to War in Vietnam* (Berkeley: University of California Press, 2005).

2   Frank Logevall, *Choosing War: The Lost Chance for Peace and the Escalation of War in Vietnam* (Berkeley: University of California Press, 1999).

3   H. R. McMaster, *Dereliction of Duty: Lyndon Johnson, Robert McNamara, the Joint Chiefs of Staff, and the Lies that Led to Vietnam* (New York: Harper Collins, 1997). Ian Roxborough, in "Learning and Diffusing the Lessons of Counterinsurgency: The US Military from Vietnam to Iraq," *Sociological Focus* 39 (2006): 335, notes McMaster's book "is a travesty of the truth. The blame game gets in the way of serious analysis. The brute fact is that the Army simply refused to put counterinsurgency doctrine into effect in Vietnam, despite the urging of President Kennedy. Instead, under General Westmoreland, it chose to fight the war in the way it wanted to, the way that it found most familiar, as a conflict with an enemy 'army.' "

more concerned with what US adversaries, above all the Soviet Union, thought of his toughness than he was worried about allies. This leads Goldstein and Bundy to conclude that George Ball, the main advocate of withdrawal within the Johnson administration, made a strategic error in proposing negotiations as the alternative to war, since Ball was never able to convincingly explain how Johnson could force a negotiated solution that would preserve a neutral South Vietnam.[1] Logevall, in contrast, contends North Vietnam as well as the USSR and China would have accepted a neutral South Vietnam over the long term. Ball would have done better, in Goldstein and Bundy's retrospective views, to have made a realpolitik argument: The war was "a loser—so lose it as cheaply as you can."[2]

In any case, Bundy makes clear that the real negotiations were between McNamara and William Westmoreland (the commander of US forces in Vietnam) over the minimum number of new troops Westmoreland would accept. Johnson shaped his war strategy in 1965 and afterward "to sustain a consensus among General Westmoreland, the Joint Chiefs of Staff, and the civilian leadership of Pentagon,"[3] a view that undercuts McMaster's picture of a subservient or divided Joint Chiefs. Johnson needed the generals' consent to the end:

> Johnson had won the partial bombing halt [announced in the same March 31, 1968, speech in which he declared he would no longer be a candidate for reelection] by a vote [of the Joint Chiefs of Staff] of three to two, but explained now that if he had pursued a compete cessation he would have lost, four to one.[4]

Porter and Logevall's opposing interpretations of American motives both find support in government documents as well as in Bundy's memoir. Successful politicians like Johnson are highly skilled at taking varying and even opposed positions with different

1    Gordon Goldstein, *Lessons in Disaster: McGeorge Bundy and the Path to War in Vietnam* (New York: Holt, 2009).

2    Ibid., 159.

3    Ibid., 188.

4    Jeff Shesol, *Mutual Contempt: Lyndon Johnson, Robert Kennedy, and the Feud That Defined a Decade* (New York: Norton, 1997), 442.

audiences, and in all these books analyses of original documents are overlaid with officials' post-hoc efforts to exaggerate their contemporaneous concerns and premonitions about the war and/ or to guard the Kennedy legacy. Nevertheless, Porter, Logevall, and Bundy/Goldstein all agree that the high command of the US military was confident that the war could be won and remained so even well after Tet, which they interpreted as a fatal blow to the Viet Cong.

Ultimately, it did not matter whether or not the generals had a viable strategy to win the war, as John Nagl[1] claims, or, as it turned out, were delusional about the nature of the enemy they faced, the weakness, cowardice, and corruption of their South Vietnamese allies, and the actual capacities of US forces.[2] President Johnson felt he could not deny their requests for troops, even when prediction after prediction of success made by the generals proved wrong. Only in the face of mounting popular protests, business elite disquiet, and some divisions within the military (motivated more by fears of enlisted men's mutinous conduct than over the prospects of victory) was Johnson able to deny Westmoreland's 1968 request for 200,000 more troops on top of the 550,000 already in Vietnam.

Kennedy was able to deflect demands for massive numbers of combat troops, but he made clear that he did not feel he could abandon South Vietnam or even deescalate until he had been safely reelected, and it remains unknowable if, in a second term, he would have dared to take a different course from the one Johnson ended up following, or what the consequences of such a decision would have been for him and his party politically. Nixon too remained stuck in Vietnam for another four years and signed off on various harebrained schemes dreamt up by the generals to win a lost war, most notably the invasion of Cambodia. We need to remember that more than 20,000 American soldiers died after Johnson left office and was replaced by Nixon.

President Obama, despite his boasts of having read histories of the

---

1   John Nagl, *Learning to Eat Soup with a Knife: Counterinsurgency Lessons from Malaya and Vietnam* (Chicago: University of Chicago Press, 2005).
2   Yingling, "A Failure in Generalship."

Vietnam War and learned from them, agreed to a surge in Afghanistan.[1] He also signed off on the reintroduction of "advisors" in Iraq in the hopes that a few thousand advisors could rout ISIS when over a hundred thousand troops had failed to defeat the insurgency under Bush. Perhaps, for a brief time, Obama convinced himself that the Joint Chiefs and David Petraeus had a viable strategy to win in Afghanistan, but even after he realized he had been fooled (or that the generals were fooling themselves), he dared not deny the generals.[2]

Similarly, the United States has vastly expanded its military presence in Africa despite the United States Africa Command's (AFRICOM's) almost perfect record of failure. In 2010, General Carter Ham, testifying before the Senate Armed Services Committee on his nomination to head AFRICOM, identified al-Shabaab as the major threat in Africa and one largely confined to Somalia. Three years later, his successor, General David Rodriguez, said, "A major challenge is effectively countering violent extremist organizations, especially the growth of Mali as an al-Qaeda in the Islamic Maghreb safe haven, Boko Haram in Nigeria, and al-Shabaab in Somalia." And then in 2016, Rodriguez's successor, General Thomas Waldhauser, repeated almost word for word Rodriquez's observation: "A major challenge is effectively countering violent extremist organizations, especially the growth of al-Qaeda in the Islamic Maghreb, Boko Haram in Nigeria, al-Shabaab in Somalia, and ISIL in Libya."[3]

Evidently, the only change was the addition of ISIL in Libya, which came into existence after the United States and NATO engineered the overthrow of Muammar Gaddafi. Thus, the growing web of US bases, agreements with militaries in more than two dozen African countries, and hundreds of Special Forces missions and drone attacks each year have resulted in a rapid *increase* in the number and lethality of terror

---

1   See David Samuels, "Barack and Hamid's Excellent Adventure," in *Harper's Magazine*, August 2010, for a bemused account of how Obama got taken by his own generals and Hamid Karzai.

2   Bob Dreyfuss, "The General's Revolt: *Rolling Stone's* 2009 Story on Obama's Struggle with His Own Military," *Rolling Stone*, October 28, 2009.

3   Nick Turse, "The US Military Pivots to Africa and That Continent Goes Down the Drain," TomDispatch, August 2, 2016.

threats. President Obama and Congress did not conclude that the US military presence in Africa should be reduced, nor have any of the AFRICOM commanders been dismissed or even criticized for their failures.

Elected civilian officials at best share with the military a role in deciding when, where, and how many American troops to commit to foreign wars. However, the details of how to fight those wars remain in the hands of the generals, and once the war begins the role of civilian officials is diminished. Even when civilian officials were more eager to fight a war than the generals, as with Iraq, once the decision to invade had been made, the generals asked for a far larger fighting force than Bush and his aides allowed.[1] The generals remained confident of victory despite repeated setbacks, and eventually wrested control of the war away from Bush, Cheney, Rumsfeld, and their civilian aides. However, by then strategic decisions, omissions, and blunders, along with policies (which we examine below) that ensured the alienation of Iraqi elites and armed opposition from the mass of Iraqis, made it impossible for the United States to achieve its aims in Iraq.

Donald Rumsfeld famously said, in response to the complaints of soldiers heading for Iraq that they lacked armor to protect their vehicles from bombs planted in roads, "You go to war with the army you have, not the army you might want or wish to have at a later time."[2] Of course, the US Army is a product of past spending decisions. Let us now examine who makes those decisions and what sort of weaponry the United States has bought with its massive expenditures.

### Contracts and Careers

The way I estimated my fees for the Army . . . was to dream up a figure that seemed unreal and add a zero. The Army didn't trust you if our fees weren't preposterous.

Greg Baxter, *The Apartment*

1  Thomas E. Ricks, *Fiasco: The American Military Adventure in Iraq* (New York: Penguin, 2006); Michael R. Gordon and Bernard E. Trainor, *Cobra II: The Inside Story of the Invasion and Occupation of Iraq* (New York: Pantheon, 2006).

2  Eric Schmitt, "Iraq-Bound Troops Confront Rumsfeld over Lack of Armor," *New York Times*, December 8, 2004.

The United States has consistently devoted a disproportionate share of its military spending to technologically innovative weapons rather than for simpler weapons useful in counterinsurgency wars. Similarly, soldiers are trained and promoted for their skill in using high-tech weapons rather than for interacting with local populations. C. Wright Mills[1] noted that weapons contracts for private firms gave the economic and military elites a shared interest in high military budgets. While the economic elite in general would prefer lower military spending to prevent tax increases (Mills wrote in the era before both the Reagan military buildup and the George W. Bush wars were accompanied by tax cuts and instead when the Eisenhower military was financed with taxes that topped out at 91 percent), that consideration was outweighed by the fact that military contracts then and now are abnormally profitable. Firms consistently gain far more in profits from military contracts than they, or their managers and shareholders, pay in taxes to finance the Pentagon budget. Thus, private firms come to have an interest in, and lobby for, military budgets weighed toward weapons procurement, and especially toward the purchase of innovative weapons, rather than for personnel.

America's invention of nuclear weapons, and its improvement of German-developed missiles, sparked a "military revolution"[2] that made possible a strategy of projecting power on a worldwide basis, premised on having those new weapons always ready for use. That strategy reinforced the preference for investment in high-tech weapons rather than personnel and, in turn, required constant technological innovation, especially after the Soviet Union developed its own nuclear arsenal. While America's perpetual technological lead and always greater resources dictated the Soviets' responsive nuclear strategy, the United States as the technological and geopolitical leader had strategic options. However, those options were shaped by the interests of defense contractors in winning and maintaining lucrative long-term contracts for high-cost, high-volume, high-profit weapons

1    Mills, *Power Elite*, 212–19.
2    Williamson Murray and MacGregor Knox, "Thinking about Revolutions in Warfare," in *The Dynamics of Military Revolution, 1300–2050*, ed. MacGregor Knox and Williamson Murray (Cambridge: Cambridge University Press, 2001), 1–14.

systems[1] and by the career trajectories of the growing cadre of military officers who inhabit four distinct services. Together officers' institutional cultures and interests and defense contractors' sway over Congress combine to shape the budgetary decisions and determine the efficacy of America's armed forces.

The military is not a unified organization. Rather, Carl Builder[2] found that the Navy, Army, and Air Force each had a "personality" that had been developed over decades and that was expressed in a hierarchy of weapons preferences. Thus, the Navy seeks to maximize its number of ships, especially of capital ships (i.e., the largest ship that takes the leading fighting role in wars, actual or planned, which, since World War II, have been supercarriers). The Air Force cares most about technology and procuring the most advanced planes, even if it has to trade quantity for quality. Repeated efforts to develop "jointness" among the military branches[3] have mostly failed.[4]

"Service ascendancy," i.e., the organization of all weapons purchases and career pathways, and the planning of war strategies, in terms of the interests and desires of four autonomous military services, has endured despite the Goldwater-Nichols Department of Defense Reorganization Act of 1986, which had the avowed purpose of better coordinating war plans and weapons procurement through a Joint Chiefs of Staff that was supposed to override the parochial interests of each service.[5] Builder thinks interservice rivalry was reduced by "a long history of budgets, roles, and missions [that] has brought considerable stability, harmony, and cooperation in their relations with one another." However, he also identifies the limits to such cooperation:

1   Seymour Melman made this point a half century ago in *Pentagon Capitalism: The Political Economy of War* (New York: McGraw-Hill, 1970) when he analyzed defense contractors' "cost-maximizing" logic.

2   Builder, *Masks of War*.

3   Don M. Snider, "The US Military in Transition to Jointness," *Airpower Journal* 10 (1996).

4   Brendan McGarry, "Army Considers Ending Joint Basing," Military.com, October 13, 2013.

5   Brad Amburn, "The Unbearable Jointness of Being," *Foreign Policy* (2009); Colin S. Gray, "Strategy in the Nuclear Age: The United States 1945–1991," in *The Making of Strategy*.

"But if the issues get too close to their vital institutional interests—their budgets, independence, or control—then barriers are likely to come up, and the threatened service typically withdraws within itself rather than striking out at the other."[1]

Builder sees these preferences as matters of institutional culture, reinforced by officers' personal experiences of devoting long years of their careers to particular weapons systems. For example,

> The ardent advocates of the new ICBM were committed to that cause because they could not be otherwise. They had devoted their professional lives to those machines. Their own personal worth and the worth of ICBMs had become intertwined in a way that could not be easily separated ... For their sense of personal worth, people will fight hard and long.[2]

However, personal preferences and officers' senses of self-worth are fortified and given material bases by the ways in which military careers are structured.

Officers' careers are organized in terms of the weapons systems they command, more than in relation to the men and women they lead. Technical expertise in a single weapons "platform" is valued over "joint, interagency, and international experience."[3] Officers are assigned to units that man and deploy specific weapons systems. A naval officer, for example, commands submarines designed to fire nuclear missiles or aircraft carriers built to allow fighter planes to shoot down enemy air forces or bombers to destroy land targets. A decision to invest in mine sweepers to counter the sort of low-cost and low-tech challenge most likely to be posed by actual enemies at the expense of submarines or carriers would stymie the careers of officers attempting to rise in the resultantly stagnant submarine or carrier corps. For that reason, "mine warfare is a stepchild of the navy, despite those who

---

1 Builder, *Masks of War*, 154.
2 Ibid., 41.
3 James Stavridis and Mark Hagerott, "The Heart of an Officer: Joint, Interagency and International Operations and Navy Career Development," *Naval War College Review* 62 (2009).

warn that it could, and has occasionally, become the central aspect of naval warfare."[1]

During the Iraq War, mines did become central. Ian Roxborough argues that the deployment of mines by Saddam Hussein's forces at the outset of the war prevented the arrival of relief supplies, fatally poisoning the atmosphere in Iraq against US forces. He sees that as one of the crucial causes of the defeats suffered by the United States after its initial success.[2] Had the US military invested in cheap minesweepers rather than the multibillion-dollar vessels preferred by naval officers and military contractors, the mines could have been removed to allow the rapid arrival of goods.

For another, more recent example, Admiral Harry Harris, the former commander of the US Indo-Pacific Command, complained to the House Armed Services Committee in April 2017 that "Critical munitions shortfalls are my top warfighting concern. Munitions are a large part of determining combat readiness in pursuit of national strategic objectives. We are short in 'here-and-now' basic munitions like small diameter bombs."[3] The immediate cause of the shortfall was the need to shift bombs stored in the Pacific to the Middle East for use there in the small-scale wars the United States is fighting in Syria and Iraq. These bombs are cheap, do not use impressive new technologies, and therefore are neither sources of high profits for defense contractors nor platforms on which officers can make dynamic careers. Thus, these weapons are underfunded, underproduced, and become scarce after only a few months of stepped-up fighting in small, low-intensity wars of the sort the United States is fighting in the Middle East.

Officers almost never receive further promotions and often have to leave the military if they transfer from one weapons system to another, hence their reluctance to take command of forces devoted

---

1   Builder, *Masks of War*, 131.

2   Ian Roxborough, "Iraq, Afghanistan, the Global War on Terrorism, and the Owl of Minerva," *Political Power and Social Theory* 16 (2004).

3   Harry B. Harris, Jr., "Statement of Admiral Harry B. Harris, Jr., US Navy Commander, US Pacific Command before the House Armed Services Committee on US Pacific Command Posture, 26 April 2017."

to counterinsurgency,[1] civilian administration, or low-tech weapons designed for actual combat. Roxborough shows that the Army and Marines abandoned thinking about and training for counter-insurgency at the end of the Vietnam War, returning to their preferred focus on "high-tech conventional warfighting."[2] The Air Force promotes officers who are expert in the technology of specific weapons rather than "defense intellectuals" who understand overall strategy.[3] The Army is "a collection of tribes . . . The largest are built around weapons systems."[4] Officers are not willing to leave their "tribe" and abandon command of high-tech weaponry for the more difficult and probably time-limited task of counterinsurgency, even if that is needed to win a war since such operations, unlike weapons designed for fantasy wars with the former Soviet Union or China, are funded only during wartimes and thus cannot sustain officers' decades-long careers. As one Iraq War combat veteran put it, "The officer corps is willing to sacrifice their lives for their country, but not their careers."[5]

Weapons systems also reward officers in their retirement. Mills viewed the circulation of individuals among the military, political, and economic elites as a key basis of those elites' harmony.[6] Defense firms often hire military officers after their retirement, and the promise of high corporate salaries to supplement their pensions gives officers a powerful incentive not to question the worth of expensive weapons systems, nor to dispute contractors' bills and pricing decisions. "The number of retired three- and four-star generals and admirals moving into lucrative defense industry jobs rose from less than 50

1  Deborah Avant, *Political Institutions and Military Change: Lessons from Peripheral Wars* (Ithaca: Cornell University Press, 1994), chapter 3.

2  Roxborough, "Learning and Diffusing the Lessons of Counterinsurgency," 331.

3  Charles J. Dunlap, Jr., "The Air Force and Twenty-First-Century Conflicts: Dysfunctional or Dynamic?" in *Lessons for a Long War.*

4  David Cloud and Greg Jaffe, *The Fourth Star: Four Generals and Their Epic Struggles for the Future of the United States Army* (New York: Three Rivers Press, 2009).

5  Thom Shanker, "Third Retired General Wants Rumsfeld Out," *New York Times,* April 10, 2006.

6  Mills, *Power Elite,* chapter 12.

percent between 1994 and 1998 to a stratospheric 80 percent between 2004 and 2008." When former generals themselves cannot lobby Congress, the major defense contractors make use of former congressional staff members, who make up the bulk of their Washington lobbying offices.[1]

Officers' opportunities for career advancement, and hence each service branch's opportunities to reward institutional loyalty, have been fortified by the remarkable expansion in the number of top-ranked officers.

> America's military is astonishingly top heavy, with 945 generals and admirals on active duty as of March 2012. That's one flag-rank officer for every 1,500 officers and enlisted personnel. With one general for every 1,000 airmen, the Air Force is the worst offender, but the Navy and Army aren't far behind. For example, the Army has 10 active-duty divisions—and 109 major generals to command them. Between September 2001 and April 2011, the military actually added another 93 generals and admirals to its ranks (including 37 of the three- or four-star variety). The glut extends to the ranks of full colonel (or, in the Navy, captain). The Air Force has roughly 100 active-duty combat wings—and 3,712 colonels to command them. The Navy has 285 ships—and 3,335 captains to command them. Indeed, today's Navy has nearly as many admirals (245 as of March 2012) as ships.[2]

Since US military preeminence is based ultimately on nuclear superiority, military officers gained the greatest prestige and rose in rank most swiftly and surely by commanding nuclear weapons. Officers therefore demanded that each branch of the service (Army, Navy, Air Force) control its own system of nuclear weapons, giving rise to the "nuclear triad" of missiles, submarines, and bombers.

Presidents have found it impossible to eliminate any part of the triad even though bombers are less powerful and more expensive than

1   Citizens for Responsibility and Ethics in Washington, "Strategic Maneuvers: The Revolving Door from the Pentagon to the Private Sector," November 10, 2012.

2   W. J. Astore, "Sucking Up to the Military Brass: Generals Who Run Amuck, Politicians Who Could Care Less, an 'Embedded' Media . . . And Us," TomDispatch, November 29, 2012.

land or submarine-based missiles (and their pilots are exposed to death or capture if shot down, which then leads the military to invest in stealth technology that both vastly raises the cost of each plane and increases the likelihood of technical failure). The vulnerability of land-based missiles means that the United States, Russia, and China have only minutes to decide if a rival has launched an attack that could destroy their missiles. This has led William Perry, defense secretary from 1994 to 1997 in the Clinton administration, among others, to argue that scrapping nuclear missiles entirely would eliminate the greatest danger of accidental nuclear war without reducing America's retaliatory capacity.[1] Such a decision would be an assault on the Army's prestige and on its nuclear officers' careers. No senior official has proposed taking this step while in office, as opposed to Perry, who made the proposal two decades after his retirement from government service.

Officers' desires for ever-greater technological complexity have raised the costs of weapons far faster than inflation or GDP. The costs of fighter and bomber planes, for example, have escalated from $50,000 each during World War II, when the United States purchased 75,000 per annum,[2] to $100 million for the F-15I and $2 billion for the B-2 in 1995 when "the United States Air Force bought exactly 127 aircraft . . . including helicopters and transports."[3] Such weapons are not suited to attacking terrorists of any stripe or to subduing populations in countries identified as dangerous by the United States. For example, the B-2 could not be deployed abroad because "the skin of the plane cannot handle the heat or the damp or the rain." As a result, "The Air Force issued a statement today saying that, for now, it will cancel plans to station the bombers overseas. 'It would be difficult to operate the B-2 from a deployed location,' the Air Force statement said."[4] As of 2009, the most popular military fighter planes were the

---

1    William Perry, "Why It's Safe to Scrap America's ICBMs," *New York Times*, September 30, 2016.

2    Kennedy, *Rise and Fall of the Great Powers*, table 34.

3    Martin van Creveld, *The Rise and Decline of the State* (Cambridge: Cambridge University Press, 1999), 345–6.

4    Tim Weiner, "The $2 Billion Stealth Bomber Can't Go Out in the Rain," *New York Times*, August 23, 1997.

F-18 Super Hornet for the Navy at $93 million each, the F-22 Raptor, with a unit price of $355 million, and the F-35, with a $134 million unit cost, none of which are suited for counterinsurgency warfare.[1]

Presidents seeking Senate ratification of treaties to limit the number of nuclear weapons needed to elicit support from the Joint Chiefs, through their testimony that the treaties would not weaken US security. That testimony could be bought only with promises to invest in existing or new weapons systems, promises that also were of interest to senators with weapons plants or nuclear laboratories in their states, in other words, almost all senators. Thus, the Obama administration, in return for Senate ratification of the New START (Strategic Arms Reduction Treaty) in 2010, which makes only modest cuts to nuclear weapons, agreed to a massive modernization of US nuclear weapons and production facilities that is projected to cost $900 billion to $1.1 trillion over the next thirty years.[2] As a result of that deal, in 2014 the United States spent more (adjusted for inflation) on nuclear weapons research, development, testing, and production than in any previous year,[3] even more than in the Reagan or George W. Bush military buildups.

Conventional and nuclear weapons were developed to either repel a Soviet offensive or to counter Soviet weapons designed to impede a

---

1   Defense Aerospace, "Cost of Selected US Military Aircraft," April 30, 2010.

2   Jon B. Wolfsthal, Jeffrey Lewis, and Marc Quint, "The Trillion Dollar Nuclear Triad" (Monterey: James Martin Center for Nonproliferation Studies, 2014). This deal was similar to the promises President Kennedy had to give to win support for the Partial Test Ban Treaty of 1963: "The [Joint] Chiefs were bribed for their support with promises of unfettered underground testing, and hawkish senators were bribed with promises of lavish defense increases down the road" (Carroll, *House of War*, 288). The promises of underground testing were kept; those of increased defense spending, as we saw in table 7.2 above, were not. Similarly, Nixon approved new weapons systems (the B-1 bomber for the Air Force, the Trident submarine for the Navy, and the Abrams tank for the Army) in return for the Joint Chiefs' endorsement of the SALT (Strategic Arms Limitation Talks) 1 and ABM (Anti-Ballistic Missile) treaties (Carroll, *House of War*, 347). However, Nixon's drastic cuts in overall military spending left no room for actually building expensive new weapons systems. Carter canceled the B-1 before it went into production. It was revived under Reagan, but only one hundred copies of the new version were built. Both the Trident and Abrams were manufactured mainly during the Reagan military buildup.

3   William J. Broad, and David E. Sanger, "US Ramping Up Major Renewal in Nuclear Arms," *New York Times*, September 21, 2014.

US attack. Since the Soviet Union had more troops in Europe than the United States, officers and firms lobbying Congress had a strategic justification to direct ever more resources into nuclear and other advanced weapons designed to counter or preempt the Warsaw Pact's manpower advantage over NATO by achieving first-strike capability. The weapons currently in development, which absorb most of the military's procurement budget, are still being designed to counter Soviet or Chinese forces rather than for the sorts of counterinsurgency wars the United States actually fights. Military officers demand and firms are paid

> to produce weapons that are too expensive, too fast, too indiscrimi-
> nate, too big, too unmaneuverable and too powerful to use in real-
> life war. It makes even less sense to design weapons whose develop-
> ment costs are such that they can only be produced on condition that
> they are sold to others; particularly since lead times are now so
> long—ten to fifteen years—as to make it likely that some of the
> buyers will have become enemies.[1]

The end of the USSR removed any strategic justification for these weapons, yet their development and production continued.

The F-35 Joint Strike Fighter, the most expensive weapon in development (in total, not unit cost), is emblematic of the constraints on US weapons procurement that have held since the start of the Cold War and of the institutional barriers to reform. The F-35 was conceived to save money with a single design that would be used by all branches of the military. However, the Air Force, Navy, and Marines were able to demand variants of the plane that would meet their particular needs. This produced the worst of both worlds: The plane is more complex and heavier than separate planes for each branch would otherwise be, since the F-35 needs to include features for each service branch in a plane that will be used by all three, and, at the same time, three variants will be manufactured, losing much of the hoped-for cost savings of a single plane. The complexity of the plane increases the difficulty of manufacturing it without fatal defects. The F-35

---

1   Van Creveld, *Transformation of War*, 210.

prototypes have failed to meet its performance objectives and in war games simulations were easily shot down by existing Chinese and Russian fighters. Nevertheless, Lockheed Martin has convinced Congress and the Pentagon to move ahead with production even before the design flaws are resolved. American allies, such as Australia, have paid for a portion of the design costs and are committed to buying the planes, even though the versions they will get (which are in addition to the three variants for the US military) will lack some of the most advanced features, making them even more likely to be "clubbed like baby seals" in actual combat.[1]

One additional requirement of all new US weapons systems augments their complexity, expense, and likelihood of breakdown: the necessity of rendering the soldiers who man them invulnerable to enemy efforts to kill or capture them. Thus, the F-35 employs stealth technology; tanks are ever more heavily armored, which makes them slower and also consumes vast quantities of fuel that, as was demonstrated in Afghanistan and Iraq, can only be delivered to the front lines at huge expense and by exposing US troops or contractors to a high likelihood of ambush.

Weapons systems are almost never canceled, despite technical failures, lack of use in the wars the United States actually fights, or rising costs that then lead the military to buy fewer of each plane, missile, gun, or ship, which thereby increases the per-unit cost as the massive research and development expenses are divided among fewer units. Conversely, the Air Force has repeatedly tried to phase out the relatively cheap and effective A-10 "Warthog" attack jet so funds can be diverted to the far more expensive F-35.[2] Despite campaigning, twice, on a platform of military restructuring, President George W. Bush succeeded in canceling only the Army's Crusader artillery system. All

---

1   David Axe, "F'd: How the US and Its Allies Got Stuck with the World's Worst New Warplane," *Medium*, August 13, 2013; see also Michael P. Hughes, "What Went Wrong with the F-35, Lockheed Martin's Joint Strike Fighter?" *The Conversation*, June 13, 2017; Paul Barrett, "Is the F-35 a Trillion-Dollar Mistake?" *Bloomberg Businessweek*, April 4, 2017; and W. J. Astore, "The F-35 Fighter Program: America Going Down in Flames," *The Contrary Perspective*, February 18, 2014.

2   Dan Grazier, "The Air Force Is Slowly Killing Off the A-10 Warthog," *The National Interest*, January 18, 2018.

other Cold War weapons systems inherited from previous administrations continued in production during the Bush years.[1] Obama was somewhat more successful and "killed weapons programs that have survived earlier attempts at termination, among them, the F-22 fighter jet, the VH-71 presidential helicopter and the Army's Future Combat System."[2]

Efforts to reduce costs by using "off-the-shelf" technology, developed for civilian purposes by private firms, have been limited so far.[3] The Strategic Capabilities Office (SCO), founded in 2012 during the Obama administration specifically to buy or adapt commercial products for use by the military, has grown rapidly since then but still commanded a budget of only $907 million in 2017.[4] SCO's efforts face resistance from defense contractors that would lose business selling their high-priced custom components and systems to cheaper civilian competition and from officers whose careers are built on their command of highly complex, service-specific weapons. In addition, military officers have pointed out that civilian information technology is easily hacked, raising a security objection to the use of off-the-shelf components and systems. Recent efforts to use commercial drones, which are orders of magnitude cheaper than custom-made military drones, have foundered on the military's belief that all its drones need to be able to operate indoors as well as outside and must contain complex target recognition software that is beyond the capacity of existing civilian drones and that would add greatly to their cost and complexity. Similar objections stymied an earlier effort at the outset of the Clinton administration to replace military-specific production lines with ones that produce both civilian goods and military components.[5]

1   David S. Cloud, "Pentagon Review Calls for No Big Changes," *New York Times*, February 2, 2006.

2   Jonathan Weisman, "Democrats' Quiet Changes Pile Up," *Wall Street Journal*, November 2, 2009.

3   Markusen and Yudken argue that the "business culture" of military contractors "is ill-suited to engage in commercial production and vice versa" (*Dismantling the Cold War Economy*, 69 and passim).

4   Sandra Erwin, "Pentagon Taking a More Serious Look at Off-the-Shelf Technology," *National Defense*, December 12, 2016.

5   *New York Times*, "Tank Parts, Off the Shelf," April 6, 1993.

Defense contractors have an interest in using their political power to preserve funding for every weapons system. The United States is unique in that private, for-profit corporations produce almost all of its weapons, whether cutting-edge or pedestrian. As we noted earlier, this gives the firms' managers and shareholders an interest in supporting military leaders' requests for innovative and expensive weapons that will continue in production for many years and that can be sold to allies as well. Military contractors' power to sway congressional votes on the Pentagon budget is derived from their locations, and relationships with subcontractors, throughout the United States. Thus, almost all senators and representatives have business owners and workers in their states and districts who benefit from the continuing production of weapons systems, regardless of their effectiveness or their expense. Indeed, the more expensive the weapon, the more the firms and workers benefit. As we noted in the previous chapter, defense workers are disproportionately unionized, which gives all unions and even unionized workers in non-defense industries an interest in supporting large military budgets.

Two developments since the end of the Cold War have fortified and deepened the connections between economic and military elites. First, the push, under the George H. W. Bush and Clinton administrations, to consolidate defense firms (in the hopes that a few gigantic firms would be more innovative and efficient than smaller firms, a hope that has not been borne out),[1] led banks to lend acquiring corporations large sums to pay for their purchases of smaller firms. (Of course, the military mergers paralleled those in other sectors, which we discuss in chapters 6 and 8). This meant that banks came to have an interest in ensuring that the defense budget, and profits from weapons contracts, remained high enough to service the debt taken on by the merged defense firms.

Second, tasks that were once carried out by military personnel have been transferred to for-profit firms. The duty of guarding American diplomats, and even commanding officers, as well as the job of protecting high officials of the US-supported governments in

---

1  Lawrence Korb, "Merger Mania: Should the Pentagon Pay for Defense Industry Restructuring?" Brookings Institution, June 1, 1996.

Afghanistan and Iraq, which in previous wars would have been carried out by enlisted American soldiers, was contracted out to private firms, most notoriously Blackwater, that relied on retired US soldiers and foreign mercenaries. The work of hauling fuel and other supplies to US troops and preparing meals, doing laundry, delivering mail, and more were also contracted out to private firms, such as Halliburton (which Dick Cheney headed before he became vice president).[1] In 2001, the Pentagon's contracted workforce exceeded civilian defense department employees for the first time.[2] There were 9,200 contract employees in the Gulf War, but by 2008 there were at least 100,000 in Iraq.[3] In 2010 contractors made up 48 percent of the combined contractor and uniformed personnel workforce in Afghanistan and and Iraq.[4]

Beyond the opportunities for enriching private firms, there are actual policy reasons to privatize some military functions: First, privatization reduces the number of troops needed for the armed forces. Every cook, driver, technician, or guard supplied by a private firm is one less soldier the military needs to recruit, train, and eventually support in retirement or disability. Steinmetz describes this as a military version of "post-Fordist 'just-in-time production.'"[5] Singer argues that these firms hold down costs by being "virtual" and hiring

1   In 1962 Halliburton absorbed Brown and Root, "holder of [Lyndon] Johnson-arranged government contracts and receiver of Johnson-arranged government favors amounting to billions of dollars . . . [and whose owners, George and Herman Brown] became in return the principal financiers of Johnson's rise to national power" (Robert. A Caro, *The Path to Power: The Years of Lyndon Johnson* [New York: Knopf, 1982], xvi). This was a merger of crony capitalist firms, or what Weber (*Economy and Society*, 166), would describe as "politically oriented capitalism."

2   Deborah Avant, *The Market for Force: The Consequences of Privatizing Security* (Cambridge: Cambridge University Press, 2005), 147.

3   Dina Rasor and Robert Bauman, *Betraying Our Troops: The Destructive Results of Privatizing War* (New York: Palgrave, 2007), 7.

4   Moshe Schwartz, *Department of Defense Contractors in Iraq and Afghanistan: Background and Analysis* (Washington, DC: Congressional Research Service, 2010), 5.

5   George Steinmetz, "Imperialism or Colonialism? From Windhoek to Washington, by Way of Basra," in *Lessons of Empire: Imperial Histories and American Power*, ed. Craig Calhoun, Frederick Cooper, and Kevin W. Moore (New York: New Press, 2006), 154.

employees just for specific contracts who then can be dismissed at the end of a war.[1] In that way, those employees are like draftees who are demobilized at the end of each war, but without the political cost of having to force civilians to serve and risk their lives. However, we need to distinguish these firms' support personnel from the armed guards they provide. The former are drawn from civilian life and often are non-Americans, and their diversion from the civilian workforce has little effect on the domestic economy since most are low skilled and many were un- or underemployed before being enticed to go to Afghanistan or Iraq. On the other hand, some of the guards are former military men who were trained at great expense by the US government. As they are drawn out of the military and into private firms, the military's savings are more than overwhelmed by the loss of skilled soldiers and the high cost of recruiting and training their replacements.[2] In addition, these guards are not under direct control of the military command, and therefore they can end up working at cross-purposes to the US military, as when they kill local civilians.

Certainly, the George W. Bush and Clinton administrations pushed to privatize many government functions, in part from their ideological commitment to neoliberalism, but it is a mistake to see the path of privatization as part of a post-Fordist or neoliberal master plan. Privatization was pushed as much by opportunistic private firms, eager to realize the high profit rates of military contracts, as by government officials. Firms like Halliburton and Blackwater build political support for continued privatization through time-honored methods that have served defense contractors so well: making contributions to political candidates and hiring former military officers and civilian officials at multiples of their public salaries. Thus, once the initial decision was made to privatize military functions, the firms created and maintained political and often corrupt alliances that ensure these services will never again be performed by civilian or military employees of the Defense Department.

---

1   Peter W. Singer, *Corporate Warriors: The Rise of the Privatized Military Industry* (Ithaca: Cornell University Press, 2003).

2   Allison Stanger, *One Nation under Contract: The Outsourcing of American Power and the Future of Foreign Policy* (New Haven: Yale University Press, 2009), chapter 5.

There is one additional and compelling reason for using contractors rather than soldiers: Contract employees killed in combat zones
are not included in the counts of US war dead, and their fates almost
always go unreported and so are invisible to the American public.[1]
The military's need to minimize casualties, and its effect on war strategy, is the topic of the next section.

No American elite has an interest in changing US military strategy
and the procurement budgets that maintain the reliance on high-tech
weaponry. As we will see in the next section, efforts to fight wars with
sustained commitments of ground troops, either conscripts or volunteers, has provoked increasing resistance from Korea to Vietnam to
Iraq. Instead, the US military has looked for technological substitutes
for soldiers. Already half a century ago, in Vietnam,

> Igloo White, which cost $7 billion [placed] tens of thousands of
> sensors . . . around the jungles of Vietnam and Laos in the hope of
> locating and targeting enemy supply columns on the Ho Chi Minh
> trail. But the Vietnamese quickly learned to move the sensors or
> make them send false signals.[2]

Grandiose claims for the effectiveness of smart weapons during the
Gulf and Iraq wars, and in the air war over Serbia, turned out to be
vastly exaggerated.[3] The latest technological fix—the Predator
drones—"turned out to be expensive and delicate instruments."[4] Both
the Iranians and North Koreans figured out by 2011 how to jam the
drones' GPS systems, although technologically less sophisticated

1   The 2004 episode in which four American employees of Blackwater were
killed by Iraqi insurgents, who then hung the contractors' bodies from a bridge in
Fallujah, is the only case that received wide publicity. The attention was in part fortu-
itous in that journalists from the United States and elsewhere were in the city and so
in a position to photograph or film the hanging bodies, and the display of the bodies
was grisly and visually compelling.
2   Andrew Cockburn, "Drones, Baby, Drones," *London Review of Books* 34
(2012); see also Alfred W. McCoy, "Imperial Illusions: Information Infrastructure
and the Future of US Global Power," in *Endless Empire* for a fuller account of the
failure of America's use of information technology in Vietnam.
3   Thomas X. Hammes, *The Sling and the Stone: On War in the Twenty-First
Century* (St. Paul: Zenith, 2004).
4   Cockburn, "Drones, Baby, Drones."

militants in Afghanistan, Pakistan, Yemen, Somalia, and other places with weak or disintegrated states have yet to figure out how to shoot down drones.

Drones and all other smart weapons depend on intelligence, and accurate intelligence requires American troops or spies on the ground (or intelligence from allies more reliable than the South Vietnamese, Iraqis, or Afghans proved to be). The difficulties in finding Osama bin Laden, and then the decision to use Special Forces rather than drones or Pakistanis to kill him, demonstrate the limits of technological fixes, as do the numerous cases of drones that hit the wrong target, or hit a target chosen on the basis of faulty intelligence. As late as 2013, almost 90 percent of those killed by drones in Afghanistan were not the intended targets, although the United States classifies any "military-age male" hit as an "enemy killed in action" except in the rare cases where the identity of the dead man can be determined and there is strong evidence he was "not an unlawful enemy combatant."[1] When the United States is trying to win "the hearts and minds" of the civilian population of an occupied or battleground country, drone hits on innocent civilians serve to undermine that goal.

Nor have the few successful hits on actual insurgent fighters rather than civilians managed to blunt the insurgencies in Afghanistan or Iraq, as demonstrated by ISIS's explosive success in 2014–15 and the Taliban's spreading control. The Defense Department itself concluded that drone attacks in 2012–13 had only a "marginal" effect in killing "key" insurgents or disrupting Al-Qaeda or the Taliban's use of Afghanistan as a safe haven.[2] In 2017, General John Nicholson, the new American commander in Afghanistan, stated, without irony, in testimony to the Senate Armed Services Committee, "Of the 98 US designated terrorist groups globally, 20 operate in the Afghanistan-Pakistan region. This is the highest concentration of terrorist groups anywhere in the world."[3] Thus, for counterinsurgency wars and for other military confrontations such as in the Balkans, there remain no

---

1   Ryan Devereaux, "Manhunting in the Hindu Kush: Civilian Casualties and Strategic Failures in America's Longest War," *The Intercept,* October 15, 2015.
2   Quoted in Ibid.
3   Testimony of General John Nicholson before the Senate Armed Services Committee, February 9, 2017 (audio recording).

substitutes for fielding armies with significant numbers of troops,[1] which is why General Nicholson advocates for an increase in American troops in Afghanistan. Unless and until the United States admits defeat in Afghanistan, Nicholson's successors will issue similarly bleak assessments and call for further reinforcements.

The focus on high-tech weaponry thus undermines US capacity to win wars in three ways. First, America's overwhelming qualitative and quantitative edge over all other countries creates an arrogant belief, present from Vietnam to Iraq, that the United States can defeat any rival. This leads military and civilian leaders to commit to wars that, if they undertook a sober analysis of each side's actual capacities, would lead them to avoid conflicts with little chance for American success. Second, once the decision to fight a war is made, US troops arrive with the wrong weapons and without the extensive training needed for counterinsurgency. Finally, as the prospect for victory recedes, American commanders rely on ever-greater doses of firepower, which serve only to further antagonize the local population.

### CASUALTY AVOIDANCE AND THE NEW CULTURE OF AMERICAN LIFE

Despite all the high-tech weapons, most wars still require that troops be sent into battle at the risk of dying. However, the US public's willingness to tolerate American casualties declined as opposition to the Vietnam War deepened. Despite both President Bushes' claims that they had overcome the "Vietnam Syndrome," the American public has become ever more averse to casualties. In response, the US military has intensified its efforts to minimize American war deaths and to glorify both the dead and soldiers' bravery in protecting one another. Those efforts have the effect of further undermining public support for military strategies that put American lives at risk.

Americans' casualty aversion matters because the insurgents the United States fought in Vietnam, Afghanistan, and Iraq were willing to endure massive casualties over long periods of time. This is

1  Martin van Creveld, *The Changing Face of War: Lessons of Combat from the Marne to Iraq* (New York: Ballantine, 2006), 5.

evidenced in the insurgents' seemingly endless capacities to recruit new soldiers to replace those killed and injured. During the Vietnam War, the US command touted the high enemy body counts as a harbinger of impending victory. In retrospect, the massive imbalance in casualties was a sign of the very different levels of commitment on the part of Americans waging offensive wars of choice that were, at best, tenuously if not totally falsely linked to US security, and Vietnamese who were fighting for what they saw as their class interests as well as for national self-determination. Similarly, Afghan and Iraqi insurgents see victory over the American invaders as the necessary condition for their ability to determine any and every aspect of their life. It is no wonder the insurgents in all three countries were willing to pay such a high price and to do so for as long as was required.

American weapons designed at great expense to protect American soldiers, heavy investments in helicopters to evacuate the wounded, and field hospitals to quickly treat them with advanced techniques, many of which were developed by the military, have greatly reduced the death rate of wounded soldiers. Nevertheless, Afghanistan resulted in the death of 2,417 American troops, and Iraq of 4,563, as of January 15, 2019.[1] Those numbers are far lower than the 58,220 who died in Vietnam or the 36,574 in Korea. Even though the recent war deaths have been relatively few, they have received far more media coverage and that coverage has been much more emotionally charged than for deaths in previous wars.

Much attention was given during the Iraq and Afghan wars to a ban, instituted by George H. W. Bush's administration during the Gulf War and continued by his son's government, on news media access to and photographs of the coffins of dead Americans being returned to the United States.[2] This effort to hide the consequence of "wars of choice" has been contrasted to the supposed coverage of returning bodies in earlier wars.

1   See icasualties.org for a running tally of US military fatalities in Iraq and Afghanistan.

2   Elizabeth Bumiller, "Pentagon to Allow Photos of Soldiers' Coffins," *New York Times*, February 26, 2009. The ban was ended in the first months of the Obama administration.

In fact, there was very little media attention to American war dead during the Vietnam War. Instead, most of the coverage focused on the outcomes of battles rather than casualties. Indeed, even the weekly reports of war deaths, announced on the three networks' evening news shows, with the dramatic ratios of North Vietnamese and Viet Cong deaths to those of Americans, were understood, at least until Tet, as a measure of the war's progress more than of its human costs. Public reaction was strongest in the rare weeks when US deaths exceeded those of the South Vietnamese because those reverses called into question the Johnson administration's claim that the South Vietnamese were bearing the brunt of the war.

*The New York Times'* coverage of the Vietnam War is a good measure of the stoic view of casualties that still prevailed in that era. Of the 5,651 articles the *Times* published on the war from 1965 through 1975, only 1,936 include any mention of Americans killed. Only 726 American dead were named in those articles, in a war in which 58,267 died. Biographical information was included about sixteen soldiers, and photos of fourteen. There are only five references to the reactions of the families of the dead and only two articles mention the suffering of injured American soldiers. Two other articles discuss the funerals or burials of the dead. This restrained coverage is far different from that of the *Times* or any other media outlet during the Afghan and Iraq wars, with frequent lists of the names, ages, and hometowns of Americans killed, and numerous stories on grieving relatives, funerals, and the struggles of injured or psychologically traumatized soldiers.

Our current and anachronistic view of public concerns over soldiers and their lives during the Vietnam War era has been shaped by later developments, most notably the Vietnam Veterans Memorial, which has become the template for how Americans think about their war dead. Indeed, the memorial has displaced Arlington National Cemetery, the Tomb of the Unknown Soldier, and all other sites as the most visited memorial in the United States. In so doing, it has altered the relationship between the individual and the nation. Unlike the dead citizen-soldiers of all previous American wars, whose worth and sacrifice, and those of their families, were ratified by their connection to and subsumption in a national cause, the Vietnam War dead are just dead individuals whose lives are given meaning only in the memories and suffering of their families and friends. In contrast to every previous war memorial, the Vietnam Veterans Memorial makes

> no symbolic reference to the cause or country for which they died, [and instead] immediately highlights the individual. But, once it has been determined that the individual will overshadow cause and country, the task of constructing that individual becomes the primary concern.[1]

The Vietnam Veterans Memorial's focus on individual suffering and familial grieving is compatible with the ways in which American prisoners of war were perceived and politicized during the Vietnam War. POWs became a political issue during the Vietnam War as pro-war politicians in the United States, above all Nixon, used them to sustain support for the war and to falsely assert that anti-war activists were unconcerned with the prisoners.[2] George McGovern, in one of his few witticisms, mocked this by saying, "You'd think we fought the Vietnam War to get our prisoners back." The concern with POWs had the unintended effect—unintended by the war hawks who hyped this issue—of deepening Americans' empathy for soldiers' human suffering and that of their families, and led them to be seen as victims as well as heroes, ultimately weakening support for Vietnam and any other war that put American soldiers in harm's way. The POW "issue" is a rare case of a right-wing strategy that boomeranged.

This line of thinking continued with the image of the yellow ribbon, which Americans first wore to express their concern for the hostages (government employees rather than soldiers) held in Iran in 1979–81. Any geopolitical meaning to the hostages' ordeal was submerged in the drama of the fifty-two individuals held in Tehran. The yellow ribbon has since become a symbol of concern for any Americans in danger abroad. Yellow ribbons were tied to trees,

1 Robin Wagner-Pacifici and Barry Schwartz, "The Vietnam Veterans Memorial: Commemorating a Difficult Past," *American Journal of Sociology* 97 (1991), 400.
2 H. Bruce Franklin, *M.I.A. or Mythmaking in America* (Brooklyn: Lawrence Hill, 1992).

attached to cars and trucks, and worn on shirts during the Gulf, Afghanistan, and Iraq wars.

The use of yellow ribbons to express concern for soldiers sent into combat by their own government suggests a surely unintended equivalence between the radicals who held the hostages in Iran and the US government that sent troops to the Gulf, Afghanistan, and Iraq. The crucial point, for those who display the yellow ribbons, is that Americans are in danger: The ribbons express above all else a desire that the individual soldiers return home safely from Iraq or Afghanistan, as the hostages did from Iran. Yet if the American public's desire is merely for their soldiers' safety rather than for victory, then each casualty is seen as an unjustifiable loss.

Certainly, many relatives remember the Vietnam War dead, and those who died in Afghanistan and Iraq, as patriots; the most common souvenir left at the memorial is the American flag, but the focus on grieving survivors in retrospective coverage of Vietnam and of all subsequent wars downplays the solace of patriotism. This is seen in Jim Sheeler's *Final Salute*, a book-length elaboration of his Pulitzer Prize–winning series of articles for the *Rocky Mountain News*. Sheeler follows "casualty assistance calls officers (CACOs)," the men who knock on doors to inform the "next of kin" that their relative has died in Iraq. Tellingly, this personal form of communication was adopted only toward the end of the Vietnam War;[1] before that, families were informed by letter. The timing of that change suggests that the Defense Department lost confidence that relatives would accept their soldier's death as the tragic fulfillment of patriotic duty. Nor has the military recovered that confidence since. Indeed, the *Casualty Assistance Calls Officer Student Guide* advises CACOs to "avoid phrases or platitudes that might appear to diminish the importance of the loss . . . Pointing out positive factors such as bravery or service may be comforting later, but are usually not helpful at this time."[2] There is no other mention of patriotism, service, or duty in the *Guide*, which otherwise is filled with

1 Jim Sheeler, *Final Salute: A Story of Unfinished Lives* (New York: Penguin, 2008).

2 Commander, Navy Region, Mid-Atlantic, Casualty Assistance Calls/Funeral Honors Support Regional Program Manager, "Casualty Assistance Calls Officer Student Guide."

advice on how to cope with grief and arrange funerals, and offers a summary of survivors' benefits.

The military not only reflects, but also contributes to, the public's heightened sensibility toward the human worth of its soldiers. This is seen in the growing investment in weaponry and medical services to save American soldiers' lives as well as in the deployment of casualty assistance calls officers. It is also expressed in the military's concept of heroism. We can see the military's increasing focus on the worth of their soldiers' lives in the criteria for awarding the Medal of Honor, the highest award for bravery in the US military. Medals are explicitly designed to serve an inspirational role, encouraging new acts of bravery and self-sacrifice from soldiers in ongoing and future wars as well as memorializing past actions. Thus, medals convey more focused and changeable messages than other forms of commemoration, such as military cemeteries and war memorials. Medals thus are illustrative of the values the military wishes to convey, both to its soldiers and to the civilian public.

Medals of Honor were awarded primarily, from World War I through Korea, for "offensive bravery," a soldier's willingness to risk or lose his life in the effort to defeat and kill enemy forces. Examples of offensive heroism include charging the enemy during battle, rallying one's fellow troops to fight harder, and killing large numbers of enemy soldiers alone.[1] A minority of the citations from those wars was for defensive heroism, instances when a soldier risks or loses his life to bring wounded comrades or the bodies of dead fellow soldiers to safety. The most common example of defensive heroism was that of soldiers who threw themselves onto a hand grenade or other exploding devices in order to absorb the blow and save fellow soldiers. Some of the citations noted both offensive and defensive actions.

---

1  Most of the Civil War and other nineteenth-century Medal of Honor citations were brief and did not detail the actions for which the honorees received the medal. Phrases such as "extraordinary heroism," "distinguished gallantry," "conspicuous coolness and heroism," and "bravery in a dangerous situation" appear repeatedly. Richard Lachmann and Abby Stivers, in "The Culture of Sacrifice in Conscript and Volunteer Militaries: The US Medal of Honor from the Civil War to Iraq, 1861–2014," *American Journal of Cultural Sociology* 4 (2016), label such unspecific citations as awards for general bravery.

Vietnam marked a clear turning point. Beginning in 1967, a majority of the citations were for defensive heroism; by 1969, two-thirds were for risking one's life protecting fellow soldiers rather than killing the enemy. Thirteen of the eighteen medals given since Vietnam, for Somalia, Afghanistan, and Iraq, were for defensive heroism. Only one was exclusively for offensive heroism, and the other four were for both.

Table 7.3:  **Criteria for Medal of Honor**

|  | General Bravery | Offensive Heroism | Defensive Heroism | Both |
|---|---|---|---|---|
| Civil War | 1227 | 150 | 148 | |
| World War I | | 86 | 31 | |
| World War II | | 314 | 101 | 13 |
| Korea | | 94 | 36 | 2 |
| Vietnam | | 83 | 133 | 32 |
| Somalia | | | 2 | |
| "War on Terror" | | 1 | 11 | 4[1] |

The military's narrative of defensive heroism, enshrined since Vietnam, has undermined the potential for the US government to use the widening social distance between volunteer soldiers and the civilian population to fight wars in ways that risk the lives of large numbers of American soldiers. In its efforts to extract a heroic narrative from Vietnam, the military enshrined defensive heroism in a way that elevates the protection of American soldiers' lives to the supreme marker of military conduct and honor. The medals, along with other forms of commemoration, above all the Vietnam Veterans Memorial,[2] convey to civilians as well as soldiers a narrative of war that gives primacy to US soldiers' deaths and to efforts to save fellow soldiers' lives. To the extent that policymakers accept this narrative, or are bound by the preferences of soldiers and civilians who accept that narrative, this standard is applied to US foreign policy and war planning and requires civilian and military leaders to minimize casualties,

1   Source: Lachmann and Stivers, "The Culture of Sacrifice in Conscript and Volunteer Militaries," table 2.
2   Wagner-Pacifici and Schwartz, "The Vietnam Veterans Memorial."

no matter how that narrows the ways in which the United States can intervene militarily around the world or affects the prospects of success.

Casualty avoidance is not just a reflection of public opinion but is now embedded within the military ethos as reflected in the criteria for selecting recipients of the Medal of Honor. The military's success or failure at avoiding casualties, more than its ability to realize strategic objectives, now shapes the ways in which news media report American wars. As a result, the military has no choice but to adopt "risk-transfer warfare,"[1] strategies that minimize American casualties, even at the cost of increasing the deaths of civilian non-combatants in the countries that the United States attacks, and thereby further angering the local populations. In the next section, we analyze how risk-transfer warfare combines with US efforts to impose neoliberalism, and how those two pillars of American strategy ensure resistance to US occupations.

## NEOLIBERALISM, PLUNDER, AND RESISTANCE

The US invasions of Afghanistan and Iraq initially produced relatively low casualties and not much resistance. In both countries, armed opposition to the US occupation developed even though the killing and destruction ended once the old governments had been deposed, and even though in both cases the United States pledged to leave when a new government of its liking had been established.

Perhaps nationalism now is such a powerful force that no peoples will tolerate invasion and occupation by foreign forces, but if that was the case, why didn't the Iraqis and Afghans wait for the Americans to leave, as the United States initially promised to do, and likely would have if the local populations had acquiesced in the governments the US imposed? Why did Afghans and Iraqis risk their lives to challenge troops that had an overwhelming advantage in firepower?

The Bush administration first answered those questions by claiming that ideologically addled dead-enders from the old Ba'athist and

---

1   Martin Shaw, *The New Western Way of War: Risk-Transfer War and Its Crisis in Iraq* (Cambridge, MA: Polity, 2005).

Taliban regimes animated the resistance in both countries. At other times, Bush officials argued that the resistance in both countries was supported and directed by foreign powers: mainly Iran in Iraq and Pakistan in Afghanistan. The problem with either of those explanations is that remnants of the old regimes and foreign assistance for insurgencies materialized only well after (months in Iraq and years in Afghanistan) the Taliban and Ba'athist governments had fallen. Resistance in both countries began with local opposition to the American occupation.

The Bush administration, and journalistic and (retired) military commentators,[1] later offered a second explanation for the insurgency: The United States botched its initial occupation. Defense Secretary Rumsfeld's desire to demonstrate that the US military had been (or was in the process of being) transformed by its investment in high-tech weaponry and information technology led him to demand that the invasion be carried out with a much smaller force than his generals requested. Rumsfeld at first seemed to have won that bet with the rapid collapse of Saddam Hussein's military, but that meant US forces were inadequate for the job of occupying the country. Rumsfeld himself denied that he had miscalculated, and instead famously said, "stuff happens" and "freedom's untidy"[2] as Iraqis looted government ministries and other facilities not destroyed by US bombing. As we noted above, Roxborough argued that the US military's lack of minesweepers prevented the arrival of relief supplies, fatally poisoning the atmosphere in Iraq against US forces.

The Bush administration eventually responded to the disorder in Iraq, and thereby at least implicitly accepted the view that the US invasion force had been too small, with the 2007 "surge," the decision to temporarily send 20,000 more troops to Baghdad and Anbar Province

---

1   The most comprehensive accounts are found in Thomas E. Ricks, *Fiasco: The American Military Adventure in Iraq* (New York: Penguin, 2006); Michael R. Gordon and Bernard E. Trainor, *Cobra II: The Inside Story of the Invasion and Occupation of Iraq* (New York: Pantheon, 2006); and Daniel Bolger, *Why We Lost: A General's Inside Account of the Iraq and Afghanistan Wars* (Boston: Houghton Mifflin, 2014).

2   Sean Loughlin, "Rumsfeld on Looting in Iraq: 'Stuff Happens,'" CNN.com, April 12, 2003.

and to lengthen the deployment of the troops already there. Violence eventually diminished in Iraq, although it is impossible to determine if, or the extent to which, that was due to the surge, to US payoffs to Sunni tribal leaders previously in opposition to the occupation (the so-called Sunni Awakening), Muqtada al-Sadr's unilateral cease-fire in the face of an expanded US troop presence and decreased sectarian attacks from Sunnis, or because Shia militias had by then succeeded in their ethnic cleansing of much of Baghdad. Regardless, the surge was a political coup for the Bush administration, enabling it to convince most mainstream US journalists,[1] members of Congress—including then-senator Barack Obama, who "said the surge had 'succeeded beyond our wildest dreams' "[2]—and through them a majority of the American public,[3] that the invasion and occupation of Iraq ended up as a success. This allowed Republicans, including the then-retired architects of the Iraq war,[4] to fob responsibility for the ultimate collapse of order on the Obama administration.[5]

---

1   Typical coverage of the surge includes Bob Woodward, "Why Did Violence Plummet? It Wasn't Just the Surge," *Washington Post*, September 8, 2008; and Dexter Filkins, "Exiting Iraq, Petraeus Says Gains Are Fragile," *New York Times*, August 20, 2008.

2   Quoted in Greg Muttitt, *Fuel on the Fire: Oil and Politics in Occupied Iraq* (New York: New Press, 2012), 243.

3   Polls show a clear majority of Americans considered the surge a success when asked in 2008, 2009, and 2010 (PollingReport.com, "Iraq," 2015).

4   David Petraeus, "How We Won in Iraq," *Foreign Policy*, October 29, 2013.

5   The status of forces agreement, signed by the Bush administration and the Iraqi government right after Obama's election as president in November 2008, was in substance a document of unconditional surrender by the US to Iraqi nationalist demands. It set a hard date of December 31, 2011, for the withdrawal of all US troops. More significantly, it stated that the bases the United States had built in Iraq at a cost of many billions of dollars, and which the Bush administration planned to use to station planes and troops at the center of the Middle East and thereby intimidate neighboring countries, could not be used to attack any other country without permission of the Iraqi parliament, permission that in light of domestic Iraqi and regional political realities would never be granted. Nevertheless, the agreement was a political masterstroke for Bush and the Republicans. "Deferring the agreement would have given newly elected Barack Obama an opportunity to end the occupation, blaming its sudden end and all the consequences on his predecessor. By securing the continued occupation, the form and timing of any withdrawal would now be entirely Obama's responsibility," (Muttitt, *Fuel on the Fire*, 247) even though Obama in fact was conforming to the ultimate December 31, 2011, deadline negotiated by Bush.

Invaders are successful when they bring enough force to conquer foreign lands, but they only succeed in maintaining control in the long term by enlisting local support. The United States in Iraq, like the empires we explored in previous chapters, depends on local elites to assume most of the administrative work and eventually to constitute an indigenous armed force to take over the tasks originally assumed by the conquering force. Ultimately, such arrangements between invaders and locals are far more essential to continued control than the conquering power's willingness and ability to maintain large numbers of troops or administrators abroad. Thus, rather than asserting that "a peculiarity of American imperialism—perhaps its principal shortcoming—is its excessively short time horizon,"[1] we need to find out why the administrators and soldiers the United States sent to Iraq, and to Afghanistan and Vietnam, were so ineffective from the start at building and maintaining local allies who could be counted upon to do America's bidding while successfully suppressing their non-elite compatriots.

In Iraq and Afghanistan, as in Vietnam, the local elites proved to be massively corrupt, and their armies unwilling or unable to suppress insurgencies. Such weaknesses are inevitable: After all, who would ally with a foreign conqueror unless they saw it as a path to enrich themselves? And since almost no one is willing to die to preserve foreign domination, indigenous puppet armies are destined to be cowardly and to constantly weigh the likelihood that their foreign protectors will depart and leave them to the mercies of nationalists who will spare the local quislings only if they, in fact, secretly collaborated with the insurgency.

President Trump's immigration policies will make it harder to recruit local allies on any terms.[2] Since the United States has such a poor record of winning wars, local collaborators need to plan on leaving their

---

1   Ferguson, *Colossus*, 13; for a similar argument, see Bolger, *Why We Lost*.

2   This point was made in a letter to President Trump signed by 130 former generals and State and Defense Department officials from both Democratic and Republican administrations. The letter phrased opposition to Trump's ban in terms of America's image in the Muslim world and that "the Iraqis who risked their lives to work with the U.S . . . will be left in harm's way" (*New York Times*, "Letter from Foreign Policy Experts on Travel Ban," March 11, 2017.

country when the war is lost. Trump's "Muslim ban" originally included Iraq, which meant that local collaborators were blocked from coming to the United States. While Afghanistan was not one of the seven banned countries, the US embassy in Kabul stopped taking applications because the number of Special Immigrant Visas, reserved for such collaborators, had been exhausted. This cannot be blamed on Trump alone. Congress allocated only 1,500 visas over four years for this program, even though 10,000 Afghans are thought to be eligible.[1]

Thus, the fate of the US occupations in Iraq, Afghanistan, and Vietnam, like those of the British in India, in the thirteen American colonies and anywhere else in their empire, or the Dutch, French, and Spanish in their colonies, depended on the occupiers' abilities to offer sufficient incentives to local elites. Those incentives need to be rich enough and appear enduring enough to overcome collaborators' fears of retaliation by the compatriots they betrayed.

The United States faces greater difficulties in recruiting and retaining collaborators in Iraq and Afghanistan in the twenty-first century than it or its imperial predecessors did in earlier centuries because of increased American corruption due to privatization[2] and the Bush administration's commitment to instituting a sort of neoliberalism (a commitment continued under Obama) that robs local elites of opportunities for enrichment that were available to their Cold War counterparts in Vietnam[3] and elsewhere.

---

1  Fahim Abed and Rod Nordland, "Afghans Who Worked for US Are Told Not to Apply for Visas, Advocates Say," *New York Times*, March 10, 2017.

2  The Americans who ran the Coalition Provisional Authority (CPA) were appointed because of their political loyalty to the Bush administration and fealty to Republican policies, including opposition to abortion (Rajiv Chandrasekaran, *Imperial Life in the Emerald City: Inside Iraq's Green Zone* [New York: Knopf, 2006]). Most CPA officials were Republican Party operatives and as such had a continuing career interest in ensuring that firms and individuals who contributed to the party and its candidates received contracts for military and civilian work in Iraq, regardless of the contractors' competence or corruption.

Private firms were largely immune to reviews of their contracts and bills by government auditors in both Iraq and Afghanistan (Chandrasekaran, *Imperial Life in the Emerald City*; Peter van Buren, *We Meant Well: How I Helped Lose the Battle for the Hearts and Minds of the Iraqi People* [New York: Metropolitan, 2011]; Stanger, *One Nation under Contract*), allowing them to siphon off monies from both military services and development programs.

3  Douglas C. Dacy, *Foreign Aid, War, and Economic Development: South*

The neocons who advocated, years before 9/11, a US invasion of Iraq to overthrow Saddam Hussein, and hoped for a series of wars that would replace the governments in Iran and Syria, proposed a frankly colonial project. Their neoliberal plan for the Middle East would not be just an effort to privatize state firms (a process that elsewhere in the world has enriched local as well as American elites), cut social benefits, and ensure the free flow of financial capital. Rather, they saw the series of invasions as a way to enrich Americans, who would gain control of the massive Iraqi and Iranian oil reserves and of other assets.[1]

Brenner observes that neoliberalism in both the core and periphery enables "mechanisms of politically constituted rip-off."[2] The redistribution of Iraqi wealth advocated by the neocons and that the Americans attempted to implement in decrees by the Coalition Provisional Authority was not designed to, nor did it, lead to economic growth. Rather, it was a zero-sum redistribution from Iraqis to Americans. As a result, the Americans could count on less elite or mass Iraqi support than US occupiers in earlier wars not guided by

---

*Vietnam, 1955–1975* (Cambridge: Cambridge University Press, 1986) provides the best overview of US aid and economic policy in Vietnam and how Vietnamese elites were able to exploit those programs to enrich themselves.

1   The process of renegotiating the debt Iraq accumulated under Saddam Hussein provided another avenue for private enrichment. Such debt could have been renounced under the "odious debt doctrine" recognized in international law. "In its classic formulation, the doctrine provides that a regime's debt is odious, and thus unenforceable, if the state's people did not consent to the debt, the proceeds from the debt were not used for the benefit of the people, and the regime's creditors had knowledge of the first two conditions" (Jai Massari, "The Odious Debt Doctrine after Iraq," *Law and Contemporary Problems* 70 [2007]). However, the United States appointed James Baker, secretary of state under George H. W. Bush, to represent Iraq in debt negotiations. Baker simultaneously represented Saudi Arabia, the largest holder of Hussein-era debt (Justin Alexander, "Downsizing Saddam's Odious Debt," MERIP, March 2, 2004). The end result was that 20 percent of the uncollectable debt had to be repaid, sapping Iraqi government revenues for years, and the rest forgiven only if Iraq adopted IMF conditions, including an end to most subsidies and also ratificaiton of an oil law opening Iraqi oil to foreign firms (Muttitt, *Fuel on the Fire*, 149–50). The subsidies were ended, leading to a drastic increase in unemployment and to rapidly rising prices. Since the oil law was never passed by the Iraqi Parliament, the status of the remaining 80 percent of Hussein-era debt remains unresolved since, thanks to Baker, none of it was ever declared odious.

2   Robert Brenner, "Introducing Catalyst," *Catalyst* 1, no. 1 (2017): 11.

such neocon aspirations. Correspondingly, the United States needed to rely almost exclusively on military force, a force that was less effective and available in fewer numbers and for a shorter period of time than in previous wars.

Private firms, especially when they are largely immune to reviews of their contracts and bills by government auditors, as was the case in both Iraq and Afghanistan, have more scope to siphon off monies from both military services and development programs than do corrupt government employees. Most critically, private firms are able to import employees and goods and, in that way, bypass the local politicians, landowners, and businessmen with whom American officials in Vietnam had to deal. Thus, privatization removes the paths through which the US government in Vietnam, Korea, and elsewhere in the twentieth century offered stable and enduring opportunities for local collaborators to enrich themselves. In the absence of such paths, local elites will do better for themselves by allying with insurgents, or at least standing back and allowing insurgents to push the United States out of Iraq and Afghanistan, rather than allying with the occupiers.

Local elites may support, acquiesce in, or even lead insurgencies, but they are too few to provide the fighters needed to push an occupying army to withdrawal or outright defeat. Thus, we need to ask why ordinary Iraqis and Afghans were willing to risk their lives confronting the most powerful military force in the world rather than bide their time and wait for the Americans to leave. While elites' unwillingness to police the mass of people is part of the answer, US-imposed neoliberalism provided the spark of desperation and urgency that fueled the insurgency.

Michael Schwartz provides the most comprehensive analysis of US political and economic policy in Iraq.[1] In addition to the oft-discussed decision by Paul Bremer to dissolve the Iraqi army, leaving thousands of well-trained and armed soldiers unemployed and with a grievance against the United States, Schwartz shows that Bremer and his staff

---

1  Michael Schwartz, *War Without End: The Iraq War in Context* (Chicago: Haymarket, 2008); "Neo-Liberalism on Crack: Cities under Siege in Iraq," *City* 11, no. 1 (2007).

moved to forbid the reopening of government-owned firms in all sectors of the Iraqi economy. In other words, the CPA determined that Iraqis would work for and buy goods and services from private, mainly foreign-owned enterprises, or not at all. The impetus for those decisions was partly ideological, a commitment to eliminating the example of state-owned firms that survived if not thrived through years of embargoes and wars, bringing Margaret Thatcher's TINA ("there is no alternative") to one of the few remaining bastions of state-owned enterprises in the post-Soviet era.

Expectations of practical economic benefits for the United States, however, were even more important than making ideological points. As state-owned firms were closed, opportunities were created for foreign, mainly US, firms to provide, at first with US government subsidies, the goods and services Iraqis once produced for themselves. As US firms built, or imported and installed, electrical generators, sewage treatment plants, hospitals, schools, and more, Iraq became dependent on American workers and firms to run those plants. Iraqis who had worked in those sectors had become expert at repairing and jerry-rigging old facilities that employed Soviet, French, and other older technologies purchased before the embargo that followed the 1991 Gulf War. As those machines were replaced with new American ones, Iraqi employees became obsolete and unemployable. Hence the desperation to end the occupation before the technological and ownership transfers could be effected, or at least to create a level of disorder that would prevent American contractors from installing US facilities.

Schwartz shows how neoliberalism interacted with the corruption of US contractors to both spark the insurgency and ensure that the reconstruction projects paid for with US government funds (or with Iraqi funds that had been frozen in US accounts since Saddam Hussein's invasion of Kuwait in 1990) were wasted. American officials in Iraq tolerated shoddy and incomplete work while paying US firms up front before the work was inspected or bills could be audited. In the majority of cases where the projects were never finished or were poorly constructed, the resulting work was unrepairable by Iraqis who had no knowledge of or training in US technology. In any case, the American firms never instructed Iraqis how to operate what had been installed, since the firms planned to profit far into the future through contracts to service the plants and did not want to be undercut by skilled Iraqis. This, rather than the supposed naivety of State Department officials emphasized by Peter van Buren,[1] himself a career Foreign Service officer, explains the anger that the American occupation aroused in Iraqis.

The US government's turn to a plunder neoliberalism in its dealings with all but the most powerful and autonomous countries in the world undercuts the efforts of counterinsurgency warfare to win support from local populations. What the United States did in Iraq was different from the sort of neoliberalism it fostered in much of the rest of the world, most notably Russia, where state-owned firms were sold to local capitalists (if often with American partners). In Iraq, locals were largely frozen out as the Bush administration sought to create an Iraqi economy dominated entirely by US firms. The plan was for American oil firms to extract energy and use the profits from that to pay other US firms to build and manage infrastructure and import American consumer products. Iraqi capitalists and workers would be entirely frozen out of the major sectors of that new Iraqi economy. This form of neoliberalism would have eliminated most opportunities for the United States to offer paths to wealth for elites and destroyed the jobs and small businesses that ordinary people depend upon for their livelihoods, including those of oil workers who were heavily unionized and pushed back. The United States' ability to force through privatization failed in the face of such resistance.

When neoliberalism is imposed at arms length through trade deals, debt restructuring agreements, or the seemingly implacable workings of markets, it is impossible for affected populations to take revenge on the bankers, business executives, and government officials who orchestrate those policies. However, when the United States moves to eliminate enemy governments and then to quickly restructure economies, as it has done most recently in Iraq and Afghanistan, then American troops are present to become targets of insurgents. When neoliberal policies are combined with plunder and corruption on the part of US contractors and the misfocused investments in

---

1   Van Buren, *We Meant Well.*

weapons and training we analyzed above, the price of American occupations in dollars and in the lives of US soldiers becomes
unsustainable.

So far, the United States has not attempted to impose plunder
neoliberalism except in Afghanistan and Iraq, both projects of the
Bush administration. It remains to be seen if the United States will
attempt to reproduce this project elsewhere or if it will alter its goals in
future wars, or indeed if there will be further invasions. After all,
almost thirty years passed from the final communist victory in
Vietnam in 1975 to the invasion of Iraq in 2003. How long will it be
before the United States attempts an invasion or counterinsurgency
war again?

## WHAT CAN AMERICAN MILITARY POWER STILL ACCOMPLISH?

After World War II, the United States was able to (1) undermine the
Soviet Union and then China as well, (2) select the governments of
countries it dominated, or at least remove governments it did not like,
(3) defeat most major Third World national revolutions, and (4) assign
countries to positions in a global economy designed and directed by
the United States. Since the collapse of the Soviet Union, the United
States has been able to ensure almost the entire world submits to a
neoliberal order that prevents governments from nationalizing firms
or blocking the flow of financial capital.

Yet, in most of the world, US power was hegemonic more than
coercive. The United States' offer to serve as policeman of the world
has been accepted by a majority of the world since 1945, and by
almost the entire world after 1991. Many countries look to the US
military's command of the commons (the world's airspace and seas
as well as outer space) to ensure global order and to protect them
from nearby regional powers that, in the absence of American military dominance, could dominate or invade their neighbors. Thus,
communist Vietnam, after decades of fighting and millions of deaths
to free itself from US domination, eagerly signed up for the Trans-
Pacific Partnership and is considering allowing the United States to
base warships at Cam Ranh Bay to deflect Chinese power—and of

course each and every Eastern European country begged for admission to NATO and the EU, just as Western European governments positioned themselves after World War II within a geopolitical and economic structure designed and controlled by the United States in return for protection from the USSR. American aid through the Marshall Plan came after the recipient governments had already cast their lot with the United States.

American power has been welcomed by capitalists around the world, whose property and commercial freedoms have been protected by the United States. Any costs the United States imposed on its allies have, at least for capitalists, been outweighed by the value of its military protection services for the integrity of countries' borders and for capitalists' property rights and market access.

In the face of continuing US power, are the defeats in Afghanistan and Iraq anomalies or harbingers? I have analyzed why the US military is particularly ill suited to wars against insurgencies, so in that sense those wars are anomalous. If other powers see those wars as categorically different, they would conclude that the United States still could easily defeat them and refrain from provocative actions. So far, with the exception of Russia's invasion of Crimea, established governments have not seen those defeats as signs that they can attack weaker neighbors, although Russia, China, and Iran have been more aggressive in seeking to dominate nearby countries.

Invasions and wars against resulting insurgencies could become less anomalous if neocons, or others who believe that US financial and geopolitical health can be augmented only by embarking on new neocolonial ventures, control US foreign policy. That would resume a cycle of defeats that further undermines Americans' willingness to endure war casualties and that would provide new demonstrations of American military weakness, encouraging other countries to become more assertive themselves.

Such defeats will matter if US economic decline, or a decisive move to privilege American capitalists at the expense of their counterparts elsewhere in the world (by neocolonial invasions or other means), leads more governments to try to assert interests at odds with US geopolitical and economic designs for the world. Such challenges, as opposed to countering massive cross-border invasions, are precisely the ones the United States demonstrated in Iraq and Afghanistan that it cannot overcome with its military. Small countries would then look to regional powers rather than to the United States for protection. Indeed, they might look to lesser powers for protection from the United States itself. At that point, its inability to invade and reshape other countries would mean the United States would have to rely on bluster and bluffs or use the weaponry to which it has devoted most of its resources to launch a catastrophic war.

# 8

# The American Economy: Financial Cannibalization

The United States emerged from World War II as, by far, the dominant economic and military power. The United States used that power to recast relations among nation-states, including the decolonization of its wartime allies' empires. US economic policy did not, and still does not, attempt to create zones of exclusive American influence. Rather, US policy was directed at "creating openings for or removing barriers to capital in general, not just US capital."[1] However, the global financial architecture that was created at the 1944 Bretton Woods Conference mandated fixed exchange rates that were pegged to the US dollar, which in turn could be converted into gold at a fixed rate. The International Monetary Fund was created to offer loans to countries to bridge balance of payments deficits in the hope such credit would remove the temptation to devalue currencies unilaterally. The agreement empowered, but did not require, the governments that signed the agreement—the United States, Canada, Japan, Australia, and most of Western Europe—to restrict the movement of capital across borders.[2] That decision reflected the shared view of New Deal and conservative Democrats (and some Republicans) in Congress and the executive branch under both Roosevelt and Truman that such

---

1   Leo Panitch and Sam Gindin, *The Making of Global Capitalism: The Political Economy of the American Empire* (London: Verso, 2012), 11.
2   Eric Helleiner, *States and the Reemergence of Global Finance: From Bretton Woods to the 1990s* (Ithaca: Cornell University Press, 1996), 25–50; Martijn Konings, *The Development of American Finance* (New York: Cambridge University Press, 2011), 87–99; Gérard Duménil and Dominique Lévy, *Capital Resurgent: Roots of the Neoliberal Revolution* (Cambridge, MA: Harvard University Press, [2000] 2004), 162; Rawi Abdelal, *Capital Rules: The Construction of Global Finance* (Cambridge, MA: Harvard University Press, 2007).

limits on investment and speculation were needed to allow governments in Western Europe and Japan to pursue "embedded liberalism,"[1] i.e., Keynesian social welfare to stimulate growth so as to undermine leftist parties for Cold War geopolitical reasons.

> The cold war also ensured that economic growth, not deflation, was the prime objective for US strategists in the State Department as a means of fostering political stability in Western Europe and offsetting the strength of the Communist party in countries such as Italy and France.[2]

The United States also gave priority to the economic and political integration of Europe over convertibility of their currencies with the dollar.

The priority given to geopolitics over finance, and to growth over deflation, reflected the balance of elites in the United States. At war's end, the military commanded enormous resources and the State Department and aides in the White House assumed responsibility for ensuring that America retained and expanded its network of alliances in the postwar era, a desire that came to be seen as a necessity with the advent of the Cold War. Military and foreign policy elites' capacity to shape America's stance at Bretton Woods and after was reinforced by the political weakness of New York bankers (the financiers with the interest and capacity to profit from foreign loans or currency speculation). Big banks in the 1940s remained discredited by their role in the financial fraud that contributed to the 1929 stock market crash and ensuing Great Depression. The economic recovery powered by military spending benefited industrialists rather than financiers, making them the dominant American capitalists by the end of World War II.

Bankers accrued some power because industrialists needed the big commercial banks to provide them with funds to pay back federal Defense Plant Corporation loans that had enabled them to convert to munitions production for World War II[3] and thereby escape

---

1   Helleiner, *States and the Reemergence of Global Finance*, 1–22.
2   Ibid., 63.
3   G. William Domhoff, *State Autonomy or Class Dominance?: Case Studies on Policy Making in America* (Hawthorne, NY: Aldine de Gruyter, 1996), 215–18; Gregory Hooks, "The Weakness of Strong Theories: The US State's Dominance of the World War II Investment Process," *American Sociological Review* 58 (1993).

government control and partial ownership after 1945. Of course, industrial firms relied on bank loans as well as retained earnings for their expansions in the decades after World War II. However, big corporations had an array of commercial banks from which they could borrow money, a majority of which lacked the interest or capacity to engage in international finance and so did not expend political capital in the first postwar decades on trying to shape federal policy in the international arena. As we saw in chapter 6, the New Deal regulatory system served to protect regional and local banks that acted as a financial and political counterweight to the big commercial banks, which meant that Congress did not champion New York bankers' policy preferences.[1] This balance of power ensured that industrialists' concern with building markets for exports took precedence over New York bankers' desires to profit from international transactions.

New York bankers were not totally powerless, and federal officials, somewhat under Roosevelt and more so under Truman, saw "embedded liberalism" and capital restrictions as temporary expedients that would no longer be needed once Europe recovered and the political threats from communist and socialist parties receded. As a result, capital controls were never comprehensive enough to prevent capital flight from Europe and were progressively weakened in the 1950s as the balance of power shifted within the United States and as the British government took advantage of its right to end capital controls in an effort to preserve London's position as a world financial center, albeit one that had to cede first place to New York.[2]

Postwar capital controls were undermined almost immediately when the Treasury Department, the federal agency most amenable to New York bankers' pressure, opted not to cooperate with European efforts to prevent capital flight.[3] Tax treaties that the United States

1  Konings, *Development of American Finance*, 80–84; Kurtuluş Gemici, "Beyond the Minsky and Polanyi Moments: Social Origins of the Foreclosure Crisis," *Politics and Society* 44 (2016); Davis, *Managed by the Markets*, 109–10.

2  Aaron Major, *Architects of Austerity: International Finance and the Politics of Growth* (Stanford: Stanford University Press, 2014), 23–45; Helleiner, *States and the Reemergence of Global Finance*, 1–22.

3  Panitch and Gindin, *The Making of Global Capitalism*, 76–80.

negotiated with other governments required the United States to share any information it had on foreigners holding investments and earning income in the United States with the home countries of those investors. The United States avoided that obligation, and thereby encouraged foreigners to send money to America, by requiring American banks to report only on US citizens' accounts. In that way, the US government had no information on foreigners to share with other governments, and foreigners could hide income in the United States, a maneuver the United States continued into the twenty-first century.[1]

The failures of capital controls led to massive capital flight from Europe to the United States, threatening Western European governments' ability to rebuild their economies and eventually stimulate demand for US exports. New York bankers successfully blocked demands by Europeans to force repatriation of capital sent to the United States. The crisis was resolved by the Marshall Plan, which, despite its size, made up for only part rather than all of capital flight to the United States.[2] This was the first postwar instance of using US government funds rather than regulations that could lessen private profits to achieve economic stability. However, both government funds and private profits were sacrificed when the United States pressured other European countries and banks to suspend (and ultimately to forgive) all prewar German debts, a benefit that was even more valuable than the Marshall Plan for Germany.[3]

---

1   Nicholas Shaxson, *Treasure Islands: Tax Havens and the Men Who Stole the World* (New York: Palgrave Macmillan, 2011), 119.

2   Helleiner, *States and the Reemergence of Global Finance*, 51–77.

3   Compare the American government's stance toward German debt in the 1940s with its approach to Iraqi debt after the 2003 invasion, which we examined in the previous chapter. In both cases, foreigners held the debt, so its cancellation would not cost American financiers. The United States had no hesitation in making European governments and bankers pay to further the American goal of rebuilding the Germany economy, while James Baker worked to protect foreign, mainly Saudi, holders of Iraqi debt with the result that the Iraqi economy and the new Iraqi government's capacities were weakened to the severe detriment of US strategic objectives. The difference in approach epitomizes the shift, over a half century, in the US government's relation to elites and in the agents it employs to affect policy. In the 1940s, geopolitical concerns could and did override private profit, and civil servants and appointees who for the most part did not have private financial interests in the

The postwar international financial system was highly successful in fostering economic growth in both Europe and the United States in the "thirty glorious" years after 1945. We saw in chapter 6 that US growth was much faster and shared far more equitably before 1974 than after. Similarly, Western European GDP enjoyed annual average compound growth rates of 4.08 percent for 1950–73 but only 1.78 percent for 1973–98. The comparable figures for Japan are 8.05 percent and 2.34 percent. For the world as a whole they are 2.93 percent and 1.33 percent.[1] Bretton Woods was successful at limiting if not blocking capital flows and modulating changes in exchange rates, preventing the banking crises that emerged after 1970 with unrestrained speculation in currencies and the enormous growth in "hot money." Worldwide, there were at least 124 financial crises from 1970 to 2007.[2]

American hegemony over the global financial system outside the Soviet sphere thus was far more successful at fostering growth, equality, and financial stability prior to 1970 than it was afterward. We need to explain first why that successful system came undone and why the United States has managed to sustain financial hegemony despite the instability and failures of the different system it created after its destruction of Bretton Woods. Once we clarify the United States' role in both the old and new global financial regimes, we will be in a position to identify the continuing bases for US hegemony and offer predictions of the future length and strength of American power in an era of domestic political paralysis and limited military efficacy.

We first examine the workings of Bretton Woods and its relation to both the international trade system it fostered and internal US fiscal policy, and identify the sources of instability in each element of this system and in their interactions. We next trace the effects upon finance

---

outcomes implemented policy. In the 2000s, private actors who stood to profit from their simultaneous representation of private, and foreign, investors, in this case James Baker, were the implementers of policy. State and other private elites now lack the cohesion to counter corrupt alliances between self-dealing government agents and domestic and foreign investors.

1   Maddison, *World Economy*, volume 1, table 3-1a.
2   Major, *Architects of Austerity*, 203.

and trade of Nixon's decision to abandon fixed exchange rates and the convertibility of dollars into gold. We are especially concerned with understanding how the United States led the construction of a new global financial architecture, how the dollar remained the privileged currency in the world, and why the United States was able to, and remains able to, attract unlimited foreign capital to fund its trade deficits and governmental debt. Then, we will identify points of weakness in US financial hegemony by examining the sources, course, and resolution of the 2008 financial crisis. Throughout, we are concerned with identifying the elites who enacted and benefited from each financial system because that will allow us to determine who had the power to take measures to protect their interests even at the expense of domestic or global economic growth and stability. This analysis will allow us to specify the limited remaining bases of US dominance in finance and how that financial power will interact with America's domestic political economy and its space to use military power to sustain global geopolitical dominance.

## DOMESTIC STABILITY AND GLOBAL PRESSURES UNDER BRETTON WOODS

The global system created under American leadership at the end of World War II was grounded in a set of institutions that were designed to foster economic growth and to deal with the pressures trade and balance of payments deficits would put on fixed exchange rates and on countries' gold reserves. The World Bank loaned money, first in Europe and then to Latin America and newly independent countries in Asia and Africa. The International Monetary Fund (IMF) was given the job of "settl[ing] international accounts and provid[ing] financing to countries running severe payments deficits."[1] At first, as we saw earlier, the United States dealt with European countries' deficits directly through the Marshall Plan. However, congressional support for such expenditures quickly waned, falling from more than 2 percent of GDP during the Truman administration to less than 1 percent in

---

1   Major, *Architects of Austerity*, 24.

the era from Eisenhower through Nixon,[1] and the World Bank and IMF instead took up their intended roles.

The Bretton Woods system was hegemonic in that its institutions granted real roles and degrees of decision-making to other countries, albeit in service to overall goals that the United States had set at war's end and then revised in light of shifts in geopolitics and in response to changes in the balance of power among domestic American elites. Unlike the United Nations Security Council, which was paralyzed from the outset by the vetoes that the five permanent members each could exercise, the international financial agencies, most importantly the World Bank, the IMF, and the Bank for International Settlements (BIS), gave disproportionate, though not controlling, power to the United States. Other countries were able to protect their particular interests through those institutions, and the policies enacted under American leadership also fostered European and Japanese prosperity.

During the first decade after World War II, the US government worried, with real justification, about communist or socialist parties entering Western European governments. However, as European economies recovered and conservative governments, albeit ones committed to expansive social welfare programs and relatively egalitarian economies, became dominant in most of Western Europe, the "State Department, which was more concerned with opening up the world economy than it was with complex monetary arrangements to promote embedded liberalism,"[2] became the principal government agency setting US policy in international organizations and focused more on expanding US influence to the Third World of newly independent colonies in Asia and Africa than on undermining the ever more moderate leftist parties in Europe.

Financial elites in the United States and Europe were opportunistic in pressing for liberalization of currency controls. Helleiner notes that currency and other financial controls suffer from an inherent collective action problem, which he argues explains why finance was liberalized more quickly than trade.[3] As soon as one country

---

1 Tarnoff and Nowels, "Foreign Aid," 16.
2 Major, *Architects of Austerity*, 34.
3 Helleiner, *States and the Reemergence of Global Finance*, 1–22.

liberalized finance, money would pour in from abroad, drawing business and profits away from banks in other countries. Britain was the weak link: London had been the world financial center before 1914, and even in the interwar years London bankers and the Bank of England profited from currency transactions and the pound's role as the main international currency. Financial liberalization allowed London to profit first from wealth that flowed in from former colonies. Later, London leveraged its place in the EU, and also became the sun around which tax havens in British crown dependencies, overseas territories, and former colonies orbited. This funneled money, often the result of tax avoidance in other countries or the proceeds of outright criminal activity, into vehicles managed by British banks that became the source of great profit to British financiers.[1] As I noted in chapter 6, the United States and Britain are the two major holdouts from EU and OECD efforts to force offshore banks to disclose the true owners of shell corporations, the essential precondition for collecting taxes.

Despite London's ability to secure a highly lucrative, if more than a little shady, second position in world finance, New York became the financial center of the world in 1945 by default because it was the only place where firms and banks could issue bonds, since only Americans had the wealth to buy such bonds in the early postwar years and the dollar was the only safe currency with enough volume to accommodate the global demand for credit. That economic power, combined with America's geopolitical supremacy, gave US negotiators at Bretton Woods the leverage to demand that the dollar, not a new international currency, become the reserve currency. This gave the United States the benefits of seigniorage that it continues to enjoy today.[2] As America began to run trade deficits, the growing foreign dollar holdings could

1  Shaxson, *Treasure Islands*; Research Centre on Transnational Crime, *Euroshore: Protecting the EU Financial System from the Exploitation of Financial Centers and Offshore Facilities by Organized Crime* (Trento: University of Trento, 2000). As I was working on this book, *The Guardian* reported that London banks had laundered at least $740 million in money from Russian criminals (Luke Harding, Nick Hopkins, and Caelainn Barr, "British Banks Handled Vast Sums of Laundered Russian Money," *Guardian*, March 20, 2017).

2  Leonard Seabrooke, *US Power in International Finance: The Victory of Dividends* (Houndmills: Palgrave, 2001), 53.

be invested in the continually growing market for US government short-term notes. That market ensured that no other currency would be able to compete with the dollar in later decades to become the world reserve currency.[1]

New York bankers continually pressured their government to match British liberalization so that they could retain the dominant position they had achieved in 1945. The American and British governments were joined in efforts to weaken capital controls by Switzerland, which had always been a place for foreigners to hide money, and Germany and the Netherlands, which looked to exports more than internal demand to boost their postwar economies.[2]

The goal of freeing capital was compatible with the United States' and allied governments' efforts to liberalize trade. A treaty establishing an International Trade Organization was rejected by the Senate in 1948 because Republicans opposed the trade concessions the United States would have had to make in signing the agreement and conservative Democrats saw the proposed ITO as too internationalist, in the sense that the United States would have had to submit to regulations from an international agency.[3] They were encouraged in this stance by American manufacturers who worried that the advantages they received from their (then) technological superiority and their vast home market would be compromised by policies such an international organization could set.

In the absence of an ITO, the United States sought to build on the bilateral agreements the Roosevelt administration had signed with twenty-eight countries between 1934 and 1945 with a series of multilateral General Agreements on Tariffs and Trade (GATT).[4] GATT gave little power to its governing agency since signatories could withdraw from agreements at any time, and the agreements of each GATT "round" were in fact a set of specific deals between signing countries that left room for protecting powerful domestic industries. Nevertheless, the GATT agreements from 1947 through the Kennedy

---

1   Konings, *Development of American Finance*, 87–99.
2   Helleiner, *States and the Reemergence of Global Finance*, 81–100.
3   Panitch and Gindin, *The Making of Global Capitalism*, 91–6.
4   Nitsan Chorev, *Remaking US Trade Policy: From Protectionism to Globalization* (Ithaca: Cornell University Press, 2007), 40–68.

Round of 1964–67 managed to reduce tariffs by a third in total on average (i.e., from 22 percent to 15 percent); the effects were mainly on trade in manufactured goods among the United States, Western Europe, and, from 1956 on, Japan.[1] Other countries received little benefit from GATT until it expanded to include 102 countries in the Tokyo Round of the 1970s.

While governments favored the freer movement of capital and increasing trade, they remained, through the 1950s and '60s, committed to maintaining fixed exchange rates, which limited countries' abilities to export inflation or to compete for markets (and beggar each other) by devaluing their currencies. The IMF had been created to deal with the pressures that free trade and capital movements would place on currencies by offering loans to central banks to temporarily cover trade deficits. Countries, however, were reluctant to go to the IMF since the public grant of loans would indicate economic weakness and spark further currency declines. Instead, the central banks of European countries and the US Federal Reserve dealt with crises quietly by loaning one another currency and allocating gold from a joint pool.[2] These maneuvers strengthened links among finance ministries, central banks, the OECD, IMF, BIS, and the World Bank, allowing these organizations to collectively set monetary and regulatory policies and override the preference of actors within individual countries.[3]

The stratagems designed to preserve Bretton Woods shifted the balance of power among government agencies within and among countries. Since exchange rates were fixed, disputes centered on interest rates. By the early 1960s, the United States was running consistent trade deficits and needed loans from European central banks so that the outflow of dollars would not be presented to the Federal Reserve for conversion into gold. Europeans used their leverage to demand fiscal restraint from the United States. Germany and Switzerland especially did not want the inflow of dollars to create inflation in their

---

1   Chad Bown and Douglas Irwin, "The GATT's Starting Point: Tariff Levels circa 1947," National Bureau of Economic Research Working Paper no. 21782 (2015).

2   Major, *Architects of Austerity*, 38–45.

3   Helleiner, *States and the Reemergence of Global Finance*, 81–100.

countries.[1] "The US payments deficit, once vital to European recovery, was now a threat to many countries' growth models."[2]

More specifically, European industrial firms pressured their governments to demand that Kennedy's proposed stimulus (which was enacted under Johnson in 1964) be tailored so that US consumers could buy more European exports, rather than to help US manufacturers to modernize so that they could undercut newer European factories. Thus, Germany and Switzerland stated their willingness to hold dollars provided the United States increased interest rates and restricted credit. This swayed the Federal Reserve's Federal Open Market Committee in 1962–63 to adopt "Operation Twist," an effort to raise short-term and lower long-term rates to restrict credit.

> This forced banks to find new, innovative ways to take in deposits and lend money and made speculative dealings in short-term markets more lucrative relative to the stagnant returns offered in the long-term credit market. Over subsequent years these innovations would put the American financial sector on an increasingly fragile footing, threatening the commercial Keynesian growth program and the social democratic goals of Lyndon Johnson's Great Society.[3]

While Bretton Woods ultimately proved unsustainable, with the free flow of capital, expanded trade, and the resulting American trade deficits, the efforts in the late 1950s and 1960s to preserve fixed exchange rates had consequences that lasted beyond Nixon's abolition of Bretton Woods. Economic policy in the United States and Western Europe increasingly was made by central banks rather than elected officials. Central bankers gained leverage within their own countries by coordinating actions with one another, above all the currency swaps that stabilized exchange rates, and by conducting economic research and analysis, through the BIS.[4]

---

1  Ibid., 101–11; Matusow, *Nixon's Economy*, 117–48.
2  Major, *Architects of Austerity*, 134.
3  Ibid., 156 and passim.
4  Panitch and Gindin, *The Making of Global Capitalism*, 122–7.

Central banks' increasing power pushed national economic policies away from Keynesianism, not just in the United States but in much of Western Europe as well,[1] with the pressure to turn toward austerity hitting countries most strongly when they suffered from trade or budget deficits. Central banks' coordination with one another and through the BIS and IMF blunted nationalist rivalries among those banks.[2] Economic stability became understood in financial terms, which meant price stability got priority over growth or the reduction of poverty and inequality. "National governments' dependency on foreign monetary authorities to mitigate the effects of transnational capital flows was a powerful mechanism of coercion that could be used to push national policy making into the path of orthodoxy through austerity."[3]

Pressures from the Fed and from allied central banks heightened institutional as well as economic tensions within the United States. Operation Twist created a credit crunch since the booming American economy, stimulated by the Great Society and Vietnam War spending, encouraged firms to borrow for new facilities. The Fed, responding to savings and loans' still strong political power, refused to raise interest ceilings on deposits under Regulation Q. American commercial banks moved to raise capital, and outflank the Fed, by offering CDs, which were not covered under Regulation Q and which drew funds away from S&Ls. Rising interest rates in the United States attracted Eurodollars (dollars that accumulated in Europe due to US trade deficits and from American investments in European firms) back to the United States, often through branch offices that American commercial banks opened in Europe to compete with London bankers for the Eurodollar market,[4] and that allowed American banks to escape regulation by their own government.[5] State and local governments in the United States also found it hard to compete with private

---

1   Major, *Architects of Austerity*.
2   Panitch and Gindin, *The Making of Global Capitalism*, 122–7; Major, *Architects of Austerity*, 189–208.
3   Major, *Architects of Austerity*, 194.
4   Ibid., 157–88.
5   Seabrooke, *US Power in International Finance*, 58–61.

borrowers,[1] which spurred those governments to adopt innovative and risky financing techniques.

The New Deal balance between commercial banks and S&Ls was permanently disrupted, despite the continuation of Regulation Q until it was phased out in the 1980s. The pressures on S&Ls and the incentives for financial speculation, as we will see in the next section, were intensified by rising inflation. US commercial banks increasingly became international entities and therefore required and demanded different policies from the United States, ones that Nixon found were compatible with his deep desire to ensure a strong economy for his reelection.

## NIXON AND THE RECASTING OF GLOBAL FINANCE

Nixon, early in his presidency, had to confront the effects of the inflation sparked by Vietnam War spending (which Johnson and congressional majorities refused to counter with an income tax surcharge until 1968, well after inflationary pressures had become self-sustaining) and by workers' ability to demand wage increases and costly improvements in benefits thanks to their militancy and to the very low unemployment rates of the late 1960s.[2] Efforts by the Fed to counter inflation through higher interest rates led to a liquidity crisis and the bankruptcy in 1970 of Penn Central, then the largest railroad company in the United States. European employers faced similar pressures from rising labor costs but did so without the cushion American capitalists had received from the profit spurt of 1964–66. Profits in Europe had stagnated during those years.[3] European governments, which were angered by America's ability to "export" inflation through fixed exchange rates, retaliated by demanding that the US government exchange Eurodollars for gold, opening the possibility that US gold reserves could be exhausted if enough foreign dollar holders made such demands. Germany sought to reduce its

---

1   Krippner, *Capitalizing on Crisis*, 58–85.
2   Konings, *Development of American Finance*, 109–30.
3   Panitch and Gindin, *The Making of Global Capitalism*, 135–41.

exposure to American inflation by letting the mark float. Switzerland followed suit.[1]

Nixon resolved the immediate crisis with his New Economic Policy in August 1971 (yes, Nixon really did use the same name as Lenin had for his 1921 shift away from War Communism!). Nixon's NEP suspended the Bretton Woods system of fixed exchange rates and the convertibility of dollars into gold, neither of which were ever revived. He also imposed a ninety-day wage and price freeze and a 10 percent import tax. Politically, Nixon's policy was a great success. The wage and price freeze and subsequent controls did bring down inflation and allow for tax cuts that stimulated the economy, creating a boom that ensured Nixon's reelection in 1972.[2]

The New Economic Policy enhanced US leverage over Europeans. No longer could Europeans use the threat of their own devaluations or presenting dollars for exchange into gold to pressure the United States.[3] The 10 percent import tax undercut European and Japanese manufacturers. The Europeans and Japan agreed to a "massive devaluation of the dollar against the mark (by a total of 50 percent between 1969 and 1973) and the yen (by a total of 28.2 percent between 1971 and 1973)"[4] in return for the end of the American import tax.[5]

The United States successfully blocked efforts in 1973 by the Europeans and Japan to revive cooperative capital controls.[6] The United States also torpedoed a plan to deal with the enormous growth of petrodollars after the 1973 oil shock through the IMF. US opposition ensured that American, and to a lesser extent British, banks would

---

1   Matusow, *Nixon's Economy*, 117–48.
2   Ibid., 149–213.
3   Arrighi, in *Adam Smith in Beijing*, argues that America's defeat in Vietnam caused a general crisis of hegemony. What Major (*Architects of Austerity*) and the other analysts cited here show is that America's trade deficit undermined America's ability to maintain economic hegemony under the rules of Bretton Woods. Fiscal pressures and Nixon's desire for an economy strong enough to ensure his reelection were motives enough to account for his New Economic Policy, regardless of Vietnam. As we saw in the last chapter, Nixon addressed the problems stemming from the loss in Vietnam with his Nixon Doctrine of arming proxies like Iran.
4   Ibid., 104.
5   Matusow, *Nixon's Economy*, 149–81.
6   Helleiner, *States and the Reemergence of Global Finance*, 101–11.

handle the flow and reap profits from recycling oil money into loans.[1] The Treasury saw oil countries as buyers of US government debt.[2] These stances against international financial cooperation, except to deal with the consequences of banking crises, became the guiding star of US policy from Nixon to the present, and ensured that (mainly American) financiers would be the principal beneficiaries of deregulation. However, as we will see in the following sections, deregulation was not uniform or automatic. We need to identify the actors who had the power to force new policies, and we need to trace the chains of contingent change that led to outcomes that to a large extent were unanticipated by the advocates of deregulation.

Beyond Nixon himself, we can identify short-term and long-term beneficiaries (and losers) of his New Economic Policy. American manufacturers gained over their foreign competitors. Brenner, as we saw in chapter 6, identified the late 1960s as a turning point in global capitalism, when overproduction meant that capitalists in each country would have to fight one another over a shrinking pool of profits. However, as we noted, Brenner fails to identify the American actors who were able to force foreigners to absorb the fall in profits. While Nixon as president could be regarded as the instrument of American capitalists, we need to recognize that the temporary bump in profits and economic growth was not sustained. In the long term, Nixon did not solve American manufacturers' problems, and he certainly did not solve inflation, which surged when wage and price controls were relaxed in early 1973, after Nixon had been safely reelected. The continuing dollar devaluation further fueled inflation.[3] All economic measures for the United States were worse for 1973–79 compared with 1950–73: GDP growth per annum fell from 2.2 percent to 1.9 percent, inflation rose from 2.7 percent to 8.2 percent, unemployment rose from 4.8 percent to 6.5 percent, and productivity fell from 2.6 percent to 1.1 percent.[4]

--------

1   Ibid., 111–15; Mann, *Sources of Social Power*, volume 4, 144.
2   Konings, *Development of American Finance*, 109–30.
3   Matusow, *Nixon's Economy*, 214–400.
4   Panitch and Gindin, *The Making of Global Capitalism*, 142.

The decline in the dollar did raise demand for US manufacture, but not enough to entice large firms to invest in technological innovation in the face of global overproduction.[1] The main beneficiaries of the falling dollar were US farmers or, to be more precise, large landowners who were able to ride out and profit from interest rate and commodity price fluctuations, which became even more volatile once Nixon's détente made possible Soviet purchases of American grain that varied widely from year to year depending on the unpredictable Soviet harvests.[2] Small farmers who lacked access to capital or the reserves to weather fluctuations increasingly were bankrupted, allowing large farmers and corporate firms that invested in farms to consolidate land ownership.

Nixon's desire to undercut his rival Nelson Rockefeller and help his base of capitalist supporters in the South and West at the expense of New York bankers led to a series of regulatory changes that culminated in the Securities and Exchange Commission's "big bang" of 1975, which "dramatically shifted away from its long-maintained support for the cartel-like structures of brokers, investment banks, and corporate managers that had dominated capital markets since the 1930s" and were based mainly in New York.[3] This, combined with the relaxation of antitrust under Nixon that we noted in chapter 6, had two principal effects: first, the one intended by Nixon, which was to allow the consolidation, through mergers and buyouts, of large regional banks to rival the big New York banks that had been the central nodes of director interlocks and that had been the exclusive American intermediaries with global finance. Second, this liberalization, like the relaxation of currency controls in the 1960s, spawned new regulatory capacities that created new contingent chains of organizational innovation that favored particular interests not always anticipated by those who initially fostered the liberalization.

Nixon's partial dismantling of the New Deal financial architecture combined with resurgent inflation to create volatility in financial

---

1    Konings, *Development of American Finance*, 109–30; Brenner, *Boom and the Bubble*.

2    Matusow, *Nixon's Economy*, 214–40.

3    Panitch and Gindin, *The Making of Global Capitalism*, 149.

markets that disrupted the ability of large and small firms, farmers, state and local governments, and of course individual consumers and savers to make long-term financial plans. Firms and farmers reacted to instability by seeking to hedge risk with new financial instruments that banks and other financial institutions were allowed to offer. It is a mistake to see Nixon's moves as mere deregulation. The end of New Deal controls was accompanied by congressional passage in 1974 of amendments to the Securities Act that created the Commodity Futures Trading Commission (CFTC).

> State Agencies like the CFTC were keen to promote the spreading and hedging of risk, including by the many non-financial corporations that invested in derivatives ... The CFTC [allowed] space for self-regulation and innovation in derivative markets ... It was on this foundation that the internationalization of the derivatives markets took off in the next decade [of the 1980s].[1]

Nixon's dismantling of Bretton Woods and the creation of the CFTC were the first steps in a decades-long interaction between federal stratagems to boost domestic economic indicators while preserving American geopolitical dominance, financial elites' efforts to profit from the new openings created by those federal policies, and attempts by the United States and other governments and by international agencies like the IMF and BIS to solve the crises their policies and capitalists' opportunistic responses created. Thus, financialization and neoliberalism were not the unfoldings of ideological master plans, even though an increasing number of government officials and capitalists subscribed to what Hacker and Pierson label "hard Randianism,"[2] the belief that the rich are deservedly rich because they contribute more than others to national well-being and the poor are deservedly poor because they are stupid and lazy and are parasites on the national economy.

Nixon, his advisors, and their successors groped for solutions to the crises that erupted during their tenures in office. They were limited

---

1  Ibid., 150.
2  Hacker and Pierson, *American Amnesia*.

by the changing capacities of other American and foreign actors to guard their particular interests and by the US government's circumscribed resources. Thus, we need to account for the distinct steps of deregulation, and for the government interventions that sought to restore stability and to protect privileged actors. That will provide the bases to understand how the United States maintained financial hegemony up to and beyond the 2008 crisis, and how financial success has coexisted with relative decline in other sectors of the economy.

## FINANCIALIZATION AND THE TRANSFER OF RENTS FROM FIRMS TO INDIVIDUALS

US economic strategies evolved, were revised, and were reworked yet again during the 1980s and 1990s.

> Three major political-economic turning points mark this ebb and flow of currency devaluation and revaluation: the Reagan-Thatcher monetarist "revolution" of 1979–80, which reversed the devaluation of the US dollar of the 1970s; the Plaza Accord of 1985, which resumed the dollar devaluation; and the so-called "reverse Plaza Accord" of 1995, which again reversed the devaluation.[1]

Paul Volker directed the first turning point. As president of the Federal Reserve Bank of New York and then appointed by President Carter in 1979 as Federal Reserve Chair and reappointed by President Reagan, Volker spearheaded a drastic increase in interest rates in 1978–79. His strategy succeeded in breaking the inflationary spiral that had been set

---

1  Arrighi, *Adam Smith in Beijing*, 107. Duménil and Lévy, *Capital Resurgent: Roots of the Neoliberal Revolution* (Cambridge, MA: Harvard University Press, 2004) see financialization as a strategy capitalists pursued in the 1980s and 1990s to wrest income away from both workers and managers. However, the analysis in both their books is highly abstract and theoretical. They show the results of financialization in terms of the income of the top 1 percent, which, unfortunately for their argument, includes both capitalists and managers. They have almost nothing to say about the political struggles that produced changes in state policies that made financialization possible, and as a result they do not build a causal argument and are unable to explain differences between nations.

off in the late 1960s and accelerated by the oil shocks of 1973 and 1979, although at the cost of a severe recession. In addition, rising interest rates drew funds from around the world into the United States and reversed the dollar deflation that Nixon had engineered. This made it more difficult for US firms to compete with their European and Japanese counterparts, once again raising the trade deficit.[1] Volker's policies combined with Reagan administration attacks on unions to break workers' abilities to preserve their share of national income in the United States and in other OECD countries. However, as we examine later, "debt took the place of wage income as a main source of consumption capacity. This created a debt bubble that eventually imploded in 2008."[2]

High interest rates made the New Deal banking system, with limits on deposit interest rates, untenable.[3] The Fed and both commercial and regional banks pushed Congress to deregulate interest rates with the 1980 Depository Institutions Deregulation and Monetary Control Act, which phased out Regulation Q's limits on interest and mortgage rates.[4] This change put S&Ls at a fatal disadvantage since they still were restricted mainly to mortgage loans, which were long term, and most of the mortgages held by S&Ls had been written when interest rates were lower. S&Ls had the political power, since they were among the larger enterprises in many districts, to compel Congress to pass the 1982 Garn–St. Germain Depository Institutions Act, which allowed the S&Ls into new lines of business.[5]

While each of these policies addressed specific economic problems and responded to particular domestic elite interests, as a whole,

the essence of the monetarist counterrevolution was a shift of US state action from the supply side to the demand side of the ongoing financial expansion. Through this shift, the US government stopped

1   Krippner, *Capitalizing on Crisis*, 86–105.

2   Ho-fung Hung and Daniel Thompson, "Money Supply, Class Power, and Inflation: Monetarism Reassessed," *American Sociological Review* 81, no. 3 (2016), 462 and passim.

3   Konings, *Development of American Finance*, 131–52; Helleiner, *States and the Reemergence of Global Finance*, 123–45.

4   Krippner, *Capitalizing on Crisis*, 58–85.

5   Panitch and Gindin, *The Making of Global Capitalism*, 164–83.

competing with the growing private supply of liquidity and instead created brisk demand conditions for the latter's accumulation through financial channels

by offering higher interest rates on US government bonds than investors could get in other countries from either bonds or investments in private firms whose profits were squeezed by high interest rates combined with the earlier problem of overproduction.[1]

Despite the harm Volker's monetarism did to many large and small industrial firms, capitalists as a whole benefited from the effect that tight money had in undermining workers' bargaining power. Wages, which had risen in tandem with productivity, began their long stagnation in the 1970s, as we discussed in chapter 6. Monetarism, along with the concentration of Reagan's tax cuts on high-income individuals rather than on corporations, had the effect of advantaging capitalists as individual investors over corporations as continuing entities. This fundamental shift in who benefited from US government economic policy disrupted the regulatory, fiscal, and monetary policies that had sustained the industrial elite and opened opportunities for individual financiers with the foresight and leverage to profit from new conditions.[2]

American manufacturers gained only limited market share at home and abroad from the decline of the dollar and from protectionist measures, in part because demand fell as most Americans' incomes did not grow during the Reagan years and foreign producers continued to be able to undercut American firms in quality and price. The rate of profit of the US non-financial corporate business sector, which

---

1   Arrighi, *Adam Smith in Beijing*, 160.
2   The rise of American financiers in the 1980s and 1990s parallels the explosive success of Russian oligarchs after the dismemberment of the Soviet Union (David T. Hoffman, *The Oligarchs: Wealth and Power in the New Russia* [New York: Public Affairs, 2002]; Andrew Spicer, "Deviations from Design: The Emergence of New Financial Markets and Organizations in Yeltsin's Russia," in *The Emergence of Organizations and Markets*, ed. John F. Padgett and Walter W. Powell [Princeton: Princeton University Press, 2012]). While the processes were dramatically different, in both cases an elite of new men attained extraordinary wealth because they figured out how to take advantage of political and financial opportunities that had not previously existed and, therefore, that old elite actors were unprepared to navigate.

had fluctuated between 12 percent and 17 percent in the 1950s and 1960s fell into the 10–12 percent range under Nixon, dipped to 8 percent in the recession at the start of the Reagan administration, recovering only to 10–11 percent in the Reagan boom. It took until the Clinton bubble of the late 1990s for the rate of profit to briefly exceed 12 percent, a level that was typical of *recession* years in the 1950s.[1] US industrial firms nevertheless retained enough domestic political power in the 1980s to force the federal government to address its profits crisis, and the United States had enough leverage over Europe and Japan to force them to accept the Plaza Accord of 1985, which, by devaluing the dollar, restored the advantage Nixon's New Economic Policy had given US industrial firms over their European and Japanese competitors.

Similarly, the United States in alliance with Britain was able to set the terms of the 1988 Basel Accord, which changed banks' capital requirements to varying levels depending on the riskiness of their assets. The effect was to force Japanese banks to increase their capital, and they could do that most easily by buying US Treasury bonds, which Basel had enshrined as the safest asset in the world.[2] However, despite the advantage that American manufacturers gained due to their government's global power, the overall thrust of government policies discouraged corporate investment in factories and instead fostered a turn toward financial engineering.

High interest rates pulled money out of the stock market, which had already been dragged down by stagnant profits and unionized workers' abilities to win wage and benefit increases that matched or exceeded inflation rates, and into government bonds.

> Instead, as Volker decisively restored the value of money, firms and households alike quickly abandoned the economy of goods and services, channeling capital into financial markets . . . The result was to transfer inflation from the nonfinancial to the financial

---

1   Kotz, *Rise and Fall of Neoliberal Capitalism*, figure 4.1.
2   Konings, *Development of American Finance*, 131–52; Seabrooke, *US Power in International Finance*, 112–50; Helleiner, *States and the Reemergence of Global Finance*, 146–68.

economy . . . [This led to] surging asset prices [that] encouraged a debt-financed consumption boom in the US economy[1]

that continued even when interest rates fell after inflation was tamed.

Inflation and high interest rates encouraged a fundamental shift in corporate managers' strategies during the 1980s. Nixon's relaxation of antitrust laws had allowed firms to pursue a strategy of growth through acquisition in the 1970s. Firms in different industries bought one another or merged, creating ever-larger conglomerates that made no strategic sense since they operated in unrelated areas and were hard to manage. As a result, acquiring firms' stock prices usually fell after a merger. However, top executives benefited because in the 1970s corporate boards still set managers' pay by the size of the firm they managed.[2]

Large, diversified firms were hard for investors and analysts to value. Stock prices therefore were largely determined by book value, which managers did not adjust to account for inflation since an increase in book value would translate into a lower profit margin, and by earnings per share, which were held down by increasing global competition and workers' rising wages. Overly depressed share prices created an opening for "hostile takeover" firms that realized they could make money if they bought the underpriced shares of conglomerates and then sold off the parts of those firms.

Such a strategy was made possible by three factors: First, court decisions allowed takeover firms to mount hostile takeovers and pay for shares with junk bonds. Second, the Reagan administration further relaxed antitrust laws, allowing mergers among competitors in the same industry.[3] Mergers jumped from around 100 per year under Carter to almost 3,000 by the end of the Reagan administration; they then peaked at almost 5,000 per year during the second Clinton

---

1  Krippner, *Capitalizing on Crisis*, 103–4.

2  This and the following seven paragraphs are based on Frank Dobbin and Dirk Zorn, "Corporate Malfeasance and the Myth of Shareholder Value," *Political Power and Social Theory* (2005); Stearns and Allan, "Economic Behavior in Institutional Environments;" and Neil Fligstein, "The End of (Shareholder Value) Ideology," *Political Power and Social Theory* 17 (2005).

3  Khan and Vaheesan, "Market Power and Inequality."

administration.[1] Such horizontal integration created oligopolies that could fix prices, justifying the high prices paid to hostile takeover firms for the desired division of a conglomerate. Finally, declining interest rates created an appetite among investors for "high yield," i.e., junk, bonds. New financial firms acted as intermediaries between takeover firms and investors, most notably Drexel Burnham Lambert and its leading partner Michael Milken.[2]

The dismemberment of conglomerates, like the privatization of public firms and property in the former Soviet bloc and in Western Europe, were one-time opportunities. By the late 1980s, there were few conglomerates left, and the rising stock market meant that few firms were so undervalued that they could be taken over and quickly resold for large profits. Takeover firms and the brokers that floated junk bonds mainly were partnerships, so the key employees reaped most of the profits from such financial engineering, rather than the shareholders of the conglomerates that got bought out or the holders of the junk bonds, whose default rates ate up much of, and sometimes more than, the difference between the high marginal rates of junk bonds and the lower returns on absolutely safe Treasuries.

Mergers in the late 1980s and since have been consummated to achieve vertical or horizontal integration and have mostly met with little challenge by the federal government. Investor returns from the stock market (or, more precisely, the inflation-adjusted Standard & Poor's 500 Index with full dividend reinvestment) realized their greatest average annual returns in the 1950s, 16.7 percent, declining to 5.2 percent for the 1960s and -1.4 percent for the 1970s. This reflects the fact that the S&P's 1968 peak, which itself was hardly higher than the 1965 peak, was not reached again until 1986.[3] Average annual returns were 11.6 percent for the 1980s, 14.7 percent for the 1990s, and -3.4 percent for the 2000s. The stock market was a profitable investment in the 1945–65 and 1983–2000 periods, but flat from 1965 to 1983 and

---

1   Kotz, *Rise and Fall of Neoliberal Capitalism*, figure 2.2.
2   Stearns and Allan, "Economic Behavior in Institutional Environments."
3   "S&P  500:  Total  and  Inflation-Adjusted  Historical  Returns," SimpleStockInvesting.com.

since 2000. Despite a 176 percent increase under Obama, the largest of any post–1945 president except Clinton, it remained below the 2000 peak.[1] The Trump bull market of 2017–18 took the S&P 500 only to 8.8 percent above the Clinton peak.[2]

The takeover wave coincided with the transfer of stock ownership from individual to institutional investors (pension funds and mutual funds), which controlled 60 percent of the shares of large corporations in 2000, up from 20 percent in 1980.[3] Institutional investors are paid and attract clients based on their performance, which is measured by their return on investment over time (usually measured quarterly and over one, three, and five years). As these funds have grown larger it becomes ever more difficult to find alternatives to the existing array of large corporations to park their money. Fund managers therefore have shifted from selling shares in underperforming firms to demanding reforms.

Fund managers and the executives of the firms whose shares they held were disciplined by the growing corps of securities analysts. Analysts initially catered to individual investors in corporate shares but then expanded to evaluate mutual funds as well. Securities analysts specialize by industry, "so analysts were less likely to cover conglomerates [which thus were less likely to be subjects of 'buy recommendations'] than single-industry firms,"[4] providing yet another incentive to dismember firms that spanned industries.

Analysts' purported expertise was their ability to predict future share prices, which were based on projections of earnings. Firms therefore created the position of chief financial officer (CFO) to communicate with analysts and guide their projections. Analysts were most positive about firms that had steadily increasing earnings, which were seen as preferable to more volatile results, even if the latter ultimately produced greater overall returns. Steady results were easier to predict and were less likely to leave analysts in the embarrassing position of having over- or underestimated quarterly results.

1  "S&P 500 Performance by President," MacroTrends.net.
2  "S&P 500 Return Calculator, with Dividend Reinvestment," DQYDJ.com.
3  Dobbin and Zorn, "Corporate Malfeasance," 188.
4  Ibid., 191.

Firms and their CFOs accommodated analysts by manipulating profits to meet or slightly exceed expectations, even if that required cooking the books to hide one quarter's overly large profits and instead report them later. Such manipulation led, especially at some high-tech firms and most notoriously at Enron, to outright accounting fraud. In the July 1, 2000, to June 30, 2001, fiscal year, NASDAQ firms reported losses

> of no less than $148.3 billion [much of it due to the need to "restate" earnings from previous years]. This was a little more than the $145.3 billion in profits these same companies had reported in the entire period from September 1995 through June 2000! As one economist pithily put it, "What it means is that with the benefit of hindsight, the late 90s never happened."[1]

As analysts' recommendations and stock prices came to depend on predictable and steadily increasing quarterly earnings, corporate boards adopted the doctrine of "shareholder value," the notion that top executives should be rewarded solely on the basis of their firms' stock price, and that the best way to "align" executives' interests with those of shareholders was by offering those executives massive stock options. In fact, stock options did not really align managers' and shareholders' interests. Instead, managers manipulated profits to run up their firms' stock prices and then sold their options as soon as they could. As we saw in chapter 6, stock options amounted to "one fifth of non-financial corporate profits (net of interest) [in 1999] . . . Whereas in 1992, corporate CEOs held 2 per cent of all equity outstanding of US corporations, by 2002 they owned 12 percent."[2] A 2014 study found that

> The average annual dilution among S&P 500 companies relating to executive pay was 2.5 percent of a company's shares outstanding. Meanwhile, the costs of buying back shares to reduce that dilution equaled an average 1.6 percent of the outstanding shares. Added

1   Brenner, *Boom and the Bubble*, 295.
2   Ibid., 299.

together, the shareholder costs of executive pay in the S&P 500 represented 4.1 percent of each company's shares outstanding [each year].[1]

A second way to run up a stock's price was to announce a buyback. Buybacks were limited by the SEC and treated as stock manipulation

> until 1982 ... [when] the S.E.C., under the chairmanship of the Reagan appointee John S.R. Shad[2] gave companies so-called safe harbor against charges of manipulation if they bought their stock in the open market under certain circumstances. (The provision is known as Rule 10b-18).[3]

The mere announcement of a stock buyback would cause a firm's share price to rise, even if the buyback never took place.[4] Buybacks had the effect of reducing a firm's capital, precisely the opposite of stock markets' purported purpose. This reduces funds available for investment in facilities and research and development.[5]

> James Crotty ... has calculated for American corporations other than financial the amount of what he defines as 'payments to financial markets"—interest (net), dividends, and share buy-backs—as a proportion of cash flow (profits plus depreciation). Again a steady increase. In the early 1960s, the proportion was around 20%. In the 1970s, the figures were around 30%, with a clear rising trend taking off in 1984, culminating in a 1990 peak of 75%. Thereafter there was a sudden plunge in the mid-1990s but the figure was back up to 70% at the end of the decade ... These figures are symptomatic of a transformation in American capitalism, a shift in power from managers

---

1    Gretchen Morgenson, "Investors Get Stung Twice by Executives' Lavish Pay Packages," New York Times, July 8, 2016.

2    Shad was "a former vice chairman of E. F. Hutton and the first Wall Street insider to lead the commission in 50 years" (Lazonick, "Profits Without Prosperity").

3    Andrew Ross Sorkin, "Stock Buybacks Draw Scrutiny from Politicians," New York Times, August 10, 2015.

4    Davis, Managed by the Markets, 97.

5    Lazonick, "Profits Without Prosperity."

whose expertise lies in their intimate knowledge of the operations of the organization they run, to owners and representatives of owners who closely monitor their activity with an eye to maximizing the returns to capital.[1]

Cronyism among CEOs, the directors of their firms, and analysts at banks and brokerages became endemic in the 1990s and has continued ever since. The average compensation for directors of S&P 500 firms reached $251,000 in 2012.

> Who makes decisions about director pay? The directors ... Shareholders can sit back and say "These directors are being paid so well that I can't see them ever questioning management on anything because this is a gig they would hate to lose."[2]

Directors, in turn, ratify CEOs' pay packages based on the recommendations of consultancy firms, which are hired based on their reputation for finding that the "market rate" for CEO pay is moving ever upward, and then are rewarded for their recommendations with much larger contracts "for providing other services."[3]

Directors' decisions to increase the pay of CEOs and other top executives are supported as well by the managers of the mutual funds that hold most US shares and vote those shares at corporations' annual meetings. As funds have ever-greater amounts of capital to invest, they are no longer able to pick and choose among firms and instead come to hold shares in all the firms in each industry. Fund managers thus have no choice but to "aim to maximize the value of their entire stock portfolio, rather than the performance of individual firms within that portfolio. Because fierce competition between portfolio firms reduces the value of the entire portfolio, it is in the asset managers'

---

1   Ronald Dore, "Financialization of the Global Economy," *Industrial and Corporate Change* 17 (2008), 1102.

2   Jeff Green and Hideki Suzuki, "Board Director Pay Hits Record $251,000 for 250 Hours," *Bloomberg Technology*, May 30, 2013.

3   Committee on Oversight and Government Reform, United States House of Representatives, "Executive Pay: The Role of Compensation Consultants," 2007, govinfo.gov/content/pkg/CHRG-110hhrg46535/pdf/CHRG-110hhrg46535.pdf.

interest to structure executive pay in such a way that managers have weakened incentives to compete aggressively against their industry rivals. In short, high levels of common ownership rationalize performance-insensitive pay."[1]

Analysts are pressured to generate "buy recommendations" for the firms they cover because those firms can reward the analysts' banks and brokerages with the highly lucrative businesses of underwriting mergers and bond issues and serving as advisors in financial transactions. The top executives of corporations that send their financial business to Wall Street firms in turn are rewarded with access to the IPOs (initial public offerings) of new firms, which those executives can immediately sell for quick profits.[2]

Self-dealing by Wall Street analysts and investment bankers was facilitated by the transformation of the large Wall Street investment banks. When firms were partnerships, partners could withdraw their share of the profits only over the long term, and often only when they reached retirement age. This gave employees a decisive interest in making their careers in a single firm and in managing the firm's affairs to preserve its long-term profitability and viability, which was based in large part on their firms' reputation for honest dealing. As all the major Wall Street firms became publicly held companies from the 1970s to the 1990s, existing partners reaped windfalls as their partnership holdings converted into shares they could sell. Incentives were different in publicly held companies; bankers were paid based on current year profits and so they pushed for innovative new securities products that could be quickly marketed.[3]

Corporate executives and Wall Street bankers and analysts thus receive repeated incentives to collude with one another, to manipulate financial statements and analyses, and to report rising quarterly profits, even at the expense of their firms' long-term profitability and viability, as we saw earlier with the restatement of tech firms' profits in 2000–01, and as we will see later in the financial collapse of 2008.

---

1 Miguel Anton et al., "Common Ownership, Competition, and Top Management Incentives," Ross School of Business Working Paper no. 1328 (2016), 1.
2 Davis, *Managed by the Markets*, 96–9.
3 Ibid., 122–31.

Financiers' incentives and career paths, whether they work as corporate CFOs or directly for financial firms, undermine their firms' institutional cohesion and long-term interests, albeit in different ways than those of military officers described in the previous chapter. Incentives in both sorts of institutions encourage specialization: spending an entire career commanding a single weapons system or working in a single market. Both military and financial careers advance at the expense of institutional interests: Officers seek to maintain existing weapons systems even when they divert funds and personnel from potentially more effective strategies. High-level employees at financial firms make investments that maximize their own incomes in the short term and build their prestige in the eyes of others who invest in the same market at other firms, even as they greatly magnify risk for their own firms and for the economy as a whole.

Such decisions make sense because

> the primary relationship of most people in big finance is not to their employer but to their market . . . the people who work inside the big Wall Street firms have no serious stake in the long-term fates of their firms. If the place blows up they can always do what they are doing at some other firm—so long as they have maintained their stature in their market. The quickest way to lose that stature is to alienate the other people in it. When you see others in your market doing stuff at the expense of the broader society, your first reaction, at least early in your career, might be to call them out, but your considered reaction will be to keep mum about it. And when you see people making money in your market off some broken piece of internal machinery— say, gameable ratings companies, or riggable stock exchanges, or manipulable benchmarks—you will feel pressure not to fix the problem, but to exploit it.[1]

If a firm implodes, many of the top executives and their most valuable employees do not even need to use their market connections and reputations to find new jobs because they already have made their

---

1   Michael Lewis, "Occupational Hazards of Working on Wall Street," *Bloomberg View*, September 24, 2014.

"number," i.e., accumulated an amount that if invested conservatively will produce enough income to support their and their heirs' future (luxurious) spending needs in perpetuity. Executives have accumulated such vast fortunes due to the richness of stock options (discussed earlier) and to Wall Street firms' practice of devoting a fixed percentage, which varies somewhat among firms but usually is a majority, of their annual profits to bonuses for their employees, with most of that going to their top-level traders, analysts, and executives. In 2015, the bonus pool for "broker/dealer operations of New York Stock Exchange (NYSE) member firms" was $25 billion, while those firms' profits after paying out the bonuses was $14.3 billion.[1] In other words, 64 percent of Wall Street firms' profits went to employees' bonuses and 36 percent to shareholders.

Such within-and-between-firm rent-seeking and outright corruption makes sense of the otherwise surprising finding that the increase in the top 1 percent's share of national income "from 1970 to 2010 is accounted for by: increased inequality within labor income (68 percent), increased inequality within capital income (32 percent), and a shift in income from labor to capital (0 percent)."[2] The income from labor of the top 1 percent increased 195 percent from 1970 to 2012 compared to a 65 percent increase for capital income.[3] The restructuring within and among corporations and financial firms that we examined in this section explains much more of the shift in labor income than does the stagnation of educational attainment that gets pride of place in Claudia Goldin and Lawrence Katz's determined effort to ignore the role of capital and political power in the distribution of income.[4]

Furman and Orszag note that the rate of return on invested capital has been steady, at around 10 percent per annum for the median US publicly traded nonfinancial firm in the half century from 1965 to

1    Thomas DiNapoli, "Wall Street Bonuses and Profits Decline in 2015," Office of the New York State Comptroller, March 7, 2016.

2    Jason Furman and Peter Orszag, "A Firm-Level Perspective on the Role of Rents in the Rise in Inequality" (presentation, "A Just Society" Centennial Event a Honor of Joseph Stiglitz, Columbia University, October 16), 2015, 3.

3    Ibd., 4; see also Piketty and Saez, "Income Inequality in the United States;" and Piketty, Saez, and Zucman, "Distributional National Accounts."

4    Claudia Goldin and Lawrence F. Katz, The Race Between Education and Technology (Cambridge, MA: Harvard University Press, 2008).

2015. However, returns have risen sharply for firms in the 90th percentile from a range of 20–25 percent in the years from 1965 to 1985 up to 30–35 percent in the twenty-first century.[1] The ability of certain firms to maintain consistently higher profit margins is not necessarily a sign of rents, although the growth of monopolies and monopsonies certainly has created opportunities for rent-seeking. Note that Furman and Orszag's data exclude financial firms, so the concentration of profits is even sharper than their figures indicate. FIRE (finance, insurance and real estate) firms' share of US corporate profits rose from around 20 percent in the 1969–83 period (it was lower in the previous twenty years) to 30 percent in 1990 and 45 percent by 2001.[2] Financial firms accounted for more than 50 percent of US corporate profits abroad by 1999.[3] Even these data understate financial profits since industrial firms like GE generated an increasing share of their profits from financial activities in recent decades. The shift into finance has the additional benefit of facilitating the smoothing of quarterly profits, such as GE's much celebrated fifty-one consecutive quarters of earnings growth between 1981 and 1994 under then-CEO Jack Welch.[4]

While the shift of brains and capital from manufacture into finance has greatly enriched a corporate elite fortified with new men (and a few women), the shift of income upward and toward financial firms has not served to foster overall economic growth. Stephen Cecchetti and Enisse Kharroubi conclude from their comparative analysis of the twenty-one wealthiest OECD countries,

> The growth of a country's financial system is a drag on productivity growth. That is, higher growth in the financial sector reduces real growth ... Credit booms harm what we normally think of as the engines for growth—those that are more R&D-intensive.[5]

1   Furman and Orszag, "A Firm-Level Perspective," 10.
2   Krippner, *Capitalizing on Crisis*, 33.
3   Ibid., 50.
4   Thomas O'Boyle, *At Any Cost: Jack Welch, General Electric, and the Pursuit of Profit* (New York: Vintage, 1999), 332.
5   Stephen G. Cecchetti and Enisse Kharroubi, "Why Does Financial Sector Growth Crowd Out Real Economic Growth?," Bank for International Settlements Working Paper no. 490 (2014), 25.

They attribute this effect in part to the diversion of the most skilled and capable employees into finance.

Cecchetti and Kharroubi's explanation for the deleterious effect of financialization on national economic growth is supported by Wall Street veterans who observe that before 1980 the smartest Ivy grads went into law and medicine. Wall Street "then was considered a place that you went if you couldn't get into any place else . . . People just didn't make that much money on Wall Street."[1] With the end of the Cold War, physicists went to Wall Street: PhDs became PSDs—

> people who were "poor, smart and with a deep desire to get rich" . . .
> This trend brought two things to Wall Street: a whole new level of intellectual horsepower—the upper reaches of the IQ scale—and a new layer of important players who had no reason to doubt that markets worked as formulaically as the weapons systems they had once puttered over.[2]

Physicists have been supplemented by mathematicians, who apply their abilities to writing trading programs and algorithms designed to profit from small discrepancies across markets rather than, as their predecessors did, to solving scientific or governmental problems or developing goods and services for the real economy.

Elites' structural positions within firms, and their capacities to reorder relations among firms, have become primary causes of the polarization of income over the past forty years. Financialization was the result of those elite actors' successes in forcing organizational transformations, and winning governmental consent for those innovations, that created opportunities for them to enrich themselves. Yet, as we will see, financialization created volatility within national economies and by the early twenty-first century created a level of instability as great as that Nixon faced in the 1970s, although the

---

1  In the introduction, we heard Derek Bok describe the widening chasm between lawyers' salaries in the public and private sector, and we added that even the salaries corporate firms pay to law school graduates have been eclipsed by the incomes BA graduates can earn on Wall Street.

2  Michael Hirsh, *Capital Offense: How Washington's Wise Men Turned America's Future Over to Wall Street* (Hoboken, NJ: Wiley, 2010), 61, 177.

governmental responses since 2008 have neither sought nor achieved the transformative effects accomplished through Nixon's New Economic Policy.

## FINANCE AND TRADE UNDER CLINTON AND BUSH II: LIBERALIZATION AND SPECIAL INTERESTS

As the weight of power shifted within and among firms and industries, US government policy in the financial and trade realms changed as well. Policy initiatives occurred in reaction to economic crises, but elites' shifting interests shaped those responses. Above all, elite pressure on government increasingly came from self-dealing managers and financiers who see firms and markets as targets for manipulation and dismemberment rather than (as was the case in earlier decades) from corporations that were protected by networks of directors centered around large banks that, through their loans, had an overriding interest in the long-term preservation of their corporate clients' institutional integrity.

American banks and other financial firms were able to take advantage of the global opportunities their government had opened for them through the twinned processes of deregulation and de facto government guarantees. Bank regulators, in the growing list of countries that adopted the 1988 Basel Accord, determined the strength of their nations' banks through capital-asset ratios rather than cash reserves. This made the loans and other instruments packaged by American financial firms attractive to foreign buyers, allowing American banks to take ever-greater risks, knowing that there would be foreign markets for their bets.[1]

US banks were encouraged in their risk-taking by the Fed's decision to bail out big American banks endangered by the 1982 Mexican debt crisis. The Fed has continued this policy ever since. That has

---

1 This and the following two paragraphs are based on Konings, *Development of American Finance*, 131–60, and Raghuram G. Rajan, *Fault Lines: How Hidden Fractures Still Threaten the World Economy* (Princeton: Princeton University Press, 2010).

made it possible for banks to create and speculate in new forms of financial instruments, most significantly derivatives. The Fed's decision in the 2000s to consider mortgage securities as a low-risk and liquid asset encouraged originating banks to keep them on their balance sheet, and made them attractive to other banks and pension funds in Europe as well as the United States. "The mark—basically anyone with money to invest and trust in investment banks and in ratings agencies—was apparently known generically in the industry as 'Düsseldorf.'"[1]

Each crisis and the growing interconnectivity of US and foreign banks and financial firms increased the Fed's power. The Fed could manipulate interest rates with subtle signals; its power was enhanced by Fed chair Alan Greenspan's huge reputation for economic wisdom. (Although the 2008 crisis and Greenspan's confession that the collapse left him "in a state of shocked disbelief"[2] demonstrated that his image as "the maestro" of a stable and endlessly growing US economy was vastly exaggerated if not totally undeserved.) The Fed could not control the amount of credit,

> but it developed an extraordinary capacity to steer, manage, and stabilize flows of credit. And it could use this capacity to solve market bottlenecks and promote ongoing financial expansion, thus ensuring that liquidity creation would not spillover into the real economy and cause inflation.[3]

The Fed's power was demonstrated by its ability to control the effects of the 2000 dot-com crash and 9/11 on the financial sector, although in the former instance a general recession did follow the NASDAQ crash.

At the macroeconomic level, the US Treasury and Fed adopted new fiscal and monetary policies in the 1990s to address the threats to "international financial stability"[4] that were legacies of the Plaza

---

1   Galbraith, "The Great Crisis and the Financial Sector," 238.
2   Edmund Andrews, "Greenspan Concedes Error on Regulation," *New York Times*, October 23, 2008.
3   Konings, *Development of American Finance*, 149.
4   Arrighi, *Adam Smith in Beijing*, 111 and passim; see also Brenner, *Boom and the Bubble*.

Accord. As we discussed earlier, the Plaza Accord's de facto devaluation of the US dollar after 1985 allowed American firms to capture export markets at the expense of the Europeans and Japanese. However, Japanese firms' loss of markets to American rivals led, by the early 1990s, to a recession in Japan and with it the danger of a global financial crisis if the Japanese government and investors sold their holdings of US Treasuries to bail themselves out. The solution to this danger was the Reverse Plaza Accord of 1995, which, by boosting the value of the dollar while keeping American interest rates generally low up to the present, ensures that Americans will buy foreign goods and all but a few technologically advanced sectors of American industry will be uncompetitive globally.

Ho-fung Hung concisely sums up the consequences of this macroeconomic strategy:

> For decades, the US has been running the largest trade deficit with the world, while every other major economy (Europe, China, Japan, etc.) has been running surpluses of different sizes. Since the 1980s, the US has been leading the world into globalization through opening its own market for foreign manufactured exports in exchange for its trading partners' openness to US investment. The result is a massive exodus of US manufacturers to low wage countries like Mexico and China, manufacturing consumer goods there and exporting them back to the US ... The US is always "the consumer of last resort" for the global economy. Without US consumers, there will be no globalization.[1]

David Autor et al. provide data showing the impact of US trade deficits with China on American workers' earnings and calculate that each $1,000 per worker increase in imports from China during 1990–2007 led to an "earnings loss per adult of $213 per year."[2]

How do American capitalists benefit from this system? And how are American consumers able to buy manufactured products from the

1   Ho-fung Hung, "Can We Have Globalization Without the US?," *Policy Trajectories,* February 10, 2017.

2   David H. Autor, David Dorn, and Gordon H. Hanson, "The China Shock: Learning from Labor Market Adjustment to Large Changes in Trade," National Bureau of Economic Research, Working Paper no. 21906 (2016), 32, 31.

rest of the world if their wages are stagnant? The answer to the first question, in two words, is financial speculation, and the answer to the second question, in a word, is credit. Let us examine the mechanisms that sustained the US economy from the 1990s to 2008 by allowing ordinary Americans and their government to borrow ever more money, and thereby made it possible for financiers to get rich from matching American debtors with foreign creditors seeking to recycle the dollars they realized from the trade surpluses they ran with America.

As we saw in the introduction, federal government debt as a percentage of GDP more than doubled from 31.7 percent in 1981 to 67.7 percent in 2008. Government debt, however, was far outpaced by private debt. "Between 2000 and 2007—the total [of household debt] doubled to $14 trillion and the household debt-to-income ratio skyrocketed from 1.4 to 2.1."[1] The fastest increase in debt was on the part of financial firms, which rose from 19.7 percent of GDP in 1979 to 117.9 percent in 2007.[2]

Monica Prasad[3] provides historical context to that enormous expansion of mortgages and consumer credit over the past quarter century. The US government stood apart from other rich states throughout the twentieth century for its extensive measures to make credit available, first to farmers who were at the forefront of movements in the 1890s and 1930s to demand credit to deal with falling commodity prices brought on by their ever-higher productivity, and then to more citizens through New Deal, veterans', and then more general federal programs of subsidized mortgages and small business and student loans.

These programs, in the extensiveness of credit available and the liberality of terms for such loans, differentiated the United States from Europe. Prasad[4] argues that the greater diffusion of credit meant that when the United States followed the same track of banking deregulation as Europe in the 1980s, there was much more debt in America,

---

1    Mian and Sufi, *House of Debt*, 4.
2    Kotz, *Rise and Fall of Neoliberal Capitalism*, 129.
3    Monica Prasad, *The Land of Too Much: American Abundance and the Paradox of Poverty* (Cambridge, MA: Harvard University Press, 2012).
4    Ibid.; see also Rajan, *Fault Lines*; Mian and Sufi, *House of Debt*.

and it fueled an explosion of speculation that made possible the 2008 financial collapse.

Banks could make risky loans to consumers, homeowners, and businesses only as federal regulators loosened restrictions. The Fed's overall goal through the 1990s and 2000s was to encourage growth while preserving the low level of inflation it had created in the 1980s. Easy monetary policy has become the primary and most effective way of stimulating the US economy since job recovery following the 1990–91, 2001, and 2008 recessions was slower and weaker than after earlier recessions.[1] The decimation of the safety net under Reagan reduced the countercyclical effect of federal programs, most notably unemployment insurance, which covered only half of those who lost their jobs in the 1990–91 and 2001 recessions. That fraction climbed to two-thirds after 2008, thanks to the expanded benefits made available in the American Recovery and Reinvestment Act of 2009, i.e., the Obama stimulus.[2] Thus, except in 2009, the Fed was the principal and often the only source of stimulus in recessions, leading it to respond with dramatic rate cuts. For example, after the NASDAQ crash of 2000–01, the Fed cut short-term interest rates from 6.5 percent in January 2001 to 1 percent in June 2003.[3]

The injection of massive amounts of credit into the US economy had destabilizing effects worldwide. Prolonged low Fed rates pushed money abroad in search of higher yields, and the highest yields were found in low- and middle-income countries, which suffered seventy-two financial crises in the 1990s. In contrast to the crises of the 1980s, which were due to countries, most notably Mexico, and their private firms overextending themselves and taking on debts that could never be repaid, most of the 1990s crises were caused by rapid moves of "hot money" out of countries as investors looked for even higher yields, panicked at speculative dips in the borrowing country's currency or rises in US or European interest rates, or came under pressure as other speculators shorted that country's bonds.

---

1   Rajan, *Fault Lines*, chapter 4.
2   Casey Mulligan, "Unemployment Compensation over Time," *New York Times*, December 21, 2011.
3   Rajan, *Fault Lines*, 105.

Again, in contrast to the 1980s, when banks extended loans directly to Third World governments, in the 1990s money moved through New York banks in the form of short-term bonds that passed risk from banks to bondholders. "Bond debt rose from 20 percent of total private credit to 'emerging market' countries in 1990 to 70 percent in 1997."[1]

Even though the use of bonds rather than loans guaranteed that American banks were not directly at risk in most of the 1990s crises, the US Treasury intervened in many of those crises with the goal "to ensure that these countries avoided lasting expulsion from international capital markets [and] to ensure that these countries were able to access the ever more liquid instruments that increasingly predominated in these markets."[2] The Treasury acted unilaterally because members of Congress didn't want to go on record as voting for foreign bailouts, but they were willing to stand by as the Treasury exerted authority it had never been granted explicitly in law. The Fed also intervened during crises by reducing US interest rates to pull capital back into, and thereby calm, emerging markets.

At the same time, foreign governments' central banks, wanting to keep their currencies low so they could continue to export, bought up dollars and invested them in US government bonds.[3] In rich countries, especially Japan and Germany, private banks bought US securities with dollars deposited by their clients. Thus, Americans invested in unsafe instruments abroad while money came back to safe US investments. "In some ways, Federal Reserve policy was turning the United States into a gigantic hedge fund, investing in risky assets around the world and financed by [safe] debt issued to the world."[4] The intermediary in this financial arbitrage became the US housing market through mortgages. The Fed encouraged this process because

as nominal interest rates fell, homeowners refinanced mortgages, shifting considerable purchasing power away from rentier interests

---

1   Panitch and Gindin, *The Making of Global Capitalism*, 248, 249.
2   Ibid., 248 and passim.
3   Ho-fung Hung, *The China Boom: Why China Will Not Rule the World* (New York: Columbia University Press, 2016).
4   Rajan, *Fault Lines*, 109.

and towards individuals with a higher propensity to consume goods, services, and housing. This consumption in turn generated new employment through standard Keynesian multiplier effects, sustaining the expansion by helping shift the US federal budget into surplus and thus enabling the Federal Reserve to continue lowering interest rates.[1]

American banks' opportunities to attract and profit from the recycling of other countries' trade surpluses, and from hot (and often illicit) money, was made possible by trade treaties that opened foreign markets to American financial firms. Those treaties also disadvantaged American manufacturers, creating the trade surpluses in the first place. Trade negotiations inevitably require concessions, and each country's negotiators must decide which of its industries it will favor and which it will sacrifice in return for gains in other sectors. Changes in America's goals from 1945 to the present reflect shifts in the balance among US elites. In essence, the United States in the GATT rounds from 1949 through 1979, and before that in the bilateral treaties negotiated by the Roosevelt administration, channeled the interests of US manufacturers.

The Trade Act of 1974 was the first instance in which financial firms' interests were recognized, albeit in balance with industry. The 1974 Act made it easier for the "executive to act against dumping and illegal subsidies" by foreign nations, which served to weaken manufacturers' opposition to further trade liberalization treaties. The Act also allowed presidents to negotiate treaties that addressed "non-tariff barriers. [In addition, the Act created] a 'fast track' procedure [that] did not allow Congress to modify US international trade concessions, only to accept or reject the international trade agreement as a whole."[2] Fast track, combined with specific concessions and subsidies for key industries like steel and textiles, allowed presidents to push one trade treaty after another through Congress.[3]

---

1   Schwartz, *War Without End*, 268.
2   Nitsan Chorev, "Fixing Globalization Institutionally: US Domestic Politics of International Trade," *International Sociology* 25 (2010): 63.
3   Ibid.; Panitch and Gindin, *The Making of Global Capitalism*, 223–45.

"The United States' main goal in launching a new round of multilateral trade negotiations, the Uruguay Round, was therefore to bring the so-called 'new issues'—services, investment and intellectual property—into the jurisdiction of GATT."[1] The treaty that emerged from this round, and was ratified in 1994, created the WTO (World Trade Organization), which was given the power to impose penalties for unfair trade practices. This had the effect of making it too expensive for countries to maintain trade barriers found to violate the treaty, undermining industrial firms' ability to protect their domestic markets.[2]

Global trade negotiations on a Doha Round, begun in 2001 and designed to build on the Uruguay Round, have failed to reach a conclusion.[3] However, in the meantime, the United States signed a series of bi- and multilateral trade treaties, most prominently NAFTA with Canada and Mexico in 1994, and a series of agreements with Central and South American countries as well as with Jordan, Bahrain, Morocco, Singapore, and finally South Korea in 2012. The Trans-Pacific Partnership Agreement was successfully concluded in 2016, but the next year, in his first week as president, Donald Trump withdrew the United States before it could be ratified. (It is unknowable if a President Hillary Clinton could have overcome congressional opposition, and her own criticisms of the TPP voiced during the 2016 campaign, to achieve ratification.) Negotiations on the Transatlantic Trade and Investment Partnership between the United States and the EU remained unresolved at the end of the Obama administration.

The big winners within the United States under the NAFTA and WTO regimes were Hollywood, software firms, and, above all, financial firms, which gained entrée into ever more countries around the world.[4] All trade agreements favored US and European

---

1    Chorev, "Fixing Globalization Institutionally," 64.

2    Ibid.; Panitch and Gindin, *The Making of Global Capitalism*, 223–45.

3    Kristen Hopewell, *Breaking the WTO: How Emerging Powers Disrupted the Neoliberal Project* (Stanford: Stanford University Press, 2016).

4    Malcolm Fairbrother, "Economists, Capitalists, and the Making of Globalization: North American Free Trade in Comparative-Historical Perspective," *American Journal of Sociology* 119 (2014); Tim Woods and Theresa Morris, "Fast

agriculture at the expense of farmers everywhere else.[1] In essence, manufacturing was sacrificed for the benefit of finance, a few cutting-edge high-tech sectors, and show business. However, even as the trade treaties and the ways in which they have been enforced decimate American manufacturing jobs and facilities, the firms that owned those factories or their successors still benefit from the treaties' protection of their "intellectual property." Manuel Montes and Vladimir Popov show that the enforcement of intellectual property rights costs developing countries $60 billion each year, almost all of which flows to US or European firms.[2] In essence, American manufacturing workers lost their jobs, but executives and shareholders continue to profit from their firms' patents and from the continuing ability to control supply and sales networks those "virtual firms" retain.

Consumer spending and financial engineering reinforced each other. Americans could be the world's consumers of last resort only if they continued to have access to ever-increasing amounts of credit. Financial institutions, and firms that were divesting themselves of the production of actual goods and services, needed to find new opportunities to move capital around the globe if they were to increase their profitability. The solution to the problems of both American consumers and financiers was found in the real estate sector, the largest pool of wealth held by Americans outside the top 1 percent,[3] and therefore the dominant source of collateral for loans and the prime site for speculation in the decade leading up to the 2008 financial collapse.

Tracking Trade Policy: State Structures and NGO Influence during the NAFTA Negotiations," *Research in Political Sociology* 15 (2007).

1   Hopewell, *Breaking the WTO.*
2   Manuel Montes and Vladimir Popov, "Bridging the Gap: A New World Economic Order for Development?" in Calhoun and Derlugian, *Aftermath: A New Global Economic Order?*, 127–30.
3   Emmanuel Saez and Gabriel Zucman, "Wealth Inequality in the United States since 1913: Evidence from Capitalized Income Tax Data," *Quarterly Journal of Economics* 131 (2016).

## THE POLITICAL SOURCES OF THE 2008 CRISIS

Legislation, court rulings, and deregulatory decisions by the Fed and other agencies charged with supervising banks widened opportunities for Wall Street to write and then sell toxic mortgages. More broadly, such regulatory changes and the transformation of firms (discussed above) gave financiers incentives and opportunities to manipulate the mortgage market to book often imaginary profits for their firms and thereby reap windfall salaries and bonuses for themselves, building personal fortunes even as they risked their firms' future viability. "The financialization of corporate activity and the rise of Wall Street has encouraged CEOs to focus narrowly on sustaining their stock price over a time horizon that does not exceed their own tenures at the top."[1]

Deregulation at first was designed to prevent S&Ls and other banks stuck with long-term mortgages on their books from becoming insolvent as Volker raised interest rates, as we discussed earlier. The Depository Institutions Deregulation and Monetary Control Act of 1980 blocked states from enforcing usury laws for first mortgages. The Alternative Mortgage Transaction Parity Act of 1982, part of the Garn–St. Germain Act, allowed adjustable-rate mortgages, negatively amortized mortgages, and mortgages with balloon payments. This legislation ratified earlier regulatory steps by the Federal Home Loan Bank Board, which had allowed federally chartered thrifts to write variable rate mortgages and then extended that option to state chartered thrifts, preempting state laws.

The Secondary Mortgage Market Enhancement Act of 1984 legalized a private market for mortgage-backed securities (MBS). The Tax Reform Act of 1986 allowed MBS to avoid double taxation. Together these two acts made it financially viable for private firms to take on larger and riskier mortgages than Fannie Mae (the Federal National Mortgage Association) and Freddie Mac (the Federal Home Loan Mortgage Corporation) were allowed to buy (although later Fannie Mae and Freddie Mac were allowed to take on risky, though not jumbo, mortgages).[2]

---

1   Hacker and Pierson, *American Amnesia*, 354.
2   This and the following nine paragraphs are based on Jennifer Taub, *Other People's Houses: How Decades of Bailouts, Captive Regulators, and Toxic Bankers*

Once Congress and regulators allowed banks to write risky mortgages, banks were given confidence that they could profit from such mortgages, regardless of their borrowers' obvious financial weaknesses, by a number of mutually reinforcing and cascading judicial, regulatory, and legislative decisions. A 1993 Supreme Court decision (*Nobelman v. American Savings Bank*) blocked bankruptcy judges from reducing principal on mortgages. This gave banks a false sense of security that they would be able to get their money even if individuals declared bankruptcy. The Office of Thrift Supervision (OTS) in 1996 adopted a rule permitting federal thrifts to ignore state consumer protection laws. The OTS also allowed thrifts to offer mortgages with prepayment penalties. Both those regulatory changes by the OTS widened banks' opportunities to write predatory loans that were more profitable than traditional mortgages.

In the mid-1990s, Fannie Mae and Freddie Mac, both shareholder-owned, for-profit corporations that are federally chartered and implicitly federally guaranteed, moved to buy ever-greater amounts of the mortgages banks had written with small down payments and ones without documentation of buyers' income (the aptly labeled "liar loans"). This benefited the shareholders and executives of Fannie and Freddie, because those corporations realized profits when they packaged and resold mortgages purchased from banks as mortgage-backed securities. Franklin Raines, the Fannie Mae CEO, was paid $91.1 million in salary and bonuses from 1998 through 2004,[1] based on profits that proved to be illusory. However, until the collapse and their

---

*Made Home Mortgages a Thrilling Business* (New Haven: Yale University Press, 2014), 222–46; James Crotty, "Structural Causes of the Global Financial Crisis: A Critical Assessment of the 'New Financial Architecture,' " *Cambridge Journal of Economics* 33 (2009); Hersh Shefrin and Meir Statman, "Behavioral Finance in the Financial Crisis: Market Efficiency, Minsky and Keynes," in *Rethinking the Financial Crisis*, ed. Alan S. Blinder, Andrew W. Loh, and Robert M. Solow (New York: Russell Sage, 2012); Robert A. Jarrow, "The Role of ABSs, CDSs, and CDOs in the Credit Crisis and the Economy," in *Rethinking the Financial Crisis*; and Galbraith, "Great Crisis and the Financial Sector"—except for the two paragraphs on AIG, which draw on Phil Angelides, *The Financial crisis Inquiry Report* (New York: Public Affairs, 2011), as well as Crotty.

1   Marcy Gordon, "Franklin Raines to Pay $24.7 Million to Settle Fannie Mae Lawsuit," *Seattle Times*, April 18, 2008.

takeover by the Treasury, Fannie Mae and Freddie Mac served as the buyers of first and last resort, allowing banks to find markets for toxic mortgages and thereby keep writing new ones without tying up their capital over the long term. Fannie and Freddie's support for these mortgages also served as an endorsement to private purchasers of bundled mortgages.

Regulatory changes made it possible for banks to bundle mortgages into ever more complex securities that could be sold to other financial firms. The SEC in 1992 issued Rule 3a-7, which ensured entities that created collateralized debt obligations (CDOs) would not be classified as an "investment company." This minimized SEC supervision and the likelihood that fraud would be detected in CDOs and the firms that issued them. Regulatory agencies' lax accounting rules let banks put CDOs in off-balance-sheet entities, hiding their risk to defaults. In November 2001, the Fed and three other banking regulatory agencies (the Office of the Comptroller of the Currency, the Office of Thrift Supervision, and the Federal Deposit Insurance Corporation) agreed to lower risk weighting for MBSs from 50 percent to 20 percent, thereby reducing the capital banks had to keep to cover those investments.

Banks and financial firms created credit default swaps (CDSs) that were sold to the buyers of residential MBSs and CDOs to mimic Freddie and Fannie guarantees and thereby falsely assure the buyers that their investments were safe. The Commodity Futures Modernization Act of 2000 made the CDS market possible by allowing investors to buy CDSs on a debt security they did not own, leading to an explosion of CDSs that gambled on securities without investing in them. The Act also allowed preempted state-level regulation of derivatives for municipal bonds. This let banks peddle complex pieces of financial engineering to municipal officials who were unable to understand what they were being sold.

In the resulting confusion, profits were reestablished, but incidences of corruption, fraud, and graft also increased markedly. The list of serious scandals originating in the municipal securities market during this period is daunting: pay-to-play, premium laundering, yield burning, bid rigging, excessive compensation/pay packages, and various conspiracies top the list of investigations launched by federal agencies.[1]

In essence, that Act ended all legal constraints on derivatives. Brooksley Born, who headed the Commodity Futures Trading Commission, sought to issue new regulations for derivatives. However, she was blocked in that effort during the last years of the Clinton administration by the combined opposition of Fed chair Greenspan and Treasury secretaries Robert Rubin and his successor, Lawrence Summers.

The need for such regulation was demonstrated by its absence in the saga of the American International Group. AIG was the main seller of CDSs, a business it went into heavily after the firm was caught in 2005 for cooking its books and then had to restate earnings for the past five years. AIG's accounting fraud didn't bring on closer supervision by federal regulators of AIG's new business in CDSs. In 2008, on the verge of bankruptcy for writing CDSs it could not cover, AIG received a series of bailouts from the Fed that eventually totaled $180 billion. In effect, the government nationalized AIG, taking 80 percent ownership of the firm.

After that disaster and the bailouts, AIG awarded "377 members of the [Financial Products] division a total of $220 million in bonuses for 2008" despite the fact that "the unit lost $40.5 billion" that year.[2] The next year, AIG executives received $165 million in bonuses. Efforts to pass legislation taxing those bonuses, and ones received by executives of any other firm receiving a federal bailout, failed in Congress after President Obama told bankers "he did not want to vilify" them[3] and Treasury secretary Timothy Geithner and Lawrence Summers (returned to government as Obama's director of the National Economic Council) lobbied against the bill. Some of the executives voluntarily gave up their bonuses, and in the end the government more than recouped the money it advanced to AIG, suggesting that

---

1   L. Owen Kirkpatrick, "The New Urban Fiscal Crisis: Finance, Democracy, and Municipal Debt," *Politics and Society* 44 (2016): 51.

2   Crotty, "Structural Causes of the Global Financial Crisis," 565.

3   Dave Gustafson, "Obama Prods Bankers to Do More to Revive US Economy," *PBS Newshour*, December 14, 2009.

the government would have benefited financially if it had nationalized rather than bailed out the banks.

Deregulation and the encouragement of speculation continued under the George W. Bush administration. In 2004, the SEC issued a rule that reduced the net capital needed by the five largest broker-dealers: Bear Stearns, Goldman Sachs, Lehman Brothers, Merrill Lynch, and Morgan Stanley. This was done in response to an EU directive requiring banks operating in Europe "to designate a consolidated supervisor in their home country."[1] Those five firms all picked the SEC rather than any other US regulatory agency, accurately recognizing that the SEC would not limit or investigate their activities.

Lax SEC supervision allowed the five largest broker-dealers, and lesser firms as well, to use "short-term, often overnight, repurchase agreements"[2] to borrow money. The Bankruptcy Abuse Prevention and Consumer Protection Act of 2005 encouraged the use of such "repos" by expanding "the special treatment that repo cash lenders were given in a borrower's bankruptcy."[3] However, despite these protections, repos exposed the financial firms to extreme risk since, in a market panic, they would not be able to refinance their short-term repos and would have to dump investments, causing a crash. Such disasters were averted by Fed loans and purchases of degraded assets.

The Fed's interest in keeping credit flowing to consumers through mortgages and home loans, and its (and other regulators') long-standing ties to banks and financial firms, stymied enforcement of existing regulations and blocked the promulgation of new rules designed for the new era of highly leveraged and complex financial instruments. "A major part of the reason Wall Street developed ever more complex products was precisely because it was so hard for clients—and regulators—to figure them out."[4] Clients got little help from rating agencies, which gave inaccurate labels to mortgage securities because the agencies were paid by the firms

---

1   Taub, *Other People's Houses*, 242.
2   Ibid., 242.
3   Ibid., 243.
4   Hacker and Pierson, *American Amnesia*, 285.

whose securities they rated rather than the investors who bought the securities. Thus, if any ratings agency had presented honest appraisals of mortgages, bankers would have given their business to rival agencies.[1]

The firms themselves as well as their financial products became increasingly complex, and their risks harder to access.

> Deregulation allowed financial conglomerates to become so large and complex that neither insiders nor outsiders could accurately evaluate their risk. The Bank for International Settlement told national regulators to allow banks to evaluate their own risk—and thus set their own capital requirements—through a statistical exercise based on historical data called Value at Risk. Government officials thus ceded to banks, as they had to ratings agencies, crucial aspects of regulatory power.[2]

US banking regulators, and international regulators under Basel II, used Moody's and Standard and Poor's ratings to determine the worth of mortgage securities and of sovereign debt on banks' balance sheets.[3]

Banks gained freedom from regulators as they also were allowed to take much greater risks.

> In the late 1990s, banks were allowed to hold risky securities off their balance sheets in SIVs [structured investment vehicles] with no capital required to support them. The regulatory system thus induced banks to move as much of their assets off-balance-sheet as possible. When the demand for risky financial products cooled off in mid 2007, bank-created off-balance-sheet SIVs became the buyer of last resort for the ocean of new MBSs and CDOs emanating from investment banks. At the end of 2007, J.P. Morgan Chase & Co. and

---

1   Crotty, "Structural Causes of the Global Financial Crisis"; Barry Eichengreen, *Exorbitant Privilege: The Rise and Fall of the Dollar and the Future of the International Monetary System* (New York: Oxford University Press, 2010), 97–120.

2   Crotty, "Structural Causes of the Global Financial Crisis," 570–1.

3   Abdelal, *Capital Rules*, 162–95; Jarrow, "The Role of ABSs, CDSs, and CDOs in the Credit Crisis and the Economy."

Citigroup each had nearly $1 trillion in assets held off their books in special securitisation vehicles. For Citigroup, this represented about half the bank's overall assets.

SIVs were supposed to be stand-alone institutions that paid service fees to the originating banks, but to which the originating banks had no obligations or commitments. They borrowed short-term in the commercial paper market and used this money to buy long-term, illiquid but highly profitable securities such as CDOs—a very dangerous game. To enable this commercial paper to receive AAA ratings and thus low interest rates, originating banks had to provide their SIVs with guaranteed lines of credit. This made the banks vulnerable to problems experienced by their supposedly inde-pendent SIVs.[1]

Financiers had ideological as well as criminal reasons to create complex products. Bankers could describe their new and ever more complex products as "innovations," allowing them to bask in the reflected glory of actual technical advances in biotech and informa-tion technology and to argue that greater regulation could stymie future "innovations" that, in some never-specified way, would help borrowers and the overall economy.

In fact, financiers' claims to innovation are the opposite of the truth. Thoams Philippon finds that the

sum of all profits and wages paid to financial intermediaries [which] represents the cost of financial intermediation . . . [as a share of US GDP] grows from 2% to 6% from 1870 to 1930. It shrinks to less than 4% in 1950, grows slowly to 5% in 1980, and then increases rapidly to almost 9% in 2010.[2]

The growth clearly tracks the rise of financial speculation in the 1920s and again from the 1980s on. Philippon shows that the increase in financial costs is due to increased trading and "the costs of active

1   Crotty, "Structural Causes of the Global Financial Crisis," 570.
2   Thomas Philippon, "Finance versus Wal-Mart: Why Are Financial Services So Expensive?" in *Rethinking the Financial Crisis,* 236–7; see also figure 9.1.

fund management . . . Investors spend 0.67% of asset value trying (in vain, by definition) to beat the market."[1]

There is no way to gauge how effective financiers' self-descriptions of themselves as innovators were in fending off regulation. US and European regulators had their own reasons for encouraging speculative finance even as it became an obvious bubble. Regulators were unwilling to undermine their bankers' competitive position vis-à-vis rivals in other countries to prevent what seemed to be an implausible crash at the core of global capitalism. Members of Congress happily drew on Wall Street for campaign contributions. Journalists got higher ratings, and became highly paid celebrities themselves, by covering once-boring financiers as though they were sports champions:

> CNBC was something more than a business-news cable channel. It was the winning team's locker room, a cultural phenomenon of the heady 1990's and a mainstay in bars, sports clubs and offices. It became the most-watched information source on cable as its anchors and correspondents reported on the stock market with the same cool confidence with which Internet entrepreneurs strode through Lower Manhattan. Chief executives like Jeff Bezos of Amazon and John T. Chambers of Cisco Systems were treated like rock stars on its programs as the once-stodgy lexicon of Wall Street—I.P.O., P/E ratio—became the hip new idiom of the day.[2]

Despite increasingly clear indications that speculative mortgages had become fraudulent, regulators never stepped in. "In September 2001, five hundred FBI agents were transferred from white collar crime to counterterrorism, and were never replaced despite a public FBI warning in 2004 that we faced an 'epidemic of mortgage fraud.' "[3] The Fed had authority under the Home Ownership and Equity Protection Act of 1994 to issue rules on mortgage lending to forbid, in the words of the Act, "unfair . . . deceptive [loans and] abusive lending practices, or

---

1   Ibid., 245.
2   Jim Rutenberg, "CNBC Struggles to Stay Relevant; with Stocks No Longer the Big Story, News Viewers Are Looking Elsewhere," *New York Times*, November 12, 2001.
3   Galbraith, "Great Crisis and the Financial Sector," 236–7.

that are otherwise not in the interest of the borrower." But Greenspan never acted. The Office of the Comptroller of the Currency blocked all efforts by state attorney generals to pursue deceptive lending cases against banks.[1]

James Galbraith compares the wave of mortgage fraud to a criminal ring in which

> the mortgage originators were, in effect, counterfeiters. They produced documents that resembled mortgages but which were known, by those who made them, to be fakes—destined either to be renegotiated or to default. An entire underworld lexicon described this craft: liars' loans, NINJA loans (no income no job or assets), neutron loans (that would destroy the people but leave the buildings intact), toxic waste. This fact alone reveals clearly that the participants knew what they were about. And . . . virtually all appraisers in some areas reported being pressured to inflate their appraisals to justify larger loans. There is no honest reason for an inflated appraisal.
>
> The counterfeit mortgages were then bundled and laundered—in the precise sense known to the drug trade—by the ratings agencies, who relabeled BBB paper as AAA without ever looking for, or at, the underlying documentation . . . The laundered paper was then fenced, again in the precise sense known to purveyors of stolen goods, by the large investment banks. Lehman Brothers, for instance, did the biggest trade in liars' loans. Goldman Sachs was long in toxic bonds until the end was nigh, at which point that firm went massively short, dumping its holdings on trusting clients, to their later chagrin.[2]

Banks' increasing leverage meant that even a small uptick in the mortgage default rate would tip those firms into insolvency. "Annual borrowing by US financial institutions as a percent of gross domestic product (GDP) jumped from 6.9% in 1997 to 12.8% a decade later."[3] Investment banks, which justify themselves by claiming that they provide credit to businesses, became such a huge drain on American

1   Taub, *Other People's Houses*, 222–46.
2   Galbraith, "Great Crisis and the Financial Sector," 237–8.
3   Crotty, "Structural Causes of the Global Financial Crisis," 574.

and global capital because the SEC "under pressure from Goldman Sachs chairman and later Treasury Secretary Henry Paulson" gave them permission in 2004 to increase their leverage from twelve times capital, the limit that applied from 1975 to 2003,

> to 40 times capital and made compliance [even with this high limit] voluntary. This allowed large investment banks to generate asset-to-equity ratios in the mid to upper 30s just before the crisis, with at least half of their borrowing in the form of overnight repos, money that could flee at the first hint of trouble. With leverage rates this high, any serious fall in asset prices would trigger a dangerous deleveraging dynamic.[1]

### Obama's Response to the Crisis and the Limits of American Hegemony

Housing prices peaked in April 2006, fell slightly for the next eleven months, and then plunged, reaching a low in May 2009 that was 32 percent below the peak three years earlier.[2]

> The mutual dependence of housing prices and credit supply, a direct corollary of the tight coupling between housing market and capital markets, reached an unprecedented level in the subprime segment of the housing market, where new mortgage loans were offered on the expectation of future increases in housing prices. [In other words, the only way the fraudulent mortgages could be paid, since the home buyers lacked the income to even pay the interest once the teaser rates expired, was if they could sell the home or refinance based on a then higher value for the house they had purchased. Thus] the fall in housing prices and the distress in financial markets fed each other, leading to a negative cascade in both markets. If housing market and financial markets were not tightly coupled, such a negative cascade would not ensue. Furthermore, if mortgage loans were not converted into fungible financial commodities, these loans could be

---

1   Ibid., 574.
2   Federal Reserve Bank of St. Louis, "S&P/Case-Shiller 20-City Composite Home Price Index" (2017).

renegotiated between lenders and borrowers, which would have prevented the negative cascade that fueled the increase in foreclosures ... The commodification of home loans lies at the origins of the foreclosure crisis and explains why foreclosures in the United States remained at elevated levels for a very long time.[1]

We need to supplement Gemici's analysis, which, while accurate on the mechanics of the mortgage market, does not address the political decisions made by the Fed and the Obama administration. Obama, as a senator and Democratic presidential nominee, supported the Emergency Economic Stabilization Act of 2008, which allowed the Treasury Department to spend $700 billion on the Troubled Assets Relief Program (TARP), buying "troubled assets" from banks and also from insurance companies, money market funds, and other "non-bank" entities. Obama, as president, continued the TARP program. More significantly, Obama in 2010 reappointed Ben Bernanke, initially selected by President George W. Bush in 2006, to a second term as chair of the Fed. Obama, in that decision, reaffirmed the Fed's policy of "quantitative easing," which, in three rounds, purchased $4.5 trillion of Treasury bonds and mortgage-backed securities.[2]

Quantitative easing stimulated the economy by lowering long-term interest rates, but it also helped banks in two ways. First, they were able to unload mortgage-backed securities that private buyers were unwilling to purchase in the wake of the collapse of real estate prices and revelations that many of those securities were based on fraudulent mortgages. Second, by holding down the rates at which banks themselves had to borrow money or pay depositors, the Fed widened the spread between what banks paid and what they could charge their customers, drastically increasing bank profits.

In a case of clear political malpractice, Obama failed to differentiate in the eyes of the public his stimulus from Bush's bank bailout. He never said anything along the lines of, "Bush bailed out bankers, and

---

1    Gemici, "Beyond the Minsky and Polanyi Moments," 17.
2    Binyamin Appelbaum, "Federal Reserve Caps Its Bond Purchases; Focus Turns to Interest Rates," *New York Times*, October 29, 2014.

my stimulus benefits ordinary Americans." Obama's unwillingness to express class politics (admittedly, when he once called bankers "fat cats," he was subjected to repeated harsh criticism from capitalists and journalists) left voters with the mistaken impression that the Obama stimulus was going to banks. Misperceptions of the stimulus were compounded by the low visibility of the three main sorts of stimulus spending: small-bore, "shovel-ready" projects; payments to state and local governments that averted public employee layoffs but did not visibly create new jobs for the unemployed; and tax cuts, which, in an effort to "nudge"[1] the public to spend rather than save their stimulus tax cuts, were distributed through imperceptible cuts in payroll withholding rather than in a single check mailed directly to voters. (George W. Bush, in a similar situation, had the political shrewdness to have his first tax rebates mailed in envelopes post-marked "Austin, Texas.")

Although Obama campaigned in 2008 in favor of mortgage cram-down legislation, which would have had the effect of overruling *Nobelman v. American Savings Bank* and empowering bankruptcy judges to deal with the complexities of securitized mortgages by forc-ing investors to write down mortgages to the actual value of homes after the bursting of the real estate bubble, he failed to make any effort to move such legislation as president. Indeed, in 2008, the Democratic majorities in Congress wanted to add such a cram-down provision to the TARP bank bailout legislation. Obama, by then the Democratic nominee, switched and opposed the provision, wanting it to be post-poned until 2009. However, his administration never gave that

---

1    Obama was infatuated with using policies that draw on insights from behavorial economics to nudge people to spend their stimulus money, save for retirement, exercise, use less energy, and undertake various other actions that benefit the general public along with the individuals who take up those behaviors (Richard H. Thaler and Cass R. Sunstein, *Nudge: Improving Decisions about Health, Wealth, and Happiness* [New Haven: Yale University Press, 2008]). Such policies have received criticism from the right as manifestations of a "nanny state." More accu-rately, nudge policies are expressions of liberal surrender. Rather than try to convince the public to support an expanded public sector or general social welfare policies, nudges seek to trick people into behaviors. When such measures are revealed, as right-wing media inevitably will do, the result is politically toxic, further undermin-ing sentiment in favor of liberal policies, even if some part of the public does end up with larger retirement savings or more physically fit.

measure priority, and bank lobbyists were able to defeat it in 2009.[1] Obama waited until 2013 to nominate a replacement for Edward DeMarco, the acting director of the Federal Housing Finance Agency (the agency created in 2008 to act as conservator for Fannie Mae and Freddie Mac), who blocked mortgage write-downs.[2]

Obama's failure on this issue was economic as well as political stupidity, since underwater mortgage holders' spending was permanently limited by their oversized mortgage payments, and those who walked away from their homes became cut off from future credit. The millions of homes that were in limbo or foreclosure cast a pall on many local real estate markets, which in the most depressed areas had not lifted eight years after the crash. These areas, with the highest shares of subprime loans, and therefore the slowest recoveries in real estate prices, were among the places with the biggest switches from Obama in 2012 to Trump in 2016.[3]

Most notably, the Obama Justice Department managed to convict only a single trader at Credit Suisse for mortgage fraud. No one else has been imprisoned for that vast financial fraud. In comparison, more than a thousand people went to prison for the savings and loan frauds in the 1980s. The government did collect $190 billion in fines and settlements from banks, but that money came from the banks' shareholders, not the executives who enriched themselves. Obama's first attorney general, Eric Holder, claimed

> the virtual absence of convictions (or even prosecutions) this time around did not result from a want of trying. "These are the kinds of cases that people come to the Justice Department to make," he said. "The inability to make them, at least to this point, has not been as a result of a lack of effort."

Whether or not Holder was correct about the difficulty of bringing cases against individuals, he was opposed as a matter of policy to

---

1   Taub, *Other People's Houses*, 247–66.
2   Mian and Sufi, *House of Debt*, 135–51.
3   Ben Casselman, "Stop Saying Trump's Win Had Nothing To Do With Economics," *FiveThirtyEight*, January 9, 2017.

bringing criminal charges against banks as institutions. As a deputy attorney general in the Clinton administration, Holder wrote a memo in 1999,

> warning of the dangers of prosecuting big banks—a variant of the "too big to fail" argument that has since become so familiar. Holder's memo asserted that "collateral consequences" from prosecutions— including corporate instability or collapse—should be taken into account when deciding whether to prosecute a big financial institution.

That policy blocked indictments of banks.[1]

All these factors—visible bailouts for bankers and a hard-to-notice stimulus for ordinary Americans, no relief for homeowners who were sold fraudulent mortgages, and total impunity for financiers who committed fraud—led voters to repeatedly punish Democrats. In 2010, the Democrats lost the House and a majority of state governments. In 2014, the Republicans took the Senate, and in 2016 the presidency.

Was an alternative that challenged banks feasible? While Obama did not move to take political advantage of the crisis and financiers' visible criminality, that opening was only a potential one. Unlike FDR, who became president more than three years into the Great Depression, the Great Recession was at its beginnings when Obama took office. His primary task, to ensure his and his party's political survival, was to limit and reverse the decline as quickly as possible. Obama could and did argue[2] that taking a more radical course would have been too risky, and that his critics on the left have failed to acknowledge what Obama asserts were unchangeable political realities, most notably the difficulty in convincing conservative Democrats in Congress to vote for the stimulus, the Affordable Care Act, and Dodd-Frank despite

--------

1    William D. Cohan, "How Wall Street Bankers Stayed Out of Jail," *The Atlantic*, September 2015.

2    Barack Obama, "Remarks by the President at Howard University Commencement Ceremony," (2016); Jonathan Chait, "Five Days That Shaped a Presidency," *New York Magazine*, October 3, 2016.

their limited provisions.[1] It is revealing that Obama, in making the case for his decisions, focuses entirely on Congress and never discusses what he did or more accurately did not do to mobilize public opinion behind his proposals. It is impossible to prove that, if Obama had tried to maintain or even deepen the level of mobilization that supported his 2008 election, a different course would have been feasible.

Once Obama, through some mixture of necessity and choice, decided to aid rather than confront banks, the existing power of US elites, their links to capitalists elsewhere in the world, and the structure of international institutions that the United States led but did not control combined to shape the response to and legacy of the crisis. The largest US banks were encouraged to use TARP and Fed funds to buy up smaller banks, just as the Obama administration encouraged mergers among hospitals and physicians' practices after passage of the Affordable Care Act. The largest banks, having been certified as systemically important, were accurately regarded by investors as "too big to fail" and attracted deposits and investments away from their smaller rivals who were deemed vulnerable to failure. Even before the crisis, the largest banks were getting bigger in absolute and relative terms.

> By the mid-2000s, the combined assets of the six biggest US banks represented around 55 percent of US GDP, up from less than 20 percent in 1995 ... In 2009, according to one calculation, the too-big-to-fail subsidy represented roughly half of the total profits of the eighteen largest US banks.[2]

The biggest banks' share of total banking assets, and their profit premium over smaller rivals, did not diminish over the years of the Obama presidency.[3]

--------

1   Paul Krugman in *End this Depression Now!* (New York: Norton, 2012), while emphatic that the stimulus was too small, wavers between blaming Obama's timidity and congressional Republicans' intransigence for failing to adopt a stimulus bill that would have been sufficiently large to end the Great Recession.

2   Hacker and Pierson, *American Amnesia*, 286.

3   Steve Schaefer, "Five Biggest US Banks Control Nearly Half Industry's $15 Trillion in Assets," *Forbes*, December 3, 2014.

Executives of financial firms and those of nonfinancial firms, whose outsized incomes were made possible by their firms' ability to generate profits through financial manipulation and who therefore shared an interest in limiting regulation of finance, used their unified power to limit the reach of Dodd-Frank (the Wall Street Reform and Consumer Protection Act of 2010). These executives used the method most favored by economic elites in the United States because of its effectiveness. Unable to directly block the legislation since Democrats had a filibuster-proof majority in the Senate, lobbyists and executives from the financial industry pushed to make the provisions of the bill as vague as possible and left the writing of the actual rules to executive agencies. Many of the regulations required approval of multiple federal agencies, including the Fed, the one most likely to heed the desires of the biggest Wall Street firms and banks. Financiers' hopes, which for the most part have been borne out, were that they could exert decisive influence in the writing of rules and, when the rules were unfavorable, get them blocked by federal courts stuffed with judges appointed by Reagan and the two Bushes, and Clinton and Obama judges who, while liberal on civil rights and civil liberties, often were sufficiently pro-business on economic cases, especially on the decisive US Court of Appeals for the District of Columbia Circuit.[1]

For example, the Business Roundtable broke with the Obama administration in June 2010 over a proposed provision in Dodd-Frank "that would make it easier for large, long-term shareholders to propose alternative candidates in elections to a company's board of directors."[2] The Business Roundtable lost in Congress and the provision remained in Dodd-Frank, but when the SEC formulated a rule implementing the provision, the Business Roundtable and the Chamber of Commerce sued, and the rule was overturned in the Court of Appeals for the DC Circuit. The Business Roundtable and the Chamber of Commerce could count on support from nonfinancial as well as financial corporations in these fights over regulation

---

1   The Supreme Court has the power to reverse the DC Circuit, but it rarely considers appeals from Circuit decisions, especially when those decisions are pro-business.

2   Hacker and Pierson, *American Amnesia*, 211.

because executives of nonfinancial firms increasingly got their income from stock options, and the firms themselves made money from finance.[1]

The trends of the first decade of the twenty-first century were not reversed to an appreciable extent by the crisis itself or by the Obama administration's response to the financial collapse. Dodd-Frank did lead to regulations that have to a real extent reduced banks' capacity to engage in financial speculation, although subprime and interest-only mortgages and credit cards with teaser rates for customers with poor credit ratings are returning to the United States[2] and Britain.[3] Since 2009, a growing fraction of the riskiest US mortgages are directly guaranteed by federal agencies,[4] as opposed to the implicit guarantees (redeemed in the crisis) for the financial firms that bought and sold subprime mortgages before 2009.

Of course, the regulations created under Dodd-Frank, like the regulations mandated by earlier financial legislation, depend for their effectiveness on federal agencies' interpretation and enforcement. Under Obama, Dodd-Frank has been somewhat successful at reducing banks' leverage, making derivatives trading more transparent and perhaps less risky, and imposed limited controls on ratings agencies and banks' proprietary trading. The Consumer Financial Protection Bureau, the brainchild of Elizabeth Warren, curbed abusive practices and forced unscrupulous financial firms to pay significant settlements to consumers.[5]

The long-term trend since Nixon, as we have demonstrated in this chapter, has been toward regulatory interpretations that are ever more generous toward financial firms at the same time as enforcement has become continually lighter. Democratic administrations and their

---

1   Ibid., 210–12.

2   Wolf Richter, "NY Fed Warns about Booming Subprime Mortgages, Now Insured by the Government," *Wolf Street*, June 21, 2016.

3   Emma Dunkley, "Banks Return to Riskier Lending on Mortgages and Credit Cards," *Financial Times*, June 30, 2015.

4   W. Scott Frame, Kristopher Gerardi, and Joseph Tracy, "Risky Business: Government Mortgage Insurance Programs," *Liberty Street Economics*, June 20, 2016.

5   Robert E. Litan, "The Political Economy of Financial Regulation after the Crisis," in *Rethinking the Financial Crisis*.

appointees have been somewhat stricter than their Republican counterparts, although Carter, Clinton, and Obama each went only partway toward reversing the reductions in regulation and enforcement of
their Republican predecessors. Trump, at the outset of his presidency,
has shown through his appointees that he will try to roll back Dodd-
Frank and other regulatory regimes as far as the law and federal courts
will allow. We can expect that the next Democratic president (unless
there is a new severe crisis and resulting progressive political wave)
will only be able to return partway to the level of regulation under
Obama.

## CHALLENGES TO AND BASES OF AMERICA'S
## CONTINUING ECONOMIC HEGEMONY

Repeated American financial malfeasance, even fraud that has cost
banks and governments elsewhere in the world trillions of dollars in
degraded assets and lost economic growth, has yet to undermine US
economic hegemony. The Fed remains the central and commanding
regulator of global finance, and the dollar remains the world currency.
US Treasury bonds continue to be viewed as among the world's safest
investments, and the only one capable of absorbing the vast surpluses
of other nations.

This section identifies the bases of continued US economic hegemony and examines the sources of challenge to America's ability to
shape the global economy according to its own design. It is especially
important to understand how America's global economic position
relates to its declining geopolitical power and to the paralysis of its
domestic political system. We also need to see American economic
power in relation to the capacities of its rivals, above all China.

The 2009 crisis enhanced the Fed's power to shape global finance.
The Fed proved able to create unlimited amounts of dollars that it
used to bail out foreign as well as domestic banks and financial firms,
and to stimulate demand and credit in the United States that allowed
American consumers to continue to buy products and feed the trade
surpluses of the rest of the world. However, the Fed acted in the face
of, and because of, Congress's severely limited capacity, even when it

attained large Democratic majorities in 2009, to pass significant economic measures to address the financial crisis and rapidly deepening global recession.

Thanks to the Fed's broad powers, the United States remained the lender as well as the consumer of last resort to the world, a role the European Central Bank (ECB) proved unable or unwilling to play. The ECB, along with other EU institutions, remained committed to a grim neoliberalism.[1] The IMF was authorized in 2009 to increase its lending by $1.1 trillion. But, in comparison to the $4.5 trillion spent by the Fed, the IMF's contribution was clearly inadequate, in large part because the United States was able to block a proposal by China, France, and Russia for a larger expansion of the IMF's special drawing rights, which could have acted as an alternate currency to the dollar. Countries in the Global South were hostile to any expansion of IMF resources and power because they remembered the punitive conditions the IMF had placed on loans to them in the 1990s.[2]

The dollar stood as the world currency throughout the crisis, and today there is no indication that any other currency or basket of currencies will assume that role. During the crisis, "many investors found that their attempts to extricate themselves from unfavorable positions required dollar-denominated transactions, [and] the vortex-like capacity of American financial markets to draw in foreign funds was once again confirmed."[3] This was because so much world debt, including government bonds, is denominated in dollars. Dollar-denominated bonds, above all the seemingly unlimited supply of Treasuries, remained the most attractive site of investment, especially in comparison to the European countries that were borrowing money. Italy, the largest borrower in the EU,[4] was hardly a safe investment, and the premium on Italian bonds, thanks to interventions by the

1   Wolfgang Streeck, *Buying Time: The Delayed Crisis of Democratic Capitalism* (London: Verso, 2017).

2   Eric Helleiner, *The Status Quo Crisis: Global Financial Governance after the 2008 Financial Meltdown* (Oxford: Oxford University Press, 2014), 1–91.

3   Panitch and Gindin, *The Making of Global Capitalism*, 318.

4   Helleiner, *Status Quo Crisis*, 54–91.

European Central Bank,[1] was too small to justify the risk in the eyes of most investors. Countries in the Global South also buy Treasuries, hold dollars in banks, and invest in the United States as a way to "self-insure" against runs on their currencies.[2]

Above all, the dollar's global role has been sustained by the enduring convergence of interests between the United States and China to preserve the dollar's primacy over the RMB. While the Chinese government moved forcefully, quickly, and successfully to counteract the effects of the crash with a $600 billion stimulus that revived growth within China, it did little to stimulate demand in the rest of the world, except for the raw commodities China imports, creating new bubbles in Brazil, Australia, and other countries whose economies remain largely dependent on the export of raw materials.

China's approach to the dollar and RMB are determined by its overriding goal of sustaining the export-oriented strategy it has employed in recent years, which has produced a high rate of growth by undercutting international competitors with low wages and a lack of environmental laws. The policies undergirding that strategy will continue as long as managers and owners of state and private manufacturing firms continue to hold sway at all levels of the Chinese government. China's huge and persistent trade surplus can be sustained only as long as its currency remains artificially low, which in turn requires exporters to "sterilize" the surplus by trading dollars and other foreign currency for RMBs. The government's control of what has become a multi-trillion-dollar currency reserve allows it to extend credit to state-owned banks, despite their negative equity. The banks, in turn, roll over their loans to state-owned enterprises (SOEs) that are kept in business producing more goods than domestic or international markets can absorb, because if banks were to acknowledge that those SOEs would never again become profitable, they would have to write off their loans.[3]

---

1   Lukanyo Mnyanda and David Goodman, "Italian Spread Shows Risk Premium Vanishing in Euro Area's Bonds," *Bloomberg*, February 27, 2015.

2   Julian S. Yates and Karen Bakker, "Debating the 'Post-Neoliberal Turn' in Latin America," *Progress in Human Geography* 38 (2014): 62–90; Helleiner, *Status Quo Crisis*, 54–91.

3   This and the following three paragraphs are based on Hung, *China Boom*.

There was some rebalancing of China's economy under Hu Jintao, but that effort was undercut by the use of most of the 2009 stimulus to encourage a new wave of lending by banks for yet more redundant factories, shopping malls, real estate developments, and rail lines. Despite his rhetoric, Hu's successor, Xi Jinping, has failed to summon the unity and political power to challenge local governments, SOEs, and private capitalists (many of whom are relatives of current and former high officials). The government's adherence to existing policies ensures that resources will not shift toward domestic consumption fast enough to mitigate the continuing danger of a wave of Chinese domestic bankruptcies or a collapse of global prices for manufactured goods.

The RMB is a minor player in global currency markets, mainly because China refuses to open its banking sector to global markets.[1] Such liberalization would sap the party-state's ability to use credit to control the economy. China's investments in the developing world do strengthen those countries' leverage against the United States by creating a new source of credit, which China offers on better terms than American or European banks, governments, and international agencies. However, while China helps to shift the balance of power from the First to the Third World, this, as we will see later, is felt mainly in trade negotiations rather than in the military realm. China has not yet made the military investments that would allow it to challenge the United States directly beyond East Asia, and even there it is not at all clear which power would have the edge in a confrontation.

China and the United States thus remain in a symbiotic relationship. China represses labor costs, mainly by limiting the mobility and rights of rural residents. China's undervalued RMB and the low interest paid on savings also serve to transfer income from workers and consumers to the state and large firms. Those savings partly go to build infrastructure and new factories in China, but much of it is exported to the United States. However, China's competitive advantage in so many manufacturing sectors means that it would be a poor investment to use that capital inflow for industrial investment in the United States, so it is diverted to underwriting the perpetual federal

---

1 Eichengreen, *Exorbitant Privilege*, 121–52.

budget deficit, and it helped fuel the real estate boom that collapsed in 2008. Hung's prognosis is grim: China and the United States both are likely to endure frequent recessions and financial collapses in a world-system in which Chinese domestic power relations ensure that the world's most populous country makes no serious effort to supplant America's dollar and military hegemony. Only popular mobilization within China could reorient its developmental policy in a more sustainable and egalitarian direction, but predicting that is beyond the scope of this book—and probably beyond the capacity of social science theory.

In the meantime, the Fed's power to regulate the global economy and finance remains largely unimpeded as long as the dollar remains the global currency. Basel III, whose implementation the G20 accelerated in 2009 in response to the crisis, created the Financial Stability Board, but the Board operates by consensus, allowing the United States and Britain to block any proposals that challenge US or British interests to remain the central nodes in world finance. The United States vetoed various suggestions by France and Germany and by countries in the Global South for mandatory enforcement mechanisms. In any case, the Board's policies imitate the reforms promulgated by the Fed and under Dodd-Frank.[1]

Conversely, when the United States does want to impose global standards, it uses "clubs" of invited nation-members, such as the Financial Stability Forum, to develop "more rigorous financial codes and standards across a range of issues, including banking supervision, insurance, auditing, securities, and data transparency."[2] These clubs allowed the United States to circumvent Third World countries, which were harmed by these efforts to discipline their banks and markets, from using their ability under formal or informal rules in established international organizations to block consensus around US proposals.[3] The United States also retains effective control over the World Bank and other multinational development banks (MDBs), and can demand

---

1   Helleiner, *Status Quo Crisis*, 92–164; Panitch and Gindin, *The Making of Global Capitalism*, 301–30.

2   Daniel W. Drezner, *All Politics Is Global: Explaining International Regulatory Regimes* (Princeton: Princeton University Press, 2007), 120.

3   Ibid.

those banks condition loans on recipients' willingness to privatize state-owned firms and to borrow from private (mainly New York–based) banks. The push under George W. Bush, with support from liberal NGOs and Democrats in Congress, to force the World Bank and MDBs to offer grants along with loans and to forgive or restructure past loans[1] meant that private banks would be more likely to have their loans to those poor countries repaid.

US financial standards, and those the United States deigns or desires to be created in forums that it controls, are the only operating global standards. As a result, the United States exercises the only significant sanction in global finance: exclusion from the US banking system. That punishment hits not just the direct target, but any country that attempts to circumvent an embargo the United States has placed on the marked nation. This is the mechanism the United States under Obama used so effectively against Iran to compel it to severely limit its nuclear program and submit to inspections.

Trade is the one arena in which US control over the global economy has been effectively challenged. Global South countries, led by China, India, and Brazil, were able to use their ability to block consensus in the WTO to demand that the Doha Round expand access to Western markets for their leading sectors: agricultural goods (Brazil), IT services (India), and manufacture (China). China's investments in the Third World and its selective purchases from other Global South countries enabled it to build a coalition to counter Western nations in the WTO. All the major powers, old and new, are committed to trade liberalization. But they do so "selectively," wanting access abroad for their competitive industries while protecting their laggards at home, so negotiations are stymied.[2]

As we have seen, the United States, in the era from the 1930s to the 2000s, was willing to provide access to its large home market in order to open the globe to its most lucrative sectors, above all finance. It was only in the 1960s that other countries began to develop sufficient industry that they could compete with American firms in the US

---

1    Sarah Babb, *Behind the Development Banks: Washington Politics, World Poverty, and the Wealth of Nations* (Chicago: University of Chicago Press, 2009).

2    Hopewell, *Breaking the WTO*, 11 and passim.

market. Even when US firms and workers suffered absolute losses, financial elites' growing power ensured that American trade policy remained committed to opening America's home market in return for access to foreign markets. This remains American policy,[1] but while American financial hegemony allows the United States to set the financial rules for the globe, its declining industrial power makes it harder to compel the rest of the world to sign on to one-sided trade deals that would rescue certain American sectors at the expense of foreign rivals.

In the absence of new global trade deals, and now the seeming demise of the Trans-Pacific Partnership and the Transatlantic Trade and Investment Partnership, regional trading blocs led by the EU and China, and among Latin American nations, have the ability to create commercial zones that disadvantage the United States and that offer mutual concessions to the other regional blocs. To the extent that these blocs no longer need US military protection, or in the face of repeated American military failures decide they can flout US pressures, even leading American industries could be at a disadvantage in global trade.

The strategy that emerged at the end of World War II and was supported by a bipartisan coalition in Washington and by military and economic elites, in which the United States made limited economic sacrifices to bind Europe, Japan, and later a few other strategic countries (most notably South Korea, Taiwan, and Israel) in a US-centered and -ruled hegemonic system, while American military power provided additional leverage in economic negotiations, has been undermined in recent decades. The loss of the Cold War threat, and the American military's inability to develop a strategy capable of mobilizing the proper human resources and weapons to face present-day enemies, reduces the geopolitical pressures on allies to accept US economic direction. Within the United States, as we have traced in

---

1   The Trump administration's views on this issue remain unclear and shifting as factions in the executive branch face off against one another, and Trump himself has never moved beyond campaign slogans to formulate clear policies or even goals for trade negotiations. In any case, it is uncertain whether Trump will be able to enact significant changes in trade policy that would reduce foreign access and spark retaliatory actions.

this chapter, a coherent national economic strategy has given way to opportunistic moves by corporate officers to pursue their own profit at the expense of the long-term viability of their firms. Such profits are realized in the financial arena, creating an ever more one-sided push for financial liberalization over government policies that protect industrial sectors.

Financialization, which, as Arrighi showed us, is the hallmark of hegemons in the autumn of their dominance, has become the favored government policy in the United States since the 1970s, as financial elites became increasingly dominant in the domestic economic sphere and were able to maneuver in Washington amid governmental paralysis that precluded alternate strategies to those favoring financialization. At the same time, US leverage in the nonfinancial economic realm was reduced as other countries gained industrial prowess, found ways to challenge US control over nonfinancial international agencies, and built their own investment and trade networks. America's ability to exercise unilateral control over the global financial architecture now is the remaining pillar of US hegemony.

American economic hegemony thus seems likely to endure continuing disruption as it depends on a sector that is increasingly prone to frauds, panics, and crises. America's financial supremacy today is built as much on rivals' incapacity as US capacity. Chinese economic elites' ability to maintain an export-oriented strategy prone to overproduction and financial bubbles, despite reformist campaigns by supposedly powerful leaders, reveals the divisions among Chinese elites and paralysis within the state. That is why China's efforts to forge a Beijing Consensus, built on opposition to military intervention against and trade embargoes of all but the most outrageous dictatorships and on a model of economic development different from what the United States advocates (although not too different from what the United States practiced during its rise to hegemony in the nineteenth and early twentieth centuries),[1] remain incomplete and tentative.[2]

---

1   Ha-Joon Chang, *Kicking Away the Ladder: Development Strategy in Historical Perspective* (London: Anthem, 2002).
2   Montes and Popov, "Bridging the Gap," 127–30.

As long as China restricts the global exchange of the RMB, a policy essential to its current economic development strategy, it will never have a currency that could rival or supplant the dollar. The Euro is the currency of a region with a large enough economy (comparable to that of the United States) to be a rival global currency, but, except for the European Central Bank, the EU has no reliable policy organ.[1] As we have seen, the ECB lacks the resources and capacity to compete with the Fed as a global regulator or economic stimulator. To do so, even if the EU somehow reformed itself, it would have to directly confront US control of the institutions that undergird the global financial architecture.

The dollar could cease to be the world currency without the RMB or the Euro replacing it. Continued high US budget and trade deficits could lead foreign investors, and American investors as well, to see Treasuries and the dollar as a Ponzi scheme and dump their holdings. However, direct challenges to the dollar would impose severe costs on rival nations. If China tried to dump dollars to punish the United States, as the United States did to Britain in the Suez Crisis, the Chinese government and banks would suffer massive and potentially bankrupting losses on their Treasury holdings. That punitive maneuver was open to the United States in Suez because Americans held few British bonds. In any future market panic, as in 2008–09, the Fed would counteract until the panic subsided. In such efforts, other countries, again as in 2008–09, would aid the United States since they have an interest in a high dollar.[2]

If the dollar were no longer the world currency, US firms and the government would have to issue bonds in other, more stable currencies to obtain lower interest rates. Then the Fed would be constrained by the need to maintain an exchange rate that would allow American borrowers to repay loans, or at least to pay current interest, in other currencies, and the Fed would not be able to print dollars as it did in 2008–14, and instead would be limited by its tiny reserves of other currencies. At that point, the United States would have no choice but

1   Eichengreen, *Exorbitant Privilege*, 121–52.
2   This and the following paragraph draw on Eichengreen, *Exorbitant Privilege*, 153–77.

to narrow its trade deficit, which could only be done by investment in actual productive facilities and by lowering wages and/or consumption, as Germany did after its 1990s reunification binge. Merely lowering the value of the dollar will not solve the problem, as Trump and some of his advisors believe. Nevertheless, this is a dilemma that Trump or his successors are unlikely to face as long as China and the EU limit themselves in their assumption of a global role and allow the Fed to remain the prime regulator of global financial markets.

## THE BOTTOM LINE

You will remember that in chapter 1, after a historical review of failed and successful hegemons, I presented a Boolean truth table of the factors that impede hegemony. Polities failed to become hegemons when there was (1) a high level of elite conflict in the metropole, (2) a high level of colonial elite autonomy from the metropole, (3) a unitary elite dominant in the metropole, and/or (4) a lack of infrastructural capacity to control colonial elites. The presence of any one of those four factors precluded hegemony, although in some cases more than one factor was present. Only the Netherlands, Britain, and the United States lacked all four. I then hypothesized that one of those factors would have to reemerge before Dutch, British, and American hegemony was undone.

We saw in chapter 4 that the Netherlands lost hegemony because Dutch imperial and commercial conquests disrupted stable elite relations in the metropole and created conflict among elites that each gained the capacity to block central state policies that threatened their particular interests. In other words, Dutch decline was caused by the reemergence of factor number one at home, while single elites gained control of colonies and trading companies that were autonomous from central state direction (factor number two). Britain's loss of hegemony was more complex, as we explained in chapter 5. Colonial elites, mainly in the settler colonies, achieved a high degree of autonomy (factor number two). But that mattered mainly by altering the balance of power among metropolitan British elites, allowing financial capitalists to challenge landed and industrial elites (factor number one) and pursue policies that kept taxes low and the pound high, stymieing British industry and preventing Britain from making the investments in industrial and military modernization needed to counter its rising geopolitical and economic rivals, above all Germany and the United States.

Now that we have examined the trajectory of American politics, the military, and the economy from the 1960s to the present, we are in a position to identify the factors that are causing the decline of US hegemony. Chapter 6 tracked the emergence of elite conflict within the United States. As in the Netherlands, elites gained the power to block governmental initiatives and to prevent policy changes that could cost them money. Unlike in the Netherlands, where the structure of elite relations was transformed by the weight and wealth of the Dutch empire and trading network, in the United States we saw that elite relations were remade by mainly internal domestic factors. That difference is due in part to the relative size of the metropolitan and imperial economies. For the Netherlands, wealth from colonies and trade overwhelmed the domestic economy. America was a continent-sized economy in which profits from the world contributed more modestly.

Different measures of domestic and international business, however, did not translate directly into the forms of elite conflict that arose in hegemonic Netherlands and America. Rather, colonial riches poured into a Dutch elite structure that had incorporated an empire through familial networks that were linked to one another by contracts that blocked the sorts of significant reforms needed to sustain Dutch industrial and commercial dominance and to generate the revenues and—more vitally—the coordination required for a military capable of countering Britain's rising capacity.

US elites did not face plausible foreign rivals in the way that the eighteenth-century Dutch or late-nineteenth-century British did. Instead, American economic elites worked in the domestic political arena to create and exploit opportunities to reconstitute themselves through corporate mergers and then through financial deregulation. These structural changes transformed elite interests and the lines of conflict and alliance among elites. That, in turn, made it possible for elites to appropriate federal government resources and powers, and to control markets in ways that absorbed or eliminated locally based competitors. Such political and market power allowed economic elites to enlarge their share of national income and wealth at the expense of consumers and workers. The global wealth that American hegemony ensured would flow into the United States bought off opposition to financialization by sustaining the trade and budget deficits those policies produced, creating new economy-sustaining bubbles even after previous ones collapsed.[1]

The dramatic shift in resources from ordinary citizens and the state to economic elites since the 1970s (the "Great U-Turn") has, as in late Victorian Britain, fatally reduced the revenues needed for investments to keep US infrastructure, technology, and workers competitive with rivals elsewhere in the world. Economic restructuring also reshaped the firms that produce weapons for the US military, ensuring that the lavish Pentagon budget is spent in ways better suited for fighting the long-extinct Soviet Union than the targets the United States wishes to subdue in the twenty-first century.

Yet it is a mistake to attribute America's military setbacks only to the effects of corporate interests on military procurement. As with their counterparts in the Netherlands and Britain, the American military developed its own rigidities and, as in Britain, responded to public concerns over war casualties. In the Netherlands, military rigidity was a direct reflection of civilian elites' control over military offices and ships, a control that mirrored their power over domestic and colonial offices and privileges. In Britain, officers' career interests stymied reform, and outrage at British soldiers' deaths and injuries (though not at those of soldiers from the colonies) brought early ends to the South African and Crimean wars and limited colonial ventures in ways that inhibited imperial policy and emboldened great power rivals.

US service rivalries and officers' career interests intersected with and reinforced military contractors' profit opportunities to produce unsuitable and often unusable weapons. However, public concern

---

1   This process was summed up accurately and concisely in a 2008 headline in the satirical newspaper *The Onion*, July 14, 2008: "Recession-Plagued Nation Demands New Bubble to Invest In."

about casualties in post-Vietnam America was deeper and more sustained than in Victorian Britain, and constricted American geopolitical strategy far more severely than similar sentiments did in Britain a century earlier. US military weakness, which undermines geopolitical hegemony, is a combined product of elite conflict (factor number one), which has created a military armed with weapons unsuited to the tasks at hand, and a new version of factor number four, lack of infrastructural capacity. The fourth factor today differs from its ancient and early modern manifestations in that it is a cultural creation, as American attitudes toward their own soldiers' deaths have been transformed in ways that limit the extent of combat.

Military setbacks, industrial stagnation, and governmental rigidity left finance as the only field open for expansion and renewed profitability as hegemony declined. However, the paths finance took, and the effect of that expansion on the rest of the world, differed dramatically in the three hegemons. Dutch financial innovations created the first global (or at least European) markets for commodities and for raising money for firms and governments (as opposed to markets for mere speculation, which existed at least since Renaissance city-states). Those markets enriched Dutch financiers but also served to funnel wealth from the Dutch empire to rising economies, above all Britain. Amsterdam merchants, unified in their families and in their city networks, remained capable of manipulating markets that became increasingly divorced from the rest of the Dutch and global economies. At the same time, those merchants' control over Holland's government and over a territorial empire that lasted respectively until the Napoleonic invasion of 1795 and US insistence that the Dutch grant Indonesia independence in 1946[1] provided new infusions of wealth that benefited the merchant elite but hardly stimulated the national economy.

British financial hegemony lasted beyond its loss of industrial and technological leadership, its demonstration of military weakness in the Crimean and South African wars, and increasing assertions of autonomy from its settler colonies. Britain's financial power stemmed,

---

1   Hendrik Spruyt, *Ending Empire: Contested Sovereignty and Territorial Partition* (Ithaca: Cornell University Press, 2005), chapter 5.

like the Netherlands before it, from the fact that its capital city was also the controlling market for allocating investment, drawing capital from the rest of Europe and the Empire and then sending it off to firms and governments that operated according to London financiers' strictures. Such control, in the case of formal and informal colonial governments, was reinforced by Britain's periodic military interventions.

British financial power was increasingly exercised at a level more abstracted from concrete markets in commodities and finished goods than had been the case for Amsterdam. Investments in actual firms and governments were more enduring than in the goods that flowed through Amsterdam warehouses. London remained the center of the financial world even as its centrality, by the end of the nineteenth century, became mainly a consequence of British financiers' inability to extricate themselves from investments over which they were losing control to increasingly autonomous settlers in the Empire and to firms (especially in the United States) ever more able to finance their expansions through retained earnings. British financial decline and loss of hegemony came when rivals no longer depended on London to provide capital and markets.

American financial hegemony has survived decades past the point at which the United States became a net borrower. The United States' position remains unassailable because it became the regulator of first and last resort for the world economy in 1945. The United States was able to position the dollar as the linchpin of global financial stability. Even as waves of crisis have emanated from the speculation that US control of global finance has made possible, the regulatory power of the Fed has been sustained. Indeed, the crises, as we have seen in this chapter, have strengthened the Fed and attracted more capital to investments in US government debt and in American stocks, mortgages, and real estate.

American financial hegemony thus will be ruptured in a different manner than was the case for the Netherlands and Britain. Those earlier hegemons' financial power did not survive the advent of new, larger, and economically more advanced rivals. The United States will retain financial control as long as the rest of the world depends on the dollar and the Fed to mitigate overleveraging, speculation, and recessions both by writing and enforcing regulations worldwide and by acting as the source of unlimited economic stimulation that flows into actual investment and production in much of the world while fueling waves of financial engineering and speculation in the United States.

The power of American regulation and the dollar will not be undone by elite conflict in the United States, since all elites derive their position in part from America's global financial hegemony, and their institutions are subject to Fed regulation. Nor is this power challenged by China or the EU's autonomy in other spheres, or by the growing ability of countries once under America's thumb to pursue their own interests alone or in concert. Their strategies of autonomy in all other spheres depend on world markets denominated in a stable dollar and presuppose the Fed's global regulatory role.

Only if and when a sufficient concert of other nations devises a new regulatory mechanism for global finance and creates a process to back up demand in recessions and liquidity in crises will American financial hegemony come to an end. While America's nuclear weapons pose a threat that is so nihilistic that they offer no practical response to countries that recognize and exploit the ever more severe limits of US conventional warfighting capacities, the Fed and dollar provide palpable and regular support for the interests of elites around the world. Thus, US financial hegemony endures, even as it corrodes the other pillars of American economic power and stymies the emergence of a stable post-hegemonic elite structure within the United States and of a government with enough autonomy to advance policies that could address the interests of Americans other than those elites who have built for themselves impregnable fortresses within largely autonomous institutions.

# III.  After Hegemony

# 9

# After Decline

Good evening. This is your Captain
We are about to attempt a crash landing . . .
This is your Captain—and we are going down
We are all going down, together.
> Laurie Anderson, "From the Air" (*Big Science*, 1982)

Books of this sort typically end with a chapter of recommendations and hopes. If I followed that path, I would now speak to elites and beseech them to think of the nation's interests, which are also their real long-term interests. I would offer advice to citizens at large to become more engaged in public affairs.[1] So far, authors who have

---

1     Mizruchi, in *Fracturing of the American Corporate Elite*, ends his book with such an appeal to American elites. Jeffrey Sachs, in *The Price of Civilization: Reawakening American Virtue and Prosperity* (New York: Random House, 2012), hectors elites to become less greedy and more public-minded, and voters to pay more attention to public affairs and watch less television. Edward Luce (*The Retreat of Western Liberalism* [New York: Atlantic Monthly Press, 2017]), a journalist and former speech writer for Treasury secretary Lawrence Summers, offers a highly pessimistic view of a future of elite privilege and self-regard in the United States and Europe, but nevertheless concludes with the faint hope that rich elites will make the sacrifices needed to sustain liberal democracy. In an earlier book, *Time to Start Thinking: America in the Age of Descent* (New York: Atlantic Monthly Press, 2012), Luce wisely concluded, "This is not the kind of book that ends with shopping lists of policy prescriptions," but he immediately followed that with the hope that somehow a way could be found to "channel Americans' frustrations into a more constructive and coherent force" (274). Richard V. Reeves, in *Dream Hoarders: How the American Upper Middle Class Is Leaving Everyone Else in the Dust, Why That Is a Problem, and What to Do About It* (Washington, DC: Brookings Institution Press, 2017), argues (incorrectly) that inequality is caused by the efforts of the top 20 percent of Americans to pass down their privileges to their children. As with many such authors, he gives great attention to Ivy League admissions. Be that as it may, his proposed solutions avoid mention of redistributive policies and instead he asserts, "A change of heart is needed: a recognition of privilege among the upper middle class" (14).

made such entreaties have not had a discernible effect on public debates or political outcomes. I am not under the illusion that I possess the rhetorical skills to move hearts. Few authors have that ability.

The rare books that resonated widely and propelled political action, at least in the United States, were written in the midst of already established and deeply organized social movements. *Uncle Tom's Cabin* was published two decades after the British Parliament had banned slavery throughout the Empire and in a period when the American abolitionist movement was already a powerful, though minority, position in the United States. Michael Harrington's *The Other America* appeared in 1962, in the midst of the civil rights movement and after John F. Kennedy had made the alleviation of poverty a key issue in his presidential campaign, though not of his administration. Rachel Carson's *Silent Spring* might be an exception to this pattern. It was published in 1962, well before an organized environmental movement emerged in the United States, and clearly spurred establishment of the Environmental Protection Agency in 1970, which then banned the pesticide DDT in 1972. However, pollution and pesticides, unlike slavery, segregation, or poverty, affect everyone. Books like Carson's speak to their readers' self-interest rather than seek to build readers' sympathy for victims who differ in obvious ways from them. Similarly, Upton Sinclair's *The Jungle* (1906) was written to expose horrible working conditions in meatpacking plants, but readers instead reacted to the book's depictions of contaminated food, leading to the rapid passage that year of the Federal Meat Inspection Act and the Pure Food and Drug Act, which established the agency that was the precursor to the Food and Drug Administration. As with *Silent Spring*, *The Jungle* provoked self-interest rather than altruism.

---

Conservative scholars of decline appeal for Americans to spend more on the military and less on social benefits for themselves (e.g., Ferguson [*Empire*; *Colossus*], whom we encountered in the introduction; see footnote 3 on page 64 for other examples). New books exhorting Americans to save their country are being published almost weekly. Perry Anderson, in "Consilium" (*New Left Review* 83 [2013]: 163–7), offers an overview of prescriptions from US foreign policy intellectuals. For a fuller analysis of declinist narratives, see Richard Lachmann and Fiona Rose-Greenland, "Why We Fell: Declinist Writing and Theories of Imperial Failure in the *Longue Durée*," *Poetics* 50 (2015).

Sinclair himself wrote, "I aimed at the public's heart, and by accident I hit it in the stomach."[1]

If I am not going to exhort readers, then what can I do in this final chapter? I assume I have made the case that now America's decline, like that of Britain and the Netherlands before, is irreversible. Therefore, the question is not how we can reverse decline, but instead how decline will affect America's political economy, its geopolitical role in the world, and the quality of life for elites and non-elites. To answer that, I begin by examining what happened in the Netherlands and Britain after their losses of hegemony. Like America, those two polities underwent gradual declines. There were not any sudden collapses of elites or major military defeats (or victories) in post-hegemonic Netherlands and Britain that could have ushered in major social reforms or political restructurings such as occurred in various countries following the two world wars.

I compare post-hegemonic Netherlands and Britain along three dimensions: the extent to which inequality rose or declined, whether tax policy was used to reduce inequality and whether social programs were initiated or expanded, and if military and foreign policies were revised to reflect those polities' reduced circumstances. I then look at the same three dimensions in the contemporary United States and reflect on whether current trends are likely to continue. I seek to identify forces that could push the United States toward greater equality, expanded social programs, and a less aggressive and imperial foreign policy. The possibility of such a hopeful future depends largely on the revitalization of American democracy, and so I examine the prospects for such a renewal. I end with a consideration of the paradoxical coexistence of American elites' seemingly unchallenged power and their growing fears for the future.

---

1  Arlene Finger Kantor, "Upton Sinclair and the Pure Food and Drugs Act of 1906: 'I Aimed for the Public's Heart and by Accident I Hit it in the Stomach,' " *American Journal of Public Health*, 1976 (December) 66 (12), 1202–5.

## ELITE PRIVILEGE AND INEQUALITY AFTER DECLINE

The end of hegemony closed opportunities for the sorts of windfall profits created by empire or the domination of trade networks. Yet, as Arrighi shows us and we discussed at the end of the last chapter, declining hegemons remain for a time at the center of global financial networks, which create different although still highly lucrative profit opportunities. And, in any case, some Dutch and Britons retained capital accumulated during the years of dominance that provided rentier income. Let us see how the Dutch and British economies did after hegemony, and most importantly who suffered as their nations lost the benefits of hegemony.

The Dutch income advantage over Britain lasted more than a century and a half after the Dutch had lost hegemony. The Dutch, as measured by per capita income, remained the richest Europeans, ahead of the British until the mid-nineteenth century, at least three decades *after* Britain had become the hegemon.[1] That prosperity was a legacy of the vast stores of capital the Dutch accumulated during their hegemony and their ability to park that capital in more dynamic economies. Yet wealth was narrowly held and incomes were highly unequal as Dutch elites retained the most lucrative offices and opportunities within the metropole and empire.

Finance, the leading sector in the eighteenth and early nineteenth centuries in the Netherlands, focused investment in industrial rivals,

---

1   Per capita income in the Netherlands and Britain was even in 1500, when neither was yet the hegemon. In 1600 the Dutch were 40 percent above the British, and 70 percent higher in 1700. By 1820 the Dutch were only 7 percent ahead, and the two were even in 1850. Thereafter, the British pulled ahead rapidly, going from a per capita income 10 percent above the Dutch in 1856, to 15 percent ahead in 1870, 20 percent in 1890, and 30 percent in 1900 (Maddison, *World Economy*, volume 2, table 1c; see also Jan de Vries, "Dutch Economic Growth in Comparative-Historical Perspective," *De Economist* 148 [2000], figure 2).

Great Britain had a larger population than the Netherlands, so the gap in GDP was much greater than in per capita income. In 1500 British GDP was four times that of the Netherlands, three times as much in 1600, 2.6 times as much in 1700, nine times as much in 1820, 8.6 times as much in 1850, and 10.6 times as much in 1900 (Maddison, *World Economy*, volume 2, table 1b). In this chapter we focus on per capita income rather than total size of an economy since we are concerned with changes in the distribution of income and wealth rather than the strength of each nation's economy, which was our subject in previous chapters.

above all Britain, and in the state itself.[1] In the early eighteenth century, capital shifted from productive investment into state bonds, which were narrowly held. "After 1713, interest payments absorbed over 7 percent of Holland's tax revenue . . . For the Republic as a whole, interest payments on the public debt amounted to about 7 percent of mid-eighteenth century national income," which went mainly to a small cohort of wealthy bondholders.[2] As we saw in chapter 4, increases in government revenue functioned to funnel wealth from a mass of taxpayers hit with increasing consumption taxes, to wealthy bondholders and officials.

Ordinary people did increasingly badly in the post-hegemonic era. De Vries and van der Woude find that "from the several real wage peaks occurring between the 1680s and 1730s, a new trend of declining real wages set in, reaching its nadir after 1800."[3] The decline began earlier and was sharpest for unskilled laborers. The wage decline was from a high base, elevated enough that craftsmen's wages in the Netherlands remained higher than in southern England until the beginning of the nineteenth century.[4] Despite Dutch workers' higher average real incomes, they suffered from greater inequality than their English counterparts.[5]

Britons, like the Dutch, retained an income advantage over their global rivals even after they lost hegemony. However, the British edge over its hegemonic successor, the United States, lasted only three

---

1  Marjolein 't Hart, Joost Jonker, and Jan Luiten van Zanden, "Introduction," in *A Financial History of the Netherlands*.

2  De Vries and van der Woude, *First Modern Economy*, 681–2.

3  Ibid., 627; see also de Vries, "Dutch Economic Growth in Comparative-Historical Perspective," 457.

4  De Vries, "Dutch Economic Growth in Comparative-Historical Perspective," figure 12.6.

5  Branko Milanovic, Peter H. Lindert, and Jeffrey G. Williamson, in "Pre-Industrial Inequality," *Economic Journal* 121 (2011), table 2, Gini2 column, find that the Gini for Holland in 1732 was 61.1, compared to 45.9 for England and Wales in 1759. In 1801 England and Wales had risen to 51.5, still below the 57 for the Netherlands in 1808 (which included the less wealthy provinces in addition to Holland). Walter Scheidel, *The Great Leveler: Violence and the History of Inequality from the Stone Age to the Twenty-First Century* (Princeton: Princeton University Press, 2017), 95, using a different formula, calculates that the Gini coefficient for Holland rose "from 0.5 in 1514 to 0.56 in 1561, 0.59 in 1600, 0.61 or 0.63 in the 1740s and 0.63 in 1801."

decades after what we marked in chapter 5 as the end of British hegemony in 1873.[1] The United States surpassed Britain in per capita income
for the first time in 1901 and achieved a permanent edge by 1920, except
for the Depression years of 1932–35.[2] Thus, while the Dutch retained an
income edge after the British became hegemonic, Britons fell behind
the Americans decades before the United States achieved hegemony.

British income and wealth inequality remained high in the decades
between the end of hegemony and the start of World War I. Capital's
share of national income peaked at 43 percent in 1860, declined gradually over the next fifty years to 36 percent, reflecting declining income
from the Empire and from land, but then plunged in the decade of
World War I to 21 percent in 1920.[3] Wealth remained more stable; the
top 1 percent's share of national wealth rose from 54.9 percent in 1810
to 61.1 percent in 1870, and continued to increase to 70 percent in
1895.[4] It remained within the range of 69–74 percent from 1895 until
1910, with the top 0.1 percent holding half of that. The top 1 percent's
share fell to 67.2 percent in 1914, and to 62.6 percent in 1919. World
War I was the turning point. The top 1 percent's share fell over the
subsequent century, hitting bottom at 10.6 percent in 1988.[5]

Despite the high and rising level of British inequality during its
hegemonic heyday, and high and stable or slightly declining level in
the four decades of decline leading up to World War I, workers did
increasingly well in absolute terms. Wages, which in 1800–09 were the
same as a century earlier, rose rapidly after the end of the Napoleonic
Wars, more than tripling in the century from 1800–09 to 1900–09.[6]

Ordinary Britons' unusual prosperity, which continued even in
the face of their nation's hegemonic decline, and a degree of inequality
that was significantly higher than in the Netherlands, was not due to

---

1   From 1850 through 1870 British per capita income was 30 percent above the
United States. That edge was 21 percent in 1880, 18 percent in 1890, and 10 percent
in 1900.

2   Maddison, *World Economy*, volume 2, tables 1c, 2c.

3   Piketty, *Capital in the Twenty-First Century*, online figure S6.10.

4   Ibid., online table S10.1.

5   Facundo Alvaredo, Anthony B. Atkinson, and Salvatore Morell, "Top Wealth
Shares in the UK over More than a Century," Centre for Economic Policy Research
Discussion Paper DP11759 (2017), table G1.

6   Clark, "Condition of the Working Class in England," table A2.

Britain's economic growth rate in the post-hegemonic era. In the 1810 to 1880 period, Britain had the third highest growth, after Switzerland and Belgium, in per capita income of the twelve richest Western European nations.[1] For the 1880 to 1910 period, Britain was tied for second worst with Belgium, ahead of only the Netherlands.[2]

Two factors explain Britons' rising wages in the post-hegemonic decades. First, massive emigration reduced the growth of the British population. From 1881 to 1910, more than 5.4 million people emigrated, most of whom were working adults, which was one-seventh of Britain's population in 1900.[3] This created shortages of agricultural and industrial laborers, boosting their wages. Second, there was an upsurge in unionization in Britain in 1889–92, doubling membership to 11 percent of the labor force. Union density then rose more slowly to 18 percent in 1901 and 19 percent in 1911.[4] The threat of further unionization pushed employers to raise or at least maintain wages, though for the most part only in the sectors with high unionization rates: "coal mining, then engineering, shipbuilding and railways, then cotton, then construction and government employment."[5] However, the increases in wages did not decrease the concentration of wealth, which remained at historically high levels.

The Netherlands and Britain define the parameters of post-hegemonic prosperity and inequality. Elites in both countries widened their advantage in wealth over the rest of the population in the decades after the end of hegemony. Workers' wages diverged in the two countries. In the Netherlands, wages fell absolutely and relatively, while in Britain they fell relatively while increasing absolutely. Demographic and political forces account for the difference. Britain had created settler colonies that were congenial and prosperous lands attractive to poor Britons. The Netherlands' colonies were not inviting places for

---

1    The twelve are Austria, Belgium, Denmark, Finland, France, Germany, Italy, the Netherlands, Norway, Sweden, Switzerland, and the United Kingdom.

2    Maddison, *World Economy*, volume 2, table 1b.

3    Cain, "Economics and Empire," table 2.5.

4    Mann, *Sources of Social Power*, volume 2, 601, 608; see also Wallerstein, *Modern World-System*, volume 4, 174–6; and Beverly J. Silver, "World-Scale Patterns of Labor-Capital Conflict: Labor Unrest, Long Waves, and Cycles of World Hegemony," *Review* 18 (1995).

5    Mann, *Sources of Social Power*, volume 2, 609.

Dutch emigrants. Thus, the nature of the two empires, established centuries earlier, shaped workers' fortunes in the twilight of Dutch and British imperialism. Dutch workers of the mid-eighteenth century were disorganized in comparison to their British counterparts a century and a half later, and of course an ideological and organizational base for non-craft unions did not exist in the century when Dutch workers paid the material costs of their nation's decline.

## GOVERNMENT POLICY: TAXES AND SOCIAL BENEFITS

Did inequality become a political issue in either country, and were progressive taxes instituted or social programs established or expanded to reduce inequality or address poverty? In a word, taxes did not become redistributionist in either country during their post-hegemonic decades, while some limited social programs were instituted to address poverty and provide social benefits to a wide portion of the working population in Britain but not in the Netherlands.

In the Netherlands, the Patriot Revolution of 1780–87 amplified the grievances that had animated the smaller and more easily defeated anti-state revolts of 1702–07 and 1748, in its clear opposition to Orangist rule and to the corruption and privileges of the stadtholder and his retainers. The rebels of the 1780s were motivated by the Netherlands' setbacks and then defeat in the Fourth Anglo-Dutch War of 1780–84, which the rebels accurately attributed to the government's ineptitude and the unwillingness of the rich in the Netherlands and of the VOC to adequately finance the Dutch military. Anger was deepened by the recession that resulted from British attacks on Dutch commerce in the war, a war widely seen as caused by merchants' grasping efforts to profit from the American War of Independence. Yet the class lines between rebels and Orangists were confused with many of the poor siding with the stadtholder against middle-class rebels. The revolts all ended without realizing significant political or economic changes. The Patriots' early military successes were undone by Prussian intervention in 1787.[1]

---

1   This paragraph is based on Israel, *Dutch Republic*, 1098–130. I do not address the Batavian Republic of 1795–1805, which to a large degree sought to implement

The Netherlands was an eighteenth-century pioneer in the provision of income support to the poor, mainly lowly paid laborers but also widows, orphans, and the unemployed. As the need increased in the eighteenth century, church aid to the poor, which was funded by endowments and annual surpluses, was supplemented with direct expenditures by towns and cities. Church and state poor relief in the second half of the eighteenth century amounted to a combined "3 to 4 percent of the mid-eighteenth-century national income."[1] That amount reflected the large fraction of the population that received aid more than the modest payments given to each recipient. As the population of underemployed and underpaid rose and wages fell after 1770, the amount available for poor relief became increasingly inadequate.

"The government bond default of 1811 (the *tiercering*)" wiped out the value of the bonds that had funded church charities, and the state largely replaced churches in supporting the poor. State expenditures on poor relief more than doubled from 1815 to 1829.[2] However, most of the debate over poor relief in the late eighteenth and early nineteenth centuries was over how to reduce rather than increase poor relief. Wealthy citizens complained that charity and government aid were encouraging the poor to shun work. Poor relief did allow workers to be pickier about the jobs and wages they would accept, giving them real negotiating power with employers. In any case, the *tiercering* combined with the shrunken budgets of the Batavian Republic and its successors to ensure that nineteenth-century Netherlands would be, as the elites desired, a harsher nation for the poor and for ordinary laborers than the eighteenth-century Republic had been.[3]

Dutch public expenditures on education and public works, the government programs that benefited the general population, remained stingy through the first half of the nineteenth century, varying between 10 percent of the total budget in peacetime and 5 percent during wars.

the goals enunciated by the Patriots. However, British and above all French intervention was more determinative than internal Dutch forces.

1    De Vries and van der Woude, *First Modern Economy*, 660.
2    Ibid., 660.
3    This paragraph relies on de Vries and van der Woude, *First Modern Economy*, 654–64.

Only after William I abdicated in 1839, and a "stable, centralized and limited regime was established in 1848" that swept away many elite institutional privileges, did those expenditures reach 18–20 percent, a level it remained from 1880 until "the start of World War I."[1]

Dutch taxes remained regressive until World War I. A modestly progressive income tax was enacted during the Batavian Republic and then permanently in 1893. However, it provided only a tenth of state revenues and did not undo the overall regressive nature of the Dutch tax system until a vastly expanded income tax was introduced in 1914 to pay for the war effort.[2] Earlier efforts to create a progressive income tax were supported by popular forces that backed the Batavian Republic and "public opinion on the income tax had become generally quite favorable since 1870."[3] However, in both periods, enactment of an income tax was deflected by elite control of the central government. Before 1914, most revenue came from excise taxes on commodities that were consumed by the entire population and land taxes that were set by provincial quotas that had the effect of placing a heavier burden on the poorer provinces. The rich were targeted with land transfer taxes and death duties, but the levels of those taxes were too low to make up for the regressive nature of consumption taxes.[4]

British politics and governance, in contrast to the Dutch stasis enforced by elites, were transformed significantly in the half century before World War I. The franchise was expanded by the 1867 Reform Act and the 1884 Representation of the People Act, the former sponsored by the Tories and the latter by the Liberals. Together, they ensured that by the 1885 general election, "Sixty-six percent of adult males were now eligible to vote, including upward of 40 percent of male manual workers (although many were prevented from voting by biased registration procedures). Perhaps half the electorate were

---

1   Mark Dincecco, *Political Transformations and Public Finances: Europe, 1650–1913* (Cambridge: Cambridge University Press, 2011), 11–12.

2   Wantje Fritschy, "A History of the Income Tax in the Netherlands," *Revue Belge de Philologie et d'Histoire* 75 (1997): 1045–61.

3   Ibid., 1054.

4   't Hart, "The Merits of a Financial Revolution;" "The United Provinces, 1579–1806."

workers."[1] The growing strength of workers and their Labour Party led the Liberals to make an electoral pact with Labour for the 1906 and subsequent elections. As a result, the Liberals won the 1906 and the two 1910 elections, allowing them to govern first alone and then in a coalition with Labour, which elected twenty-nine MPs in 1906 and forty and forty-two in the two elections of 1910, and the Irish Parliamentary Party.[2] The 1911 Parliament Act, which limited the power of the House of Lords, ensured that the mass electorate's preferences, as mediated through the parties, could not be vetoed by hereditary elites.

The Liberals pushed through a raft of legislation in the years from 1908 to 1911. The Old-Age Pensions Act of 1908 provided low, means-tested pensions for those over age seventy, paid by national government, and sick pay and unemployment insurance financed by worker and government contributions. The 1911 National Insurance Act provided health insurance to be paid for by contributions from workers, employers, and the national government. In addition, "The 1906 Trade Disputes Act [gave workers] full collective organizing rights."[3]

Britain devoted 8 percent of its government spending to social benefits and another 19 percent to education in 1910, triple the Dutch percentage fifty years earlier, and slightly less than Germany. The main social expenditure by the British government in the 1870–1910 period was on education, which rose 531 percent in those forty years, a higher percentage increase than in Austria, France, Germany, or the United States.[4] Total British central government spending remained low in its post-hegemonic decades, rising from 6 percent to 8 percent of GDP in the years from 1876 to 1913, to 11 percent in 1901–02, the peak years of the South African War.[5]

--------

1    Mann, *Sources of Social Power*, volume 2, 617.
2    Ibid., 623.
3    Ibid., 620.
4    Ibid., table 11.5. Since Britain did not have conscription, it lacked the extensive benefits for veterans and war widows that existed in late-nineteenth-century France and the United States, making its social expenditures all the more impressive in comparison.
5    Mitchell, *International Historical Statistics*, 816–21, 905–13.

The Liberal reforms before World War I created a notion of social citizenship that was broader, if still less generous, than in Germany.

> Under Lloyd George, [the liberals] achieved substantial results: his 1911 scheme for health and unemployment insurance and his major switch from regressive indirect to more progressive direct taxation. The state would redistribute and encourage self-help through state-regulated insurance. Insurance covered only workers in larger firms, but brought together the state, most unions, large employers, and private insurance companies. This was the first genuine reformism, in a twentieth-century sense, to occur in any country. It had come less from labor, more from a cross-class party trying to rally workers, middle class, and some regions and religions.[1]

Despite the British creation of social citizenship, government tax policy did nothing to change the distribution of income or wealth. There was no income tax in Britain until 1909, when a top rate of 8 percent was introduced. World War I was the hinge in this respect as well. Rates reached 53 percent by 1918 and never fell below 50 percent until 1988.[2] The top inheritance rate was 8 percent until it rose to 15 percent in 1907 and 40 percent by the end of World War I.[3] As low as the top British income and inheritance tax rates were in the pre–World War I years, they were higher than in Germany, France, or the United States.[4]

Britain's electoral reforms and social welfare legislation are significant because they antedate the wave of similar progressive policies that were forced on the governments that mobilized their citizens for World War I. Several recent synthetic analyses, most notably by Piketty, identify the era from 1914 to the 1970s as unique in the centuries of capitalism and nation-states for the degree of income and wealth equality, produced in good part by unprecedentedly high tax rates on top incomes and large estates. Kenneth Scheve and David

---

1    Mann, *Sources of Social Power*, volume 2, 618–19.
2    Piketty, *Capital in the Twenty-First Century*, online table S14.1.
3    Ibid., online table S14.1.
4    Ibid., tables 14.1 and 14.2.

Stasavage find that income tax rates were not related to suffrage or to whether left parties were in power. Instead, the variance is explained entirely by whether countries drafted their citizens for the world wars *and* were electoral democracies (i.e., Germany, Austria, and Italy all conscripted but were not democracies during World War I and thus did not impose high taxes on their rich).[1]

Scheve and Stasavage show that legislators in Britain, France, and the United States who advocated high taxes on the rich during the world wars framed those impositions as compensatory conscription of wealth to match the conscription of men. They conclude that in the last decades of the twentieth century, after the end of conscription, leftists were reduced to making vague arguments for "fairness" that were vulnerable to the counterargument that it is unfair to tax the rich at higher rates than others. Scheidel argues that the end of mass mobilization warfare and therefore of conscription has removed the most convincing argument for redistributive taxes.[2]

In any case, the end of conscription allowed conservatives to abandon support for high taxes on the rich. As American leftists love to note, the top tax rates they advocate today are well below those maintained throughout the 1950s during Republican Dwight Eisenhower's presidency. While Scheve and Stasavage, like Scheidel, cannot quantify the effect of the rhetoric equating conscription with taxation, they are able to show that the top rate of income tax fell in the twenty richest countries in the last quarter of the twentieth century.

## MILITARY AND FOREIGN POLICY AFTER DECLINE

Dutch elites, as we saw in chapter 4, were unwilling to raise taxes to pay for an army and navy capable of playing a decisive or even significant role in the European wars of the eighteenth century. The Netherlands remained neutral in the Seven Years' War.[3] The Dutch

---

1  Kenneth Scheve and David Stasavage, *Taxing the Rich: A History of Fiscal Fairness in the United States and Europe* (Princeton: Princeton University Press, 2016).

2  Scheidel, *Great Leveler*.

3  Fritschy and van der Voort, "From Fragmentation to Unification."

instead focused their limited military investment on retaining their colonies and trade routes in Asia and the Americas. This decision reflected elites' rational and reasonable appraisal of their power and resources relative to Britain and France. It also reflected the fact that elites profited from their access to other European markets, an access that would have been threatened by a more aggressive foreign policy, and that could be maintained without applying military force.

Similarly, in the colonies, the Netherlands and the VOC assumed a largely defensive posture by the mid-eighteenth century.[1] Thus, the Dutch did not intervene or try to take advantage of the British-French conflict over India during the Seven Years' War (1756–63). The Netherlands lost control over trade among its Asian colonies and with Europe as the British were able to commercially and diplomatically penetrate those territories. The VOC was forced to grant ever-greater autonomy to its agents in Asia, in the hopes that the company could still realize profits from acting as a conduit between its self-dealing and self-financing agents and the European markets in which the greatest profits could still be realized.[2] The VOC's successor, the Nederlandsche Handel-Maatschapij (NHM) was, in essence, a joint venture of Dutch colonial officials and Javanese nobles to enforce a monopoly on exports from that island that served to enrich those elites as well as Dutch and Chinese merchants and industrialists back in the Netherlands who got first access to the Javanese exports that they then processed and sold in Europe. The Dutch-Javanese elite alliance was able to impose higher taxes in Java that allowed the post-1848 liberal Dutch government to cut domestic excise taxes, boosting the home economy and pleasing ordinary consumers.[3]

The one exception to this cautious foreign policy came when Amsterdam merchants broke the British embargo and supplied commercial and war-related goods to American revolutionaries and to France. Amsterdam's unilateral actions were opposed by the stadtholder but supported by the merchant-dominated States General, which ordered the stadtholder to provide naval escorts for the

1   De Vries and van der Woude, *First Modern Economy*, 681–3.
2   Nierstrasz, *In the Shadow of the Company*.
3   Zanden, *Rise and Decline of Holland's Economy*, 142–51.

merchants' commercial ships, which the stadtholder did half-heartedly. Nevertheless, Dutch state actions were enough that Britain responded with a declaration of war in 1780.

The Fourth Anglo-Dutch War of 1780–84 was a geopolitical and economic disaster for the Dutch. Britain won control of the Netherlands' Indian colonies and access for its merchants to the Dutch East Indies, most importantly to Batavia (present-day Indonesia).[1] Dutch failure in the war, and the depression that resulted from the wartime disruption of trade, provoked popular protest. The Patriots opposed the stadtholder, initially with support from the Holland regent elite, but then in 1787 the Patriots turned on the regents. By this point, foreign powers became decisive in determining the outcome of Dutch domestic conflicts. The Prussians restored the stadtholder and crushed the Patriots in 1787, while Napoleon forced the stadtholder to flee in 1795.[2]

The Netherlands was never the dominant military power in Europe, even when it was the hegemon. Britain was the hegemonic naval power, which gave it the advantage beyond Europe, while on the Continent its army was never able to dominate. Instead, as we saw in chapter 5 in our analysis of the basis of its hegemony, Britain relied on allies to do most of the land fighting in Europe and weakened enemies with naval blockades. The British government, like most elements in the fragmented Dutch polity, recognized that it was ever more unable to assert its authority over rival European powers, and in the case of Britain, the United States as well.

The British government's increasingly realistic approach to geo-political realities in the late nineteenth and early twentieth centuries was aided, as we saw in chapter 5, by elites' unwillingness to pay higher taxes for a military buildup and by mass opposition to conscription, which mattered when the franchise was widened. Self-interested colonial businessmen and officials undermined restraint, but they were concerned mainly with strategically marginal lands in Africa. But even in Africa, Britain was careful not to provoke rival powers. Thus, when Britain intervened in Egypt, which was considered vital

---

1  De Vries and van der Woude, *First Modern Economy*, 683–7.
2  Israel, *Dutch Republic*, 1098–130.

geopolitically and to its bankers, it mollified Germany by supporting its colonial ambitions.[1] Similarly, Britain relied mainly on diplomacy rather than military intervention to manage its competing interests with Russia as the Ottoman Empire weakened, and Britain negotiated with the other major powers to divide China into spheres of influence.[2]

For both the Netherlands and Britain, geopolitical realities, and an inability or unwillingness to spend enough to overpower their European rivals, limited the terrain on which narrow elites could play outside of Europe. The Dutch, with the exception of its commerce with France that led the British to declare war in 1780, kept itself neutral in European wars once it had become a second-level military power. British officials, in contrast, did not limit the scope of commitments state officials made within Europe.

"Nineteenth century liberals pinned hopes on the predominantly transnational organization and 'interdependence' of capital" to prevent war,[3] just as late-twentieth-century neoliberals did, and still do. While no Briton was as simplistic as *New York Times* columnist Thomas Friedman, who wrote in 1996 that "No two countries that both have a McDonald's have ever fought a war against each other,"[4] faith in the pacific effects of free trade did blind British elites to the dangers of their nation's participation in the system of alliances in Europe.[5]

While those hopes were dashed in 1914, Mann reminds us that the main competitors for colonial territory—Britain, France, and Russia—"actually fought as allies."[6] Britain was pulled into war by its European, not its colonial or commercial, commitments. Despite ongoing policy debates within the government and in civil society from the 1870s until the day World War I began, Britain never made concessions (which of course might have proven to be never enough) to Germany's

1   Porter, *Lion's Share*, 111–18; Mann, *Sources of Social Power*, volume 2, 777.
2   Porter, *Lion's Share*, 152–67.
3   Mann, *Sources of Social Power*, volume 2, 776.
4   Thomas L. Friedman, "Foreign Affairs Big Mac I," *New York Times*, December 8, 1996.
5   Friedberg, *Weary Titan*.
6   Mann, *Sources of Social Power*, volume 2, 777.

rising power on the Continent. Friedberg and Porter,[1] who provide the best overviews of the protagonists and positions in those arguments, agree that the debates did lead to British restraint in the colonial sphere and to justifications for cuts in military spending, but they do not identify any restraints in British assertions of its interests in Europe.

Britain ended up fighting in what became World War I, a war that, in combination with round two in 1939–45, ensured the destruction of the British Empire and the triumph of American rather than German hegemony. Yet that disastrous war was not sparked by any combination of British capitalist elites, unlike the way in which Amsterdam merchants' greed set off the Fourth Anglo-Dutch War. British elites' abilities to pursue their particular interests in the post-hegemonic decades of decline meant that capitalists mattered mainly in their demands for low taxes and extensive colonial commitments, which underfunded Britain's military and diverted forces from Europe, and in their inability to cohere to challenge the autonomous decisions British diplomats and politicians made that propelled their nation into war with Germany.

## THE FUTURE OF INEQUALITY IN AMERICA

We saw that the Netherlands was highly unequal in its hegemonic era and remained roughly the same in decline, while Britain became slightly more equal after a wave of unionization in the 1890s. Ordinary Dutch people became absolutely less well off in the era of decline, while Britons became better off.

Americans, as we discussed in previous chapters, have become less equal since the 1970s, and the majority have become absolutely less well off since 2000. The low level of unionization forecloses the most likely path to reducing inequality in the future. While, as we saw earlier, Obama and his Democratic predecessors did nothing to strengthen unions, when and wherever Republicans take power, they take actions to weaken unions. In recent years this has manifested in

1   Friedberg, *Weary Titan*; Porter, *Lion's Share*.

state governments using their legal power to restrict the union rights of their employees and by passing right-to-work laws in Republican-controlled northern industrial states. Neil Gorsuch's appointment to the Supreme Court provided the fifth vote in the 2018 *Janus v. American Federation of State, County and Municipal Employees* decision (an outcome that was averted in 2016 by Antonin Scalia's timely death) that will allow workers to assert that their free speech rights are being violated if they are forced to pay dues to unions for collective bargaining on their behalf, thereby undermining the remaining public-sector unions, and which if extended to private sector unions would decimate them as well.

In other spheres of governmental activity, the same pattern occurs: Republican policies widen inequality to an extent that is only partly reversed when Democrats are in office. The 2017 Tax Cuts and Jobs Act, like earlier Republican tax cuts, provides the lion's share of the benefits to the rich. In this case, the top 0.1 percent gets 10 percent of the cuts, and the top quintile two-thirds.[1] These tax cuts, like the Reagan and Bush cuts, will deepen the deficit, resulting in cuts to programs that benefit lower- and middle-class Americans. Deregulation in finance and other sectors will allow an upsurge in predatory and fraudulent business practices that transfer income from the mass of citizens to the managers and owners of firms who are able to engage in those maneuvers.[2]

Can these regressive policies be countered? As we noted in chapter 6, labor law reforms that could aid unions have failed to pass under Democratic as well as Republican governments, and union decline has continued under each administration since the 1970s. Some activists argue that workers should organize outside the confines of the National Labor Relations Act (NLRA). However, their proposals depend on the as-yet-unrealized potential of "workers' centers,

---

1 Tax Policy Center, "Distributional Analysis of the Conference Agreement for the Tax Cuts and Jobs Act" (2017).

2 Trump's, or, more accurately, House Republicans', plans to repeal Obamacare also would have widened inequality since they combined tax cuts for the rich, in the form of a repeal of a surtax on investment income that funds the Affordable Care Act's subsidies for low-income Americans' insurance premiums, with cuts in the Act's benefits.

community and occupational groups, and identity caucuses that can work in partnerships with established unions; class action plaintiffs' firms dedicated to enforcing workplace rights; and government agencies and [state] attorneys general." However, the success of these actors and any strategies they will develop depend on federal judicial recognition of "more robust constitutional protection for group action in its many forms [which] is essential to create breathing space for worker mobilization. That protection can and should be founded upon the First Amendment freedom of assembly."[1] But those protections, in Crain and Matheny's analysis, would need to be granted by federal courts, the very ones being packed with right-wing judges who are highly hostile to union rights and indeed to public demonstrations of any kind. Of course, workers could strike and occupy workplaces without relying on legal protections, as workers did in the 1930s before passage of the NLRA and in the face of judges and state governments that were usually ready to repress strikes. Such action would require an escalation of currently almost invisible levels of worker identity and mobilization.

## THE FATE OF AMERICAN SOCIAL WELFARE

Dutch, British, and American decline each came at different moments in the history of social welfare. Social benefits were essentially nonexistent at the end of Dutch hegemony, and the Dutch government's piecemeal and inadequate additions to poor relief were not innovative, but neither were they retrogressive. The British social programs established before World War I were, along with those in Germany, unprecedented in scope, although they were still a small part of the state budget and did little to reduce inequality or improve Britons' living standards or life chances. US decline is occurring after decades of neoliberalism. The era of "conscription of wealth," instituted during the world wars, ended with serial cuts in top income and inheritance tax rates since the 1970s, in much of Europe as well as in the United

---

1   Marion Crain and Ken Matheny, "Beyond Unions, Notwithstanding Labor Law," *UC Irvine Law Review* 4 (2014): 564.

States.[1] While much of the social welfare state has survived, albeit with cuts that vary among wealthy nations, there has not been significant expansion of benefits in any OECD country in recent decades. Thus, to expect new social benefits in post-hegemonic America would be to predict the United States would move against the political economic trends of this era, and from a lower base than in other wealthy countries. The question is not whether benefits will expand, but how drastically they will be cut.

The United States has a history of social innovation at the state level, but most of that occurred in the period from the 1890s to the advent of the New Deal. Today, state and local governments are in perpetual fiscal crisis, and the political base for tax increases large enough to fund state-level social benefits is almost nonexistent. New York state in 2017 made public universities free (albeit only for full-time students, which excludes many of the poor who need to work and study at the same time). New York City created a free preschool program for four-year-olds in 2016, and in 2017 Mayor Bill de Blasio, who made the existing program the centerpiece of his 2013 election platform, proposed extending it to three-year-olds. However, it is important to note that de Blasio's proposal to fund preschool with an income-tax surcharge on the rich was rejected by the New York state legislature. Funding for preschool in New York City and the rest of the state comes from the general state budget and so is vulnerable to future fiscal crises. A few—very few—other states have offered similar piecemeal extensions of social benefits that, at least up until now, have had no discernible effect on national politics. The states as "laboratories of democracy," a phrase coined by Louis Brandeis, is an anachronism in the twenty-first century.

Republican efforts under George W. Bush to privatize Social Security failed after the Senate voted unanimously against the plan, and there is no evidence that there would not be massive opposition to a renewed plan. Despite House Republicans' deep desire to privatize Medicare, that too would be almost impossible to enact, in part because Medicare is vital to the profitability of hospitals, physicians, and pharmaceutical firms. Privatization would be not so much a

---

1   Piketty, *Capital in the Twenty-First Century*, tables 14.1 and 14.2.

transfer of the financial burden of medical care from government to patients as a decimation of the medical industry, since the federal government is, in essence, the payer of last resort for that sector of the economy because few elderly Americans could afford private insurance or pay bills out of pocket.

The existing universal social welfare programs, above all Social Security and Medicare, are widely popular, as are programs like federally subsidized student loans and mortgages, and also, it now appears, the Affordable Care Act, even though it came into effect just in 2014. However, the long gaps between the establishment of the New Deal and Great Society programs, and then the almost fifty-year gap until the Affordable Care Act, demonstrate the difficulty in adding new programs despite the popularity and effectiveness of existing ones. Political struggles will revolve around preserving existing programs or preventing cuts to them rather than expanding benefits. Entirely new national programs, like free college, which was espoused by Bernie Sanders in his 2016 presidential campaign, or universal childcare, will have to await a political turn that is at least as drastic as the Democratic sweeps of 2006–08 or 1964 and would need to be accompanied by a wave of popular mobilization not seen since the 1960s. Any such gains would not return the United States to the forefront of social welfare it occupied in the 1930s but instead would, as Obamacare did, partly narrow the gap between America's backward social welfare state and those of other rich nations.

## EMPIRE ON AUTOPILOT

Just as the British acted in its empire and in Europe without acknowledging its economic and military weakness or the rise of Germany, so too the United States today pursues a geopolitical strategy that assumes continuing military supremacy and economic preeminence. Unlike the rethinking and restructuring that occurred under Nixon, Obama did not attempt to recast America diplomacy or reduce its military stance.

The post–World War II and post-USSR eras of new international treaties, spearheaded by the United States, came to an almost total halt under Obama, with the exception of the Paris climate accord and the nuclear agreement with Iran, which Obama used executive actions to join since there was no prospect that the Senate would ratify either. Similarly, the Trans-Pacific Partnership (TPP) was unlikely to have been ratified even under a Hillary Clinton administration, so Trump's withdrawal from the treaty made no substantive difference. Bilateral trade treaties have also slowed. Obama managed to ratify only three treaties, with Panama, Colombia, and South Korea, far fewer than under Bush. The waves of NATO expansion under Clinton and Bush have almost entirely ended.

China has stepped into the breach with its Regional Comprehensive Economic Partnership (RCEP), which is moving toward a final agreement in the wake of the demise of the TPP. This new agreement, like TPP, would do little to deepen and accelerate the already dense trade links among the signatories. Rather, the RCEP would be the first step in moving China to a central position in the regulation of global trade and finance. At the same time, China's huge investments in infrastructure in Southeast and South Asia and in the Middle East through the "One Belt, One Road" scheme could lock in the economies and trade networks of countries throughout Eurasia with China, permanently disadvantaging the United States and impelling the EU to, at least in part, shift its focus from North America to China.

We examined at the end of chapter 8 the reasons why China is unlikely to become globally hegemonic in the financial realm despite its growing power and economic centrality in Eurasia. Giovanni Arrighi[1] argued that the United States, after the debacle in Iraq, was unlikely to confront China directly and instead would seek to build an alliance of Asian nations as a counterweight to China. The demise of the TPP undermines that option. The danger remains that the United States will stumble into a military encounter with China as it asserts the right to send military vessels and planes right up to China's sea and air borders, or as it defends other Asian nations' claims to parts of the South China Sea. More likely, those nations will resolve or muffle their geopolitical differences with China as part of their strategic move away from the increasingly unpredictable and frightening US

1   Arrighi, *Adam Smith in Beijing.*

government and as the importance of trade with China grows ever larger. In any case, the American generals who now largely run their nation's foreign policy never were committed to Obama's "Asian pivot" and instead focus their plans and weapons procurement on maintaining an abstract geostrategic "full-spectrum dominance" and on counterinsurgency in the Middle East and Africa. Neither objective would be advanced by an exchange of fire with China.

The United States, despite recent and forthcoming diplomatic reverses, remains in a far stronger geopolitical position than Britain held in 1914. Most of the strong military powers are American allies, and neither Russia nor China has any plans to confront the United States or to attack smaller countries that would provoke the United States into war, as Britain was by Germany's invasion of Belgium. The realignment of trade and diplomacy in Asia likely eliminates the possibility of war between China and its neighbors. Neither the United States nor NATO regarded Russia's intervention in Ukraine as a casus belli, and that assessment most likely will not change. Nor will Russia, whose army depends largely on volunteers and professionals since it reduced the length of conscription to twelve months and broadened exemptions in 2008, risk fighting a war against a hostile populace backed by NATO in the Baltic nations. Thus, the United States has no fear of being drawn into a war with any nation that has a significant military.

The real risk the United States faces, like Britain in the second half of the nineteenth century, is of its interests in peripheral lands leading to escalating commitments of American forces. The Afghan and Iraq wars, which were greatly deescalated under Obama, became sites of reescalation toward the end of Obama's second term, and the generals asked Trump to authorize further troops supplements in those two countries and in Syria.

Hendrik Spruyt, in his study of British, French, Dutch, and Portuguese decolonization after World War II, offers a useful template for understanding when imperial powers maintain their colonial presence and when they withdraw (albeit in many cases to sustain a degree of dominance through informal means). Spruyt finds that "the more fragmented the decision-making process in the core, the greater the resistance to change in territorial policy and decolonization."

Multiple elites, especially if they commanded "veto points," were able block majority preference for compromise with nationalists or secessionists in colonies. The elites with the potential to block decolonization were "business interests with direct investment in the contested territories and settler populations."[1] Corporatist or autonomous militaries were veto players in authoritarian states, and militaries exercised that power because they could and did lose resources and prestige when colonies were surrendered. Thus, Britain, whose army was under civilian control and where executive and legislative power were united in a Parliament with two strong parties that alternated in power, decolonized more easily than the other European powers. That decision reflected the civilian government's judgment about its resources and postwar geopolitical standing and British investors' view that the best way to save their colonial assets was through concessions to moderate native forces.

The French Fourth Republic was divided among actors commanding numerous veto points, multiple parties in the National Assembly, and a weak president. Colonial military forces and settlers enjoyed strong enough autonomy to block efforts to decolonize, leading to wars in Vietnam and Algeria. A similar situation in the Netherlands would have led to a prolonged war in Indonesia except that the United States, seeking to bolster its anticolonial image, forced the Dutch, on pain of losing their Marshall Plan aid, to grant Indonesia independence.

The Portuguese military, settlers, and metropolitan business interests invested in the colonies all had reasons and enough power in the authoritarian state to ensure that Portugal would fight rather than grant independence. While those actors determined policy in Lisbon, they were unable to suppress the independence movements. Rising casualties in the colonies led to a decline in applicants to officer schools from the upper-class families that had supplied all the high-level officers in the Portuguese military. This opened access to lower-class recruits and space for NCOs to be promoted up the ranks. The new, lower-class officers became the core of opposition to the colonial wars, and the revolutionaries who overthrew the regime in 1974. Some top

---

1   Spruyt, *Ending Empire*, 6, 8.

generals who saw the wars as lost and worried they'd be blamed for defeat joined the revolution. Spruyt concludes, "although the military may often be guided by narrow corporate interests, for example, in its choice of particular strategies that guarantee large budgets and military autonomy, ultimately armies need to win the war."[1]

The United States is unlikely to pull back from its efforts to dominate peripheral countries for some of the reasons Spruyt identified in postwar Europe. Specific groups of capitalists hold investments in Latin America, Africa, Asia, and the Middle East, and unless and until they are bought out by, or wiped out in competition from, Chinese or European firms, those capitalists will want the US government to restrain local governments from endangering their assets and profit opportunities. Those investors have access to enough members of Congress to block efforts to defund the military presence in those lands, and in any case the military retains its own interest in preserving the worldwide network of bases that gives it the capacity to project power throughout the globe and gives the ever-increasing number of generals and admirals their own commands.

While defeat forced the French and Portuguese out of colonies they otherwise would have retained, the US military has far more resources today than either France or Portugal had when they surrendered their colonies. Defeat has not damaged American officers' careers in the twenty-first century, nor has it led to budget cuts, in contrast to the post–Vietnam War era. As we saw in chapter 7, the United States is unable to bend resistant lands to its will and so can control only those countries that want to remain under the US security umbrella and those that are understandably scared by the destruction that the United States wrought in Afghanistan and Iraq, and which it can inflict on other resistant nations.

We can expect future American wars only in peripheral lands unwilling to kowtow to American dictates and whose peoples are willing, like the Afghans and Iraqis and the Vietnamese before them, to mount armed resistance to the United States. Those resistances will succeed when they are willing to endure death and destruction over a long enough time to allow them to inflict sufficient casualties on

---

1   Ibid., 196.

American troops that domestic American opposition forces a deescalation (as in Iraq and Afghanistan) if not a full withdrawal (as in Vietnam). Each such war will further expose the limits of American military power, deepen the global view of the United States as an immoral force acting outside international law, and further reduce Americans' tolerance for the deaths of their own citizens. However, the military's growing autonomy ensures that such wars and lesser interventions will continue to be launched even as America's geopolitical position declines.

It will be a long time before any other power or concert of powers can compel the United States to refrain from launching such wars. Nor can we look to domestic mass opposition to prevent wars. Domestic US resistance in the past has been ineffective in preventing wars or in blocking the deployments of troops or the making of threats that precipitate wars. An end or even cutback to US military ambitions would require a level of geopolitical consciousness and action among the mass of Americans equivalent to that of the Vietnam War. Even in the wake of the Afghan and Iraq wars, there is no sign of such a movement.

## AMERICAN DEMOCRACY: DEAD AFTER A LONG ILLNESS, OR MURDERED IN ITS SLEEP?

Any possibility of reversing the long slide away from egalitarian social policies and class relations, which the Republicans' return to power has accelerated and deepened, depends on an upsurge in electoral or non-electoral mobilization. As of now there is little indication that either is occurring. What are the prospects for a reversal of American political quiescence?

In chapter 6, we identified the structural changes and strategic factors that have blocked challenges from even a moderate left opposition. The restructuring of relations among capitalists increased the cohesiveness of business opposition to unions and social programs while allowing specific groups of capitalists to extract regulatory, tax, and budget favors that reduce governmental resources and capacities, further undermining the appearance and reality of the state's ability to produce either legal equality or collective benefits for most Americans. These transformations allowed employers to decimate unions while, during the same decades, mass organizations with actual local chapters lost most of their members.

These structural changes have created incentives for politicians to shift their electoral stances and governing policies to the right, and Republicans have skillfully and cynically taken advantage of these opportunities. By winning control in 2010 of state legislatures, Republicans were able to gerrymander both federal and state district lines. As a result, Democrats needed to win supermajorities when they captured control in 2018 of the House of Representatives and of seven houses of the state legislatures that will redraw district lines again after 2020. The end of equal time rules for television and radio have allowed the emergence of overtly ideological TV networks like Fox and Sinclair and of right-wing radio "shock jocks" like Rush Limbaugh and his many imitators. Such media have moved the Republican primary electorate to the right, resulting in the election of ever more intransigent congressmen, and even when such candidates lose, they make election campaigns increasingly harsh and vulgar. The vicious tone of right-wing candidates and media personalities combines with Republicans' successful obstructionism under Democratic presidents to make politics repellant to ever more Americans, pushing down voter turnout, which thereby increases the fraction of voters who are motivated by religious fundamentalism and bigotry, and further reinforces the Republican drift to the right. Capitalists' growing advantage in mobilizing campaign contributions and fielding lobbyists creates the appearance and reality of corruption in Washington and in state governments, further alienating and demoralizing voters.

The future intensity of opposition and the results of presidential, congressional, and state-level elections cannot be predicted, and I will not attempt such prognostication. Rather, what I can do is enumerate the obstacles facing such resistance. Opponents to the agenda that Trump and the Republicans are pursuing have virtually no organizations they can look to for resources or leadership. Unions are too weak now to serve that purpose, and the Democratic Party itself is merely a ballot line. It no longer has a network of local parties with either paid or volunteer workers who can meet with potential voters, ensure that they are registered, and bring them out on election days, tasks made more difficult by Republicans' enactment of ever more onerous laws for proving voters' identity. Mass media, with few exceptions, are either right-wing or adopt a supposed nonpartisan stance that legitimizes and regularizes extremist statements and policies.

Even before Trump took office, biased and shallow media already made it impossible for voters to know how well government programs are working.

> Asked how the actual cost of the [Affordable Care Act] compares with estimates prior to enactment, roughly 40 percent admitted they had no idea. Another 40 percent thought costs were higher than predicted. Only 8 percent knew that costs were substantially lower than anticipated.[1]

Similarly, voters think budget deficits increased under Obama when in fact they decreased. Voters way overestimate the portion of the federal budget spent on foreign aid (in various surveys their average guess is 15–20 percent, when actually it is less than 1 percent). Americans also underestimate the fraction of the budget that goes to the military and overestimate what is spent on the poor. Voters' preferences, when surveyed, are for substantially lower military and higher social spending as shares of the budget than was the case under Obama.[2] Republican budgets push the reality even further from public desires, but the lack of reporting on the actual situation makes it difficult for voters to make coherent demands on their elected officials or to translate their policy preferences into decisions about who they should support in presidential and congressional elections.

How will this ignorance be affected by the Trump administration's unprecedented dishonesty? While Trump will try to present himself as a success, his propaganda efforts will not spur more respect for

---

1   Hacker and Pierson, *American Amnesia*, 367.
2   Examples of research on voters' knowledge of and preferences for federal spending are Eric D. Lawrence, "What Americans Know and Why It Matters for Politics" (paper presented at the annual meeting of the Midwest Political Science Association, Chicago, April 2010); and Martin Gilens, "Political Ignorance and Collective Policy Preferences," *The American Political Science Review* 95, (2001).

government, since he will frame his supposed achievements as the result of his unique deal-making skills and not as the outcome of government capacity. When the gap between his announcements and reality becomes glaringly obvious, confidence in government will be further undermined. The current and increasingly confrontational stance mainstream media take toward Trump is limited to calling out his lies, not to explaining how government or the economy actually operates.

Disgust at Trump and rejection of his policies are unlikely to spur enduring consciousness and organization on a left that remains a diffuse collection of organizations and identities with varying interests and energies. The legacy of opposition to Bush and the Iraq War was meager. We must acknowledge, and this is the strongest basis for hope, that previous mass movements, in the United States and elsewhere in the world, often emerged rapidly and unpredictably, creating organizations and communication media of their own. More likely will be a repeat of 2006–08: Republicans will be swept out of Congress and a Democrat elected president. Without a mass movement behind them, a new Democratic majority will be able to enact only piecemeal reforms and social programs that do not significantly challenge elites' hold over resources and state powers. Such meager accomplishments, combined with relief at the departure of the loathsome Trump and his enablers, will lead voters and activists to lose the urgency and hopes that propel political action. In the absence of enduring organizations and ideologically committed media, it will be impossible to sustain involvement by all but a small minority of Americans whose personal, political, or class identities and interests should make them recruits for new or revived unions and parties.

## ELITES TO THE LIFEBOATS

Surprisingly and ironically, even as elites' command over politics and the economy becomes ever more secure and lucrative, more than a few of those privileged and powerful actors are coming to fear that they will not be safe living in the country they rule.

Élite anxiety cuts across political lines. Even financiers who supported Trump for President, hoping that he would cut taxes and regulations, have been unnerved at the ways his insurgent campaign seems to have hastened a collapse of respect for established institutions. [A lobbyist-turned-hedge-fund-manager notes,] "The media is under attack now. They wonder, Is the court system next? Do we go from 'fake news' to 'fake evidence'? For people whose existence depends on enforceable contracts, this is life or death."

As public institutions deteriorate, élite anxiety has emerged as a gauge of our national predicament. [Another hedge fund manager, this one turned think tank director, observes,] "Why do people who are envied for being so powerful appear to be so afraid? . . . What does that really tell us about our system? . . . It's a very odd thing. You're basically seeing that the people who've been the best at reading the tea leaves—the ones with the most resources, because that's how they made their money—are now the ones most preparing to pull the rip cord and jump out of the plane."[1]

Osnos and the hedge fund managers he quotes only speculate on the sources of this fear. We can expect, as the United States and the world become ever more oligarchic, more such articles and books as journalists and academics devote efforts to understanding the political and existential worldviews of the only social actors who matter in determining the futures of everyone else and of the planet on which we live. Nevertheless, even if the psychology of the ruling elites is often opaque, we can identify the material bases of their anxieties.

While Trump's election and his appointments and policies are an unexpected boon to many at the top, the raw anger his campaign exposed and the open expression of socialist ideals by Bernie Sanders and his supporters revealed to elites the thick veins of resentment and despair that a genuine right-wing populist or a leftist in control of the Democratic Party could tap to mount a successful presidential campaign in the future. Such an outcome is, as I explained above,

---

1   Evan Osnos, "Doomsday Prep for the Super-Rich," *New Yorker,* January 30, 2017.

unlikely, but the rich have a long, worldwide history of reacting fearfully to even improbable threats from below.

There are genuine material bases for linking nationalism with anti-capitalism. The United States' perpetual trade deficit is having the effect of transferring capital assets into the hands of non-Americans. In 2016, foreigners held 35 percent of US stock equity, compared with 11 percent in 1982.[1] This means that foreigners will accrue a third of the benefit from the 2018 cut in the corporate income tax rate, robbing the Treasury of funds that could support social programs for Americans. Combined with cross-border mergers, corporate inversions (the maneuver of relocating a corporation's legal domicile to a lower-tax nation), and the move of American capitalists' personal citizenship to other countries, ordinary American have increasingly real reasons for seeing wealthy foreigners (but not penniless immigrants) as the source of their powerlessness and economic immiseration. The rich are already removed in their daily lives from the experience of, and interactions with, their less fortunate fellow Americans. If they relocate to other continents, they will appear even more alien to those left behind. Of course, extraordinary wealth depends, as we have documented in this book, on political power. However, the rich are able to, and increasingly do, delegate the work of political influence to paid lobbyists who work the networks in which wealthy elites embedded themselves earlier. Those arrangements can be ordered as well from New Zealand as from New York or Chicago.

What elites cannot accomplish from afar, and what they increasingly cannot even manage up close, is to override their particular interests and mobilize their power and resources behind policies that could sustain US geopolitical or economic hegemony. Like their predecessors in the Netherlands and Britain, American elites are left to enjoy the loot they have pried from everyone else, whether they remain in a country no longer at the center of the world or relocate to what they hope is a rising hegemon or to a safe restful backwater where they can bring their capital, even though they will lack the political connections to realize superprofits. At home or abroad, those

--------

1  Steven Rosenthal, "Slashing Corporate Taxes: Foreigners Are Surprise Winners," *Tax Notes*, October 23, 2017.

who profited from the era of American hegemony and from its decline will be able to insulate themselves from the consequences of their power and greed, which will be increasingly manifest in political dysfunction, mass despair, domestic and global strife, and rising sea levels on a planet no longer able to accommodate billions of humans. The views, from their remote hilltops and guarded apartment towers, though not from bunkers, will be marvelous.

# Appendices

**Table 2A:  European Territories Gained and Lost by Great Powers, 1500–1817**

| Taken from | Lands taken by: | | | |
| --- | --- | --- | --- | --- |
| | Spain | France | Netherlands | Britain |
| Spain | | 1659: Artois, Roussillon, Dunkirk<br><br>1668: part of Flanders<br><br>1678: Franche-Comté | 1609: de facto independence from Spain<br><br>1714: Guelders province | 1714:<br><br>Gibraltar, Minorca |
| France | 1526: Milan, Artois, Burgundy, Flanders | | 1815: liberation from French rule + control of Belgium | 1544: Boulogne |
| Netherlands | | 1795: Belgium<br>1806: Netherlands | | |
| Britain | | 1559: all British holdings in France | | |
| Lesser powers | 1589: Portugal conquered until 1640 | 1516: Milan duchy<br><br>1735: Lorraine from Habsburgs<br><br>1768: Corsica from Genoa<br><br>1797: Belgium, Rhineland (part), Italy (part),<br><br>1801: Rhineland (rest), Tuscany<br><br>1806–10: Italy (rest),<br><br>1807: duchy of Warsaw | | |

Sources: Micheal Clodfelter, *Warfare and Armed Conflicts: A Statistical Reference to Casualty and Other Figures, 1500–2000*, second edition (Jefferson, NC: MacFarland, 2002); Pierre Serryn and René Blasselle, *Atlas historique* (Paris: Bordas, 1983).

Note: From 1519 until 1558 Charles I was, in addition to king of Spain, the Holy Roman Emperor and the archduke of Austria. Charles I abdicated all his thrones in 1558, leaving some to his son and a succeeding line of Habsburgs who ruled from Spain, while bequeathing his emperorship and Austrian dominions to his brother, who passed those crowns on to *his* heirs. The above table treats the territories of the Austrian Habsburgs as distinct from those of the Spanish Habsburgs following their 1558 separation.

Therefore, we could regard Spain's ceding of the southern Netherlands (Belgium), Naples, Milan, and Sardinia to Austria in 1714, of Sicily to the Holy Roman Empire in 1720, and of Tuscany and Parma to Austria in 1735 as losses for Spain, even though those territories came under the control of other Habsburgs.

**Table 2B:  Non-European Colonies Gained and Lost**
**by Great Powers, 1500–1817**

| | Lands taken by: | | | |
|---|---|---|---|---|
| Taken from: | Spain | France | Netherlands | Britain |
| Non-Europeans | 1402–95: Canary Islands | 1605–99: Canada, Mississippi Valley, Louisiana | 1615: New Netherlands | 1607–1733: thirteen colonies (gained independence 1783) |
| | 1497–1560: North African enclaves | 1625–64: seven Caribbean islands | 1605–1757: rest of Indonesia | 1610–1713: Canada |
| | | 1624: French Guiana | 1608–87: ports in India | 1612–1799: India |
| | 1511–65: Latin America, except Brazil and La Plata (Uruguay) | 1664–68: parts of southeast India | 1652: Cape Colony | 1625–66: Antigua, Anguilla, Montserrat, Tortolla, Bahamas, Barbados, Baruba, Belize |
| | | 1677: Senegal ports | 1628–48: St. Martin (half rest French), St. Eustace, Saba (British 1797–1815), Virgin Islands, Tobago, Guyana | |
| | 1564–71: Philippines | | | 1664: Gambia |
| | | | | 1788: Australia |
| | Note, 1811–36: all Latin American colonies (except Cuba and Puerto Rico) gained independence | | | |

| Taken from: | Spain | France | Netherlands | Britain |
|---|---|---|---|---|
| Other European powers | From Portugal:<br><br>1580: Cuenta (North African enclave)<br><br>1777: La Plata | | All from Portugal:<br>1605: enclave in Indonesia<br>1630: Recife, Brazil and environs (back to Portugal in 1654)<br>1638–58: Ceylon<br>1641: Malacca<br>1642: Ghana forts<br>1657: Nagapattinam (India) | Portugal: 1612: Indian ports<br>Denmark: 1797: Virgin Islands |
| Spain | | 1664: Haiti (gained independence 1804) | 1633: Curaçao, Bonaire<br>1647: Aruba (all three occupied by Britain 1800–03, 1807–15) | 1655: Jamaica<br>1739: Puerto Bello<br>1763: Florida<br>1797: Trinidad |
| France | | | 1783: Tobago | 1668: Montserrat<br>1758: Senegal<br>1759: Guadeloupe<br>1762: Grenada<br>1763: Quebec, Canadian Atlantic provinces, Mississippi valley<br>1783: Dominica, Grenada<br>1784: Montserrat<br>1794: Guadeloupe<br>1797: St. Lucia, St. Vincent<br>1809: Senegal<br>1810: Guadeloupe, Seychelles, Mauritius<br>1814: Tobago |

| Taken from: | Spain | France | Netherlands | Britain |
|---|---|---|---|---|
| Netherlands | | 1677: Tobago | | 1664: New Netherlands |
| | | | | 1672: Virgin Islands |
| | | | | 1783: Ceylon and Indian ports |
| | | | | 1797: Malaysia, Cape Colony, Guiana (part taken permanently, part occupied until 1816) |
| | | | | 1799: Aruba, Curaçao, Bonaire |
| | | | | 1796–1800 and 1810–17: Indonesia |
| | | | | 1801: Tobago |
| | | | | 1806: Cape Colony |
| | | | | 1814: Guyana |
| Britain | 1779: Florida | 1763: Guadeloupe 1779: Grenada 1783: Senegal 1795: Guadeloupe 1817: Senegal, Guadeloupe | 1628: Banda Islands and forts in Indonesia 1664: Montserrat 1667: Suriname 1682: Bantam, Java 1782: Montserrat 1803: Cape Colony 1816: Malacca, Aruba, Curaçao, Bonaire 1817: Indonesia | |

Sources: same as table 2A.

# Index